iSpeak

What makes *iSpeak* special?

iSpeak offers instructors **unmatched content and currency** in a *succinct magazine format* that engages students. *iSpeak* helps students **develop strong speech topics** by offering examples that reflect **vital personal, social, and political themes** that are played out every day on campus communities across the country.

What's Inside

Engaging pedagogy designed to be eye-catching and visually appealing can be found throughout the text. *iSpeak* shows students how they can apply their speaking skills at school and in their communities and work lives.

e-NOTE

Practicing Speeches Online

Practicing your speech for others is one of the most important steps you can take to improve the clarity of your ideas and the effectiveness of your delivery. Using YouTube and other Internet sites, you can record and upload your speech for others to view. You can ask others to view and comment on your speech and can even post your YouTube video on social networking sites likes Facebook. Using feedback from others, you can improve your speech; the mere act of recording the speech for others to view will provide a significant and realistic practice opportunity.

< E-Notes
E-Notes suggest links for exploring speech topics and connecting to community organizations.

Civic Engagement in Action >
The text offers numerous examples of actual college-based community service projects.

< Get Involved!
Get Involved sections encourage students to actively participate in issues that are relevant to them.

iSpeak

Vice President, Editorial: *Michael Ryan*
Authors: *Paul E. Nelson, Scott Titsworth, and Judy C. Pearson*
Executive Editor: *Susan Gouijnstook*
Executive Marketing Manager: *Leslie Oberhuber*
Director of Development: *Rhona Robbin*
Senior Developmental Editor: *Jennie Katsaros*
Managing Editor: *Anne Fuzellier*
Production Editor: *Margaret Young*
Production Service: *Jennifer Bonnar,*
Lachina Publishing Services
Art Manager: *Robin Mouat*
Design Manager: *Preston Thomas*
Cover Designer: *Andrei Pasternak*
Text Designer: *Maureen McCutcheon*
Photo Researcher: *Lili Weiner*
Buyer II: *Louis Swaim*
Senior Media Project Manager: *Thomas Brierly*
Composition: *Lachina Publishing Services*
Printing: *Quad/Graphics*
Cover Images: © Ocean Photography/Veer (*front cover, man*);
© Jim Goldstein/Alamy (*front cover, tablet*);
© Purestock/Getty Images (*back cover*)

Credits: The credits section for this book begins on page 319 and is considered an extension of the copyright page.

CourseSmart is a new way find and buy eTextbooks. At CourseSmart, you can save up to 50% off the cost of a print textbook, reduce your impact on the environment, and gain access to powerful web tools for learning. The iSpeak *CourseSmart eTextbook is available in one standard online reader with full text search, notes and highlighting, and e-mail tools for sharing notes between classmates. CourseSmart is the only place for faculty to review and compare the full text online, providing immediate access without the need to request a print exam copy. For further details, contact your sales representative or go to* www.coursesmart.com.

Library of Congress Cataloging-in-Publication Data
Nelson, Paul E. (Paul Edward), 1941–
  iSpeak : public speaking for contemporary life / Paul Nelson, Scott Titsworth, Judy Pearson. — 5th ed.
    p. cm.
  Includes bibliographical references and index.
    ISBN-13: 978-0-07-730953-4 (alk. paper)
    ISBN-10: 0-07-730953-7 (alk. paper)
  1. Public speaking. I. Titsworth, Scott. II. Pearson, Judy C. III. Title.

PN4129.15.N46 2011
  808.5'1—dc22

                                                                          2010044520

The Internet addresses listed in the text were accurate at the time of publication. The inclusion of a website does not indicate an endorsement by the authors or McGraw-Hill, and McGraw-Hill does not guarantee the accuracy of the information presented at these sites.
www.mhhe.com

Brief Contents

Preparing Your Presentations

[Part One]

Selecting and Arranging Content

[Part Two]

Types of Presentations

[Part Three]

Contents

[Part One] Preparing Your Presentations

1

GETTING STARTED 2

2

PREPARING YOUR FIRST PRESENTATION 26

[Part Two] Selecting and Arranging Content

5

FINDING INFORMATION AND SUPPORTING YOUR IDEAS 96

6

ORGANIZING AND OUTLINING YOUR PRESENTATION 126

7

DELIVERING SPEECHES 158

8

CHOOSING YOUR WORDS 180

9

[Part Three] Types of Presentations

10

11

PRESENTING PERSUASIVE MESSAGES 246

12

SPEAKING ON SPECIAL OCCASIONS 270

[Appendix]

1

GETTING

The purpose of this chapter is to help you face your fears, manage your anxieties, and launch your learning about effective public presentations. It also will remind you of the role public speaking plays in a democratic society at large and will encourage you to view the public speaking course as a way to learn how to be a fully functioning member of your local community. Toward the end of the chapter you will learn unique characteristics of public presentations, tips for effective talks, and techniques for keeping out of trouble with your audience.

STARTED

[As You READ

>>

1. Confront your fears about public speaking.
2. Strategize ways to reduce communication apprehension.
3. Connect to your community through public speaking.
4. Identify appropriate and vital presentation topics.
5. Define the communication process.

]

Almost anyone who becomes successful for almost any reason will be asked to speak to others about his or her experience. Danny Wong, for instance, attends Bentley University (Massachusetts), where he studies communication. As a high school student in Brooklyn, Danny co-founded an online custom dress-shirt company called Blank Label that he still runs from his college dorm room. The operation has been such a success that it's been featured in *Forbes, BusinessWeek,* and the *New York Times* among other publications.

Naturally everyone in the business world wants to know what contributed to Danny's success, and the young entrepreneur has told his story to the media in speeches and interviews a number of times. He attributes his achievements to the opportunity to attend a strong high school, to his efforts to build a network of contacts, and to reading everything he could find about how to start a small business. Asked what advice he would offer aspiring entrepreneurs, Danny recommends having realistic expectations and realizing that success requires a lot of "determination, dexterity, and sacrifice."

Whether or not you imagine yourself becoming a successful entrepreneur like Danny, over the course of your life you are likely to confront many situations in which public speaking skills can make the difference between success and failure. This book encourages you to explore the issues you care about so you can share your views with others in class and throughout your life. This chapter will help you see public speaking as an exciting and positive experience and will lead you to choose vital and appropriate topics.

How Would *You* Do It?

Refer to the chapter opening story and list a few of the characteristics or qualities of Danny Wong's story that you think make the success of Blank Label an appropriate presentation topic.

If you are reading this sentence, you are taking a class in which you are expected to deliver presentations. Which of the following comes closest to how you feel?

Speaking Excites

Student 1:   I'm eager to get in the spotlight, take center stage, and perform. I'll give a speech that will dazzle my classmates with its brilliance. I am so pleased that I am required to do something that will make me so happy.

Student 2:   I'm so scared that I think I'm going to die from fright before I ever get to the front of the room to give a speech.

Yes, these two are extreme cases, but in fact most students face a public speaking class with mixed emotions.

Typically, students who have been active in debate, individual events, theater, and musical performances are more like Student 1 above. Similarly, students who have worked full-time in responsible jobs, are married, have raised kids, or have served in the armed forces seem more likely to have confidence. Perhaps they already know more than most people about some subjects, and they are not worried about sharing their experiences.

The less you have interacted with people, the more likely you are to be worried about public speaking—like Student 2 above. People who grew up in families, cultures, and communities that value verbal communication may have been encouraged to hone their skills through such activities as debating, acting, volunteering, performing, or working. If you grew up in a family where "silence is golden" or "children are to be seen but not heard," then you may have been discouraged from developing presentation skills.

Almost anything that you do for the first time has an element of risk: the few lines you had to say in front of the class in grade school, the first date, the first kiss, the first job interview, or the first request for a raise. Interestingly, many people who claim to be afraid of public presentations probably like other experiences that scare them—for example, skiing down a steep slope, parachuting from a plane, swimming in riptides, or driving too fast. The authors recently watched an entire boatload of tourists of all ages intentionally jump off a cliff into the sea about 70 feet below, some seriously bruising themselves on splashdown. Look on your public speaking class as an opportunity to give yourself a thrill, just like many other first-time experiences. You will suffer no bruises or head traumas, but you will feel excitement.

What's the Worst-Case Scenario?

One way to face fear is to consider, "What is the worst thing that can happen?" Beginning speakers have great imaginations, especially when they fantasize about everything that could go wrong. Let's consider the possibilities:

Will you die? Comedian Jerry Seinfeld had an opening monologue in which he said, "The number two fear people have is death. The number one fear is public speaking. This means if you go to a funeral, you would rather be the person in the coffin than the person delivering the eulogy." The authors of this book have over 90 years of combined teaching experience. We have heard thousands of classroom speeches. So far, not one student has died while speaking. Nor have we ever heard of one who did.

Will you faint? One of the authors used to carry a smelling salts capsule (the kind used to revive people when they faint), just in case a student fainted while giving a speech. After several thousand student speeches the gauze-wrapped capsule started to get very dirty, but not from ever using it. The author finally threw the capsule away. None of the authors has ever seen a student faint.

Will you shake, sweat, look down, and feel your mouth go dry? Probably. Most beginning speakers feel these symptoms of anxiety, but they feel them less as they speak more. Were you as nervous on your third kiss as you were on your first? Well, you will not be as nervous on your third speech as you were on your first.

Will you blush, flush, stammer, and trip over your tongue? You might. You cannot help blushing and flushing. They are natural responses that disappear as you become more comfortable. Sometimes even experienced speakers stammer a bit and mess up on a word. You shouldn't be very concerned even if you do have minor difficulties. Even the pros trip over a word now and then.

Will you forget what you were saying? Could happen. In front of 1,200 students one of the authors used to move 40 feet from the lectern that held his notes and then forget what he was trying to explain. He would ask the class what they thought he was trying to prove, and someone in the front row always knew. In your presentations, you will likely have note cards of some sort that can help you if you get stuck. If you don't act overly concerned about the lapse, your audience won't be concerned either.

Will you survive the course? Chances are excellent that you will complete the course, learn how to reduce your fears, learn how to focus on the message and the audience, and perhaps even want to speak in the workplace or community. The vast majority of public speaking students like the course and understand that it is important—after they have completed it. In fact, our experience is that students often claim they entered the class "dreading" it, but quickly discovered that public speaking was one of their most interesting and enjoyable classes. Often your speech class is the only class in which you get to express your opinion about an important issue, and it may be one of the very few in which the teacher actually knows you. In the next section, let's address how public speaking will be one of the most useful courses you will take.

> *"Often your speech class is the only class in which you get to express your opinion about an important issue, and it may be one of the very few in which the teacher actually knows you."*

try this

Pair up with a partner and talk with each other about your feelings on taking this course. Probe a bit to find out why the other person likes or dislikes delivering public presentations. Talk for a few minutes about what you might do to increase your comfort level in the course and during the presentations.

Democracy

Studying public communication can help you exercise your constitutionally guaranteed freedom of speech. Few nations have a bill of rights that invites their citizens to convey opinions and ideas, yet freedom of speech is essential to a democratic form of government. Being a practicing citizen in a democratic society therefore depends upon knowing about current issues and being able to speak about them in conversations, in speeches, and even through the mass media. It also involves being able to critically examine messages from others. Your public speaking course can help you become a fully functioning member of your local community and our democratic society at large. Democracy presents many opportunities, but it thrives only when everyday citizens embrace its freedoms as responsibilities to actively uphold.

To apply this concept of freedom of speech to civic engagement, you should think of individuals in your school, neighborhood, or community who take risks by speaking out. Which parent dares to confront the school board about some new rule? Which worker organizes fellow workers to object to unsafe working conditions? Or which manager tells workers about the new merger, the workforce reduction, or the laying off of employees? All of these instances take some daring, but all are practical examples of how an individual can use public speaking to clarify a rule, improve the workplace, or reveal an unfortunate turn of events like the closing of an industrial plant.

Life Skills

Studying public speaking can teach you important life skills. It involves learning skills that every person will use at some point in his or her life, such as critical thinking, problem solving, decision making, conflict resolution, team building, and media literacy. Studying communication early in your college career can enhance your success throughout college, too. Consider the centrality of oral communication to all of your classes. You regularly are called on to answer questions in class, to provide reports, to offer explanations, and to make presentations. In addition, your oral and written work depends on your ability to think critically and creatively, to solve problems, and to make decisions. Most likely, you will be engaged in group projects where skills such as team building, conflict resolution, and presentation will be keys to success. These same skills will be essential throughout your life.

One of the most important life skills that you can apply immediately and every day is critical listening. Because you hear many more speeches than you give, you can frequently apply your brainpower to what other speakers say: Is the speaker telling the whole story, or is important information being omitted? Is the speaker promoting a community action that makes sense (building a new stadium, a halfway house for addicts, or a new mall), or should opposing views be heard? Civic engagement means taking a critical

Why Study Public Speaking?

" **Congress shall make no law respecting an establishment of religion, or prohibiting the free exercise thereof; or abridging the freedom of speech, or of the press; or the right of the people peaceably to assemble, and to petition the Government for a redress of grievances.** "

[The First Amendment to the U.S. Constitution]

look at which projects will do a community the most good. Maybe the new stadium will be an economic asset, but will that project also wipe out a neighborhood or two that deserve a hearing on this matter?

Work and Career

Studying public speaking can help you succeed professionally. A look at the job postings in any newspaper will give you an immediate understanding of the importance of improving your knowledge and practice of communication. The following excerpts from classified advertisements in the employment section of the Sunday paper are fairly typical:

- "We need a results-oriented, seasoned professional who is a good communicator and innovator," reads one ad for a home healthcare manager.
- Another ad, this one for a marketing analyst, reads: "You should be creative, inquisitive, and a good communicator both in writing and speaking."
- An ad for a computer-training specialist calls for "excellent presentation, verbal, and written communication skills, with the ability to interact with all levels within the organization."

As a person educated in communication, not only will you acquire the interviewing skills that will positively impact hiring decisions, but you also will have greater access to the most desirable jobs. Personnel managers typically identify effective speaking and listening as the most important reasons for hiring the people they do. Your communication skill set will continue to be important throughout your career and will always be a factor in upward mobility and successful entrepreneurship.

Do People Really Speak Anymore?

Back in the 1980s, when computers replaced typewriters, experts thought the "electronic office" would eliminate the need for paper and for secretaries. Instead, offices still have secretaries, and workers use more paper than ever before as they download information from Web sites, print electronic messages, and continue to store copies in filing cabinets. In the 1940s and 1950s, when radio and then television became common and videoconferencing became possible, experts thought nobody would be interested in paying someone to speak in person when she or he could be projected on a screen and respond interactively with an audience. On the contrary, speakers are even more in demand than before. Universities and colleges have many guest speakers; businesses invite consultants, motivational speakers, successful executives, and salespeople to speak; and every academic and business conference pays speakers to attract people to their conventions. Speaking is very big business.

Chances are excellent that you too will have opportunities to speak publicly. Peggy Noonan—speechwriter for President George H. W. Bush, President Reagan, and a host of business executives—says:

As more and more businesses become involved in the new media technologies, as we become a nation of fewer widgets and more Web sites, a new premium has been put

on the oldest form of communication: the ability to stand and say what you think in front of others.[1]

What if you could hear or see your favorite entertainer (*a*) on radio, (*b*) on TV, (*c*) on a "live" transmission via a large screen, or (*d*) in person? Which would you choose if cost and distance were not an issue? Why do we want to see politicians, athletes, and entertainers in person? We are so overexposed to people on film and video that seeing an important individual in person becomes much more special. More than ever we want to see a flesh-and-blood person talking to us.

What Is the Presentation Process?

Early in this course you need to grasp the big picture of the communication process with its component parts. Presenting is just one kind of communication context that can include many others, such as interpersonal communication, group communication, and computer-mediated communication. All of these contexts involve the seven components described below. Just as you are unlikely to understand the particulars of an automobile without understanding how horsepower, octane, torque, and exhaust contribute to speed, you are unlikely to understand the particulars of public presentations without knowing how the parts interact with each other.

What Are the Seven Components of the Communication Process?

Some basic elements are present in practically all public speaking circumstances:

1. A source, presenter, or speaker who utters the message.
2. A receiver, audience members, or classmates who listen.
3. A message: your words and ideas adapted to that audience.
4. A channel, or means of distributing your words.
5. Feedback: responses from the audience.
6. A situation: the context in which the presentation occurs.
7. Noise: any form of interference with the message.

Let's look more closely at the components of the communication process.

Source

The **source** is *the person who originates the message.* Who the sender is makes a difference in determining who, if anyone, will listen. Consider a person walking down a street in New York City. He or she would hear cell phone conversations, people hailing taxicabs, and vendors selling everything from bagels to baklava. Would you listen to the messages they are sending? Some of the talented singers, dancers, and instrumentalists might attract your attention, but few of the many contenders for your eyes and ears would succeed. Sources send messages, but no communication occurs until messages link the source and receiver.

Similarly, in the lecture hall, some professors capture your attention and leave you wishing for more ideas. Occasionally you hear delivery-challenged professors who put you to sleep in spite of their bright ideas. A source is useless without a receiver, and a speaker is useless without an audience that listens.

The source of a message has to be ethically responsible. You cannot say anything to anybody just because speech is free and its use is guaranteed. You can face charges if you incite a riot, cause a panic, or slander someone who is not a public figure. Our freedom of speech is linked to the principle of responsibility that says you are acting unethically, immorally, and possibly illegally if your message is damaging to individuals or the community in some irresponsible fashion.

Receiver

The **receiver**, listener, or audience is *the individual or group that hears, and listens to, the message sent by the source.* All individuals are unique. Receivers are individuals who have inherited certain characteristics and developed others as a result of their families, friends, and education.

The best speakers can "read" an audience; through analysis or intuition they can tell what an audience wants, needs, or responds to. This sort of group empathy allows some speakers to be seen as charismatic: they seem to exhibit what the audience feels. Even a beginning speaker can learn to see the world through the audience's eyes. Nothing helps more in the classroom than to listen carefully to your classmates' speeches, because every speech will reveal as much about the speaker as about the issue being discussed. Few speakers outside the classroom are able to hear each individual in the audience reveal herself or himself through a speech, a unique opportunity to analyze your listeners. The great benefit of speaking is that you get to respond with and to your audience, adapting and supporting your message in a way you cannot do in any other form of communication.

Message

Verbal and nonverbal messages are an integral part of the communication process. What else links the source and the receiver? Both source and receiver sense the **message**: *the facial expressions seen, the words heard, the visual aids illustrated, and the ideas or meanings conveyed simultaneously between source and receiver.* **Verbal messages** are *the words the source chose for the speech.* **Nonverbal messages** are *the movements, gestures, facial expressions, and vocal variations that can reinforce or contradict the words,* such as pitch or tone of voice that can alter the meaning of the words.

Channel

The **channel** is *the means of distributing your words, whether by coaxial cable, fiber optics, microwave, radio, video, or air.* In the public speaking classroom, the channel is first of all the air that carries the sound waves from the mouth of the source to the ear of the receiver. The type of channel might not seem to make very much difference, but messages have decidedly different impacts depending on whether they are heard from your mouth, seen on Microsoft PowerPoint, viewed on video, or heard on an iPod.

Some public speaking students discover the differences among channels when their teacher videotapes their speeches. Watching yourself electronically reproduced is not the same as watching yourself in a live performance because channels are themselves part of the message. Do you perceive a professor in a classroom the same as you do an instructor of an online course? Probably not. The channel makes a difference. Or, as Marshall McLuhan famously expressed, "The medium is the message."

Feedback

Feedback includes *verbal or nonverbal responses by the audience.* During a public speech, most of the audience feedback is nonverbal: head nodding, smiling, frowning, giving complete attention, fiddling with an iPod. All this nonverbal feedback allows the speaker to infer whether the message is being communicated to the listeners.

The question-and-answer session is a good example of verbal feedback in which the audience has an opportunity to seek clarification, to verify the speaker's positions on issues, and to challenge the speaker's arguments. In any case, feedback, like the thermostat on a furnace or an air conditioner, is the speaker's monitoring device that continuously indicates whether the message is working.

Situation

Communication occurs in a context called the **situation**—*the time, place, and occasion in which the message sending and receiving occurs.* The situation can determine what kind of message is appropriate. Only certain kinds of messages and speakers are acceptable at funerals, debates, elementary school meetings, bar mitzvahs, court hearings, and dedications. In the classroom, the situation is a room of a certain size, containing a number of people who fill a specified number of seats. The physical setting can mean that you can talk almost conversationally or that you must shout to be heard.

To apply this idea of situation in public speaking, and to link the idea to civic engagement, think of how often in your community a speech is expected. Does a politician ever make a public appearance without a speech? How often does a graduation occur without a student or guest speaker? Do you expect words to be spoken at religious services? A uniting feature in all human communities is the ritual presentation that we expect to hear to commemorate the specific occasion.

Noise

Another component of the communication process is **noise**, *interference or obstacles to communication.* Noise can be internal, in which case it can be mental (daydreaming or worry) or physical (headache or illness). Internal noise is unique to the individual. Noise also can be external, in which case it can be auditory (a jackhammer outside the window) or visual (sunlight in your eyes). External noise can affect one or many and is not unique to the individual.

The **process of communication** is *the dynamic interrelationship of source, receiver, message, channel, feedback, situation, and noise.* In actual, real-life presentations, all of these components function simultaneously and continuously. For example, let's say that you (the source) are trying to convince fellow workers (the receivers) that they should unionize (message). You argue first that the union will result in higher pay (message). The audience appears unimpressed (feedback), so you argue that the union will bring such benefits as better working conditions (message). They doze (feedback). Finally you argue that the workers will get better medical and dental plans for their families, reducing their out-of-pocket health expenses (message). This argument gets attentive looks, some questions, and considerable interest (feedback). The audience has influenced the source and the message through feedback.

The speaker conveys a message through words and action, but the audience gives meaning to that message through its own thought processes. Audiences interpret messages; they construct messages of their own from the words they hear; and they carry with them their own version of the message. Politicians slather their presentations with abstractions that audiences interpret in their own ways. The more abstract the language, the greater are the possible interpretations. "I stand for family values," says a politician. The listeners from a variety of different kinds of families can interpret this to mean that the politician is embracing their particular family.

"The speaker conveys a message through words and action, but the audience gives meaning to that message through its own thought processes."

The process of communication is a transaction between source and receivers that includes mutual influence, the interpretation and construction of meaning, and the development of an individualized message that includes how others respond. What is **communication**? *A transaction in which speaker and listener simultaneously send, receive, and interpret messages.* In public speaking, the temptation is to see the action as predominantly one-way communication: the speaker sends words to the audience. However, in many public speaking situations, the

audience influences the speaker through continuous feed-back, sometimes with words and actions and sometimes almost subconsciously.

To demonstrate the powerful effect of the audience on the speaker, a teacher challenged his class to influence his behavior. One rule was that the moment he knew they were trying to influence him, the game was over. The class had to figure out what they could do to encourage some kind of behavioral change. After 10 weeks, the teacher had not caught the class trying to influence him. They had docu-mented, however, that, when the experiment began, the teacher stroked his chin once or twice each class period. They decided that the teacher would feel rewarded if they paid more attention, asked questions, and showed interest whenever this behavior occurred. Every time the teacher touched his chin, the class subtly rewarded him with their interest, attention, and questions. By the end of the 10-week course, they had the teacher touching his chin over 20 times each class session—and the teacher was totally unaware of this influence.

The point of this anecdote is that audiences do influence speakers. In a public rally against gang proliferation and violence, they might do so with the words they yell, the movements and noises they make, or even with the signs they hold. In class, it could be the sight of heads nodding or eyes glazing over. The fact is that speakers influence audiences and audiences influence speakers, and they do so continuously in public speaking situations. See Figure 1.1 for a model of the presentation process.

Why Is Public Speaking a Unique Form of Communication?

Public speaking has some unique features that are impor-tant for you to know. However, in some ways, public speak-ing is like enhanced conversation. Teachers often praise students for using conversational, everyday language with their classroom audiences. When you meet someone for a friendly conversation, you normally greet (introduction), talk about something (body), and say goodbye (conclu-sion). Classroom presentations tend to be about serious issues, but so do many conversations. Yet, the language of conversation has fewer rules—you can say just about anything in any manner to a close friend—and conversation has turn-taking, which is usually reserved for the question-and-answer portion of a presentation. In contrast to everyday conversation, the language of presentations is more carefully chosen to appeal to a larger group. However, both in conversation and in presen-tations you basically are trying to get some message across to another person. Here are some additional unique features of public presentations, especially classroom speeches.

Time is short. Public speaking presentations typically are short. Ronald Reagan (U.S. President, 1980–1988), who was called "The Great Communicator," once said that no speech should last more than 20 minutes. He meant that 20 minutes is about all an audience can tolerate. Most of your speeches will be considerably shorter.

Simplification is necessary. You cannot say much in five minutes, especially when you consider that the introductory portion of the speech often takes one minute

Figure 1.1   **The presentation process shows a speaker and an audience simultaneously sending and receiving messages while constructing meaning.**

and the conclusion is about half a minute. How much can you say about any subject in the remaining three-and-a-half minutes? Complex topics must be simplified, complicated topics may have to be managed in parts, and deep topics may have to be introduced rather than thoroughly vetted. In his Gettysburg Address in 1863, U.S. President Abraham Lincoln delivered a "deep speech" in about three-and-a-half minutes.

Points are few. Even though bulleted lists are common and most everyone knows "The Top Ten Reasons" format, you need to limit your speech to very few main points—usually two or three. Why? Because people do not remember much. Even if you ask your audience, "What were my three main points?" you will be lucky if they remember one or two. Can you remember a politician's position on global warming, stem cell research, hate crime, or literacy? Probably not. We tend to remember brief declarations such as "No more taxes," "No more war," and "Jobs for all."

Topics are important. You need to have something important to say. A beautifully delivered speech about a trivial topic is still an empty shell, but an important or timely topic can have impact even if the delivery is uninspiring. We listen carefully to messages that are important to us.

What Topics Should You Talk About?

Our concept of freedom of speech—guaranteed by the U.S. Constitution—means that people can talk about almost anything. However, in a public speaking class, some topics work better than others. The following are some practical guidelines to help you think of topics.

Choose vital topics. This book encourages students to select topics on important issues. Among these important topics are the ones in the list to the right.

From any of these broad areas of concern, you could generate dozens of possible topics for your speeches—topics that are interesting and relevant to you and your classmates.

Choose current topics. Audiences prefer speakers who talk about issues that are relevant and timely. They like to be informed about matters that involve them. You could, of course, provide historical context about an important topic, but remember that audiences generally care about what is current.

Democracy
Environment
Technology
Education
Diversity
Ethics
Health
Economy

Choose topics that improve the audience. You will want to inform the audience about topics that will help them and to persuade them about topics that will make a positive difference in their lives. You will want to help individuals, improve the community, and serve those who need help.

You can learn to be an effective speaker by choosing vital topics, selecting a current topic, and picking a topic that improves the audience, the community, and/or the country or world.

try this

With another person in your class, make a list of some topics about which you feel knowledgeable. Then together size up some of those topics against the features mentioned above. Are they topics you should talk about or topics that invite you to reconsider?

What Should You Avoid in a Presentation?

Communication teachers believe in freedom of speech. We think that U.S. Americans should be allowed to talk about almost anything. All freedoms have limits, however. Although you can talk about almost anything in this country, here are some suggestions for topics and approaches to avoid in the classroom.

Avoid exhausted topics unless you have a new approach. Remember, your speech teacher hears many speeches. Some topics have been talked about so often without making much headway that hearing them again makes the teacher's head throb. What are some examples? Gun control and abortion rights are a couple of culprits.

Avoid illegal items lest you end up suspended or in jail. Most campuses do not allow alcohol, drugs, weapons, or bombs. So do not advocate using them, especially by showing them in class. On the other hand, you can argue that something currently illegal ought to be legalized: assisted suicide, medical marijuana, or a drinking age of 18. If you have doubts about the legality or appropriateness of your topic, then you should get your teacher's opinion.

Avoid insulting your audience. Since one of the goals of this course is to teach you how to influence others through public speaking, you need to be careful what you say about others. Ethnic slurs, cultural slights, racial epithets, street lingo, swearing, and attacks on religious beliefs of others may be legal, but they certainly are unwise choices. You can avoid insulting your audience by always approaching them with an attitude of respect.

Plagiarism: Serious Warning About Cheating

Teachers across the country are reporting an increasing number of students who get in serious trouble because they commit **plagiarism**, *the intentional use of information from a source without crediting that source.* Scholars regard plagiarism as a form of stealing, the theft of someone else's words or ideas. Because we do not want you to get into any difficulty over this offense, this warning reveals the problem and the solution.

The problem is taking someone else's words or ideas and claiming them as your own by not including a footnote or endnote in writing or an oral citation or verbal footnote in speaking.

For example, a student giving a presentation about the Supreme Court's 2010 decision on gun control finds this passage from the *New York Times*: "While such a ruling would represent an enormous symbolic victory for supporters of gun rights, its short-term practical impact would almost certainly be limited."[2] The student also finds this direct quote from the *Chicago Tribune* about ". . . this week's U.S. Supreme Court decision that gutted the city's handgun ban." That source continued: "The proposed ordinance . . . includes many limitations and requirements, including the exclusion of garages, porches and outside stairs from the definition of a home. The restrictions could trigger a legal challenge from at least some of the pro-gun forces that put the gun ban on its death bed."[3]

The student then places in his speech these words (with the material lifted from the sources above in italics):

Pro-gun forces celebrated *an enormous symbolic victory* last week when the U.S. Supreme Court *gutted* Chicago's *handgun ban* and *put the gun ban on its death bed.*

This single sentence blends the student's few words with many words from the two sources quoted above. The offense of plagiarism occurs because the speaker never indicates a source. What the speaker could have said without committing plagiarism would sound like this:

The *New York Times* last week in an article called "Supreme Court Still Divided on Guns" called the 5–4 decision "an enormous symbolic victory for supporters of gun rights." At the same time, the July 1, 2010, *Chicago Tribune*, reporting on the city gun ban being overturned, noted in an article titled "Daley Proposes New Handgun

Ordinance" that "this week's U.S. Supreme Court decision . . . gutted the city's handgun ban."

The student in this case correctly cites sources for using another's words and ideas and therefore avoids plagiarism.

The following are acts of plagiarism.

- Copying part or all of another person's speech or outline as if it were your own.
- Copying part or all of a speech or outline lifted from the Internet.
- Paraphrasing (putting someone else's words into your own words) without citing a source.

If you are unsure about whether something requires a verbal citation or a footnote, you should ask your teacher.

Every college and university has a student code of conduct that reveals the punishments for plagiarism. They often range from flunking the assignment to failing the course to being expelled. Many colleges and universities supply their faculty with software for detecting plagiarism. Finally, cultural differences occur in this issue, so international students need to be aware that colleges and universities in the United States abide by a strict interpretation of the rules against plagiarism. Do your own work, and credit others when you use their words or ideas.

Becoming an Effective Speaker

You play the most important role in making a presentation. You choose the message, you analyze the listeners, you organize the message, and you deliver the message. A presentation is always a dance, however, in which the speaker (one dance partner) uses a message (the music) to influence the listener (the other dance partner).

The Speaker's Source Credibility

Some students think they must receive a complete makeover before they can be public speakers. They may see themselves as shy, fearful of audiences, or just cautious in front of a group. They may think they have to look and sound like an entertainer, a famous preacher, or a broadcaster. Actually, the notion of a complete makeover is not possible or desirable. If all speakers looked and sounded alike, then we would grow weary of hearing them speak. If you are not funny now, this course is unlikely to make you humorous. If you are not a live wire now, this course is unlikely to make you crackle with energy. And if you lack charisma, this course is unlikely to turn you into the most popular person in the room. If you really concentrate on communicating your message to your audience in a caring and conversational manner, then you will not have to worry about how you look.

A beginning speaker can develop three areas that have been the cornerstones of public speaking for well over two thousand years. The ancient Greek philosopher Aristotle called them *ethos*, *logos*, and *pathos*. We call them source credibility, logical argument, and emotional argument. You need credibility (*ethos*) to inspire an audience to listen to an emotional story (*pathos*) that is backed by an argument (*logos*) for change. We will look most closely in this chapter at you—the source—and how "who you are" and "what you are" affect your influence on an audience. Later, in the chapter on persuasion, we will examine logical and emotional argument.

Aristotle
384–322 BCE

Benjamin Franklin likened a person's reputation to glass and china: once cracked it is never quite the same again. He was speaking of **source credibility**, *the audience's perception of your effectiveness as a communicator.* Your effectiveness is not based just on presentation or delivery skills but more on what you know and how effectively you communicate your ideas to the audience.

One means of establishing a relationship with your audience is to use **common ground**—*pointing out what features you share with your audience:* "All of us have noticed that our air quality is poor here," "We students need to balance learning with keeping physically healthy," and "What courses should qualify as general education credits?"

A second means of establishing source credibility is establishing trustworthiness. **Trustworthiness** is *the degree to which the audience perceives the presenter as honest and honorable.* A student in one author's public speaking class came unprepared. Because the assignment was brief (just the introductory portion of his presentation), he listened carefully to the first five speakers and then confidently jumped to his feet to deliver a two-minute introduction full of facts and figures. After his presentation, classmates inquired about his claim that 4,000 people died from eating junk food during the Super Bowl. The student admitted that he had made up all the facts and figures while the other students were delivering their presentations. After that, the class never fully trusted him because he had lied so obviously in his first presentation. Trust is difficult to earn but easy to lose.

A third technique for encouraging your audience to listen to you is to display **competence**, *a thorough familiarity with your topic.* For example, an agriculture major might demonstrate her competence in organic gardening by showing how to compost, irrigate, and manage pests. You can accomplish the same purpose by presenting topics about which you have some expertise beyond most people in your class, or topics that you have researched thoroughly.

**Benjamin Franklin
1706–1790** CE

"If all speakers looked and sounded alike, then we would grow weary of hearing them speak."

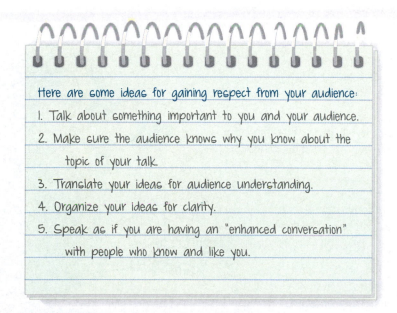

Here are some ideas for gaining respect from your audience:

1. Talk about something important to you and your audience.

2. Make sure the audience knows why you know about the topic of your talk.

3. Translate your ideas for audience understanding.

4. Organize your ideas for clarity.

5. Speak as if you are having an "enhanced conversation" with people who know and like you.

Figure 1.2   **Tips for gaining respect from your audience.**

A fourth feature that encourages your audience to pay attention to you is **dynamism**, *the energy you expend in delivering your message.* Typically, audiences are attracted by movement, gestures, facial expression, and voice variety—all delivery characteristics. Think about this comparison. Would you rather watch a presenter who is difficult to hear, rarely looks up from his or her notes, lacks facial expression, speaks in one tone, and never moves or gestures? Or would you rather watch someone who is lively and maybe even a bit dramatic, someone who can whisper and shout, someone who moves, points, and exclaims during the presentation? Listeners tend to respond favorably to presenters whose manner reflects their sincerity and conviction about the subject matter. For tips on gaining audience respect, see Figure 1.2.

The good news is that you do not have to be a top performer in all aspects of credibility. You might, for example, be exceedingly strong on trustworthiness but not be particularly dynamic, or you might be highly competent but not have much in common with your listeners. Play to your strengths without feeling that you have to be at the top of every dimension of source credibility.

Listening

Audience members decide in seconds what they think of a presenter, and what they think of a presenter may determine whether they are merely **hearing** (*receiving sound waves*) or **listening** (*interpreting the sounds as a message*). Hearing is physiological: You cannot keep from picking up the sounds unless you somehow block the sound from entering your ears. Listening is a psychological process: you need to attend to, think about, and derive meaning from the sounds. For suggestions on listening, see Figure 1.3.

You probably listen differently in different situations: passive listening to background music in your car or home and active listening when the sounds demand full attention. Active listening is characterized by posture (forward lean, head cocked for better reception), facial features (eyes alert and on the source of the message), and movement (hand cupped on the ear, hand taking notes). You might be a passive listener when your teacher is giving examples of a concept you already understand, but you are likely to be an active listener when your teacher says the words, "What I am telling you next will be on the test." Listening actively in conversation can make you a valued friend, mate, or partner. Listening

1. **Avoid Distractions.**
   Sit so the presenter is your main focus, in front of the room, away from talkative friends, away from distracting sounds and sights.

2. **Actively Engage.**
   Watch attentively, write down important points and useful observations, note what is not being said, and ask questions for clarification.

3. **Be Thoughtful.**
   What are the presenter's main points? Were they supported well? Do you agree with the message? Why or why not?

Figure 1.3 **Tips for listening during a presentation.**

actively in class is often the difference between the student who earns poor grades and the one who earns good grades. In the public speaking classroom, active listening not only allows you to learn from the content of other speakers, but it invites you to learn what delivery skills are most effective with your audience.

For more information turn to Chapter 4, "Analyzing the Audience," where you will find a section dedicated to "Listening and Public Speaking."

CULTURAL DIFFERENCES IN PRESENTATIONS

Speakers from different countries of origin often behave differently when they speak. After working with African American students at Howard University; working with students from Korea, Malaysia, and Thailand; and frequent visits to Africa and Scandinavia and forty other cultures, the authors have observed the following: Scandinavian and many Asian women cover their mouths when they smile, laugh, or giggle. Puerto Ricans, Italians, Slovenians, and Israelis tend to use gestures and facial expressions more freely than others. Finns, Swedes, Norwegians, and Native Americans are relatively unexpressive. Many Pacific Rim women are reluctant to speak loudly, and African American men and women are particularly good at being expressive.

Effective presenters learn to manage their natural nervousness so that their delivery is not damaged. In fact, they often regard "stage fright" positively. Just as athletes feel an adrenaline rush before a big game, and entertainers get "keyed up" before a performance, experienced public speakers know the initial nervousness will pass and likely will be transformed to positive energy. Although most of us feel apprehension when presenting in public, we typically get over this natural nervousness quickly. This is not to say that you will never be nervous. The point is that experienced presenters recognize that some nervousness is natural, and they take strategic steps to minimize the possibility that natural nervousness will become so severe that their delivery becomes less conversational. Let's identify these strategies, because nearly everyone experiences some fear when presenting in front of an audience.

How to Reduce Your Fear of Presenting

"Students with high levels of anxiety practically set themselves up for failure."

Understanding Communication Apprehension

The fear of presenting is called **communication apprehension (CA)**, or *an individual's level of fear or anxiety associated with either real or anticipated communication with another person or persons.*[4] Symptoms of CA include sleeplessness, worry, reluctance before you present, and "interfering, off-task thoughts" while you present.[5] Thinking "off-task thoughts" means losing focus on communicating your message to your audience by concentrating instead on sweaty palms, shaking knees, and "cotton mouth," the feeling that your tongue is swollen and your mouth is as dry as the Sahara. One wit noted that public presenters suffer so often from wet palms and dry mouth that they should stick their hands in their mouths.

What else do we know about CA? Students with high levels of anxiety practically set themselves up for failure. Students high in anxiety exhibit "less audience adaptation, less concern for equipment likely to be available when the speech was presented, less concern about the tools available to aid in preparing the speech, more difficulty in coming up with information for speeches, and greater self-doubts about one's capability as a speaker."[6] On the other hand, CA is not correlated with age, sex, or grade-point average,[7] and students with the highest anxiety in public communication courses "showed the largest improvement in perceived competence."[8]

Reducing Anxiety

What can you do to reduce the anxiety that you are likely to feel before speaking? What thoughts can you think, what actions can you take, and what precautions can you observe to help you shift attention from yourself to your message and your audience? The following six keys to confidence can help you reduce your fear of public speaking.

1. *Act confidently.* Actions often change before attitudes do. You may act as if you like others before you really do. You dress up for a party, and as a result, act in a certain way. You decide that you are going to have fun at a social event, and you do.

   You can use the same strategy when you present by thinking of public speaking as acting. You can say to yourself, "I am going to behave in a confident manner when I speak," and then proceed to act confidently even if you are not. This action is not much different from acting cool on the street, playing the role of the intellectual in class, or pretending you are a sports hero in a game. You are simply acting as if you are confident standing in front of the class. Our students suggest the following: Move to the front of the room as if you own it and act as if the audience respects you and wants to hear your words.

2. *Know your subject.* Your first presentation should be about something you know already. This early experience should not require very much research. In fact, many communication professors will ask you to talk about yourself. Whether you speak about some aspect of yourself or some other topic, you will be a better presenter if you choose a subject that you know something about.

   When LaMarr Doston, a thirty-year-old father of three, was assigned to give his first presentation, he could think of nothing about himself that he wanted to share with the class. He was glad that he did not have to do research for the presentation, but he was unhappy that he did not know what to say about himself. After two days of worrying about it, LaMarr was in his office at work when he thought of what he was going to say: "I am LaMarr Doston, the Fast Food King."

   LaMarr had worked for five different fast-food chains over the years. He worked his way from a mop jockey at one place, to counter server at another, to fry cook at a third, to night shift manager at a fourth, and now morning shift manager at the fifth fast-food chain. LaMarr was good at his work, promoted frequently, commended often, and recommended highly. He seemed to know every job there was at a fast-food outlet. He was the Fast Food King.

3. *Care about your subject.* Amanda Carroll gave an introductory presentation about being adopted and bi-ethnic. Amanda had one African American biological parent and one European American biological parent. As a baby, she was put up for adoption in a small Ohio town and raised by white parents. Amanda was very perceptive. She knew that people wondered about her origins because of her appearance. She satisfied the audience's curiosity and provided an added dimension by discussing the satisfaction of being chosen as a baby by parents who wanted and loved her.

   If your teacher wants you to speak on a topic other than yourself, you should make sure that you select one that you know and care about. Avoid, in general, politically charged issues, but do select a topic in which you are passionately interested. The more you care about your subject, the more you are going to focus on the message and the audience instead of worrying about yourself.

4. *See your classmates as friends.* No audience is more concerned about your success than your classmates in a beginning public speaking course. They worry about you so much that if you should falter, they break into a sweat. They care how you do. See them as friends instead of uncaring strangers, and your perceptions will help you feel confident in front of the classroom. Our own students suggest that you begin talking only when you are ready, and that you look at the people in your audience before starting. While speaking, focus on the friendly faces—those who smile, nod, and generally make you feel good about your speech.

5. *See yourself as successful.* If you are an inexperienced presenter, you may need to work at thinking positively about your prospects as a public presenter. You need to think about, and then rehearse in your mind, how you are going to give your presentation. Some people might call this "worrying," but psychologists call it "mental imaging." Whatever you call this mindfulness, you can use it to help you succeed. Consider the difference between the statements of negative and positive self-assessment in Table 1.1. Thinking about your presentation in a positive way will not eliminate all nervousness, but upbeat thinking will keep it from becoming harmful.

6. *Practice for confidence.* More and better practice reduces nervousness. Indeed, research has demonstrated that this is the case.[9] Our own students recommend having your introduction, main points, and conclusion clear in your head. The more times you practice, the less nervous you will feel. Also, the more closely your practice sessions resemble your actual speaking experience—including an audience, for example—the less nervous you

TABLE 1.1 STATEMENTS OF NEGATIVE AND POSITIVE SELF-ASSESSMENT	
STATEMENTS OF NEGATIVE SELF-ASSESSMENT	STATEMENTS OF POSITIVE SELF-ASSESSMENT
• "I will forget what I am supposed to say."	• "I can prepare well enough to succeed in my presentation."
• "I will turn red when I get nervous."	• "Each time I practiced the presentation I felt better about it."
• "My presentation will be boring."	• "People usually respect my opinion on things."
• "I do not know enough about anything to speak on it."	• "I can come up with something to say about anything."

will feel. Although you should not practice your presentation to the point of memorization, you should not overlook the importance of practicing several times over the span of a couple of days.

Make sure that you take every opportunity to stand in front of the class before class begins and as your classmates leave the room. You need to see what the class looks like before you give your speech. Unless you have been a teacher, a business trainer, or have had other opportunities to speak in front of groups, you do not know what an audience looks like from the front of the room. The more you get accustomed to that sight before you give your speech, the more comfortable you will be.

Most universities have classrooms that are empty for some hours during the day or evening. Have some of your friends listen to your presentation as you practice your message in an empty classroom. The experience will be very close to what you will encounter when you actually give your presentation. The practice will make you more confident.

You should be careful not to have unrealistic expectations. Not everyone starts from the same place. People of all ages, cultures, nationalities, and experiences populate colleges today. Some students have been active in the workplace for years. Some have come to college with half a lifetime or more of experience; others have very little experience and may even be uncertain about their command of the English language. Your job in this class is to work on building your confidence, so you can spend a lifetime working on your competence and your effectiveness with audiences in public communication situations. For example, an occasional vocalized pause may not even be noticed if you are involved with the message and the audience, and they are focused on your message. Perfection is not really the goal; communicating effectively is the aim of this course.

For
REVIEW >>

AS YOU READ

1. Confront your fears about public speaking.

2. Strategize ways to reduce communication apprehension.

3. Connect to your community through public speaking.

4. Identify appropriate and vital presentation topics.

5. Define the communication process.

SUMMARY HIGHLIGHTS

▶ Some people see their public speaking course as a fate worse than death; others see the course as a rare opportunity to perform.
  • Nearly everyone gets a rush from standing in front of an audience.
  • Nearly always, our fears before speaking turn out to be an exaggeration: nobody dies of heart failure, faints, or falls on the floor.

▶ You can reduce anxiety through several behaviors:
  • Act confidently.
  • Know your subject.
  • Care about your subject.
  • See your classmates as friends.
  • See yourself as successful.
  • Practice until confident.

▶ Your public speaking course can help you become a fully functioning member of your local community.

▶ Being a practicing citizen in a democratic society depends upon knowing about current issues and being able to speak about them in conversations, in speeches, and even through the mass media.

▶ What should you talk about in your presentations?
  • Current topics that interest your audience are a good choice.
  • Vital topics that relate to your community will engage you (the speaker) and your audience.

▶ What topics should you avoid?
  • Avoid exhausted topics unless you can offer a fresh approach.
  • Avoid topics that advocate illegal activities, including open use of firearms, illegal drugs, explosives, flammable substances, contaminated blood, etc.
  • Avoid insulting topics that disparage ethnic groups, racial groups, religions, or cultural practices.
  • Avoid plagiarized speeches.

▶ The communication process includes seven interactive components: speaker (source), audience (receiver), message, channel, feedback, situation, and noise.

Pop Quiz

1. The means of distributing the message is the component of the communication process known as the
   (A) situation
   (B) channel
   (C) feedback
   (D) noise

2. A student in the classroom coughs while the teacher is speaking. The cough is a component of communication called
   (A) feedback
   (B) noise
   (C) situation
   (D) channel

3. Which word best describes communication?
   (A) one-way
   (B) uncomplicated
   (C) transactional
   (D) simple

4. One unique feature of public speaking is:
   (A) Public speaking presentations are typically long.
   (B) Topics are trivial.
   (C) A lot of main points are necessary.
   (D) Complex topics must be simplified.

5. When choosing a topic, you should *avoid* topics that
   (A) are current
   (B) help improve the audience
   (C) have been used exhaustively
   (D) are vital

6. Using a speech, outline, or manuscript from a source other than you, without an oral footnote, is termed
   (A) dynamism
   (B) plagiarism
   (C) communication apprehension
   (D) common ground

7. Establishing trustworthiness and displaying competence comprises one's
   (A) source credibility
   (B) outline
   (C) channel of information
   (D) speech preparation

8. Hearing is _____; listening is _____.
   (A) physiological; psychological
   (B) physiological; physiological
   (C) psychological; physiological
   (D) psychological; psychological

9. Before her speech, Laura got very nervous, had sweaty palms, and her knees shook. She likely experienced
   (A) psychological trauma
   (B) dynamism
   (C) communication apprehension
   (D) common ground

10. Audience members nodding or asking questions following a presentation are examples of
    (A) plagiarism
    (B) dynamism
    (C) feedback
    (D) self-assessment

Answers: 1 (B); 2 (B); 3 (C); 4 (D); 5 (C); 6 (B); 7 (A); 8 (A); 9 (C); 10 (C)

APPLICATION EXERCISES

1. Talk in groups of three to five students for 15 minutes about what you can do to reduce your apprehension about public speaking. Have one person in each group take notes so the groups can share their best ideas with the class after the discussion. The purpose is to allow you to reduce anxiety and to learn some practices to reduce anxiety.

2. Write down as many ideas as you can remember about how to make an effective public presentation. After writing down as many as you remember, you should open the text and add as many more as you can find. The purpose is to mentally reinforce early in the course some of the guidelines for effective presenting.

3. Introduce yourself to your classmates by stating your name and whatever you want them to remember about you. Some ideas: year in school, jobs, armed forces, public service, family, place of origin, travel, languages, talents, special skills, unusual hobbies, different experiences.

KEY TERMS

Channel	Hearing	Receiver
Common ground	Listening	Situation
Communication	Message	Source
Communication apprehension (CA)	Noise	Source credibility
Competence	Nonverbal messages	Trustworthiness
Dynamism	Plagiarism	Verbal messages
Feedback	Process of communication	

get involved!

What do we mean by "vital topics"? Very simply, these are subject matters that profoundly affect a community and its individuals. As members of a democratic nation, we need to exercise our right to free speech and become engaged in issues that ultimately affect us all. Select a topic that interests you and learn more about it. To demonstrate, let's say that you select a topic that involves several vital issues like democracy, ethics, and health—a topic like gun laws. Our democracy guarantees lawful ownership of guns, some laws take an ethical stand that guns threaten lives, and some urban areas make gun laws a public health issue. To explore the issue you go to FoxNews.com where you find an astounding 721,000 items on "gun laws." In 2009 some state legislatures considered the right for students to have guns on campus.

Now you should try to select a vital topic related to the ones below.

- Democracy
- Environment
- Technology
- Education
- Diversity
- Ethics
- Health
- Economics

Then go to the Internet and access any of these sources:

www.FoxNews.com
www.washingtonpost.com
www.wsj.com (Wall Street Journal Online)
www.nytimes.com (New York Times Online)
www.cnn.com

See what you can learn about your chosen topic by exploring the many articles revealed by your search.

2

PREPARING

The title of this chapter is probably a little misleading. Odds are that everyone reading this chapter has already given speeches before: a speech to a club like 4H, a speech as a part of a high school or even elementary school class, or a speech as part of your job. All of these are real and meaningful speaking experiences. However, one of the skills you will learn and practice in this class is adaptation—how you adapt to each unique speaking situation in which you find yourself. In that sense, going back to square one and thinking about your speeches in this class as if they were among your first is probably smart. This chapter helps you reorient your understanding of public speaking by introducing you to the Five Canons of Rhetoric, a useful way of thinking about the process of preparing a speech, as well as tips for preparing your initial presentations in this class.

YOUR FIRST
PRESENTATION

As You READ >>

1. Incorporate the Five Canons into your presentation.
2. Clearly identify an introduction, body, and conclusion in your presentation.
3. Determine how you will balance clarity and ornamentation in your presentation.
4. Develop ideas for effective nonverbal behaviors in your presentation.

In 2008 Sarah Palin jumped to the forefront of the Republican Party as the vice presidential nominee with John McCain. Although the McCain-Palin ticket did not win, Sarah Palin emerged as a significant force in the GOP because she was able to connect so easily with several demographics within the Republican Party. As the Obama Administration advanced its agenda, the Tea Party movement emerged as a highly vocal condemnation of various initiatives like the 2009 Economic Recovery Act and the 2010 Healthcare Reform Act. Sarah Palin, because of her outspoken criticism of Obama and "Big Government," became a favorite of the Tea Party supporters.

On February 6, 2010, Palin gave a keynote speech at a national Tea Party convention in Nashville, Tennessee. In her speech Palin argued for stronger actions toward nations like Iran and North Korea, for less government spending, and for a return to a reliance on the free market. Near the end of her speech, Palin described her perspective on the ideals of the Tea Party:

> *The best of America can be found in places where patriots are brave enough and free enough to be able to stand up and speak up and where small businesses grow our economy one job at a time and folks, like Reagan, we know that America is still that shining city on a hill. I do believe that God shed his grace on thee. We know that our best days are yet to come. Tea Party nation, we know that there is nothing wrong with America that together we can't fix as Americans.*

Although obviously this was not her first speech, Palin followed the same advice that would be wise for a first-time speaker—she identified a few key themes and used a variety of appeals to support her views on those themes. Whether your speaking experiences number in the single digits or the thousands, starting with the foundations of public speaking will help you craft a message with a greater chance for success.

How Would *You* Do It?

Sarah Palin's speech to the Tea Party in Nashville emphasized the use of pathos to inspire audience members. For what types of speaking situations would you use pathos as a primary persuasive tool? How would you generate ideas for ways to effectively use pathos in those situations?

Foundations of Public Communication

Sarah Palin's speech in Nashville was similar in form to the types of speeches you will give in this class. The introduction to her speech oriented the audience to her message and reminded audience members of her experiences to establish credibility. The body of her presentation focused on a few key points—mostly those points were criticisms of the Obama Administration's policies. Her speech ended with memorable statements wrapping up her ideas and calling the audience to action. At one point in the presentation, Palin stated,

> Our president spent a year reaching out to hostile regimes, writing personal letters to dangerous dictators and apologizing for America, and what do we have to show for that? Here's what we have to show. North Korea tested nuclear weapons and longer-range ballistic missiles. Israel, a friend and critical ally, now questions the strength of our support. Plans for a missile defense system in Europe, they've been scrapped. Relations with China and Russia are no better. And relations with Japan, that key Asian ally, they are in the worst shape in years. And around the world, people who are seeking freedom from oppressive regimes wonder if Alaska is still that beacon of hope for their cause.

Notice how Palin used a series of short examples to evoke certain emotional reactions from her audience—this strategy is making use of pathos, something you will learn more about shortly. You see, even highly experienced speakers follow recommendations and theories guiding public speakers for centuries.

This section of the chapter introduces you to the Five Canons of Rhetoric. The Five Canons have been used since the time of ancient Greece to help students of rhetoric and oratory understand the essential principles of preparing and presenting a well-crafted speech. Although their application has been updated to reflect changing times and cultures, their straightforward presentation of the speech preparation process is a perfect place for your study of public speaking to begin.

The Roots of Rhetoric: The Five Canons

As suggested in the Sarah Palin example, public speaking is essential to the smooth functioning of democracy. Whether or not you agree with Palin and the Tea Party movement, her speeches allow her to remain significantly engaged in civic life, even though she is no longer the governor of Alaska or a vice presidential nominee. If you wanted to become civically engaged, how would you do so? You might volunteer in your community, you might donate money, but at some point you will likely feel compelled to give a speech. In fact, one could argue that meaningful civic engagement cannot happen unless one speaks out to persuade or form solidarity with others.

The **Five Canons of Rhetoric** were created by Greek philosophers to help teach civic-minded students ways in which they could use rhetoric and oratory as tools of civic life. Making speeches about the virtues of taxation, declarations of war, and maintenance of infrastructure was just as relevant in 5th-century Athens, Greece, as it is today, and the best way to guide action on these topics is to present compelling public arguments. The Five Canons are a useful starting point for your study of public speaking. Table 2.1 describes the Five Canons and suggests key skills associated with each one.

TABLE 2.1   SKILLS ASSOCIATED WITH THE FIVE CANONS OF RHETORIC

DESCRIPTION OF CANON	KEY SKILLS
1 **INVENTION** *Finding information for your presentation*	To engage in the invention process you should: • Determine the goal of the presentation. • Determine issues related to your topic. • Determine how you can use ethos, pathos, and logos in your speech. • Predict what your audience wants and needs to know. • Conduct research to supplement your personal knowledge.
2 **Organization** *Selecting an appropriate arrangement and structure for a presentation*	To engage in effective organization you should: • Prepare an introduction. • Organize main points and supporting material for the body of the presentation. • Develop a conclusion that summarizes the presentation and ends with impact.
3 **STYLE** *Using clear and ornamental language*	To effectively use style you should: • Avoid technical language unless necessary. • Define important terms. • Arrange words using patterns appropriate for oral presentation. • Use metaphors, analogy, and creative language to increase artful ornamentation.
4 **UNDERSTANDING** *Being able to recall main ideas and details in your presentation*	To effectively use understanding you should: • Prepare a planning outline of your ideas. • Prepare a shortened presentation outline that will help keep you on track during the presentation. • Engage in extemporaneous delivery to maximize eye contact and conversational delivery.
5 **DELIVERY** *Using effective verbal and nonverbal behaviors to maximize the effectiveness of your message*	To engage in effective delivery you should: • Avoid reading your presentation. • Maintain consistent eye contact. • Be natural with your use of gestures, facial expressions, and movement.

1. Invention

A common misunderstanding about public communication is that style is more important than substance—how you say your message is more important than what you say. This misunderstanding is a natural by-product of television because we constantly see politicians and other professional speakers talking in carefully edited sound bites. If you attend club meetings, classes, or civic groups, however, you will quickly see that substance is more important because few of us are expert speakers.

The substance of your presentation is directly tied to the **invention** process, which is *the art of finding information.* Invention deals with everything from selecting a topic for your presentation to locating examples, statistics, and other forms of supporting material. From ancient to modern times, speakers have used several approaches to invention.[1] In general, invention attempts to: (1) look at a problem from all sides, (2) ask the right questions, (3) select relevant information, (4) find new ways of talking about old topics, and (5) find new analogies and relationships between things.

Ran Ju was asked by her teacher to prepare a speech about an important social issue. Because she knew several people who had served in Iraq and Afghanistan, Ran Ju wanted to prepare a speech on Post Traumatic Stress Disorder, or PTSD. Although Ran Ju was very interested in the topic because of her friends' experiences, she knew that not everyone in her audience would be able to relate to the experiences of soldiers. So, after doing research, Ran Ju was able to broaden her approach to include more common triggers of PTSD as well as therapeutic approaches to helping those who have this disorder. In so doing, Ran Ju was able to maintain a focus on her friends' stories while at the same time making her speech more relevant to the majority of her classmates. Through the invention process, Ran Ju identified ways to broaden her speech by including other common examples of PTSD while focusing her speech on a few key issues that could be discussed in a short presentation to classmates.

To follow Ran Ju's lead and effectively engage in the invention process, we recommend that you ask a series of questions about your topic:

"A common misunderstanding about public communication is that style is more important than substance—how you say your message is more important than what you say."

1. *What is the goal of the presentation?* Are you primarily trying to teach, persuade, or entertain your audience? Determine what your audience expects and try to approach the topic in a slightly different way. This approach can effectively capture listeners' attention; however, the use of different "angles" should not obscure your intended objective for the presentation.

2. *What general issues are related to your topic?* By brainstorming with a concept map, you can easily identify various subtopics associated with your overall topic. **Concept maps** are *pictures or diagrams that allow you to visualize main and subordinate ideas related to a more general topic.* Narrowing your focus to one or more of the subtopics can help you effectively select relevant information and find new approaches to talking about your topic. This strategy is precisely the one Ran Ju used to talk about PTSD. Figure 2.1 provides a concept map related to her presentation. In addition to helping you narrow your focus, a concept map can also assist you in identifying points to include in your preparation outline.

3. *How can you use ethos, pathos, and logos in your speech?* Aristotle's original discussion of invention noted that speakers use three forms of proof to persuade: ethos, pathos, and logos. Ethos referes to the ethical proof, which today we tend to interpret as credibility. Pathos

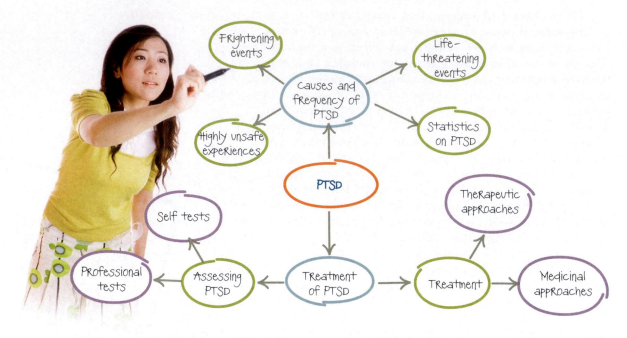

Figure 2.1   Concept map for Ran Ju's presentation on PTSD.

is when the speaker uses emotions to motivate the audience. Sarah Palin's speech shows how the emotion of fear and frustration can be used to incite action. Logos is the use of logical argument. One of the arts of speaking, according to Aristotle, is finding ways to meaningfully integrate these forms of proof. Although each speech will likely use all three, one may be emphasized more or less depending on the situation and skill of the speaker in carrying out the invention process.

4. *What does your audience need to know and want to know?* Anticipating your audience is a key presentation skill. Taking time to carefully consider your audience is wise because it allows you to adapt your message to their wants and needs.

2. Organization

Organization refers to *the arrangement and structure of a presentation.* As you will learn in detail later in the course, many presentations have an introduction, body, and conclusion. Let's begin by understanding the function of each part of the presentation.

1. *The introduction.* The purpose of the introduction is to set the stage for the whole presentation by providing a central idea or thesis statement and previewing the main ideas to be addressed. Effective introductions find a creative way to introduce the topic—often using a story, example, or audience interaction through questions and answers. Finding ways to establish credibility with your audience is also wise.

2. *The body.* Presentations typically consist of two to four main points. Selecting two, three, or four main points will enable listeners to more easily follow your presentation and remember key ideas. Carefully consider how to arrange your facts, testimony, and other evidence when outlining the body of the presentation. In particular, you should ensure that all main points have adequate supporting materials. You should start your planning process by arranging the body of your presentation because key elements of the introduction and conclusion are dependent on your main and subordinate points.

3. *The conclusion.* Effective presentations develop endings that not only summarize content, but also end with impact by using, for instance, quotations or stylistic devices such as metaphors and similes. Simply stating "That's it" or "I'm finished now" is not an effective way to end your presentation.

Knowing how to arrange presentations is challenging because any topic offers multiple options for arranging ideas and evidence, and no single approach is absolutely correct.[2] In subsequent chapters, we offer multiple options for arranging ideas; for now, we recommend that you focus on developing a distinct introduction, clear main points, and a conclusion that brings closure to the presentation by reviewing key ideas.

---

try this

Read through the eight items listed below. Then arrange them into the outline for the body of the presentation on the right. The outline should have two main points with three subpoints each.

1. Adopt-a-Block
2. Organizations related to human rights
3. Racial Fairness Project
4. Student organic farm
5. Organizations related to the environment
6. Rock the Vote
7. Campus computer recycling
8. Habitat for Humanity

I. _____
   A. _____
   B. _____
   C. _____

II. _____
   A. _____
   B. _____
   C. _____

---

3. Style

Strictly speaking, **style** refers to *the use and ornamentation of language.* Most efforts to define the concept of style have focused on using clear language. Avoid the use of jargon, define technical terms that might be unfamiliar to your audience, and use language and phrases you have in common.[3] Clarity also describes the way you arrange words. Avoid long sentences with multiple clauses so listeners can more easily follow your presentation—however, many short sentences in a row can actually cause confusion because the ideas come across as choppy and disjointed. As a practical matter, use conversational language and avoid preparing an elaborate script, because our style of writing often differs substantially from what listeners expect to hear from an oral presentation.

Using clear language, in terms of both words and arrangement, is an important skill. Yet, rhetorical scholar Ray Keesey notes that "clarity of style is the first consideration but it is ornament that, properly speaking, makes rhetoric art."[4] While clarity refers to the ease with which we interpret langauge, **ornamentation** refers to *the creative and artful use of language.* Using ornamental language is certainly one of the most advanced presentation skills that you can learn.

Fortunately, a few strategies can help you begin:

1. *Target certain areas for ornamental language.* When talking about his hobby of studying hurricanes, Steve used simple stylistic wording to improve clarity and ornamentation. His initial working outline contained this statement for the preview of his presentation:

Today I will discuss the causes and effects of hurricanes.

Steve's wording became much more effective after he edited his preview for style. After editing his initial ideas, Steve changed his preparation outline to read,

Today I will talk with you about my hobby of studying hurricanes, one of the most common and most powerful weather phenomena many of us will ever see. Since Hurricane Katrina, the impact of these weather events on our country and the world has received much attention. I hope to teach you about hurricanes by first taking you into the eye of the storm to understand how they form, and then twisting through the path of destruction that they can cause.

As you can see, Steve's stylistic approach is much more effective. Adding ornamental language greatly improves Steve's presentation by engaging the audience's imagination.

2. *Use analogies and metaphors.* Analogies and metaphors help you describe something by comparing it to something else. When introducing herself to the class, Cheri used a metaphor to describe her experience of moving to college. "My trip to college is best described as a train wreck because everything that could have gone wrong did go wrong." Such comparisons add vivid description to otherwise common experiences. Accomplished authors make use of stylistic metaphors and analogies to enhance their novels, and presenters can employ similar strategies to captivate audiences.

3. *Use narratives.* As children, we learn to love stories. Many of us cherish memories of hearing our favorite bedtime story, and this love for narrative lasts well into adulthood. Telling stories based on personal experience or other sources of information naturally adds rich description to the issues we examine during presentations. Your own experiences likely confirm this. Your most interesting teachers probably made ample use of stories and examples to enhance their classes. Effective presenters learn quickly that stories and examples bring language to life through vivid descriptions of lived experiences.

In a commencement address delivered on May 1, 2008, to students at Georgetown University, Wendy Kopp, CEO and founder of Teach for America, used narrative to illustrate how teaching can be an important form of community service.[5] During her presentation she told a story about Joe Almeida, a Georgetown graduate who entered the Teach for America program. She explained that Joe started working for a Washington, D.C., high school where students had very low expectations for their educational futures. Despite facing numerous challenges, Joe helped students at his high school envision a better future, as Kopp explained in the following narrative.

But Joe went ahead. And, he threw every bit of himself into the effort to accomplish his goals. Among other things he decided to bring all his kids here to Georgetown to help them envision their future as college-going students. When his school could not pay for all the costs of the trip, Joe just went ahead and raised all the money he needed through bake sales and the like. At year's end, Joe's students had made significant progress in catching up academically and had adopted the mindset that college was in their future. As one student said, "This is the first time anyone's expected me to go to college." A mother said, "I didn't think my son would go to college. Now I know it's possible."

By using the narrative about Joe, Kopp was able to accomplish two important tasks: First, she was able to help audience members identify with her message, since Joe Almeida was a fellow Hoya (that is, a Georgetown alumnus). Second, she was able to present an important piece of evidence using stylistic language and vivid imagery. Such evidence can bring life to a speech in ways that other forms of evidence cannot.

"Effective presenters learn quickly that stories and examples bring language to life through vivid descriptions of lived experiences."

4. Understanding

The fourth Canon of Rhetoric was originally labeled as memory. In ancient Greece, libraries and the Internet were difficult to find, so speakers relied on their memory to retain historical facts, details of current events, statistics, scientific theories, and other information necessary to develop ideas during a speech. Today, we have readily available external resources to supplement our memory. Now, all information resources on the Internet are literally with you as you walk from class to class.

Rather than relying on memory, the term **understanding** might be a more contemporary way of describing this canon. Although you do not need to memorize details to acquire encyclopedic knowledge in order to be an effective speaker, you do have a responsibility to understand ways of interpreting facts. Whereas the greatest challenge facing our parents and older generations of speakers was finding information, the challenge facing you now is making sense of the hundreds of thousands of resources available to you when researching a topic. Interestingly, communication teachers often refer to the fourth canon as "the lost canon" because the emphasis on memory is largely unnecessary, at least in the way Greek teachers of rhetoric approached the topic. When reframed as "understanding," however, this canon might be the most important.

Developing and using skills of understanding is hard to condense into a list of skills like those found in the other canons. Being able to understand the world around you requires skills developed over a lifetime. Nevertheless, here are some ideas on how you can work toward deeper understanding now as a college student.

1. *A liberal arts education is important.* Courses in your general education program help you develop perspectives and capacities for viewing the world from different perspectives. Rather than viewing your "gen ed" courses as things you have to take before you can focus on a major, view them as opportunities to help you understand your world in more detail and with greater appreciation. Even this term you will learn things in other classes that can help you understand your speech topic(s) in deeper ways.

2. *Be cognizant of current events.* A significant step in understanding the world around you is realizing that it is not simple. Following current events, reading the newspaper, listening to the news, following blogs, and even attending meetings in your community will help you gain an understanding of the systemic nature of our social world. By systemic, we mean that one small thing impacts many others. What happens when teachers are laid off to balance a school district's budget? What would happen if everything in our country was dictated by the free market? What would be the effect of fining companies who move jobs overseas? These questions have complex answers, and understanding those answers require ongoing awareness of the issues. Fortunately, as you teach yourself to be a more complex thinker about the world, the process of understanding new things gets easier.

3. *Talk with others. Understanding is not achieved in isolation.* *Talking* with others to test your ideas and assumptions is critical in helping you *refine* your ideas and understandings. John Dewey, a noted American social critic and theorist, argued that if we want a more democratic nation we have to start by having a democratic relationship with the people that we live with and next to. Taking time to have meaningful conversation is a first step in such relationships. In large part, your public speaking class gives you an opportunity to practice this exact skill!

4. *Be engaged.* Civic engagement means that you care about your community and the society in which all of us live. Engagement means that you are active in helping, however you choose to define that. As you increase your levels of civic engagement you will have a greater appreciation for and understanding of your surroundings. Take time to volunteer. Use your job as an opportunity to learn about how others work and behave. Care about the future of others as much as your own future. Tell others how you feel about things that are important. All of those steps will keep you engaged and will provide valuable learning experiences.

5. Delivery

Delivery includes *the verbal and nonverbal techniques used to present the message.* Professional speakers and politicians are paid thousands of dollars to present speeches, and we have justifiably high expectations for their delivery. The majority of us, however, cannot call upon such skill. We like to use the analogy of baseball. Watching a major league baseball game is enjoyable because the players are able to perform at a very high level—nearly mistake-free. Yet, we also think that the intimacy and humanness of a minor league, college, or even Little League baseball game makes the experience every bit as enjoyable as a trip to Wrigley Field in Chicago. We can effectively deliver presentations without approaching the skill of a Malcolm X, Barack Obama, or Newt Gingrich. In fact, the most effective presenters learn that being perfect in their delivery is far less important than being themselves.

VISUAL RHETORIC GOES GLOBAL

cultural NOTE

Discussion of the Five Canons of Rhetoric underscores the emphasis on spoken rhetoric. After all, most of the Five Canons provide advice on how to best *say* something. In fact, the dominant Western view of rhetoric places a nearly exclusive emphasis on the spoken word. Several scholars, however, have documented the role of visual rhetoric. For example, communication scholars Paul Booth and Amber Davisson analyzed how visual imagery in photographs related to Hurricane Katrina created powerful rhetorical statements that help define and provide iconic meanings for important events.[6] Such rhetorical use of visual imagery is not unique to America. During the Iranian election protests in the summer of 2009, protesters carried photos of slain protesters to highlight violent government responses.[7] Indeed, the Internet, cell phone technology, and other forms of digital media could cause visual imagery to become (if it has not already done so) even more important than the spoken word in terms of rhetorical impact.

Although you will learn several techniques for effective delivery later in the course, for now we suggest that you begin working on a couple of skills and avoid some of the worst presentation habits:

1. *Don't read your presentation.* Reading from notes is the single most common bad habit presenters develop. This one habit can literally destroy your ability to be naturally effective in your delivery. Minimize your use of notes by practicing your presentation several times. Each time you practice, try to reduce the number of notes that you need. Effective presenters should be able to deliver a five- to seven-minute presentation with only one 3" × 5" card of notes; this might not be practical for your first presentation but it should be an objective for which you strive.

2. *Maintain consistent eye contact with the audience.* Your eye contact, rather than your voice, is your "secret weapon" as a presenter. Maintaining consistent eye contact causes listeners to perceive you as more confident, competent, and charming. Glancing at your notes is necessary at times, but always looking down at them causes listeners to question whether you are truly prepared for your presentation. During most of your presentation you should look at your audience rather than at your notes.

3. *Be natural with your nonverbal delivery.* We naturally use our hands, body, and face to communicate messages that complement our verbal statements. Although some presenters plan to use various nonverbal behaviors, most presenters are simply encouraged to follow their instincts and do what comes naturally. Unfortunately, many students develop another bad habit—one related to reading their presentation—which diminishes their ability to be natural: tying their hands to a lectern. We commonly see students clutch the lectern, their notes, or even themselves in a death grip because of the natural apprehension accompanying any type of public performance. If your teacher allows you to use a lectern, we recommend that you place your notes on it for easy reference, but that you stand slightly to the side of the lectern. By doing this, you avoid the temptation to hold on to it.

We have now introduced you to five important areas in which you can develop your public speaking skills. Both accomplished and inexperienced presenters rely on these five foundational skills—sometimes implicitly and sometimes explicitly—to prepare and deliver presentations. We will revisit these skills throughout the book, but you are now armed with enough knowledge to begin preparing your first speech.

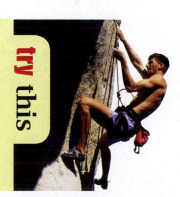

try this

You can improve your own skills as a presenter by carefully observing others. Watch a prominent speaker on television or check out a videotape from your library. Make notes on how the speaker uses nonverbal behaviors like eye contact, gestures, and facial expressions. What did you find effective or distracting about the speaker's delivery?

Tips for Preparing Your First Presentation

Now that you understand some of the foundational skills used to prepare effective presentations, you should begin thinking about how to translate your knowledge into practice and start preparing your first presentation for the class. Although teachers use a variety of approaches for the first presentation, some general strategies can help you effectively prepare for any presentation.

Tips for Planning Your Presentation

1. *Gather materials.* Especially if your first presentation is prepared entirely in class, having materials to work with is important. You should bring with you a legal pad or notebook paper to use for taking notes, a couple of 3" × 5" note cards to use for your speaking outline, and two colors of pens to prepare your presentation outline on the note cards. You can use one color to indicate main points and the other to list details or subpoints. See Figure 2.2 for an example.

2. *Carefully review the assignment expectations.* Your teacher may provide you with a written assignment description or may discuss the assignment orally in class. Before you begin working on your presentation—or before you come to class if the presentation will be prepared in class—take care to review all information about the assignment. Summarizing the key expectations in writing will help you remember exactly what you need to do when you begin working.

Figure 2.2 Sample presentation note card using two colors to distinguish between main and subordinate points.

3. *Use the invention process to accumulate information.* If your teacher allows you to prepare your first presentation outside of class, you have a full array of resources from which to select during the invention process. In addition to using information from the library or Internet, think carefully about personal experiences and local sources that may be relevant to your topic. Make sure when you use sources of information that you describe those sources during your speech.

4. *Plan to be organized.* Recall that most of your assigned presentations should have an introduction, body, and conclusion. Also remember that most presentations have two to four main points in the body. You can plan in advance by writing headings for these sections on a page in your notebook. Once you begin preparing your presentation, you will simply fill in this template.

5. *Plan to be clear.* Once you have accumulated information during the invention process, the majority of your work should center on developing a clear central idea and main points. Although you may change these points several times as you continue preparing, taking time to plan them first will help you focus your thoughts, and your work will be more efficient. For now, simple wording is most effective; later, you might edit your wording to add style.

Practicing Speeches Online

Practicing your speech for others is one of the most important steps you can take to improve the clarity of your ideas and the effectiveness of your delivery. Using YouTube and other Internet sites, you can record and upload your speech for others to view. You can ask others to view and comment on your speech and can even post your YouTube video on social networking sites likes Facebook. Using feedback from others, you can improve your speech; the mere act of recording the speech for others to view will provide a significant and realistic practice opportunity.

6. *When selecting details, focus on quality, not quantity.* Using a well-explained example or statistic is far more important than trying to impress your listeners with the scope of your knowledge. When selecting details to fit under each of your main points, try to select those which are memorable, vivid, and credible. Three quotations from a Web site such as Wikipedia are far less effective than a statement from a scientific journal or a detailed description of your personal experience because many people view "dot-coms" with skepticism.

7. *Edit for style.* Once you have planned your message, think of ways to "dress up" your style. Can you take the simple wording of your central idea and main points and make them rich by using a metaphor, analogy, or creative wording? Remember that style also involves using clear language. Don't overuse style to the extent that your message is obscured.

8. *If possible, practice, practice, practice.* Some teachers require that the first presentation be prepared and delivered during class, and in such cases, practice is difficult. But you can still practice preparing a speech and delivering it to a roommate or friend. Even if it is on a different topic than the one you deliver in class, you can still rehearse the process. If you are allowed more time to prepare your presentation, plan to practice your talk aloud a minimum of three times.

9. *Plan for effective delivery.* In advance of your presentation, you should carefully visualize what you are going to do when your turn arrives. Remember to minimize your presentation notes and to stand beside the lectern if one is present. As you are delivering your presentation, shift your focus and your eye contact among a handful of people scattered around the room. This practice will help you draw all listeners to your message. Remember that your audience does not expect perfect delivery, especially if your delivery seems natural.

10. *Enjoy the opportunity!* One of the most exciting aspects of a course in public communication is the guaranteed opportunity to talk with peers about topics of interest to you. Such experiences can be exhilarating and even give some students a "rush." If you open your mind to the possibility, we think you can experience a similar feeling. Remember that you are not trying to be a professional public speaker; you are simply trying to meaningfully connect with your listeners. Have fun with the experience!

Common Types of First Presentations

Teachers often use the first classroom presentation to accomplish two primary objectives. First, they usually want you to become familiar with the process of preparing and delivering a classroom presentation. In particular, the first presentation creates an opportunity for you and your classmates to learn more about each other—this knowledge is important because such information will better enable you to adapt future classroom presentations to the specific interests and needs of your audience. Second, teachers typically want you to begin practicing several of the skills necessary for developing and presenting effective presentations. With these two general objectives as a starting point, teachers select from a variety of presentation formats for the first classroom presentation. We provide suggestions for four of the most common types of first presentation assignments: the impromptu presentation, presenting yourself, presenting a classmate, and the demonstration presentation.

Impromptu Presentations

An **impromptu presentation** is *one that does not allow for substantial planning and practice before the presentation is given.* Although you typically are required to develop an introduction, body (with at least two main points), and conclusion, you probably will not be expected to integrate supporting materials such as detailed statistics, quotations, or multiple sources. Teachers typically use this type of assignment to provide you with the experience of presenting ideas to your classmates and to practice thinking on your feet. Impromptu presentations can take many forms. Most of the time you will have about five minutes to prepare a rough presentation outline. Most teachers will allow you to use a rough presentation outline like the one shown in Figure 2.2.

In a speech before the National Conference of State Legislators in 2009, Joan Detz,[8] a speechwriter, gave several suggestions to politicians who need to master the art of giving a strong, three-minute speech. Among her tips were:

1. *Focus your message and words.* The average American speaks at 140 words per minute. During an impromptu presentation of a couple minutes or slightly longer, you don't have much space to say what you want to say. You should limit your message to one or two specific things.

2. *Think about your audience.* In a short speech you have to connect quickly and effectively. Irrelevant examples or unclear analysis will cause audience members to tune out because they know the speech will be over quickly. However, if you pull them in effectively you will likely have undivided attention for the duration of your speech.

3. *Use style.* Light humor, simple visuals, and use of inclusive pronouns like "we" rather than self-centered pronouns like "I" are most effective. Such stylistic choices will grab attention and help audience members connect with you more quickly.

> **"As I look back upon my life, I see that every part of it was a preparation for the next. The most trivial of incidents fits into the larger pattern like a mosaic in a preconceived design."**
>
> [Margaret Sanger (1879–1966), Nurse/Advocate for Women's Health]

Presenting Yourself

Teachers often use the first presentation as an opportunity to have you introduce yourself to the class. Typically, your task in this type of speech is to prepare a presentation in which you describe your background and other meaningful things about yourself like significant experiences, hobbies, or interests.

Because you will typically have at least one evening to prepare this presentation, your teacher might expect more supporting examples and explanations than for an impromptu presentation.

- *Develop structure.* As you prepare your presentation outline, use your legal pad to develop main points. Your main points should organize information so that audience members can easily follow your train of thought. For example, you might organize your main points chronologically, beginning with early memories and working up to recent ones, or you might arrange them topically, with one point about your family and another about your hobbies and interests.
- *Focus on small details.* Because you have time to prepare, you should carefully consider ways that you can use style to improve your creative language use.
- *Be thoughtful.* When selecting stories to tell about yourself, carefully consider which stories will teach the listeners about who you are and persuade them that you are a "credible student." Carefully selecting such examples will allow you to make friends more quickly in class and will tell your teacher that you are serious about doing well in the course.
- *Make content meaningful to the audience.* Although a presentation about you will be naturally interesting, an even better one will find ways to relate your life experiences to those of your listeners. What can they learn from your stories?

Because this assignment focuses on themselves, some students assume that the presentation can easily be planned just before class. However, taking time to carefully develop and organize ideas, paying attention to small details like style, and practicing your presentation can determine whether your presentation is "excellent" or merely "average."

Presenting a Classmate

Some teachers prefer that you present information about a classmate rather than about yourself. The advantage of this approach is that the process more closely follows that which you will use in other presentations; that is, you must consult external sources during the invention process. For this presentation, you are typically asked to interview a classmate and plan a presentation about that person. In many respects, the same suggestions we provided for the self-introduction presentation apply equally well to the peer presentation. Perhaps the one additional skill necessary for this assignment is the need for effective interviewing techniques to use during the invention process.

To gather information, you must interview your classmate. A thorough analysis of interviewing skills is unnecessary for this assignment; however, the following suggestions should help you gain enough information to plan a successful presentation.

- *Plan interview questions.* The most effective strategy for conducting an interview is to preplan some questions, while remaining flexible enough to ask follow-up questions.

- *Record answers.* Effective interviewers will either tape-record or take detailed notes of answers to interview questions. A detailed recording (whether audio or written) will better enable you to select accurate information when preparing your presentation.
- *Start with the basics.* Although basic information such as a person's hometown, major, year in school, and age are potentially the least interesting facts to learn, such information is expected. Begin your interview by learning these basics.
- *Ask questions about more than the basics.* One widely supported concept in communication is that each of us has layers of information that we disclose to others. Our outer layer contains basic information and is commonly revealed to others without much forethought. Subsequent layers include information about our personal beliefs, our personal values, our goals and desires, and our self-concept. These layers of information are revealed naturally as a relationship progresses. For your presentation, you might ask your partner about some of these more personal issues so that you can do a more thorough job of introducing the individual to your class.
- *Look for the novel and unique.* Each of us has characteristics and experiences that make us unique. Although we may find our hobbies or preferences familiar or routine, others may not. Ask questions to learn details that your interview partner may find ordinary but that you think would be interesting to your classmates.
- *Be ethical.* Your short interview with your classmate could be the beginning of a solid friendship. Recognize that some information might come up during the interview that should not be divulged to the class. Moreover, your introduction of your class colleague should be done with respect and consideration.

Effective interviewing skills are valuable for careers in sales, management, health, and even teaching. Our own experience suggests that interviewing and introducing a fellow classmate is one of the more enjoyable presentation experiences you can have in class.

Demonstration Presentations

Another typical first presentation is a more formal informative speech that demonstrates something. A **demonstration presentation** *teaches audience members how something works or how to perform some task.* Students usually pick a topic with which they have ample experience. At universities in the Midwest, "country students" commonly teach "city students" how things are done "on the farm" in presentations about many rural activities, from bull riding to raising organic vegetables. Students more oriented toward the sciences might illustrate a scientific principle. Kim, for example, used a balloon and tinfoil to demonstrate how black holes develop in space. Yet other students discuss hobbies ranging from making homemade beer to competing in snowboarding competitions.

Demonstration presentations can come across as either interesting or trivial. To prepare an effective demonstration presentation, carefully analyze how you can make your topic relevant to audience members. For example, why would listeners care to learn about snowboarding competitions when most will never engage in the activity? Here are a couple other suggestions for preparing an effective demonstration presentation:

- *Organize logically.* Because even simple processes like recycling can require several steps, it can be challenging to find clear main points for a demonstration presentation. Your main points should divide and organize multiple steps into a few logical categories. To talk about composting, for instance, you might cover the following main points:

  I. Building a compost bin.
  II. "Feeding" the compost bin.
  III. Using compost in your garden.

- *Use visual aids.* One of the most effective ways to increase listeners' interest in your topic is to show them what you are talking about. Displaying diagrams and pictures often does wonders to clarify your explanation of complex or unfamiliar things. Of course, visual aids are also one of the biggest pitfalls for new presenters. In a later chapter, you will learn to effectively plan, create, and integrate visual resources into your presentation. For now, make sure that your visual resources are clear and easily seen, and that you carefully plan when to use them during your presentation.

The beginning of this chapter introduced Sarah Palin, who delivered the keynote address at a meeting of the Tea Party movement in Nashville. Regardless of how you might feel about Palin, she illustrated the power of public speaking as a form of civic engagement, and enacted many of the skills described in this chapter. Her speech used pathos, or emotion, effectively; she crafted a well-organized message that focused on a few key points; she used her own unique style to maintain interest; and, she found ways to easily connect with her audience. As you prepare your first presentation in class, be confident in the knowledge that following even a few of these suggestions will result in a very positive experience.

Sample Speech for Review and Analysis

In the spring of 2009, CNN awarded several "Hometown Heroes" awards to individuals who have made a difference helping others in their communities. One of those heroes was Anne Mahlum, founder of Back on My Feet, which uses running as a way to help homeless individuals in Philadelphia regain self-confidence and strength. Below is the text of a speech by Jessica Biel, actress and founder of the Make the Difference Network, who introduced Mahlum at the Hometown Heroes awards ceremony (this speech can also be viewed at http://www.youtube.com/watch?v=DpZrt_t6W70).

Introducing Anne Mahlum

Sometimes an idea is just so crazy it has to work. A young woman from Philadelphia walks into a local homeless shelter and says "I want to take some people running." Right there, in the middle of a place where the forgotten and downtrodden struggle to get through the day, where the outcasts and the addicts sit without their dreams, where the rejected and the ignored believed that the whole world has turned its back on them. In walks a woman filled with such a profound belief that running can be a healing force. She says, "I wanna take some homeless people running," and that's just what Anne Mahlum did. So they laced up their shoes together, they put on their new hats and T-shirts and ran a mile together. They started slow, then the group got bigger and they ran further. And some kept right on running. They kept running toward a new job. They kept running toward a new home. They kept running toward the life they had always imagined. That is why on any given morning before the sun rises you can see a group of runners: professionals, volunteers, and homeless men and women, moving through the streets of Philadelphia stride by stride. And right in the middle of this group is Anne Mahlum, our hero, with her amazing idea.

Notice in this speech how Biel used a series of narratives to tell the basic story of how Mahlum founded Back on My Feet and how that organization aims to help people who are homeless in the Philadelphia area. Biel also used repetition and ornamental language toward the end of the presentation to paint a picture of people running as she introduced Mahlum to the viewers.

For
REVIEW >>

AS YOU READ

1. Incorporate the Five Canons into your presentation.

2. Clearly identify an introduction, body, and conclusion in your presentation.

3. Determine how you will balance clarity and ornamentation in your presentation.

4. Develop ideas for effective nonverbal behaviors in your presentation.

SUMMARY HIGHLIGHTS

▶ The Five Canons provide a useful framework for understanding key skills related to successful presentations.
  • Invention is the art of finding information, and it involves everything from selecting a topic to finding examples, statistics, quotations, and other forms of supporting material. A key skill during the invention process is the ability to discover unique angles from which to approach your topic.
  • Organization describes the arrangements and structure of a presentation. All presentations should have a clear introduction, body, and conclusion.
  • Style is the clear and ornamental use of language.
  • Understanding is a key skill for extemporaneous delivery. Although extemporaneous presentations allow the presenter to prepare ideas beforehand, presentation notes are often minimal and the presenter must remember some details and descriptions.
  • Effective delivery does not require perfection, but it does stem from being natural when presenting information to listeners.

▶ Well developed presentations accomplish different objectives with the introduction, body, and conclusion.
  • The introduction should introduce listeners to the topic of the presentation, provide a central idea, and preview points covered during the talk.
  • The body of the presentation should expand on two to four main points and include appropriate supporting materials.
  • The conclusion of the presentation should summarize the content of the presentation and end with impact.

▶ Clarity and ornamentation are two stylistic elements that increase the effectiveness of any presentation.
  • You increase clarity when you avoid technical language (or carefully define terms) and take care to arrange words effectively.
  • You increase language ornamentation by using analogies and metaphors, and creatively wording certain parts of your presentation.

▶ Nonverbal delivery improves when presenters avoid overusing written notes, maintain eye contact with listeners, and use natural nonverbal behaviors including gestures, movement, and facial expressions.

Pop Quiz

1. Organizing main points and developing an introduction are skills associated with:
   (A) invention
   (B) organization
   (C) style
   (D) understanding

2. The invention process involves:
   (A) using clear and ornamental language
   (B) using effective verbal and nonverbal behaviors
   (C) finding information for the presentation
   (D) selecting an appropriate arrangement and structure

3. Which of the following statements regarding organization is true?
   (A) You should avoid using metaphors or similes in the conclusion.
   (B) The body should have five or more main points.
   (C) Not all main points need to have supporting material.
   (D) The introduction should provide the thesis statement and preview the main points.

4. Using language creatively and artfully is referred to as the canon of:
   (A) understanding
   (B) delivery
   (C) organization
   (D) style

5. A mode of delivery that involves speaking from carefully prepared notes is called:
   (A) memorized
   (B) extemporaneous
   (C) manuscript
   (D) impromptu

6. When presenting your speech, you should:
   (A) practice your presentation and minimize your use of notes
   (B) grab the podium to avoid gesturing
   (C) glance at the audience sparingly
   (D) read your presentation

7. A presentation that teaches the audience how something works or how to perform a task is a(n):
   (A) impromptu presentation
   (B) concept map
   (C) demonstration presentation
   (D) presenting a classmate

8. If you interview a classmate for an introductory speech, you should:
   (A) begin the interview with an in-depth question
   (B) divulge all information, regardless of topic sensitivity
   (C) solely ask questions about the basics
   (D) plan your interview questions

9. The impromptu presentation:
   (A) allows for substantial planning
   (B) should be clearly organized
   (C) includes numerous supporting materials and citations
   (D) should be delivered with minimal eye contact

10. Amy's speech was bland and did not include vivid descriptions or ornamental language. What canon of rhetoric does she need to improve upon?
   (A) invention
   (B) organization
   (C) style
   (D) delivery

Answers: 1 (B); 2 (C); 3 (D); 4 (D); 5 (B); 6 (A); 7 (C); 8 (D); 9 (B); 10 (C)

APPLICATION EXERCISES

1. Practice your impromptu speaking skills by preparing short presentations for each of the three quotations that follow. The presentation notes you prepare for each quote should have a thesis statement and two main points. The thesis and main points should develop an explanation demonstrating that the quotation says something about who you are as a person.
   a. "... friendship ... is essential to intellectuals. You can date the evolving life of a mind, like the age of a tree, by the rings of friendship formed by the expanding central trunk." —Mary McCarthy

b. "You don't need proof when you have instinct." —"Joe" in the movie *Reservoir Dogs*

c. "Just like a boxer in a title fight, you got to walk in that ring all alone." —Billy Joel

KEY TERMS

Concept maps

Delivery

Demonstration presentation

Five Canons of Rhetoric

Impromptu presentation

Invention

Organization

Ornamentation

Style

Understanding

get involved!

In this chapter you learned about the invention process, or the act of locating available sources of information. As part of that process you must identify salient issues, conduct research, and find supporting material. One of the best ways to begin the invention process is to talk with members of your community.

In this book we highlight several vital themes including the economy, education, medicine, and war. One way to begin your invention process is to talk with people in your community about how those vital themes are experienced by members of your community. Here are some steps you can take to begin the invention process for an upcoming speech while at the same time starting to get involved with those around you.

1. As necessary, conduct some background research on one of the vital themes so that you have a basic understanding of broad issues related to that topic.

2. Create a short set of questions that you can use to interview people about those topics. The questions should focus on how people in your community experience and are affected by issues related to the vital themes you selected.

3. Make appointments to meet with several community members to have short (30-minute) discussions about the themes. In those discussions you can ask interview questions and gain insight from your interviewees.

After meeting with several people, you will have important information that you can use to substantiate ideas in your speech. More importantly, you will have the opportunity to develop relationships and contacts that can help you become connected to your community and the people who live there.

3

SELECTING A
TOPIC &

One of the first steps in preparing a presentation is choosing a topic. You may choose to talk about a topic that is familiar to you, or you may use this opportunity to research an unfamiliar topic about which you are curious. In either case, the choice is yours. In this chapter, we will consider selecting a topic and purpose.

PURPOSE

[As You READ

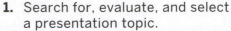

>>

1. Search for, evaluate, and select a presentation topic.
2. Identify three general purposes of public speaking.
3. Write a specific purpose for a presentation.
4. Develop a thesis statement for a presentation.

]

Tim Tolman knew he had spent too much time checking all his friends' Facebook pages when he realized how hungry he was. Shutting down his laptop and heading to the campus cafeteria, he smiled to himself as he remembered what he had recently read about Facebook—that if it were a separate country, it would be the fourth-largest nation in the world, with a population of about 400 million people.

Everyone can think of things that make Facebook appealing. Finding and keeping in touch with friends old and new is as easy as hitting a few keys. Sharing photos and videos is fast and fun. And letting everyone know about good news and big changes in your life is simple when all you have to do is make a single post for all your friends and contacts to find. In fact, 35 million people around the world find the social networking site so attractive that they log on to change their status every single day.

On the other hand, Tim mused, quite a few Facebook users forget that everything they post on the site becomes more or less public information. Tim knew about people who had been bullied or harassed online, who had been embarrassed by photos posted by others, and who had run afoul of their employers' policies by posting proprietary or inappropriate information online. A stadium worker for the Philadelphia Eagles was fired after making an angry post about the team's decision to release a player to the Denver Broncos, even though he quickly deleted it. A cop in Atlanta posted the times he would be working in plainclothes and disclosed that he was cooperating with the FBI on a drug case. He was fired too, even though his Facebook account was a private one.

Tim carried his tray over to a table where a couple of his friends were sitting. He had already decided, while choosing nachos and a drink, that Facebook would make a great topic for the upcoming speech he needed to prepare for class. He knew his audience would consider it significant and engaging—after all, every one of them had a Facebook page. He believed the topic was appropriate for the classroom setting, and that he would be able to find plenty of new information to present.

But he still needed to narrow his topic and determine the purpose of his speech. Did he want to share information about the benefits Facebook could offer, or persuade his listeners to pay more attention to the drawbacks of social networking? In this chapter, we will consider how to select a topic and purpose for your speech.

FREE SPEECH, CULTURAL RESPECT, AND CHANGING CONNOTATIONS

In the past, the term "Oriental" was used to describe people, cultures, and products that came from the East. More recently, the term "Asian" has come to replace the word "Oriental." Common usage in government documents, newspapers, magazines, and other written materials have supplanted the word "Oriental" with the term "Asian." Imagine that an older speaker who was familiar with the term "Oriental" used the word in his talk to a state legislature. When cautioned about the negative connotation of the word to members of the assembly who had Asian ancestors, the speaker claimed he learned the term "Oriental" as a child and had always used it. He went on to add that his freedom of speech allows him to use this word. He asks sarcastically, "Is the rug in my living room an 'Asian rug'"? How would you respond? Would your response depend on the ethnic makeup of the audience? Why or why not? Which is more important: respect for cultural sensitivity or free speech? Most of us would agree that both are important.

How Would *You* Do It?

Refer to the chapter opening story, and create a thesis statement for each of Tim's two topic options.

The range of topics on which you can speak is almost limitless, but sometimes you might have a difficult time identifying a topic for your speech. The First Amendment to the U.S. Constitution protects the right of free expression, saying, in part, "Congress shall make no law . . . abridging the freedom of speech."

Does the First Amendment mean that nothing is off-limits? No: Speakers cannot defame others with falsehoods, they cannot incite audiences to take illegal action, and they cannot threaten the president's life. Consider with your class the obligations associated with the right to free speech. Besides legal obligations (not labeling others, not inciting illegal or dangerous activities), what other obligations do speakers face when granted the right of free speech? Are people obligated to enact their right of free speech?

The First Amendment is often the subject of debate in contemporary society. The development of the Internet, concern for children's rights, differing views on women's rights, and incidents of hate speech by a variety of groups all fuel the sometimes fiery debate about the parameters of the First Amendment. Nonetheless, you are free to speak on almost any topic that you can identify. The authors of this text encourage you to speak on the following themes: environment, education, health, democracy, ethics, diversity, technology, and economics. Why? Because these vital topics lead you to consider subjects that are important and significant to you

Searching for a Topic

"By addressing vital issues, you avoid having to listen to speeches on trivial topics."

and to your audience. Also, by addressing vital issues, you avoid having to listen to speeches on trivial topics like the history of toothpicks, why I wore this outfit today, or why cars have tires. Check with your instructors for any particular expectations they may have. Here are some examples of vital topics:

My experience with welfare	Why people hate taxes
Reducing the federal deficit	Conservatives on bailouts
Violence and video games	Cheating on the Internet
Bias in American journalism	New restrictions on abortion
Flunking out of college	The price of prescription drugs
Problems with health care	The battle for Kandahar
Arizona immigration law	Healthcare bill

When your instructor assigns a speech, what do you do? Many beginning speakers put off the assignment as long as possible. You may consider possible topics as you go about other daily activities. How can you jump-start the process so you have more constructive time to plan your presentation?

In this section, we will discuss five methods of searching for a topic: individual brainstorming, categorical brainstorming, conducting a personal inventory, current topic identification, and Internet searching. Some of these methods will be more interesting and useful to you than others. You do not have to use all methods, but you should find one with which you are comfortable and use it.

Individual Brainstorming

Brainstorming occurs *when you try to think of as many topics as you can in a limited time.* Without judging them, you simply list all topics that come to mind. Groups frequently use brainstorming when members get together to propose a number of ideas. After the brainstorming process, which should be limited to a specific amount of time (say, five minutes), the group discusses the ideas and selects one or more by assessing their quality.

Individual brainstorming occurs when you, individually, spend a certain amount of time writing down all the possible topics you can think of. After you have completed that phase of the process, you evaluate the topics and choose two or three for further research. Select the one that works out best for you.

Categorical Brainstorming

Categorical brainstorming is similar to individual brainstorming. The difference is that *you begin with categories that prompt you to think of topics.* For example, you might think about people, places, things, and events. Begin by writing these four categories on a sheet of paper and making four columns. Then, brainstorm topics that fit in the four columns. Table 3.1 provides an example. To localize this activity, use the same categories, but generate a new table using only campus, community, or regional topics.

Conducting a Personal Inventory

Another strategy that might be helpful is conducting a **personal inventory**. *Consider features of your life such as experiences, attitudes, values, beliefs, interests, and skills.* Write down anything that describes you. Don't worry if your words don't sound like a topic for a

TABLE 3.1   TOPICS IDENTIFIED BY CATEGORICAL BRAINSTORMING

PEOPLE	PLACES	THINGS	EVENTS
Aung San Suu Kyi		climate change	Cinco de Mayo
Angelina Jolie		higher education	Halloween
Allen Toussaint		social justice	spring break
Hannah Montana		tsunamis	Earth Day
Anne Heche		immigration laws	Chinese New Year
Rush Limbaugh	Tibet	biofuel	graduation
Stephen Colbert	Nepal		Race for the Cure®
Denzel Washington	Arctic National Wildlife Refuge		
Bill Maher	Darfur		
"Tea Baggers"	Australia		
Jon Stewart	Hollywood		Election Day
George Rada	Saturn		Boxing Day
J-Lo	Napa Valley	social media	
Eric Holder	Kandahar	Facebook	concerts
	South Central L.A.	sex scandals	Nobel Prizes
	New Orleans	diversity	Groundhog Day
	Mount Rushmore	DNA	
	Central Park	bank reform	Declaration of the the Báb
		childhood obesity	

presentation. No idea should be discarded at this stage. Later you will cull this list and identify two or three topics that might work for your presentation. Here are some topics that students identified using personal inventories:

Studying abroad

Interning for your senator

Service learning with hearing-impaired children

Laser surgery for better sight

The symbols in a powwow

Being a Muslim in the United States

Rugby as exercise

Free speech in Mexico

Health care for veterans

Private versus public education

Growing up below the poverty line

Preparing for a job interview

Managing a life-threatening disease

Volunteering in a mental health facility

Current Topic Identification

Another way to approach searching for a topic is to consider topics of interest today. **Current topics** are *items that you find in the news, in the media, and on the minds of people in your audience.* Among the best sources of ideas on current topics are newspapers, magazines, TV news/discussions/documentaries, radio talk shows, and the Internet. Most students do not read newspapers or magazines, but they do watch *The Daily Show* and *The Colbert Report*, shows which report news with a comic twist. Student speech topics that originated in current topics include:

Renewable energy	Athletes as role models
Omega-3 and	Racial profiling
Omega-6	Human rights education
Rising healthcare costs	Anabolic steroids
Binge drinking	Hate crimes
Genetically modified produce	Hybrid cars
Biodiversity	Executive compensation
AIDS in the 21st century	Same-sex marriage
Technology and terrorism	Climate justice and equity
Workplace diversity	Genetic privacy
Sex scandals	Vertical farming

Internet Searching

Getting started is most important. Sure, you should think about a proper vital topic, but too many students think too long before they launch their search for information. The search for information contains both a blessing and a curse. The blessing is that never before has so much information about everything been available to so many so quickly. The curse is that same thing: we have access to so much information that selecting what to say has become a problem. That is why students who earn high grades in public speaking think quickly and then start their research early because they have too much information from which to choose. See Figure 3.1 for tips.

- Use key words to narrow your search as much as possible.
- Do not just nab the first sources that pop up because much better ones can lie beneath the surface.
- When you locate a valuable source, be sure that you copy the exact site citation to list as a reference (sometimes they are very difficult to relocate later).
- Be sure to use quote marks around anything you lift directly so that you can avoid plagiarism.

Figure 3.1   **Tips for your Internet search.**

Selecting a Topic

Now that you have identified several topics for a presentation, you will need to comb through them and select one. How can you best succeed in choosing? Here are some general guidelines for topic selection used successfully by public speaking students:

- *Speak about topics you already know.* What subjects do you know about—Web design, culinary arts, or national parks? You will save much time by choosing a familiar topic.
- *Speak about a topic that interests you.* What subjects arouse your interest—politics, social justice, or fitness? What do you like to read about? What elective courses do you choose? Selecting a topic that interests you will make the research process enjoyable.
- *Speak about topics that are uniquely your own.* If you have done a personal inventory or an individual brainstorm, examine the list for topics that might not be shared by others in the class. Consider unusual jobs or travel experiences.

Consider your unique background for ideas to share with the audience.

- *Speak about a topic that is important to your local community.* Have you heard the expression "Think globally; act locally"? How can you relate international and national issues and trends to your hometown or present community?

- *Speak about topics that your audience finds interesting—* finding work, Internet dating, or interviewing dos and don'ts. What do people in your class enjoy talking and hearing about? Which of their favorite topics could you discuss with some authority? If people tend to talk about certain topics before or after class, consider those ideas for a speech topic.

- *Speak about a topic that the audience embraces, but you do not.* Do some members of your class hold ideas that they accept without question, but which you think could be challenged? For example, people in your class might have differing views on political candidates, cohabiting, or how much alcohol they should and do drink. Try to convince members of the audience to consider your thinking on the topic.

- *Speak about a topic that is worth your time and effort and the time of your listeners.* Consider the themes that are central to this book: the environment, education, health, democracy, ethics, diversity, technology, and economics. Remember, speech is free; make it matter.

" Try not to become a [person] of success, but rather, try to become a [person] of value. "

[Albert Einstein]

Evaluating Topics

After you have identified a general topic, the next step is evaluating it. You must determine if the topic meets standards of appropriateness for the speaker, audience, ethics, and occasion.

Appropriate for You

While you should always keep your attention on the audience, you also need to determine whether a topic is of interest to you. A speech is appropriate for you as a speaker if you can generate interest in the topic. If you are interested, you can be enthusiastic, and the audience is likely to share your feelings. If you are not, the audience will probably sense it.

Imagine, for example, that you are very active in the Republican Party. Your parents are staunch Republicans and you have integrated many of their values and beliefs into your own life. When you enrolled at Blinn College in Bryan, Texas, you immediately joined the College Republicans. During your second semester at the school, you were

involved in a service learning project with the Washington County Republican Party. Although you know that not all of your classmates share your point of view, the principles of the Republican Party are important to you. This topic, therefore, would fit the criterion of being appropriate for you.

Research is every speaker's obligation. You should know something about your topic, but you should also have a sincere interest in learning more about the subject. A topic is appropriate for you if you know—or can learn—more about it than most of the people in the audience. Most of us possess only superficial knowledge of most topics. A speaker can generally learn more about a specific subject than is generally known to an audience. When you have such knowledge, you are said to have subject matter competence.

Appropriate for the Audience

A speech is appropriate for audience members if the content is both interesting and worthwhile to them. The speaker is responsible for generating audience interest. Suppose you are very interested in genetic engineering, but you realize that practically nobody else in the class holds this interest. One way to arouse audience interest might be to show how controversial genetic engineering can be. For example, consider the issue of genetically modified foods.

As you are thinking about controversial topics, consider local, state, or national figures who have advocated positions contrary to the expectations of most audience members. What are the potential advantages, disadvantages, and obligations that speakers need to consider when they select a controversial topic? What can you learn about controversy from the speeches of well-known people?

"The speaker is responsible for generating audience interest."

Also consider whether your topic is worthwhile for the audience. If the audience is already familiar with the topic, be careful about the information you are presenting. Try to present new information about familiar topics; do not repeat what the audience is already likely to know. A presentation about a topic too familiar to the audience—for example, reality television—would probably be uninformative. A presentation about a topic that is too trivial—for instance, your summer vacation at the lake—will not be worth the audience's time. A proper analysis of your audience should reveal both how interesting and how worthwhile your topic would be for them. In the next chapter, we thoroughly discuss audience analysis.

Appropriate for the Occasion

Finally, consider the topic's appropriateness for the occasion: Is the subject significant, timely, and tailored? A speech topic is *significant* if the content meets the audience's expectation of what should occur on that occasion. In a classroom presentation, for example, a common expectation is that the speech should be on a topic of importance to the class, the campus, the community, or the world. Your breakfast preferences, your date Saturday night, or your most recent argument with your kids probably do not warrant publicity; that is, a presentation about them would seem insignificant.

A speech is *timely* if it can be linked to the audience's current concerns. A student who gave a presentation about a revolution in Liberia did a fine job on the speech, but the revolution had occurred several years before and the student failed to demonstrate how the topic related to the present. Ancient history can be timely if the speaker can show how that history speaks to the present.

A speech is *tailored* if the topic is narrowed to fit the time allotted for the presentation. To cover the rise and fall of the Roman Empire in a five-minute speech is impossible, but to talk about three ways to avoid obesity through diet and exercise

1. Do you, as the speaker, have involvement with the topic?
2. Do you, as the speaker, have competence in the topic area?
3. Based on audience analyses, does this topic hold interest for your audience?
4. Based on audience analyses, is the topic worthwhile to your audience?
5. Is the topic significant in terms of the speech occasion?
6. Is the topic timely or appropriate for the speech occasion?
7. Have you appropriately narrowed and limited the topic for the occasion?

Figure 3.2   **Guidelines for topic appropriateness.**

is possible. Most speakers err in selecting too large rather than too small a topic. A narrow topic allows you to use research time more effectively; researching too large a topic will require cutting much of the material to meet the time limits of the speech.

Refer to the criteria in Figure 3.2 as guidelines for evaluating your topic for appropriateness.

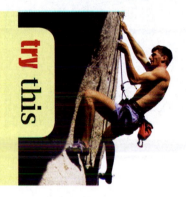

try this

After you have identified a number of topics using one or more of the methods in the section on searching for a topic, pair up with a classmate. Share your lists. Have your classmate identify topics in which she or he would be interested and that are appropriate for the occasion. Reverse roles and identify appropriate topics from your classmate's list. What does this exercise illustrate? Are either of you surprised by the other's reaction to the topics?

Purposes of Speeches

Without a map, you do not know how to get to your destination. In public speaking, without a purpose, you do not know what you should say. In this section of the chapter, we consider *purposes* of speeches and the *thesis statement*, which is a kind of short summary of your speech. Speeches have both general purposes and specific purposes. We consider both purposes here.

General Purposes

In the broadest sense, the *general purpose* of many speeches is either *to inform, to persuade,* or *to highlight a special occasion.* In class, your teacher may determine the general purpose of your speech. When you are invited to give a presentation to a particular group, the person who invites you may suggest a purpose. If you are not given a general purpose, you should consider the speech, the occasion, the audience, and your own motivations as you determine the general purpose of your speech.

The general purposes of speaking can sometimes overlap. To understand how informative speaking and persuasive speaking are interrelated, select one or more vital topics and determine how they can be approached as either an informative or a persuasive message. By using several examples, you will better be able to distinguish between speeches that are "mainly informative" and "mainly persuasive." This distinction is more difficult to recognize when engaging complex, multifaceted, or controversial topics. Most speeches, however, can be distinguished as mainly informative, mainly persuasive, or mainly special occasion.

The Speech to Inform

The **speech to inform** *seeks to increase the audience's level of understanding or knowledge about a topic.* Generally, the speaker provides new information or shows how existing information can be applied in new ways. The speaker does not attempt to persuade or convince the audience to change attitudes or behaviors. The informative speech should be devoid of persuasive tactics. The speaker is essentially a teacher. How would the following topics lend themselves to a speech to inform?

Wetlands ecology	How to prevent oil spills
Corporate accounting ethics	What is a democracy?
Wind energy	Early childhood literacy
Interviewing: Best practices	To Twitter or not to Twitter
What does it mean to be Buddhist?	Recognizing gay marriage

Keep in mind that the main idea behind the informative speech is to increase the audience's knowledge about a topic.

William B. Harrison, Jr., chief executive officer of J. P. Morgan Chase and Company, delivered a talk to the Peterson Business Award Dinner at the Greenwich Library in Greenwich, Connecticut, on March 7, 2002. Harrison began his informative talk by stating,

> Tonight I will look at how two institutions—banks and libraries—have evolved through three great revolutions in information technology. This will be a quick, even light-hearted look.

Similarly, Dr. Smith, a member of the American Society of Plastic Surgeons, began her talk,

> While statistics vary on the frequency of procedures performed, an increasing number of teenagers are seeking plastic surgery.

These two speakers give dozens of speeches each year. They demonstrate their ability to state their purpose clearly and cleverly. Professional speakers can serve as good role models for beginning speakers.

The Speech to Persuade

The **speech to persuade** *seeks to influence, reinforce, or modify the audience members' feelings, attitudes, beliefs, values, or behaviors.* Persuasive speeches may seek change or they may argue that the status quo should be upheld. Persuasive speakers attempt to add to what the audience members already know, but they also strive to alter how the audience feels about what they know and ultimately how they behave. The speaker, in this instance, is an advocate. How would the following topics lend themselves to a speech to persuade?

Reducing binge drinking on college campuses

Heart disease has origins in youth

We overmedicate the doomed

Why do we overpay executives?

The conservative cure for high taxes

Money problems plague higher education

Famous Dave's: a successful minority business

Does going global mean going broke?

Why families suffer when the economy fails

How faith-based organizations help people

State support for education

Do Americans trust big government?

How can you serve your community?

Daniel Ramirez, a student, began his persuasive presentation,

Maybe you have never thought about the safety of your automobile, but after hearing my presentation today, I hope you will. Two months ago, my wife asked me to run some errands in her new car. This automobile purchase was the result of careful research and numerous consultations with *Consumer Reports* magazine. As I sped to pick up a few groceries and two items from the drugstore, nothing was further from my mind than all the investigative work she had done prior to buying the car. But when an oncoming car hit me head on, both air bags deployed exactly as they were designed to do. The engine absorbed the impact of the collision and was driven downward rather than toward the front seat. Amazingly, I walked away without a scratch.

No one in the audience could have doubted that the purpose of his speech was to be persuasive.

The Special Occasion Speech

The **special occasion speech** *is a presentation that highlights a special event.* Special occasion speeches are quite common, but they differ in many ways from the speech to inform or the speech to persuade. Special occasion speeches are presentations designed to welcome, to pay tribute, to introduce, to nominate, to dedicate, to commemorate, or to entertain. The following topics would lend themselves to a special occasion speech.

Honoring a Boy Scout leader

A eulogy for an old friend

Celebrating Campus Compact

Roasting a retiring officer

Toasting the bride and groom

Introducing a new employee

Celebrating an anniversary

A nomination speech

Dedicating a building

An after-dinner thanks

Welcoming new members

Initiating members to an honorary

An excerpt from a special occasion speech follows:

Happy Birthday Mom!
This day means a lot to us, and I thought I'd take a few minutes today to tell you why. The most obvious explanation, of course, is that we all like an excuse for a party! But there's a more important reason. We all want you to know how much we appreciate everything you've done for us. And we all want you to know that we think you have a lot to celebrate. For starters, you've been a great provider. You've been the kind of mother who puts her family first, and does whatever it takes to make . . .

Specific Purposes

The general purpose involves nothing more than stating that your goal is to inform or to persuade. The *specific purpose* goes a step further. Here *you identify your purpose more precisely as an outcome or behavioral objective. You also include the audience* in your specific purpose. For example, a specific purpose statement might be, "My audience will be able to list the five signs of skin cancer." A specific purpose statement thus includes your general purpose, your intended audience, and your precise goal. Some additional examples of specific purpose statements might be the following.

My audience will be able to explain why violence and bullying in elementary schools are on the rise.
My audience will be able to define and identify hate crimes.
My audience will state the benefits of walking.
My audience will identify three reasons to help register persons without homes to vote.
My audience will be able to identify helpful herbs.
My audience will be able to describe ways to adopt new technologies.
My audience will stop drinking alcoholic beverages in excess.
My audience will identify three reasons to become a nurse.

When developing your specific purpose, consider the following four characteristics of good purpose statements:

1. They are declarative statements rather than imperative statements (expressing a command, request, or plea) or interrogative statements (asking a question). They make a statement; they do not command behavior nor do they ask a question.
   GOOD: My audience will be able to state some reasons for failing to graduate within four years.
   POOR: Why do students flunk out of college?
2. Strong specific purpose statements are complete statements; they are not titles, phrases, clauses, or fragments of ideas.
   GOOD: My audience will be able to defend our institution's policy on liquor on campus.
   POOR: The importance of liquor policies.

❝Statements of specific purpose guide the entire presentation like a map or blueprint.❞

[Judy Pearson]

e-NOTE

General and Specific Purpose

Find a passionate speech, such as the short message from President Ronald Reagan on January 22, 1981, as he spoke to the American hostages freed from Iran (at **http://www.reagan.utexas.edu/archives/speeches/1981/12281d.htm**). Or examine President Bill Clinton's farewell speech to the nation (available at **http://www.americanrhetoric.com/speeches/wjclintonfarewell.htm**). Or consider a famous historical speech such as Patrick Henry's "Give Me Liberty or Give Me Death," which you can access at **http://theamericanrevolution.org/ipeople/phenry.asp**. Another well-known historical speech is Elizabeth Cady Stanton's "Declaration of Sentiments and Resolutions," available at **http://gos.sbc.edu/byyears/old.html**. Can you determine the general purpose and the specific purpose of the speech you have selected?

3. They are descriptive and specific, rather than figurative and vague or general.
   GOOD: My audience will learn how to create a playlist on iTunes.
   POOR: My goal will be to demonstrate all the many things you can do with an iPod.
4. They focus on one idea rather than on a combination of ideas.
   GOOD: My audience will be able to distinguish between legal and illegal drugs.
   POOR: I want my classmates to avoid illegal drugs and possibly getting arrested; I also want them to know about legal drugs that may be useful to them as they become increasingly fit.

If your statement of purpose meets these standards, then you are ready to begin creating a thesis statement for your presentation. One speaker determined her statement of purpose as: My audience will be able to identify at least three attractions in the San Jose del Cabo, Mexico, area.

Thesis Statement

You may decide the general kind of presentation you will give and the specific goal you have before you conduct your research. However, unless you have a personal involvement with your topic, you will probably not be able to develop the thesis statement until you become more informed.

The **thesis statement** is *a summary of the speech* that typically is established early in the presentation. It is similar to the topic sentence or central idea of a written composition: a complete sentence that reveals the content of your presentation. Some examples of thesis statements follow:

- U.S. businesses need to restore trust with the public.
- Puerto Rico's Caribbean National Forest is a national treasure.

- Judges need to follow, not make, laws.
- Diversity is America's good fortune.
- Community service is essential for any successful democracy.
- Hispanics have become the largest minority group in the United States.
- Intercultural communication knowledge is essential for successful globalization.
- Over 1.2 million young people in Los Angeles are "at risk" and are in jeopardy of not reaching adulthood.
- Fear of terrorism has become absurd.
- Moral truth is not the same in every culture.

What are some qualities of a good thesis statement? (1) The thesis statement should be a complete statement rather than a fragment or grouping of a few words. (2) The thesis statement should be a declarative sentence rather than a question, explanation, or command. (3) The thesis statement should avoid figurative language and strive for literal meanings. (4) Finally, the thesis statement should not be vague or ambiguous. Let us examine some examples of poorly written thesis statements:

Implementing a job-shadowing program

The immune system is fantastic!

Are you getting enough sleep?

Television destroys lives.

The right to vote

Why are fewer men going to college?

What is wrong with these thesis statements? The first and fifth are not complete sentences. The second is an exclamation while the third and sixth are questions. The second uses language ("fantastic") that can be defined in multiple ways, while the fourth uses exaggeration to make a point. Some of these topics may also be viewed as trivial. How could we rewrite these ideas into appropriate thesis statements?

A job-shadowing program should be implemented on our campus.

The human immune system is important for homeostasis.

The human need for sleep varies with age and activity.

Excessive television viewing may lead to violent behavior.

Voting is an important element of a democratic society.

A smaller number of men than women are attending college today.

Purposes of speeches are thus general and specific. Although the general purpose is often to inform or to persuade, the specific purpose goes further. The specific purpose includes the goal of your speech as a precise outcome or behavioral objective. The specific purpose reflects considerations of your audience. The thesis statement is a one-sentence summary of the speech and should be a complete and unambiguous statement.

> **"The reason most people never reach their goals is that they don't define them, or even seriously consider them as believable or achievable."**
>
> [Denis Waitley, *The Waitley Institute*]

Let us finish this chapter by visualizing the three elements that will form the foundation of your presentation. Regardless of the purpose of your speech, all presentations usually require a topic that is appropriate for the speaker and the audience, a purpose that is consistent with the assignment of expectations of the occasion, and a thesis statement that clearly reveals the content of your presentation. Table 3.2 illustrates the three-step process for the three general purposes of speaking: informative, persuasive, and special occasion.

From Topic Selection to Thesis Statement: A Three-Step Process

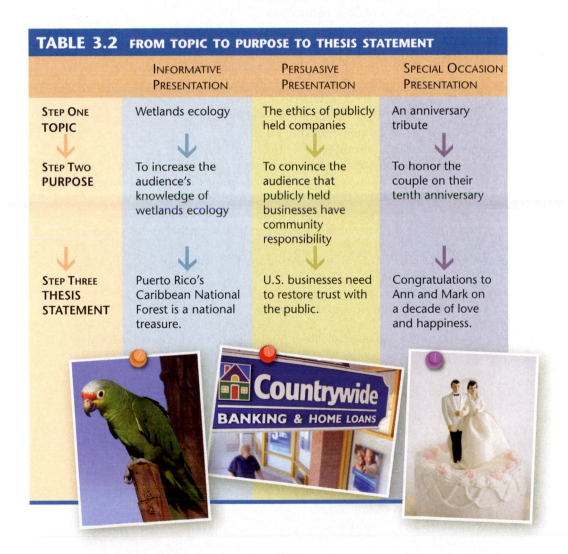

TABLE 3.2 FROM TOPIC TO PURPOSE TO THESIS STATEMENT

	INFORMATIVE PRESENTATION	PERSUASIVE PRESENTATION	SPECIAL OCCASION PRESENTATION
STEP ONE **TOPIC**	Wetlands ecology	The ethics of publicly held companies	An anniversary tribute
STEP TWO **PURPOSE**	To increase the audience's knowledge of wetlands ecology	To convince the audience that publicly held businesses have community responsibility	To honor the couple on their tenth anniversary
STEP THREE **THESIS STATEMENT**	Puerto Rico's Caribbean National Forest is a national treasure.	U.S. businesses need to restore trust with the public.	Congratulations to Ann and Mark on a decade of love and happiness.

For
REVIEW >>

AS YOU READ

1. Search for, evaluate, and select a presentation topic.

SUMMARY HIGHLIGHTS

▶ To search for a public speaking topic, you can use at least five different approaches:
- Individual brainstorming.
- Categorical brainstorming.
- Conducting a personal inventory.
- Current topic identification.
- Internet searching.

▶ To evaluate a public speaking topic, determine whether the topic meets the standards of
- Appropriateness for the speaker.
- Appropriateness for the audience.
- Appropriateness for the occasion.

▶ To select a public speaking topic:
- Speak about topics you already know.
- Speak about topics that interest you.
- Speak about topics that are important to your local community.
- Speak about topics that are uniquely your own.
- Speak about topics that your audience finds interesting.
- Speak about topics that the audience embraces but you do not.

2. Identify three general purposes of public speaking.

▶ The three general purposes of public speaking are
- To inform.
- To persuade.
- To celebrate a special occasion.

3. Write a specific purpose for a presentation.

▶ The specific purpose for a public speech includes considerations of
- Your general purpose.
- Your intended purpose.
- Your precise goal.

4. Develop a thesis statement for a presentation.

▶ To develop a thesis statement for a public speech:
- You will prepare a one-sentence summary of the speech.
- You will need to be informed on your topic.

Pop Quiz

1. Kathy tried to think of as many topics as she could in 10 minutes. She was participating in:
   - (A) conducting a personal inventory
   - (B) brainstorming for ideas
   - (C) violating the First Amendment
   - (D) a special occasion speech

2. Categorical brainstorming is when you:
   - (A) find items in the news to discuss
   - (B) consider features of your life, such as experiences, beliefs, or skills
   - (C) search on the Internet for a topic
   - (D) begin with categories that prompt you to think of topics

3. When choosing a topic, you should not speak about topics that are:
   - (A) uniquely your own
   - (B) important to your local community
   - (C) uninteresting to the audience
   - (D) embraced by the audience

4. To be appropriate for the occasion, the topic should be:
   - (A) significant, timely, and tailored
   - (B) interesting and worthwhile to the audience
   - (C) interesting to you
   - (D) ethically sound

5. The speech that seeks to increase the audience's level of understanding or knowledge about a topic is the speech to:
   - (A) persuade
   - (B) highlight a special occasion
   - (C) influence
   - (D) inform

6. Andrew gave a speech on why schools should lower tuition. This was likely a speech to:
   - (A) inform
   - (B) persuade
   - (C) introduce
   - (D) highlight a special occasion

7. An example of a speech's specific purpose is:
   - (A) "I will inform my audience."
   - (B) "The importance of an education."
   - (C) "A speech to persuade."
   - (D) "My audience will be able to identify three advantages of green tea."

8. The thesis statement:
   - (A) avoids revealing the content of the presentation
   - (B) is established in the conclusion
   - (C) is a complete statement
   - (D) uses figurative language

9. A toast at a wedding reception is an example of a:
   - (A) speech to inform
   - (B) speech to influence
   - (C) speech to persuade
   - (D) special occasion speech

10. A specific purpose statement is:
    - (A) declarative in nature
    - (B) figurative and vague
    - (C) focused on a combination of ideas
    - (D) a phrase or clause

Answers: 1 (B); 2 (D); 3 (C); 4 (A); 5 (D); 6 (B); 7 (D); 8 (C); 9 (D); 10 (A)

APPLICATION EXERCISES

1. Examine the following specific purpose statements. Identify those that are good examples and explain why the others are bad examples.

   a. The beauty of the Grand Teton National Park.

   b. My audience will be able to explain the current Homeland Security strategies.

   c. What do men want in their personal relationships?

   d. My audience will be able to identify five kinds of love.

   e. To persuade the audience to live and let live.

   f. To inform my audience about STDs.

   g. To identify the primary causes of cancer.

   h. My audience will be able to distinguish between moderate and binge drinking.

   i. To explain early baldness in men.

   j. My audience will go to graduate school or professional school.

   k. To inform my audience about weekend trips in the region.

   l. To inform my audience about the pleasures of flying one's own plane.

   m. To inform my audience about the steps to earning the Eagle Scout Award.

   n. A passion for cooking.

2. Divide a piece of paper into four columns. Write one of the following general topics at the top of each of the four columns.

   a. Job experiences I have had.

   b. Places I have traveled.

   c. City, state, or area I am from.

   d. People who make me angry.

   e. Happy experiences I have had.

   f. Unusual experiences I have had.

   g. Personal experiences I have had with crime.

   h. My involvement in marriage, divorce, or other family matters.

   i. My experiences with members of other groups—the old, the young, other ethnic groups.

   j. The effect of the drug culture on my life.

   k. My relationship to local, state, or federal government.

   l. My background in painting, music, sculpture, theater, dance, or other fine arts.

   m. My feelings about grades, a college education, sororities and fraternities, college requirements, student government, or alternatives to a college education.

   n. My reactions to current radio, television, or film practices, policies, or programming.

   o. Recent Supreme Court decisions that affect me.

   p. My personal and career goals.

Now, write down specific topics under each of the four general topic areas you chose. Spend no more than five minutes on this exercise brainstorming. Next, underline one topic in each of the four columns that is particularly interesting to you. From these four topics, select the one about which you have the most information or the best access to information. Can you adapt the topic to your specific audience?

KEY TERMS

Brainstorming	Personal inventory	Speech to persuade
Categorical brainstorming	Special occasion speech	Thesis statement
Current topics	Speech to inform	

get involved!

Service Learning is "education in action," connecting college with community, and a way to apply your education to people and projects that make the world a better place in which to live. Beyond simply volunteering for a worthy cause, service learning invites you to be mindful about your activities on behalf of others; indeed, the idea is to learn from your service.

What are some examples of service learning projects? CharityGuide.org mentions children's issues, animal welfare, community development, environment, health, and poverty. More specifically, that organization mentions saving vanishing wetlands, protecting endangered species, preventing deforestation, improving children's dental care, preventing teen suicide, and reducing identity theft.

What opportunities does your campus offer to engage your education in service to the community? The National Youth Leadership Council (**www.nylc.org**) says "Serve-Learn-Change the World" and "work across generations and cultures to strengthen your community." Google "Service Learning" for project ideas.

4

ANALYZING

Effective presenters try to learn as much about the members of their audience as they can before communicating. As beginning speakers, we too often focus on our own concerns and interests. We speak on our favorite topics without considering what the audience might want or need to hear. We use language that we understand without considering that the audience might not understand it. Perhaps the individualistic culture of the United States invites more attention to self and less to audience than might be the case in more collectivist cultures, such as those represented by many Arab, African, Asian, and Latin American countries.[1]

THE AUDIENCE

[As You READ

 >>

1. Determine how audience and context affect presentations and how speakers adapt to each before and during their presentations.
2. Explain the effects of audience worldview on topic selection and treatment.
3. Identify five methods for analyzing an audience and understand the ethics of audience analysis.
4. Explain the role of listening in public speaking.

Ami was deep in thought as she left the community center, her head full of ideas and plans. For her political science seminar in public policy, she had just volunteered to give a talk to the community's senior group in a couple of weeks, to help them understand how the government's new healthcare bill would affect them and their health insurance and medical prescriptions. She knew she had a lot of homework to do on the topic before she made her presentation in a couple of weeks, but what concerned her now was how she could best reach her audience.

"Remember, Ami," the young director of the center had told her, "our members are seniors, but they don't think of themselves as old! Most of them are retired, and some are widowed, but they're active people who travel often and have a lot of outside interests. In fact, some of them are getting out and about with their friends more often now than they did when they were still in the workforce. Please don't underestimate them."

Ami had nodded her understanding and had taken a couple of quick notes.

"On the other hand," the director continued, "they're worried. None of them really understand how health care is going to change, and they're going to have a lot of questions for you. That's one reason we're so glad you stopped by today to volunteer. There's a real need for information and reassurance.

"Now, what else can I tell you about our members?"

How Would *You* Do It?

Refer to the chapter opening story, and list some of the questions you think Ami should ask the director of the community center about the senior group she's going to address. What would you like to know about them if you were in her place?

Audiences for Great Speeches

If you would like to know more about history, public speaking, and audience analysis, you should go to **www.americanrhetoric.com/top100speechesall**, where you will find the top 100 great American speeches. Among them are: Elie Wiesel, holocaust survivor, on "The Perils of Indifference"; union leader Cesar Chavez's "Speech on Ending his 25-day Fast"; Lou Gehrig's "Farewell to Baseball" address; black activist Stokely Carmichael's speech on "Black Power"; Hillary Clinton's "Women's Rights Are Human Rights"; and President Richard Nixon on "The Great Silent Majority." You can listen to one or more of these speeches for their historical value, but for purposes of this chapter you should listen for what these top speeches assume about their listeners. Nixon's speech, for example, assumed that America was full of fed-up voters who were saying little but feeling much frustration. He was so good at analyzing his audience that he was elected president largely based on how accurately he articulated a frustrated public.

Audience Analysis

What is audience analysis? **Audience analysis** is *discovering as much as possible about an audience for the purpose of improving communication with them.* Audience analysis occurs before, during, and after a presentation. Why should a speaker analyze an audience?

Think of public speaking as another version of the kind of speaking you do every day. Nearly always, when you meet a stranger, you size up that person before you disclose your message. Similarly, public speaking requires that you meet and know the members of your audience so you are able to create a message for them. Public speaking is not talking to oneself in front of a group; instead, it is effective message transmission from one person to many people in a setting in which speaker and audience influence each other.

Let us consider the wide variety of audiences you might face in your lifetime:

Your classmates	A political group
Fellow workers	A board of directors
Members of a union	A group of children
A civic organization	Community members
A religious group	A school board
Retired people	A committee of professors
A group of friends	A social club

Would you talk to all these audiences about the same topic or in the same way? Of course not. Your choice of topic and your approach to that topic are both strongly influenced by the nature of your audience. We focus on the audience in a presentation by learning the nature of that audience.

When we talk to individuals, we are relatively careful about what we say and how we say it. We speak differently to strangers than to intimates, differently to people we respect than to people we do not respect, and differently to children than to adults. Similarly, we need to be aware of audience characteristics when we choose a topic and when we decide how we are going to present that topic to the audience.

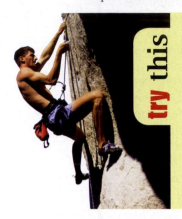

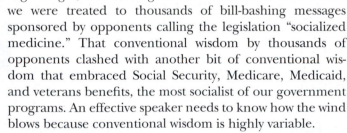

try this

You have already talked to multiple audiences, especially in informal settings (planning an evening with friends, discussing an adventure with other couples, speaking up at a parent-teacher meeting). How many of these audiences can you recall? How would you describe some of these audiences? Provide as much detail as you can about these audiences. Then compare notes with a classmate to see what assumptions you made about your audiences. Remember that one danger in audience analysis is **projection**, the belief that others believe as you do when actually they may not.

Imagine that you are about to speak to a new audience. How would you learn about the people in your audience? First, you could rely on "conventional wisdom." Second, you could consider a demographic analysis of the characteristics of the people, such as their gender, age, and ethnicity. Let's examine each of these general ways of learning more about an audience.

Conventional Wisdom

Conventional wisdom is *the popular opinions of the time about issues, styles, topics, trends, and social mores, the customary set of understandings of what is true or right.* Conventional wisdom includes what most people are said to think. *Newsweek* magazine devotes a few column inches each week to conventional wisdom about people and issues. Sometimes the president of the United States gets an arrow up (positive sign) one week and an arrow down (negative sign) the next week—on the same issue. Let's look at how conventional wisdom relates to audience analysis.

Conventional wisdom is a gross oversimplification often based more on a whim than on deep-seated convictions. Look at the popularity of entertainers: one minute they are on top of the world with hit songs and endless concerts; the next minute they are in the Dumpster, facing charges, and seeking rehab. In the healthcare debate

we were treated to thousands of bill-bashing messages sponsored by opponents calling the legislation "socialized medicine." That conventional wisdom by thousands of opponents clashed with another bit of conventional wisdom that embraced Social Security, Medicare, Medicaid, and veterans benefits, the most socialist of our government programs. An effective speaker needs to know how the wind blows because conventional wisdom is highly variable.

How can a speaker use conventional wisdom? An excellent way to demonstrate your critical thinking ability is to challenge conventional wisdom. If people are getting too comfortable with government intrusion, then make a reasoned case for why we don't need Big Government. If conventional wisdom is against taxation, then inquire how to pay for all the services the public demands. And, if conventional wisdom says no more war, then make a spirited case for a vigorous national defense.

Demographics

What are some aspects of an audience that can affect how they interpret your message? The **demographics** (which literally means "characteristics of the people") of an audience *include gender composition, age, ethnicity, economic status, occupation, and education.* You can learn the demographic features of your campus or community by getting data from the campus office for institutional research and/or the Census Bureau. From this information, a complete demographic profile of your campus or community emerges. Consider how demographic patterns might be relevant to topic selection and other issues related to audience adaptation.

Gender Composition

Why would a speaker care whether the audience is composed of men, women, or a mixture of the two? With some topics, the gender composition of the audience may make no difference at all. With other topics, gender representation may make all the difference in the world.

You may need to consider whether your topic is gender-linked or gender-neutral, and modify your treatment of the subject when speaking before generally male, generally female, or mixed-gender audiences. Consider the factors that may cause women and men to react differently to certain topics. Be aware that some women and some men feel that women have been victims of discrimination. They will be watchful for signs of discrimination from speakers.

e-NOTE

Facts About Women

Here are some demographics about women according to the U.S. Department of Labor:

- Women by 2016 will account for nearly 50 percent of the increase in the labor force.
- The top three occupations for women are secretaries and administrative assistants, nurses, and elementary and middle school teachers.
- The top three high-paying jobs for women are pharmacist, chief executive officer, and lawyer (all three groups are paid more than female engineers or physicians).
- The women with the most education are more likely to be in the labor force.
- The women with the most education are least likely to be unemployed.

Learn to use the Internet to find authoritative sources of information for presentations.

(All information from U.S. Department of Labor's Women's Bureau Web site.)

Try to avoid relying on stereotypes to help you determine an audience's needs based solely on gender. For example, if you were a student at Marquette University in Milwaukee, Wisconsin, you might have participated in a service learning project at the Milwaukee Women's Center, which provides a safe haven for women who have been verbally or physically abused. In considering your topic, you might think that this would not be appropriate for your audience because nearly half your class is made up of men. However, you may not know that many

of the men in your class are majoring in sociology and have taken classes on gender inequality, and that two of the men have actually worked for similar agencies.

Age

The 2010 census is most likely to show an increase in the over-80 group, an increase in the Hispanic group, a decrease in the proportion of whites, and a dramatic increase in the number of retired individuals. These figures become important in audience analysis because older folks may still read newspapers, while young adults are more likely to actually use the apps on their cell phone, know how to make a DVD, and get their news on the Internet. An effective presenter has to take the audience's level of experience and wisdom into account.

Look at the topics listed below and decide which are more appropriate for young adults, middle-aged people, or the elderly. The age of your audience members will affect the topic you choose and how you treat a particular topic. Be wary of stereotyping as you consider the list.

Placing your kids in college	Plastic surgery	Competitive sports
Selecting a career	Body piercing	Choosing a major
Managing your time	Enlisting in military service	Animal rights
Saving dollars from taxes	Voting	Health care in hostels
Choosing a college or university	Selecting a tattoo	Domestic violence
Investment opportunities	Cell phones	Downsizing
Social Security reform	Selecting software	Dating issues
	Traveling in Europe	Day care facilities
		Community service

You might speak about selecting a career to a younger audience but reserve the topic of cashing in your annuities for an older audience. On the other hand, you might discuss affordable housing with either younger people or older people. However, your approach will be different if you know that your audience consists of 19-year-old undergraduates or members of the AARP who are in their 60s and 70s. Considering age is part of audience focus, a primary ingredient in audience analysis.

Ethnicity

Knowing the ethnic makeup and identity of your audience members can make an important difference in your effectiveness. **Ethnicity** identifies *people who are united through "language, historical origins, nation-state, or cultural system."*[2] Ethnic groups preserve communication traditions that affect the way their members speak and listen; some are only partially shared with other groups.

People exhibit and prefer different conversational patterns and expectations because of their ethnic identity. For instance, African Americans and European Americans, while sharing aspects of U.S. culture, each have unique styles of communicating. Sometimes dialects differ, sometimes conversational rules and expectations differ, and sometimes interactional styles such as use of argument and discussion differ between the two groups.

As you consider speeches that you might give at work, on campus, or in your community, you recognize that a number of different co-cultures will be part of your audience. First, list any possible co-cultural groups that may be in your audience. Next, consider the topics that members of that co-culture might consider important or "vital." Be sure that you avoid stereotypical statements and favor fact-based statements about the co-cultures in your community or on your campus.

As speakers, we need to be sure that we do not accidentally or needlessly injure or insult audience members who have ethnic backgrounds different from our own. Members of the dominant culture of the United States have had tumultuous relationships with members of smaller **co-cultures**, or *groups that are similar to the larger culture but are distinguished by background, beliefs, and behaviors.* For example, Cuban Americans, native Hawaiians, Puerto Ricans, Vietnamese, and Appalachians are just a few of the groups that have been excluded from many of the privileges members of the dominant culture enjoy. Members of various ethnic groups are sensitive to the discrimination that has limited their people.

Sometimes even experienced public presenters make errors that are outrageous to members of ethnic co-cultures. Well-meaning people can accidentally use metaphors, figures of speech, language, or examples that members of co-cultures find offensive. You can learn to be more sensitive to other groups by practicing your presentation with friends who have backgrounds different from your own or by interviewing and observing other people to determine the kind of language they avoid and the types of examples, analogies, and metaphors they employ.

CO-CULTURAL BELIEFS ABOUT SPEAKING

Some co-cultures in the United States have different ideas about public speaking. The Blackfeet Indian Nation in Montana, for instance, values public speaking skills but reserves them for leaders, like tribal elders.[3] Furthermore, Blackfeet see silence as a way to connect with another person—unlike European-Americans who dread silence and value a continuous flow of words. A member of the Blackfeet Nation might feel presumptuous speaking in front of a group and might feel uncomfortable about communicating so much with words. This group's different ideas about public speaking underline the importance of knowing ethnic makeup in selecting topics and in choosing an approach for your presentation.

"As speakers, we need to be sure that we do not accidentally or needlessly injure or insult audience members who have ethnic backgrounds different from our own."

Economic Status

According to the U.S. Census Bureau, the annual median income for a four-person family is $67,019. However, this number varied by state in the nation. For example, families in Connecticut, Maryland, and New Jersey had the highest median incomes, while families in the District of Columbia, Mississippi, and New Mexico had the lowest median incomes. (For more information, see www.census.gov/hhes/www/cincome/4person.html.)

What is the economic status of your audience? Are they primarily wealthy individuals or are they from lower economic groups? People who are wealthier tend to be more conservative, are often older, may have more education, and have probably traveled more than less wealthy people. Wealthy people may be less open to new ideas because they are accustomed to being treated deferentially, with courteous submission to their wishes or judgments. They may be more difficult to persuade because they feel that they have already made good choices. On the other hand, less wealthy people may be more liberal, younger, and may be less educated because of their age. Less wealthy people may be more open to new ideas and may be more easily persuaded because they have less to lose and more to gain.

Some topics are appropriate for more affluent audiences, while other topics are right for less financially successful people. Consider the possible economic differences in your classroom. Do some students have jobs and families? Are some students from affluent families that pay their tuition and expenses? Do other students depend entirely on their own income from one or more jobs? However, a person's or audience's economic status alone is not sufficient to select or discard a topic.

For example, if you attend Ivy Tech, an Indiana community college with 120,000 students on 23 campuses that caters to working adults, you find that the college's strategic plan includes civic engagement and economic development. You can learn about people in need so you can speak with authority about people's economic problems, one of the vital speech topics advocated in this text.

Occupation

Whether you speak in the classroom, in the workplace, or in the community, the kinds of jobs people have are important to audience analysis because occupation influences both delivery and content of presentations.

First, occupations influence the way we talk to each other. Dockworkers are predominantly males who talk to each other at union meetings. Secretaries and administrative assistants are predominantly females who talk to each other at meetings about using new software, new procedures, new forms, and self-development. Sales managers motivate their sales personnel, and managers meet often to face issues. When you present in the workplace, you need to be highly aware of how to present yourself—everything from what you wear to how you talk.

Every business has its own culture that determines everything from what employees wear to work to how they talk to each other. From a communication perspective, language is the important aspect to recognize. Every job has it jargon, but the trouble comes when two sets of jargon intersect. Someone from tech services is supposed to tell the secretaries how to use the new software system. The secretaries know computers well, but the technology and computer security folks have a language that they use with each other that does not communicate well with others. So, a presenter always has to know how to cross code, how to translate one culture's technical jargon into language compatible with another culture's language. That task is almost always more difficult than it sounds.

For now just remember that every job has its own culture, its own way of talking, and its own language. The effective presenter is a skilled translator: a person who can successfully communicate between cultures.

Education

The most recent information on educational attainment in the United States shows that 85 percent of all adults 25 years of age and older have completed at least high school. More than one in four (27 percent) have received at least a bachelor's degree. Education makes a great deal of difference in earning power. In 2004, adults without a high school diploma earned an average of $21,600 per year; with a high school diploma, the average earnings were $30,800. Those with some college work earned an average of $35,700, while those who completed college earned an average of $49,900. If you are interested in tracking these numbers, a good source is the U.S. Department of Commerce, Bureau of the Census, which is available online.

Educational level also differed based on ethnicity and area of the country. Asians and Pacific Islanders had the highest proportion of college graduates (47 percent), followed by non-Hispanic whites (29 percent), African Americans (17 percent), and Hispanics (11 percent). The Northeast region had the highest proportion of college graduates (29 percent), followed by the West (28 percent), the Midwest (26 percent), and the South (25 percent). Even though these percentages seem quite close, the large numbers from which they are derived make them statistically different. (For more information, see www.census.gov.)

Educational attainment is frequently related to economic status and occupation. A person's level of education may tell you very little about his or her intelligence, ambition, or sophistication. However, people with more education tend to read and write more, are usually better acquainted with the news, are more likely to have traveled, and are more likely to have higher incomes. What are some of the implications of educational level for the way you approach your audience?

- People who read and write regularly tend to have more advanced vocabularies, so adjust your language choices to the educational level of your audience.
- People who are receptive to new information need less background and explanation on current issues than those who are not.
- People who have seen more of the world tend to be more sophisticated about differences between people and cultures.

Most important of all, you need to take into account how much your audience already knows about your topic. Knowledge is not necessarily the same as education in analyzing an audience. For example, an auto mechanic might not have a degree from a university, but she clearly would have knowledge about repairing a car, and thus terms relating to auto mechanics would not have to be defined. The opposite, of course, would be true in the case of an educated audience with no background in auto mechanics, for whom all technical terms would require definition.

"Knowledge is not necessarily the same as education in analyzing an audience."

In addition, is the audience likely to have a position on your issue? If so, how might their knowledge level affect your attempt to increase what they know or to change their minds on the issue? For example, if you are talking to a group of older individuals, they may have established opinions on Medicare, Social Security, and the inflated costs of drugs. A younger group of people might not have strong opinions on these matters, but they may care about a poor job market, high bills, and tuition costs.

CO-CULTURES CAN DISCOURAGE DISCOURSE

Some co-cultures in the United States do not encourage skills like public speaking because the very act of speaking out is regarded as acting bigger than, better than, or more important than others. One example is the Germans from Russia, a group of ethnic Germans who spent a century in Russia until Stalin killed many and sent the rest to Siberia. The ones who escaped to North America live in communities from North Dakota to Texas, right down the middle of the United States. Even though these hardy individuals are very successful as a group, they are almost absent from the political arena because of their perception that such aspirations could be viewed as being uppity. You may know of other cultures and co-cultures that similarly discourage people in the group from standing up, speaking out, and taking leadership, even in a democratic country.

Worldview

An important point to consider is that every individual has his or her own personal experience that shapes a perspective or point of view about the world. In that way we are all different from each other. At the same time we have commonalities, characteristics that we all share. In audience analysis the challenge is to merge perspectives: to discover what we have in common so we can build on that commonality.

In the workplace everyone has had different experiences. Some of your fellow workers were loved in their family of origin; others may have come from dysfunctional families. Some grew up privileged; others were poor and emerged from tough neighborhoods. But in the workplace these individuals with such different experiences are in a common cause to advance the goals of their business. The effective presenter builds on the common goal to seek innovation, advance sales, and improve customer satisfaction. In other words, good audience analysis allows the presenter to transcend differences and to go beyond commonality to new levels of accomplishment. Knowing your audience well can allow you to boost their accomplishments and yours.

Physical Characteristics

Physical characteristics include height, weight, style, fitness, gender display, and obvious disabilities. Imagine that you were going to speak to an audience of the American Federation of the Blind, to a group of individuals in wheelchairs, or to people who had another specific physical disability. How would you adjust your presentation? Most of us would do a poor job of adapting to these situations. Although members of such audiences generally ask that they be treated like those without disabilities, we tend to speak louder, perhaps unnecessarily, enunciate more clearly, or make other changes. We need to guard against language usage that disparages specific people, and we should be sensitive to negative stereotypes that we unintentionally may use. Even if your audience does not include people with physical disabilities, ridding yourself of negative stereotyping is important. People do negative categorizing so routinely that they do not even realize they are guilty of perpetuating myths about individuals with disabilities. For example, in his presentation "Language and the Future of the Blind," Marc Maurer, president of the National Federation of the Blind, discussed one of the stereotypes that he found particularly offensive: the idea that people who are not sighted are incompetent.

Recently an advertisement appeared from the Carrollton Corporation, a manufacturer of mobile homes. Apparently the Carrollton Corporation was facing fierce competition from other mobile home builders, who were selling their products at a lower price. Consequently, the Carrollton Corporation wanted to show that its higher priced units were superior. In an attempt to convey this impression, the company depicted the blind as sloppy and incompetent. Its advertisement said in part: "Some manufacturers put out low-end products. But they are either as ugly as three miles of bad road, or they have so many defects—crumpled metal, dangling moldings, damaged carpet—that they look like they were built at some school for the blind." What a description! . . . It is not a portrayal calculated to inspire confidence or likely to assist blind people to find employment.[4]

Clearly, you must adjust your language to any perceived physical characteristics of your audience, but going beyond that, rid your presentation of all negative, offensive stereotyping.

Methods of Audience Analysis

Some speakers seem to be able to analyze an audience intuitively, but most of us have to rely on formal and informal means of gathering such information. Individuals in advertising, marketing, and public relations have developed complex technological means of collecting information from audiences before, during, and after their message.[5] However, most of us usually collect information about audiences through observation, group identification, interviews, and questionnaires. Table 4.1 summarizes the advantages and disadvantages of these methods of audience analysis.

TABLE 4.1 THREE LEVELS OF AUDIENCE ANALYSIS			
METHOD	MEANS	ADVANTAGE	DISADVANTAGE
Eyeball or Observation	Scan the audience	Quick and easy	Can be inaccurate and stereotypical
Group Identification	Informant inquiry	Knowing group's values	Presenter as an outsider
In-Depth Inquiry	Interviews and questionnaires	Deeper understanding	Time and effort required

Observation

Observation, or *watching and listening,* reveals the most about the audience before and during the presentation. Looking at audience members might reveal their age, ethnic origin, and gender. More careful observation may reveal marital status by the presence or absence of rings; materialism by conspicuous brand names and trendy jewelry; and even religious affiliation by such symbols as a cross, skullcap, or headscarf. Many people in an audience advertise their membership in a group by exhibiting its symbols.

In the classroom, you have the added advantage of listening to everyone in your audience. Your classmates' speeches—their topics, issues, arguments, and evidence—all reveal more about them than you could learn in a complex questionnaire. Your eyes and ears become the most important tools of audience analysis that you have.

Group Identification

When you speak in the workplace, to a group to which you belong, or to a community organization, you need to meet the expectations of the group. Even in the workplace people at different levels in the organization may dress differently (bosses are sometimes even called "suits"), talk differently (educational differences), and even think differently (operational vs. visionary leaders). Even in your own workplace you have to adapt to the specific audience. Outside your own workplace, a key to audience analysis is knowing what a group values so you can adapt your presentation to their expectations.

The easiest way to gain such knowledge is through an **inside informant**, *someone who belongs to the group who can tell you what the group stands for.* You want to know what the group values not so you can merely mimic what they already believe but so you can adapt your message for maximum effectiveness. Service groups like Rotary, Lions, and Kiwanis have in common their generosity to causes like defeating polio worldwide, providing glasses for all, and building parks and recreational areas. Religious groups are relatively transparent in their beliefs about many matters, both moral and political. Unless you share some value with a group, you are unlikely to be invited to speak. But for any presentation to a group you must tailor your message to build on what the group already values. Here are some possible questions to ask of an inside informant:

1. How will this audience respond to my topic?
2. How does my topic relate to what this group values?
3. What are the characteristics of the audience?
4. How long does the audience expect me to speak?
5. What is the setting or the occasion for the presentation?

You really do need to know some answers before you face the audience with your message.

Interviews

Discover information about your audience by interviewing a few members of the group. These **interviews**—*inquiries about your audience directed at an audience member*—should typically occur far in advance of the speech. However, many professional speakers gain some of their most relevant material during the reception or the dinner before the presentation. The competent speaker takes advantage of this time with the audience to learn more about them, their needs, and their interests. Whether it takes place well in advance of the presentation or just before the time you will speak, an interview for information on the audience should focus on the same questions listed in the preceding section on group identification.

When you are conducting an audience analysis for a classroom presentation, you can talk to a few people from class. Try to discover their opinions of your topic, how they think the class will respond to it, and any helpful suggestions for best communicating the topic. Interviews take time, but they are a great way to learn more about your audience.

To understand the role of the interview in preparation for your presentation, arrange to interview at least one person in your community. Consider people who may have information on your topic that will be relevant to your preparation. Next, consider their probable contribution and availability: Your roommate might not offer a unique perspective, and an important elected official may not have any free time in his or her schedule.

Questionnaires

Whereas interviews take more time to execute than to plan, **questionnaires**—*surveys of audience opinions*—take more time to plan than to execute. The key to writing a good questionnaire is to be brief. Respondents tend to register their distaste for long questionnaires by not filling them out completely or by not participating at all.

What should you include in your brief questionnaire? That depends on what you wish to know. Usually you will be trying to discover what an audience knows about a topic and their attitude toward it. You can ask open-ended questions, yes-or-no questions, degree questions, or a mixture of all three—as long as you do not ask too many questions.

Open-ended questions are *like those on an essay test that invite an explanation and discourage a yes-or-no response.* Examples include:

> What do you think should be done about teenage pregnancies?
>
> What do you know about alternative energy sources?
>
> What punishments would be appropriate for plagiarism?

Closed or **closed-ended questions** *force a decision by inviting only a yes-or-no response or a brief answer.* Examples include:

> Should all public schools offer art and music education?
> _____ Yes _____ No
>
> Should a man be allowed paternity leave from his job when his child is born or adopted?
> _____ Yes _____ No

Degree questions *ask to what extent a respondent agrees or disagrees with a statement:*

> I believe that all people deserve housing.
> Strongly agree   Agree   Neutral   Disagree   Strongly disagree

Or degree questions may present a continuum of possible answers from which the respondent can choose:

> Which of the following would be an appropriate punishment for an embezzlement of $5,000?
>
> $5,000 fine $4,000 fine $3,000 fine $2,000 fine $1,000 fine
>
> 1 year jail   2 years jail   3 years jail   4 years jail   5 years jail
>
> How much paternity leave from the workplace do you think men should receive?
>
> None One week Two weeks One month Two months Six months

These three kinds of questions can be used in a questionnaire to determine audience attitudes about an issue. A questionnaire, such as the one in Figure 4.1, administered before your presentation, can provide you with useful information about your audience's feelings and positions on the issue you plan to discuss. All you have to do is keep the survey brief, pertinent, and clear.

Questionnaire: Same-Sex Marriage

1. I think that same-sex couples should be allowed to marry.
   _____ Yes _____ No

2. I think that same-sex couples should be permitted to have legal connections, but should not be allowed to marry.
   _____ Yes _____ No

3. At what point should same-sex couples be allowed to marry?
   _____ Whenever they choose _____ After cohabiting for a year
   _____ After cohabiting for _____ Never
   six months

4. Our society actively punishes gays, lesbians, and same-sex couples.
   Strongly agree   Agree   Neutral   Disagree   Strongly disagree

5. What social support, if any, do you feel should be extended to gay and lesbian individuals? _____
   _____
   _____
   _____

Figure 4.1   **Sample questionnaire.**

Analysis of the Situation

Five factors are important in analyzing the situation you face as a speaker: the size of the audience, the environment, the occasion, the time, and the importance of the situation.

Size of Audience

The *size of the audience* is an important situational factor because *the number of listeners* can determine your level of formality, the amount of interaction you have with the audience, your need for amplification systems, and your need for special visual aids. Larger audiences usually call for formality in tone and language; smaller audiences allow for a more casual approach, a less formal tone, and informal language. Very large audiences reduce the speaker's ability to observe and respond to subtle cues, such as facial expressions, and they invite audience members to be more passive than they might be in a smaller group. Large audiences often require microphones and podiums that can limit the speaker's movement, and they may require slides or large posters for visual aids.

Speakers need to be flexible enough to adapt to audience size. One of the authors was to give a presentation on leadership to an audience of over 100 students in an auditorium that held 250 people. Only 25 students appeared. Instead of a formal presentation to a large group, the author faced a relatively small group in one corner of a large auditorium. Two hours later, the author was to speak to a small group of 12 or 15 that turned out to be 50. Do not depend on the planners to be correct about the size of your audience. Instead, be ready to adapt to the size of the audience that actually appears.

Environment

You also must be prepared to adapt to environmental factors. Your location may be plagued by visual obstructions such as pillars and posts, an unfortunate sound system, poor lighting, a room that is too warm or too cool, the absence of a podium or lectern, a microphone that is not movable, or a lack of audiovisual equipment. If you have specific audio, visual, or environmental needs, you should make your requests well in advance to the individual who has invited you to speak. At the very least, you will want to inquire about the room in which you are to speak.

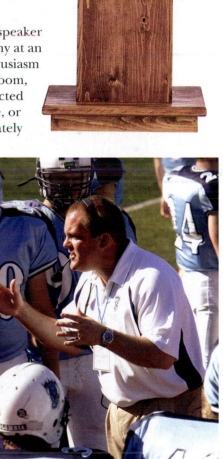

Occasion

The *occasion* is another situational factor that makes a difference in how a speaker adapts to an audience. The speaker is expected to be upbeat and even funny at an after-dinner speech, sober and serious at a funeral, full of energy and enthusiasm at a pep rally, and prudent and factual in a court of law. Even in the classroom, a number of unstated assumptions about the occasion exist. You are expected to follow the assignment; not break laws or regulations of the campus, state, or nation; maintain eye contact; keep to the time limit; and dress appropriately for the occasion.

Outside the classroom, the confident presenter learns about the expectations for the occasion. Consider for a moment the unstated assumptions about these public presentation occasions:

- A high school commencement address.
- A persuasive message at a town meeting.
- A talk with the team before a big game.
- A demonstration of how to accurately read blood pressure.
- A motivational talk to your salespeople.
- An informative presentation on groundwater quality issues.
- An announcement of layoffs at the plant.

Each of these occasions calls for quite a different kind of presentation, the parameters of which are not clearly stated but are widely understood. Our society seems to dictate that you should not exhibit levity at funerals, nor should you be too verbose when you introduce another person. The best way to discover information about the occasion and expectations for it is to question the individual or the organization inviting you to speak.

Time

A further aspect of any speaking situation that makes a difference to a speaker is when and for how long the presentation is given—the *time*. Time can include the time of day, the time that you speak during the occasion, and the amount of time you are expected to fill. Early morning speeches find an audience fresh but not quite ready for serious topics. After-lunch or after-dinner speeches invite the audience to sleep unless the speaker is particularly stimulating. The optimal time to speak is when the audience has come only to hear the speaker and nothing else.

"The speaker is expected to be upbeat and even funny at an after-dinner speech, sober and serious at a funeral, full of energy and enthusiasm at a pep rally, and prudent and factual in a court of law."

The time you give the presentation during an occasion can make a big difference in audience receptivity. You will probably find that people are genuinely relieved when a presentation is shorter than expected, because so many speeches are longer than anyone wants. To overestimate our knowledge and charm and how excited an audience is to hear from us is easy. Audiences will be insulted if you give a presentation that is far short of expectations—5 minutes instead of 30—but they will often appreciate a 45-minute presentation when they have expected an hour.

Importance

The final situational factor is the *importance* of the occasion, the significance attached to the situation that dictates the speaker's seriousness, content, and approach. Some occasions are relatively low in importance, although generally the presence of a speaker signals that an event is not at all routine. An occasion of lesser importance must not be treated like one of great importance, and an occasion of greater importance should not be treated lightly.

What are the responsibilities of a speaker in a classroom setting, which is generally viewed as "less important" than many public speaking situations? The classroom talk may be viewed as relatively routine compared with a televised town hall debate. Are the obligations that you have in the classroom different from those that you would have if you were a community leader or activist?

We usually perceive rituals and ceremonial events as high in importance. We see the speaker at a university commencement exercise, the speaker at the opening of a new plant, and the speaker at a lecture as important players in a major event. Speakers at informal gatherings or local routine events are somewhat further down the scale. Nonetheless, a speaker must carefully gauge the importance of an event so the audience is not insulted by his or her frivolous treatment of what the audience regards as serious business.

The Uniqueness of the Classroom Audience

Students sometimes think of the speeches they deliver in public speaking class as a mere classroom exercise, not a real speech. Perhaps this is partly because they know that they have a grade riding on their speech. They may therefore be more concerned with the grade than with communicating their message effectively to the class.

Viewing the classroom speech as a mere exercise is an error. Classroom speeches are delivered to people who are influenced by what they see and hear. In fact, your classmates as an audience might be even more susceptible to your influence because of their *uniqueness* as an audience. Table 4.2 illustrates some of the unique characteristics of classroom audiences.

The classmates who make up your audience might have their own knowledge about and positions on issues, but they are capable of changing, too, as they listen and learn. Next we will look at how you can adapt to this unique audience.

TABLE 4.2 UNIQUENESS OF THE CLASSROOM AUDIENCE	
CHARACTERISTICS OF THE CLASSROOM AUDIENCE	IMPLICATIONS FOR THE COMMUNICATOR
1 The classroom audience, because of the educational setting in which the presentation occurs, is exposed to messages it might otherwise avoid: the audience is "captive."	May add interactivity to increase interest and engagement.
2 The size of the audience tends to be relatively small (usually 20 to 25 students) and constant.	You can use more personal information and you can avoid microphones and other amplifying devices.
3 Classroom audiences include one person—the professor—who is responsible for evaluating and grading each presentation.	You might need to analyze the professor more carefully as an audience member than you do other members of the audience.
4 Classroom speeches tend to be short.	You must consider topics that can be managed in a brief period of time.
5 The classroom speech is nearly always one of a series of speeches in each class period.	You might keep in mind that visual aids, a dynamic delivery, and stylistic language are even more important than in other situations.
6 The speaker has an opportunity to listen to every member of the audience.	You can learn a great deal about your classmates' opinions, beliefs, and values and do a highly skillful audience analysis.
7 The classroom audience may be invited to provide written and/or oral feedback on the speech.	You can increase your skill as a communicator by carefully heeding any advice or criticism you are given.
8 The classroom speaker has more than one opportunity to influence or inform the audience.	You can show improvement over time.

Think of how you should look and act when you speak to your class. Would you look and act the same if you were going to make a presentation to (a) friends in a residence hall; (b) a group of schoolchildren; (c) administrators at your institution; (d) your parents and parents of others in your neighborhood; or (e) small business owners who live and work near your campus? Describe the differences.

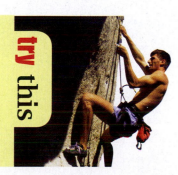

try this

Adapting to Your Audience

This chapter has characterized several tools—observation, informants, interviews, and questionnaires—to use in analyzing your audiences. These tools of analysis and audience demographics will not be beneficial, however, unless you use them for the purpose of audience adaptation. **Audience adaptation** means *making the message appropriate for the particular audience by using analysis and applying its results to message creation.*

In the case of an informative presentation, adapting to the audience means *translating ideas.* Just as a translator at the United Nations explains an idea expressed in English to the representative from Brazil in Portuguese, a speaker who knows about baud rates, kilobytes, and megabytes must be able to translate those terms for an audience unfamiliar with them. Perhaps you have already met some apparently intelligent professors who know their subject matter well but are unable to translate it for students who do not. An important part of adapting an informative speech to an audience is the skill of *translating* ideas.

Your instructors—from kindergarten through college—are essentially informative speakers. You have heard people communicate informative material for 13 years or more. Consider some of your best instructors. Why were they effective in the classroom? They probably took the time to illustrate their points, instead of simply presenting information as an endless list of facts. This is translation.

Now consider those instructors you would deem poor teachers. What did they do that invites you to rate them lower? Did they talk "over your head" and use sentence structure and language that you did not understand at the time? They may have used examples from events that occurred years before you were born and provided no context for them. They might have used a great deal of jargon that confused you and seemed unapproachable.

In the case of persuasive presentations, adaptation means *adjusting your message both to the knowledge level of the listeners and to their present position on the issue.* Use the tools introduced in this chapter and the audience characteristics you discover to help you decide where you should position your message for maximum effect. Too often speakers believe that the audience will simply adopt their point of view on an issue if they explain how they feel about the topic. Actually, the audience's position on the issue makes a greater difference than the speaker's does, so the speaker has to start by recognizing the audience's view. For example, if you believe the audience agrees with you, you can place your message early. If you believe they are in disagreement, you may need to proceed more cautiously.

Two students in a public speaking class provided excellent examples of what happens when the speaker does and does not adapt to the audience. Both speakers selected topics that seemed to have little appeal for the audience because both appeared to be expensive hobbies. One of the students spoke about raising an exotic breed of dog that only the rich could afford. The entire presentation was difficult for the listeners since they could not see themselves in a position of raising dogs for the wealthy.

The other student spoke about raising hackney ponies, an equally exclusive business. However, this student started by explaining that he grew up in a poor section of New Haven, Connecticut. His father was an immigrant who never earned much money, even though he spoke six languages. This student came from a large family, and he and his brothers pooled their earnings for many years before they had enough money to buy good breeding stock. They later earned money by selling colts and winning prize money in contests. By first explaining to the audience that he was an unlikely breeder of expensive horses, the speaker improved the chances that the audience could identify with him and his hobby. He adapted his message to the unique audience.

What kinds of messages influence you? Consider the variety of persuasive speakers you have heard—ministers, priests, rabbis, and other clergy; salespeople; teachers and parents; politicians and elected officials of our own and other countries; people lobbying for a special interest group; and people trying to convince you to change your cell phone service or to buy a home gym.

What kinds of appeals work for you—emotional appeals or logical ones? Do you need to believe in the ethical standards of the speaker before you will listen to what he or she has to say? Do you like to hear the most important arguments first or last? Do you tend to believe authorities, statistics, or other kinds of sources? If you use your own experiences and thoughtfully reflect on them, you may be able to understand better how others might respond favorably to you as a persuasive speaker and adapt your message to them.

Audience adaptation occurs before, during, and after a presentation. Central to your ability to adapt to your audience are your listening skills. In the classroom, listening to other speakers reveals information that will be valuable as you prepare your own presentations.

The Importance of Listening

Both speaking and listening are essential components of public speaking. In the past, public speaking focused more on speakers and the creation and transmission of messages than on listeners and their active participation in the process. The role of the listener in communication has gained more importance. Indeed, current experts believe that listening is essential to the development of citizenship and a civil society.[6] If you are interested in further exploring the role of listening in a civil society, visit http://www.listen.org and consider its characterization of listening as the "language of peace."

You learn more by listening than by talking. Every speech you hear and every question asked and answered provides information about the people who will become your audience. Your serving as an audience member during your classmates' speeches provides you with an opportunity to analyze their choice of topics, the way they think, and the approaches they use. In short, being an audience member invites you to analyze your audience throughout the course.

You may not have thought of this fact when you enrolled in a public speaking class, but you will listen to many speeches for every speech you deliver. Over the course of the school term, you will likely hear between 100 and 200 speeches in your public speaking course. You will learn ways to evaluate speeches and ways to improve your own speeches. And you will learn methods of argument that you can employ.

Listening and Public Speaking

Becoming a Better Listener

How can you improve your listening skills? Consider the many situations in which you listen: when you attend class and listen to an instructor, when you learn how to read to children from the director of the volunteer literacy program, or when you attend a lecture and listen to a visiting speaker. Your purpose is to understand the information the speaker is presenting. You may try to understand relevant information about the speaker and factors that led to the speech, as well as the central idea of the speech itself. Listening requires a high level of involvement in the communication process. The following suggestions, which are also summarized in Figure 4.2, should help you become a more effective listener.

Suspend judgments about the speaker. Suspend your premature judgments about the speaker so you can listen for information. Wait until you have heard a speaker before you conclude that he or she is, or is not, worthy of your attention. If you make decisions about people because of their membership in a particular group, you risk serious error. For example, gays or lesbians could be against same-sex marriage, members of fraternities may not be conformists, and artists are often disciplined.

Focus on the speaker as a source of information. You can dismiss people when you categorize them. When you focus on a speaker as a valuable human resource who can share information, ideas, thoughts, and feelings, you are better able to listen with interest and respect. Every speaker you hear is likely to have some information you do not already know. Try to focus on these opportunities to learn something new. Resist categorizing the speaker and dismissing his or her message as a consequence.

Concentrate your attention on the speaker. If you find yourself dismissing many of the speeches you hear as boring, consider whether you are overly egocentric. Perhaps your inclination to find your classmates' speeches boring is due to your inability to focus on other people. Egocentrism is a trait that is difficult to overcome. The wisest suggestion, in this case, is to keep in mind one of the direct benefits of concentrating your attention on the speaker: if you focus on the other person while she is speaking, she will probably focus on you when you are speaking. Even more important, you will come across better as a speaker if others perceive you to be a careful listener. Nothing else you can do—including dieting, using makeup, wearing new clothing, or making other improvements—will make you as attractive to others as learning to listen to them.

Listen to the entire message. Do not tune out a speech after you have heard the topic. More than likely, the speaker will add new information, insights, or experiences that will shed light on the subject. One professor teaches an upper-division argumentation course to twenty students each quarter. She assigns four speeches, but every speech is given on the same topic. In a ten-week period, students hear eighty speeches on the same topic, but every speech contains some new information. The class would be dismal if the students dismissed the speeches after hearing they would all cover the same topic. Instead of considering the speeches boring, students find them interesting, exciting, and highly creative.

Focus on the values or experiences you share with the speaker. If you find you are responding emotionally to a speaker's position on a topic and you directly oppose what he or she is recommending, try to concentrate your attention on the attitudes, beliefs, or values you have in common. Try to identify with statements the speaker is making. The speaker might seem to be attacking one of your own beliefs or attitudes, but, if you listen carefully, you may find that the speaker is actually defending it from a different perspective. Maximizing our shared ideas and minimizing our differences result in improved listening and better communication.

Focus on the main ideas the speaker is presenting. Keep in mind that you do not have to memorize the facts a speaker presents. Rarely will you be given an objective

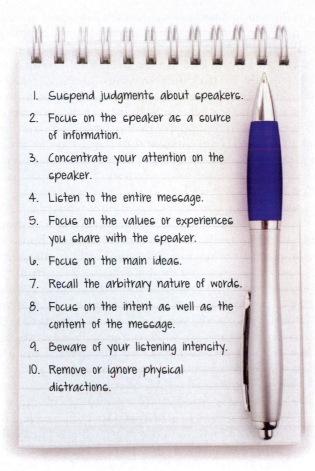

1. Suspend judgments about speakers.

2. Focus on the speaker as a source of information.

3. Concentrate your attention on the speaker.

4. Listen to the entire message.

5. Focus on the values or experiences you share with the speaker.

6. Focus on the main ideas.

7. Recall the arbitrary nature of words.

8. Focus on the intent as well as the content of the message.

9. Beware of your listening intensity.

10. Remove or ignore physical distractions.

Figure 4.2   **Guidelines for becoming a better listener.**

examination on the material in a student speech. If you want to learn more about the information being presented, ask the speaker after class for a copy of the outline, a bibliography, or other pertinent documentation. Asking the speaker for further information is flattering; however, stating in class that you can recall the figures cited but have no idea of the speaker's purpose may seem offensive.

Recall the arbitrary nature of words. If you find that you sometimes react emotionally to four-letter words or to specific usage of some words, you may be forgetting that words are simply arbitrary symbols people have chosen to represent certain things. Words do not have inherent, intrinsic, "real" meanings. When a speaker uses a word in an unusual way, or when you are unfamiliar with a certain word, do not hesitate to ask how the word is being used. Asking for such information makes the speaker feel good because you are showing interest in the speech, and the inquiry will contribute to your own knowledge. If you cannot overcome a negative reaction to the speaker's choice of words, recognize that the emotional reaction is yours and not necessarily a feeling shared by the rest of the class or the speaker. Listeners need to be open-minded; speakers need to show responsibility in word choice.

Focus on the intent as well as the content of the message. As you listen to a speaker, focus both on what is said and why it is said—the speaker's intent. Instead of embarking on mental excursions about other topics, focus on all aspects of the topic the speaker has selected. Consider the speaker's background and his or her motivation for selecting a particular topic. Try to relate the major points the speaker has made to his or her stated intentions. By refusing to consider other, unrelated matters, you will greatly increase your understanding of the speaker and the speech.

"You need to become a good judge of how intensely to listen and to learn ways to alter your listening intensity."

Be aware of your listening intensity. You listen with varying degrees of intensity. Sometimes when a parent or roommate gives you information, you barely listen. However, when your supervisor calls you in for an unexpected conference, your listening is very intense. Occasionally we trick ourselves into listening less intensely than we should. Everyone knows to take notes when the professor says, "This will be on the test," but only an intense listener captures the important content in an apparently boring lecture. You need to become a good judge of how intensely to listen and to learn ways to alter your listening intensity. Sitting on the front of the chair, acting very interested, and nodding affirmatively when you agree are some methods that people use to listen with appropriate intensity.

Remove or ignore physical distractions. Frequently you can deal with physical distractions, such as an unusual odor, bright lights, or a distracting noise, by moving the stimulus or yourself. In other words, do not choose a seat near the doorway that allows you to observe people passing by in the hall, do not sit so that the sunlight is in your eyes, and do not sit so far away from the speaker that maintenance noises in the building drown out her voice. If you cannot avoid the distraction by changing your seat or removing the distracting object, try to ignore it. You probably can study with the radio or television on, sleep without having complete darkness, and eat while other people are milling around you. Similarly, you can focus your attention on the speaker when other physical stimuli are in your environment.

Consider whether you would be able to concentrate on the speech if it were, instead, a movie you have been wanting to see, a musical group you enjoy, or a play that has received a rave review. One man said that when he had difficulty staying up late to study in graduate school, he considered whether he would have the same difficulty if he were on a date. If the answer was no, he could then convince himself that the fatigue he felt was a function of the task, not of his sleepiness. The same principle can work for you. Consider whether the distractions are merely an excuse for your lack of desire to listen to the speaker. Generally you will find you can ignore the other physical stimuli in your environment if you wish to do so.

Evaluate Your Listening Skills

How well do you listen? Consider a recent experience when you listened to a presentation by another person. Alternatively, use this self-evaluation when you listen to the next classmate to give a speech:

1. Did you find something to arouse interest in the speech?
2. Did you find the subject interesting?
3. Did you listen to the message rather than to how it was delivered?
4. Did you listen with a purpose?
5. Did you listen for major ideas and relationships among various points?
6. Did you sit in a place where you could both hear the speaker and listen to the speech?
7. Did you avoid or ignore distractions?
8. Did you subordinate specific words to the total meaning of the content?
9. Did you pay close attention so that at any point you could summarize the speaker's main ideas up to that point in the talk?
10. Did you listen to all the speaker had to say before criticizing it?

Ethics and the Audience

As you prepare to speak to a particular audience, remember ethical considerations, those moral choices you make as a speaker. Audiences expect different levels of truthfulness in different situations. A comedian is expected to exaggerate, distort, and even fabricate stories. A salesperson is expected to highlight the virtues of a product and think less of the competition. A priest, a judge, and a professor are expected to tell the truth. In the classroom, the audience expects the speaker to inform with honesty and to persuade with reason.

Most speakers have a position on an issue. The priest tries to articulate the church's position, the judge follows a body of precedents, and the professor tries to reveal what is known from her discipline's point of view. You, too, have reasons for your beliefs, your positions on issues, and the values you espouse. The general guideline in your relationship with your audience is that you should have the audience's best interests in mind.

Next Steps in Audience Analysis

In this chapter, we talked about audience analysis and audience adaptation. Keep in mind that this process continues as you prepare your presentation. You will apply what you learn about the audience to the research you conduct, the kinds of supporting materials you choose, and the arguments you make. In the next chapter, you will learn about why you will benefit from conducting research for your speech. Armed with the information on audience analysis and adaptation in this chapter, you will be ready to make ethical and informed decisions on using your own experiences, the Internet, and the library for conducting research.

For REVIEW >>

AS YOU READ

1. Determine how audience and context affect presentations, and how speakers adapt to each before and during their presentations.

2. Explain the effects of audience worldview on topic selection and treatment.

3. Identify four methods for analyzing an audience, and understand the ethics of audience analysis.

4. Explain the role of listening in public speaking.

SUMMARY HIGHLIGHTS

▶ To give a successful presentation, know your audience and be aware of the setting in which you deliver your speech. This will ensure your presentation addresses your audience's interests and concerns and respects their worldviews.

▶ The demographic features of an audience include:
  • Gender
  • Age
  • Ethnicity
  • Economic status
  • Occupation
  • Education
  • Shared experiences

▶ Situational analysis includes:
  • The size of the audience
  • The environment
  • The occasion
  • The time
  • The importance of the situation

▶ Your topic selection and approach should take into account differences and similarities in worldview between you and your audience, as well as within the audience itself.

▶ Four methods of audience analysis that a speaker can use are:
  • Observation
  • Informants
  • Interviews
  • Questionnaires

▶ Speakers need to apply ethical principles to their audience analysis and adaptation. It is important to avoid stereotyping when selecting an appropriate topic for an audience.

▶ The importance of listening is:
  • Essential to citizenship and civil society
  • Essential to success in your public speaking course

Pop Quiz

1. The popular opinion of the time about issues, styles, and trends is termed:
   (A) demographics
   (B) audience analysis
   (C) conventional wisdom
   (D) co-cultures

2. Gender composition, age, ethnicity, and occupation comprise an audience's:
   (A) situational analysis
   (B) ethical principles
   (C) informants
   (D) demographics

3. When speaking to an audience comprised of college first-year students with undecided majors, you should:
   (A) use very specific examples
   (B) avoid including all audience members
   (C) tell generic anecdotes
   (D) use jargon relevant to the communication studies field

4. Groups that are similar to the larger culture but are distinguished by background, beliefs, and behaviors are also called:
   (A) co-cultures
   (B) conventional wisdom
   (C) worldview
   (D) audience adaptation

5. Mark watches and listens to the audience before he gives his presentation. He is utilizing a method of audience analysis called:
   (A) group identification
   (B) observation
   (C) interviews
   (D) questionnaires

6. The person who invites you to speak at an event can be considered your:
   (A) observation specialist
   (B) surveyor
   (C) interviewer
   (D) informant

7. "Do you like dogs?" is an example of a(n):
   (A) open-ended question
   (B) closed-ended question
   (C) observation
   (D) environmental factor

8. Audience size, environment, occasion, time, and importance are factors that are important in:
   (A) ethnicity
   (B) critical listening
   (C) one's worldview
   (D) audience analysis

9. Justin modified his speech on healthy eating to include nutritional choices that can be made at the local campus dining halls. This is an example of:
   (A) audience adaptation
   (B) worldview
   (C) audience analysis
   (D) observation

10. To become a better listener, you should:
    (A) concentrate your attention on something other than the speaker
    (B) focus on the speaker as a source of information
    (C) judge the speaker immediately
    (D) focus on the details in the speech

Answers: 1 (C); 2 (D); 3 (C); 4 (A); 5 (B); 6 (D); 7 (B); 8 (D); 9 (A); 10 (B)

APPLICATION EXERCISES

1. Given the observations listed below, what do you think would be the audience's probable response to a presentation on Social Security issues, world hunger, the erosion of the environment, or changing sexual mores? For each statement about the audience, state how you believe they would generally feel about the topic.

   a. The audience responded favorably to an earlier informative speech on race relations.

   b. The audience consists mainly of urban people from ethnic neighborhoods.

   c. The audience consists of many married persons with families.

   d. The audience members attend night school on earnings from daytime jobs in factories and retail businesses.

   e. The audience members come from large families.

   f. The audience includes many people from developing countries.

   g. The audience consists of people from ages 18 to 29.

2. Determine answers to the following questions for your class:

   a. What is the age range of the members of the class audience?

   b. What are the economic backgrounds of the class?

   c. Describe classmates with any obvious disabilities.

   d. What styles of clothes do the audience members wear?

   e. Describe other features of the students' appearance such as style, gender-display, and fitness.

   f. How much do class members interact before and after class?

   g. How much time do classmates spend on Facebook?

   h. What interests or hobbies do the students discuss?

   i. Describe other behavior, both verbal and nonverbal, of the class members.

   j. Are various ethnic groups or co-cultures represented?

   What are the implications you might draw from these observations? How should you adapt your speech based on these observations?

3. The audiences you face today may not be identical to the audiences you will face in the future. Review the list of audiences on page 71, and add to this list three audiences to whom you foresee yourself presenting in the next ten years.

4. Listen to a speech in the classroom, on the Internet, or elsewhere on campus. Using a scale of 1–5 (1 = poor; 5 = excellent), rate your ability to listen on the following dimensions:

   _____ a. suspending judgments

   _____ b. regarding the speaker as a source of valuable information

   _____ c. concentrating on the speaker

   _____ d. listening to the entire message

   _____ e. focusing on shared values and experiences

   _____ f. focusing on the main ideas

   _____ g. focusing on the intent of the message

   _____ h. removing or ignoring physical distractions

KEY TERMS

Audience adaptation	Conventional wisdom	Interviews
Audience analysis	Degree questions	Observation
Closed or closed-ended questions	Demographics	Open-ended questions
Co-cultures	Ethnicity	Projection
	Inside informant	Questionnaires

get involved!

You might want to learn more about persons with disabilities. You might try to find information online. On Web sites you may find state and local programs for persons with disabilities. Does your school currently have service-learning projects that engage persons with disabilities?

Groby Community College in the United Kingdom holds a Walk & Fun Day in June to attract support for Special Olympics; Mesa Community College in Arizona hosts the summer Special Olympics; and Lorain County Community College in Ohio holds a Special Olympics basketball tournament. Does your school have some community involvement programs in which you can engage?

How can your selected speech topic be relevant to a service-learning project? Knowing what you do about your topic and your audience, how can you make a difference in your community?

5

FINDING
INFORMATION

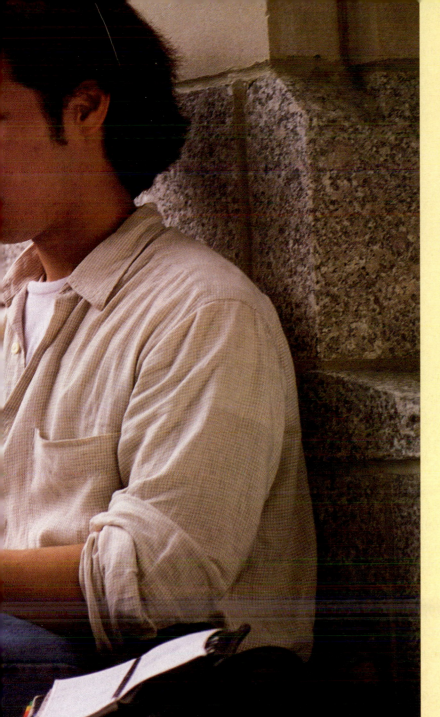

This chapter will help you find information you need for your presentations. We discuss how you can use various strategies—including personal experience, interviews, and your computer—to find information. You'll also learn about evaluating sources of information and about different types of supporting material found in presentations.

AND SUPPORTING
YOUR IDEAS

As You READ

>>

1. Think about how you will use research to prepare, organize, and deliver your presentation.
2. Identify personal experiences, potential interviews, and library and Internet resources that will support and be appropriate for your speech.
3. Understand how to critically evaluate Internet resources.
4. Practice citing information correctly in your outline and oral presentation, and gain an understanding of the ethical obligations associated with using sources and supporting materials.

A recent conference held at the Earth Institute showcased the work of student interns who analyzed several indicators of climate change within the vicinity of New York City. One of those students, Brian Hoyer, reported on a project analyzing water quality within the Hudson River watershed near the city. In his presentation, Hoyer explained how real-time, 24-hour data collection allows precise monitoring of several key indicators like water temperature, dissolved oxygen, salinity, turbidity, and chlorophyll. The ability to monitor water quality in specific watershed locations will allow scientists to better understand how changes in sea levels, temperature, and other climactic factors impact local water quality. Such information can assist in planning and mitigation efforts well into the future. You can watch the presentation by Hoyer and other students at http://www.earth.columbia.edu/articles/view/2465.

Hoyer's presentation relied on a specific type of evidence: scientific data collected from highly precise monitoring equipment. By using such evidence, Hoyer was able to present highly credible information describing the quality of water in the Hudson River. Also, through carefully prepared visual aids, he was able to describe the environmental impact of pollution and runoff from the city.

Hoyer selected scientific evidence because he was speaking to experts in environmental science. When you prepare your speech, you must select evidence appropriate for both your purpose and your audience. This chapter teaches you how to develop and execute a research plan so that you can use effective supporting material in your speeches.

How Would *You* Do It?

You just read about Brian Hoyer, who gave a presentation for the Earth Institute about the effects of climate change on the Hudson River. Hoyer's presentation emphasized the use of scientific evidence that he and others collected. If you were giving a speech on the effects of climate change in your region, what types of supporting material would you use?

Why You'll Benefit from Research

When Walter Cronkite passed away in July of 2009, several colleagues recounted stories illustrating Cronkite's commitment to responsible reporting. One person who worked behind the scenes at CBS News explained how Cronkite would often arrive at the news set just minutes before the show aired. As the producer went on to explain, Cronkite and his writers often waited until the last minute to receive a second confirmation on a story before allowing the story to be aired. Using independent confirmation was important to Cronkite because he wanted to be accurate. This is exactly the same approach you should use when planning your speeches: use multiple sources of evidence to ensure that you are presenting accurate information. By knowing where to locate information and how to evaluate sources, you will be able to use evidence effectively in your presentations.

In Chapter 2, you started learning about the metaphorical lifeblood of speechmaking—the invention process. As you recall, invention involves taking ideas and giving them substance through supporting materials like narratives, quotations, statistics, and so on. Whereas other chapters have taught you how to brainstorm and then narrow your ideas, this chapter is specifically focused on research, the process of finding and using supporting material.

Good research is essential to good speaking. To be more specific, you must find a variety of high-quality sources and then think carefully about how to best integrate information from those sources into your speech. For any given speech topic—take coal mining, for example—you can obtain information from a variety of sources ranging from personal experiences and interviews to magazines, academic journals, and government documents. There are even YouTube videos showing the process of hill removal in certain regions where coal mining takes place. As a speaker, your first task is to obtain all of those materials and to carefully evaluate their accuracy, credibility, and usefulness to the point you want to make. Second, you must determine how to most effectively use information from those sources in your speech.

"Good research is essential to good speaking."

When doing research you should find information supporting, clarifying, and adding interest to the points you want to make during your presentation. Regardless of whether you are making arguments or teaching, supporting material provides the basis for ideas, thoughts, and positions that you develop. Think of your speech as a series of main and subpoints that form the basis of your position. Each of those points and subpoints need to have the adequate support or your position will fail. More broadly, Table 5.1 shows that effective research can positively impact nearly every element of your speech.

TABLE 5.1 RESEARCH AND THE PRESENTATION PREPARATION PROCESS	
PREPARATION STEP	**BENEFIT OF RESEARCH**
1 Topic selection	Research helps you discover and narrow topics.
2 Organizing ideas	Research helps you identify main and subordinate points.
3 Supporting ideas	Research provides facts, examples, and definitions to give substance to your points.
4 Preparing introduction and conclusion	Research may reveal interesting examples, stories, or quotes.
5 Practice and delivery	Because your speech is well researched, you will feel more confident and will seem more credible.

Finding Sources of Information

> **" The outcome of any serious research can only be to make two questions grow where only one grew before. "**
>
> [Thorstein Veblen (1857–1929), U.S. economist and social philosopher]

Effective speakers achieve success through well-crafted presentations that contain compelling evidence and support. Advances in technology, in particular the Internet and online databases, help smart researchers find high-quality information very quickly. Not all research, however, requires a mouse and keyboard. In this section, you will learn about a variety of research tools, ranging from yourself to highly specialized databases.

Personal Experience

Your **personal experience**, *your own life as a source of information,* is something about which you can speak with considerable authority. One student had once worked as a "headhunter," a person who finds applicants for companies willing to pay a premium for specific kinds of employees. This student gave a presentation from his personal experience of what employers particularly value in employees. Another student had a brother who was autistic. In her informative presentation, she explained what autism is and how autistic children can grow up to be self-reliant and successful in careers. Your special causes, your job, and your family can provide you with firsthand information that you can use in your presentation.

Before basing your presentation on personal experience, however, you should ask yourself critical questions about the usefulness of this information. Some of your experiences may be too personal or too intimate to share with strangers or even classmates. Other experiences may be interesting but irrelevant to the topic of your speech. You can evaluate your personal experience as **evidence**, *data on which proof may be based,* by considering the following questions:

1. Was your experience typical of what other people experience?
2. Was your experience *so typical* that it will bore the audience?
3. Was your experience *so atypical* that it was a chance occurrence?
4. Was your experience so personal and revealing that the audience may feel uncomfortable?

5. Was your experience one that this audience will appreciate or from which this audience can learn a lesson?
6. Does your experience really provide proof of anything?

Considering the ethics of using your personal experience is also important. Will it harm others? Is the experience firsthand (your own), or is it someone else's experience? Retelling the experiences of a friend or even family member is questionable because secondhand information is easily distorted. Unless the experience is your own, you may find yourself passing along incorrect information. Also, personal experience is different from personal opinion. Using additional research to clarify personal experience might be necessary.

Library Resources

A second source of information is all the resources that are available at your school's library—magazines, journals, newspapers, books, videotapes, and government documents. Be sure to check with a **reference librarian**, *a librarian specifically trained to help find sources of information*, if you are unfamiliar with resources available at your library. The reference department in your library has many useful sources. In addition to specialized encyclopedias, there are specialized dictionaries, yearbooks, books of quotations, biographical sketches of prominent individuals, and atlases. A reference librarian can quickly help you determine whether these specialized reference resources are helpful for your presentation topic.

Most libraries offer a number of indexes and catalogs you can use to locate sources of information. Indeed, modern libraries offer so many options for finding information, the most difficult task is often knowing where to begin. Library Web sites typically offer two general options for locating information: the holdings database and electronic periodical indexes. You might need to consult with a librarian or with other students to learn how to access them.

The Holdings Database

Libraries are organized using a **holdings database**, which *indexes all books, journals, periodicals, and other resources owned by the library*. The holdings database is a common starting point for finding information and it organizes materials by subject, author, title, and call number. The call number is used to find the physical location of resources in the library. Most databases also provide links to electronic versions of resources if they exist. When you search for a topic using the holdings database you can begin by typing in a keyword for your topic. Depending on how broad or narrow your keyword is, the database will return a list of subtopics or a list of resource titles (e.g., books, reference resources, etc.) relevant to your topic. For example, if you type in a keyword like "business ethics," the database might return several books with that phrase in the title. Figure 5.1 illustrates the information you might see if you click on one of those resources, in this case a book by Linda Treviño and Katherine Nelson. Notice that the holdings information shows the exact title, call number, and publication information for the book as well as telling you that the book is "available" for checkout.

Holdings databases are not just for locating books. Most libraries allow patrons to search for titles of periodicals and other resources as well. Although the holdings datbase will not allow you to search for specific articles in a magazine or technical journal, you can use the database to physically locate the source. In some cases, the database will provide a link to an electronic full-text version of the periodical so that you can browse for articles.

Figure 5.1   **Bibliographic information from a holdings database.**

TABLE 5.2 COMMON PERIODICAL INDEXES

INDEX NAME	INDEX DESCRIPTION
Academic Search Premier and Academic Search Complete	Excellent for basic research on various topics, the Academic Search Premier provides citations and full-text articles for more than 7,000 scholarly publications ranging from arts and literature to the sciences.
Communication and Mass Media Complete	This database provides citations and full-text articles on topics related to communication and mass media issues.
ERIC	ERIC indexes over 900 scholarly sources covering topics generally related to education.
Humanities Abstracts	Humanities Abstracts cites articles from over 500 periodicals relevant to various humanities topics like the arts and literature.
Lexis-Nexis	This substantial database provides full-text articles from newspapers and magazines as well as transcripts of news broadcasts, legal cases, and testimony before Congress.
Medline	A premier index for medical issues, this database offers citations and some full-text articles.
Reader's Guide	This source indexes articles from 1901 to the present. Most are from popular U.S.-American magazines.
Social Sciences Index	With citations and full-text articles, this index covers a broad range of social-scientific topics including politics, social psychology, and crime.

Periodical Indexes

Periodicals are *sources of information that are published at regular intervals.* Magazines, newspapers, and academic journals are all examples of periodicals found in your library. Periodicals are a different kind of resource than books because you are often interested in specific stories or articles in them rather than the entire issue or edition as with a book. For that reason, you must use specialized databases to locate specific articles on your topic. Table 5.2 lists several of the most common databases and describes the types of information for which they are useful.

Although the indexes listed in Table 5.2 provide access to hundreds of thousands of citations, you may wish to consult even more specialized databases to which your library subscribes. If your topic is very specialized, consultation with a reference librarian could point you in the direction of valuable resources. Periodical indexes work like most search engines on the Internet. Effective researchers often use more than one periodical index to find information. For example, if your presentation deals with a medical topic like obesity, starting with a general index like Academic Search Complete or LexisNexis and then moving to a specialized index like Medline is an effective approach. Also, not every library has all these databases—a reference librarian can help you find alternatives if your library does not subscribe to a particular database.

The Internet

The Internet has become the default gateway for conducting academic research for students and faculty alike. Whereas in the mid-1990s teachers could make easy distinctions between the Internet and "library research," those distinctions have become increasingly blurred as most libraries now have Web-based portals where patrons can access library services from any computer in the world. Besides library resources, the Internet provides unparalleled access to multimedia files (e.g., YouTube), pictures, and other types of information.

Even with the many advantages that the Web has to offer, you have to be careful when using the Web. University of Georgia Professor Joseph Dominick[1] says, "Some have described using the Internet as trying to find your way across a big city without a map. You'll see lots of interesting stuff but may never get to where you're going." The trick to not getting lost while researching on the Web is to keep some simple ideas in mind. First, you should remember that there is a difference between "free" and "fee." The best information on the Web comes from high-quality sources that cost money. Fortunately, your library likely already pays for several Web-based services that you can access. Second, start at a good landmark. Google and other "free" search services are less effective starting points than is the Library of Congress or your university library. Third, verify what you find. If you use a free search service like Google, take extra time to thoroughly verify what you find.

To maximize the variety of sources that you can use in your speech, you will likely spend some time using more common Web search tools like Google or Yahoo! The following steps describe a strategy that you can use to improve your Web search approach:

1. Begin by using a **search engine**, which is *a Web site on the Internet that is specially designed to help you search for information.* Although search engines will locate thousands of Web sites that contain the word or phrase you are searching for, one criticism of search engines is that they return hundreds of irrelevant Web sites. An alternative to using a search engine is to use a **virtual library**, which *provides links to Web sites that have been reviewed for relevance and usability.* Table 5.3 provides Web addresses for several popular search engines and virtual libraries. Meta-search engines are useful because they combine the results of individual search engines like Yahoo! and Excite.

2. Many search engines give you two options for accessing information. One option is to click on one of the several topical categories displayed on the home page of the search engine site. By following progressively more specific subcategories you can locate Web sources on a relatively specific concept, person, object, hobby, and so forth.

   The other option is to conduct a keyword/Boolean search. If you are still in the initial stages of selecting and narrowing a topic, you might want to use the first option—the organized list of categories might help you in

TABLE 5.3 WEB SEARCH RESOURCES

META-SEARCH ENGINES

Google: www.google.com

Dogpile: www.dogpile.com

MetaCrawler: www.metacrawler.com

Bing: www.bing.com

COMMON SEARCH ENGINES

Yahoo!: www.yahoo.com

AltaVista: www.altavista.com

Encyclopedia Britannica Internet Guide: www.britannica.com

Excite: www.excite.com

Lycos: www.lycos.com

HotBot: www.hotbot.com

VIRTUAL LIBRARIES

The WWW Virtual Library: www.vlib.org

Galaxy: www.galaxy.com

Yahoo! Libraries: http://dir.yahoo.com/Reference/Libraries

"One of the problems with using the Internet for information is that this medium is unregulated. The information may be biased, or just plain wrong."

that process. You should use the second keyword/Boolean search option once you have identified and narrowed a topic.

Figure 5.2 shows you what the directory page of Google looks like—notice the topical categories listed. By clicking on the categories, you will find information that is more specific. If you click on the "Biology" link under the "Science" category, you can then select from a number of subtopics related to biology. Figure 5.3 shows the list of topics related to "Genetics," which was a subcategory of Biology. Using the search feature to look for Web pages on genetics will return a greater variety of sites, some of which may not be relevant to your speech. Table 5.4 on page 106 provides recommendations on how to more effectively narrow your searches.

3. Carefully *evaluate all sources of information* you find on the Internet, especially when you locate the sources through a public domain search engine rather than your university library's home page. Suggestions for evaluating Web sources and other types of information are provided in subsequent sections of this chapter.

4. Print and bookmark good sources so that you can easily reference them while planning your presentation. By bookmarking the Web page, you can easily access the site later without having to retrace the steps of your search.

5. In addition to printing and bookmarking your sources, you can subscribe to an RSS (Really Simple Syndication) feed, which will allow you to receive and save up-to-date information from that site. You can add RSS feeds to your home page or other XML-capable personal Web pages.

One of the problems with using the Internet for information is that this medium is unregulated. The information may be biased, or just plain wrong, because no authority monitors the content of the sites. How do you determine

Figure 5.2   **The Google directory page.** Notice that each topic area is a hyperlink where you can "drill down" for more detailed information.

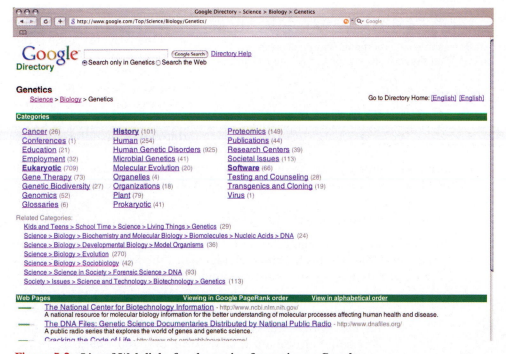

Figure 5.3   **List of Web links for the topic of genetics on Google.**

what information is accurate and credible? Ultimately, *you* will have to make that decision. Ask yourself whether someone would have reason to present biased information. If at all possible, verify the information through other sources, such as newspaper or

TABLE 5.4 TOOLS FOR NARROWING YOUR WEB SEARCH

WORD STEMMING

By default, browsers identify any Web page containing the word you entered in the search box. For example, if you want to search for the speech acronym "INFORM," the search engine would return sites with the words informative, information, informal, informing, and so forth. To prevent this result, type your search term with a single quote at the end.

Example: inform'

PHRASE SEARCH

If you are looking for a phrase, put the phrase in quotation marks. For example, simply typing in *homeless youth* would return all sites that contain the two words "homeless" and "youth" anywhere on the site. Placing the phrase in quote marks will return only sites using the phrase "homeless youth."

Example: "homeless youth"

BOOLEAN OPERATORS

Boolean operators allow you to specify logical arguments for what you want returned in a list of matching Web sites. When multiple terms are typed in a search box (e.g., "tobacco addiction"), the default Boolean operator is to place "AND" between the terms. Returned Web sites will contain both tobacco AND addiction somewhere on the page. Other Boolean operators include NOT (e.g., "PowerPoint NOT Microsoft"), which will return Web sites with the term before the operator but not sites with the term after the operator. You can also use the operator OR to find sites with one of two possible terms (e.g., "Gauguin OR van Gogh").

PARENTHESES

Using parentheses allows you to nest Boolean search arguments. In the following example, the search argument will look for Web sites containing the terms "media" and "violence" but not "television."

Example: (media AND violence) NOT television

---

magazine articles. If the source is a scholarly article, check for a list of references, and if a list of references is provided, try to determine whether the list is credible by verifying some of the sources. Finally, credible sources often provide the credentials of the individual(s) who wrote the article. If no source is provided, be cautious. Moreover, Web sources should be evaluated like any other source.

One additional point to remember is that people have different motives for creating Web pages. Some Web sites intend to provide information, others intend to persuade, and others are profit-driven. Some Web sites try to conceal their true motives—a Web site might look informative but is actually telling only part of a story to persuade you to purchase a service or product. One way to understand the motive of a Web site is to pay attention to the server extension. Table 5.5 explains the parts of a Web address and the characteristics of Web addresses with different types of server extensions. No single type of Web address—based on the server extension—is always better than another. Although knowledge of different types of Web addresses can be valuable, all Web resources deserve scrutiny.

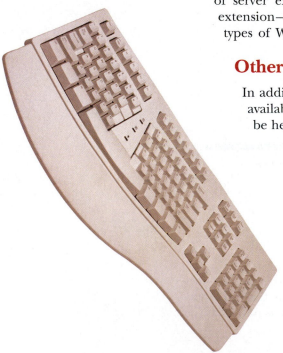

Other Resources on the Web

In addition to search engines, several reference and primary resources are available. Although this list could change daily, the following sources may be helpful depending on your presentation topic:

- *USA.gov* (www.usa.gov). A topical guide and search engine for all public resources on the Web from the U.S. government.
- *Fedstats* (www.fedstats.gov). A government Web site providing access to statistical information from over 100 federal agencies.
- *SearchGov* (www.searchgov.com). This search engine provides access to federal, state, and local government Web sites. The site also provides links to commonly accessed Web sites and the ability to search military Web sites.
- The CIA World Factbook (www.cia.gov/cia/publications/factbook/). You do not have to be a secret agent to access the resources of CIA headquarters in Langley, Virginia. The CIA

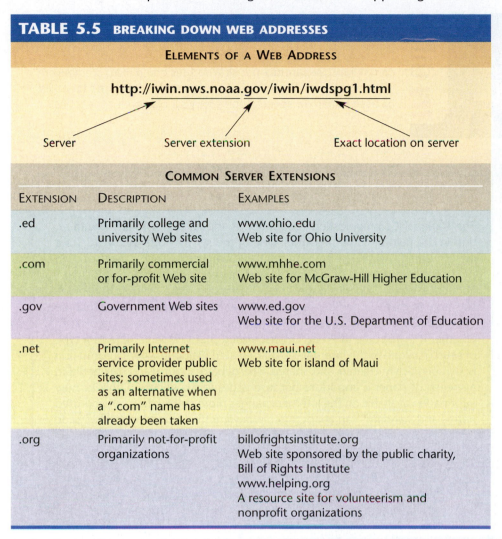

TABLE 5.5	BREAKING DOWN WEB ADDRESSES	
ELEMENTS OF A WEB ADDRESS		
http://iwin.nws.noaa.gov/iwin/iwdspg1.html		
Server	Server extension	Exact location on server
COMMON SERVER EXTENSIONS		
EXTENSION	DESCRIPTION	EXAMPLES
.ed	Primarily college and university Web sites	www.ohio.edu Web site for Ohio University
.com	Primarily commercial or for-profit Web site	www.mhhe.com Web site for McGraw-Hill Higher Education
.gov	Government Web sites	www.ed.gov Web site for the U.S. Department of Education
.net	Primarily Internet service provider public sites; sometimes used as an alternative when a ".com" name has already been taken	www.maui.net Web site for island of Maui
.org	Primarily not-for-profit organizations	billofrightsinstitute.org Web site sponsored by the public charity, Bill of Rights Institute www.helping.org A resource site for volunteerism and nonprofit organizations

World Factbook contains detailed information about every country in the world as well as "global" statistics like the total landmass in the world, the global economy, and the current estimated population of Earth.

- *Reference Resources at Yahoo!* (http://dir.yahoo.com/Reference/). If you need a dictionary, a thesaurus, an almanac, quotations, or other reference resources, Yahoo! has an excellent set of links to browse.

Even for specialized topics such as multiculturalism, co-culture, or ethnicity, the Web is an excellent resource. If you need to research various cultural issues, try these sources:

- *Yahoo! Regional* (http://dir.yahoo.com/Regional/). This Yahoo! directory provides links to information on various countries and regions of the United States.
- *The WWW Library—Native Americans* (www.hanksville.org/NAresources/). This site provides links to information about Native Americans on the Web.
- *Black History Quest* (http://blackquest.com). Resources on African American history and culture.
- *Latin American Network Information Center* (http://lanic.utexas.edu). Information on Latino history and culture in the United States.
- *Asian-Nation* (www.asian-nation.org). This Web portal provides links to resources addressing Asian American history and culture.

try this

Use Yahoo! to find information about an issue relevant to your community. Be careful—not all Web sites come from credible or reliable sources. What did you learn from this exercise that could be used to narrow speech topics for your classroom speeches?

e-NOTE

The Wikipedia Controversy

The National Communication Association is the largest scholarly organization in the field of communication. One of the services offered by NCA is a listserv called CRT-NET (Communication Research and Theory Network). In the spring and summer of 2009 there was an ongoing discussion in CRT-NET about the use of Wikipedia in speeches. On one side of the controversy professors argued that Wikipedia is largely unregulated and nothing more than an encyclopedia, a type of source that is discouraged in speeches regardless of whether it is from the Internet. Others argued that Wikipedia reflects a type of source unique to the Internet—a user-created dialogue where information is democratically created and shared. The debate about using Wikipedia in a speech or paper is important because issues in the debate highlight how information available on the Internet changes more rapidly than our accepted norms and standards can adapt. After reviewing the "About Wikipedia" page on the Wikipedia Web site, consider these questions:

1. In what instances, if any, would an encyclopedia be an effective source for a speech or paper?

2. What are the advantages and disadvantages of using an open-source information site like Wikipedia as supporting material?

3. What special obligations should a speaker/writer face when using Wikipedia?

4. Should norms in speaking and writing be such that use of Wikipedia as a source is discouraged?

Interviews with Others

Another important source of ideas and information for your speech is other people. With its faculty, staff, and numerous students, your campus has many experts on particular subjects. Your community, likewise, is populated with people who have expertise on many issues: government workers on politics; clergy on religion; physicians, psychologists, and nurses on health care; engineers on highways and buildings; and owners and managers on industry and business.

At the beginning of this chapter you read about Brian Hoyer's speech at the Earth Institute conference. The director of the Earth Institute, Dr. Jeffrey Sachs, is very skilled at using other people's stories in his speeches about Darfur, global pollution, and other world crises. If you have a chance, you should visit the Earth Institute Web site and watch one of the several videos of Dr. Sachs speaking. If you do that, you will notice that Sachs masterfully uses information that he obtains through his contact with others as evidence in his presentations. When talking about Darfur, for instance, he might recount a story about his experiences in the region. Many of his stories recount conversations that he has had with people who live in the areas he is concerned about. Although you may not have the chance to visit Darfur yourself, you might have the opportunity to interview someone who has, and consequently, can use stories similar to those of Dr. Sachs.

You will discover that interviewing is an efficient way to gather information on your topic. The person you interview can furnish ideas, quotations, and valuable leads to other sources. First, however, learn when and how to prepare for the interview, conduct the interview, and to use the results.

Preparing for the Interview

Most students are surprised that important people at their university or in their community are more than willing to talk with them about their presentation. Because the person is doing you an important favor, you have a responsibility to carefully prepare for the interview. Following the suggestions below will help ensure that your interview is productive:

- *Start early.* Professionals have calendars that, believe it or not, are even more packed than most college students' calendars. You should contact potential interviewees at least one week in advance so that the two of you can find a mutually agreeable time for the interview.

- *Determine the purpose for the interview.* Using your source to find out information easily obtained from other sources like the library or the Internet is a waste of time. Use your interview to gather important analysis, clever quotations, and personally relevant stories.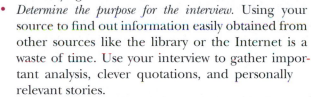

- *Do your homework.* You must have some understanding of the topic to know the right questions to ask. Taking time to carefully research your topic before the interview will enable you to ask good questions.

- *Plan questions in advance.* Effective interviewers take time to plan primary questions—questions that introduce new areas of discussion—in advance of the interview.

- *Gather equipment.* The best strategy for interviewing another person is to record the interview so that you can play it back later. You cannot write fast enough to take detailed notes, and interviewees will likely get frustrated if you keep asking them to repeat their statements. Of course, you should get the person's permission to record the interview beforehand.

Conducting the Interview

Once you have scheduled and prepared for the interview, your next task is to conduct it professionally. You will find this task to be fun and engaging. Besides dressing professionally and being on time, keep in mind the following:

- *Be polite and respectful.* Interviews rarely start with the first question. Instead, expect the interviewee to express curiosity about you and your project. Be perfectly frank about your purpose, the assignment, and the audience. The interviewee is doing the verbal equivalent of a handshake with the questioning.

- *Be careful about the tone of your questions and comments.* You are not in the role of an investigative reporter performing an interrogation. Instead, you are seeking information and cooperation from someone who can help you. Your tone should be friendly and your comments constructive.

- *Be flexible.* Even though you have prepared questions, you may find that one response may answer several of your planned questions, or that your preplanned order is not working as well as you expected. Relax. Check off questions as you ask them or as they are answered. Take a minute at the conclusion of the interview to see whether you have covered all of your questions.
- *Practice active listening.* Show an interest in the person's answers. If you are recording the interview, you should provide nonverbal feedback and concentrate on generating follow-up questions to gain even more valuable information. Be alert to nonverbal cues revealed by the interviewee, including those indicating that it is time to conclude the session.
- *Remember to get the basics.* Make sure that you have the accurate *citation information,* your interviewee's name and title, the name of the company, agency, or department, and so on. You will be citing this person's words and using oral footnotes to credit him or her, so you need correct source information.
- *Finally, remember to depart.* Give your interviewee an opportunity to stop the interview at the designated time. The interviewee—not you—should extend the interview beyond that, if anyone does. The interviewee will appreciate your gracious good-bye and gratitude for granting the interview. As a parting gesture of good will, thank the secretary, or anyone else who has helped you, as well.

Using the Interview

After you have conducted the interview, you should immediately take time to listen to the interview tape and jot down quotations and ideas from the interview onto notecards so that you can arrange those ideas with other supporting materials you find. Don't let your memory of the interview grow cold. The longer you wait, the more likely you are to forget how you wanted to use information from the interview.

Evaluating and Using Sources of Information

The University of California library has developed a very thorough guide for evaluating sources that you find on the Internet. If you visit the UC Web site (http://www.lib.berkeley.edu/TeachingLib/Guides/Internet/Evaluate.html) you will learn effective tips for making sure that any Internet sources that you use are reliable, trustworthy, and credible. In addition to carefully analyzing Internet sources, you should carefully consider any source before including the information in a speech, presentation, or paper. This section explains how you should evaluate sources and cite them correctly in your outline and presentation.

Criteria for Evaluating Sources

Just finding sources does not ensure that you have effectively researched your presentation. You must carefully evaluate each source for its credibility and usefulness. The *Style Manual for Communication Studies*[2] recommends that you use the following criteria when evaluating sources:

1. *Is the supporting material clear?* Sources should help you add clarity to your ideas rather than confusing the issue with jargon and overly technical explanations.

2. *Is the supporting material verifiable?* Listeners and readers should be able to verify the accuracy of your sources. Although verifying information in

a book is easy—the book can be checked out and read—verifying information obtained from a personal interview with the uncle of your sister's roommate is not.

3. *Is the source of the supporting material competent?* For each source you should be able to determine qualifications. If your source is a person, what expertise does the person have with the topic? If your source is an organization, what relationship does the organization have with the issue?

4. *Is the source objective?* All sources—even news reports—have some bias. The National Rifle Association has a bias in favor of gun ownership; Greenpeace has a bias in favor of environmental protection; TV news programs have a bias toward vivid visual imagery. What biases does your source have, and how might those biases affect the way these organizations or people frame information?

5. *Is the supporting material relevant?* Loading your speech with irrelevant sources might make the speech seem well researched; however, critical listeners will see through this tactic. Include only sources that directly address the key points you want to make.

These criteria are not "yes or no" questions. Sources will meet some criteria well and fail others miserably. Your job as the speaker is to weigh the benefits and problems with each source and determine whether to include the source in your speech. Indeed, you have a key ethical responsibility to carefully evaluate sources. Moreover, these criteria assume that you will take time to find out information about each source that you are using. Understanding who the author or sponsoring organization is, whether the site bases claims on supporting material or on opinion, and how recently the site has been updated are all important factors to consider.

Find a Web site on a potential topic for your presentation and use the above five questions for evaluating sources to analyze the quality of the Web site as a source of information. Based on your analysis, would you use the Web site in a speech?

try this

Source evaluation is one of the most valuable skills you can learn. Because the Internet has dramatically increased the quantity of information available to researchers, your ability to sift through multiple sources and pick out the very best is critical.

Citing Sources of Information Correctly

Once you find source material, you must provide references for the source both on your outline and in your speech. **Bibliographic references** are *complete citations that appear in the "references" or "works cited" section of your speech outline (or term paper).* Your outline should also contain **internal references**, which are *brief notations of which bibliographic reference contains the details you are using in your speech.* Internal and bibliographic references help readers understand what sources were used to find specific details like statistics, quotations, and examples. Most teachers require students to use a specific style guide for formatting bibliographic and internal references. The two most common types of style guides are the American Psychological Association (APA) and the Modern Language Association (MLA). Figure 5.4 provides sample citations for five types of sources following APA and MLA styles.

APA

Newspaper
Zibel, A. & Webber, T. (2009, July 17). Joblessness helping fuel foreclosure crisis. *Boston Globe*, p.9.

Academic Journal
Condit, C. M. (2008). Race and genetics from a modal materialist perspective. *Quarterly Journal of Speech, 94,* 383–406.

Book
Sala, O. E., Meyerson, L. A., & Parmesan, C. (Eds.). (2009). *Biodiversity change and human health: From ecosystem services to spread of disease.* Washington DC: Island Press.

Web Page
Kelly, R. (2008, July 5). *Civic engagement.* Retrieved 20 July, 2009, from Faculty Focus web site: http://www.facultyfocus.com/articles/philosophy-of-teaching/best-practices-in-teaching-civic-engagement-2/

Personal Interview
Striley, K., Phalen, S., & Weiderhold, A. (2009, August 1). Personal interview. Athens, OH: Ohio University.

MLA

Newspaper Article
Zibel, Alan, and Tammy Webber. "Joblessness Helping Fuel Foreclosure Crisis." *Boston Globe* 17 July 2009: 9. Print.

Academic Journal
Condit, Celeste M. "Race and Genetics from a Modal Materialist Perspective." Quarterly Journal of Speech 94.4 (2008): 383–406. Print.

Book
Sala, Osvaldo E., Meyerson, Laura A., and Camille Parmesan, eds. Biodiversity Change and Human Health: From Ecosystem Services to Spread of Disease. Washington DC: Island Press, 2009. Print.

Web Page
Rob Kelly. "Civic Engagement." Faculty Focus. Maginta Publications, 5 Jul. 2008. Web. 20 Jul. 2009.

Personal Interview
Striley, Katie, Phalen, Steve, & Anna Weiderhold. Personal Interview. 1 Aug. 2009.

Figure 5.4 **Five sources following APA and MLA styles.**

TABLE 5.6 EXAMPLES OF ORAL CITATIONS

TYPE OF SOURCE	EXAMPLE
Newspaper article	"Jayne O'Donnell, writing in the September 6th edition of *USA Today*, pointed out that lead paint tastes sweet, which makes the poison particularly dangerous to young children who are more likely to suck on tainted toys."
Research study	"A 2009 study published in the **Howard Journal of Communication** argued that government messages about natural disasters need to be adapted to have meaningful outcomes for non-whites, people who live in poverty, and other marginalized populations."
Web page	"A story on the American Red Cross Web site, published on February 9, 2009, described how a teacher at the Decatur Area Technical Academy in Decatur, Illinois, used volunteering for the Red Cross as a way to help her students understand the importance of community responsibility."

In addition to citing sources in your outline, you must also provide verbal citations during your presentation. Unlike the readers of a paper or presentation outline, audience members are less concerned with page numbers and titles of articles. Rather, an **oral citation** tells listeners *who the source is, how recent the information is, and the source's qualifications.* The examples listed in Table 5.6 illustrate how to orally cite different types of sources. Notice how the examples provide information about the sources as well as the key point being made by the source. These example statements could be followed by direct quotations or more detailed explanations.

Oral source citation is a skill unique to public speaking. Although written style guides like APA and MLA offer specific rules for how to internally cite sources in a written document, use of oral citations is more fluid and must be adapted to the audience, occasion, and source being used. Generally speaking, oral citations emphasize the credibility of the source being used. To capitalize on the credibility of your sources you should emphasize their qualifications, the timeliness of the information, the reputation of the outlet, and other characteristics of the source that will make them more credible from the perspective of your audience. The goal of oral source citations should be to build the credibility of your sources, which in turn will build your credibility as a speaker.

In 2005, Thomas Friedman's book *The World Is Flat* presented a compelling argument that convergence in communication technology—the Internet, computers, etc.—has not only resulted in fundamental changes in how we communicate, but has also fundamentally changed how the world works.[3] Friedman suggests that information technology "allow[s] us to think about the world differently—to see it as more of a seamless whole."

Identifying Appropriate Supporting Materials

Friedman's metaphor of the world being flat is actually a complex argument about how communication, economic activity, social relationships, and geopolitics have all converged to reduce hierarchy and separation. What this means for you and me is that our lives are linked to people across the globe in ways never before imaginable: We might get a telemarketing call from someone in Bangalore, India, have our medical labwork reviewed by a doctor in Australia, or "go to work" with a company in the Netherlands without ever leaving our hometown.

Because of the widespread impact that a flattened world will have on our lives, it should come as little surprise that a flattened world can influence how we locate and use evidence in our speeches. If, as Friedman predicts, a flattened world does break down divisions and hierarchies, the way that we research speeches ten or even five years from now will likely be vastly different. For instance, when doing an informative speech on Singapore, you would typically use various Web sites and library resources to accumulate factual information about the country and its people. In a flattened world, it is just as likely that you would find ways to e-mail and even video-chat with someone from Singapore to find out about the country and what it is like to live there. One possibility is that in a flattened world the use of personal narratives and direct connections with others will become increasingly important as a source of acceptable (if not expected) evidence for public speeches.

In fact, there is already some indication that the flattening of the world has changed how we view evidence. As recently as 2005, our colleagues developed strict policies "banning" the use of Wikipedia and other "wikis" in speeches, citing fears that "anyone can make things up and post them." While you should be cautious about any online information, scholars in communication and sociology are now documenting how wikis in general, and Wikipedia in particular, can actually be useful sources of information. In fact, many scholars who specialize in library and information sciences have readily adopted wikis as a primary way of disseminating information.

The remainder of this chapter teaches you about various types of **supporting material**, or *information you can use to substantiate your arguments and clarify your position.* As you learn about examples, surveys, testimony, statistics, analogies, and definitions, think about how the ways that you locate and use such information might change in the flattened world described by Friedman.

"Use of personal narratives and directconnections with others will become increasingly important as a source of acceptable (if not expected) evidence for public speeches."

Examples

Examples, *specific instances used to illustrate your point,* are among the most common supporting materials found in presentations of all types. Sometimes a single example helps convince an audience; at other times, a relatively large number of examples may be necessary to achieve your purpose. For instance, the argument that communities need to do more to stop environmental pollution could be supported by citing several examples of hazardous waste sites in your community or state.

Be careful when using examples. Sometimes an example is so unusual that an audience will not accept the story as evidence of anything. A student who refers to his own difficulty in landing a job as an example of problems with the economy is unconvincing if more general statistics do not support his claim. A good example must be plausible, typical, and related to the main points of the presentation.

Two types of examples are factual and hypothetical. A *factual* example is just that—a fact. It can be verified. A *hypothetical* example cannot be verified. It is speculative, imaginative, fictional. The example can be brief or extended. The following is an example of a brief factual example:

> According to the August 5, 2005, issue of *The Chronicle of Higher Education*, the time students spent volunteering in 2004 was worth almost $4.5 billion.

Here is an extended hypothetical example:

> An example of how nanotechnology could be used is in the case of oil spills. Suppose that billions of tiny robots, smaller in diameter than a human hair, were released at the site of an oil spill. These robots are programmed to seek out and digest oil molecules into pieces of silt that fall harmlessly to the bottom of the ocean. In less than one day, all evidence of the oil spill has been magically gobbled up by these minuscule workers. Two days later, the robots run out of energy and join the digested oil molecules on the ocean floor. In their short life span these nano-machines saved countless creatures from an ugly death and prevented millions of dollars in destruction.

The brief factual example is *verifiable*, meaning the example can be supported by a source that the audience can check. The extended hypothetical example is *not* verifiable and is actually a "what if" scenario. Explaining to the audience that an example is hypothetical is important. Presenting a hypothetical example as a *real* example is unethical, and your credibility will be questioned if the audience learns that they were misled.

Narratives

Whereas examples provide specific illustrations, **narratives** provide *an extended story showing how another person experienced something*. In speeches, narratives serve important roles in helping audience members learn information and emotionally connect with your ideas. If you recall from your childhood, children's stories are often written in ways that teach readers about values, norms, and ways people can relate to one another. As we grow older, we still rely on others' stories to learn scripts for life events, a process that social psychologist Albert Bandura calls vicarious learning. Using narratives in your speech will literally allow audience members to learn from the experiences of others through vicarious learning. For instance, if you were giving a speech on the topic of spirituality you might tell the story of someone who was able to combat addiction by turning to spiritual guidance and practices.

In addition to helping audience members learn, narratives also integrate emotion into a presentation because they humanize topics. Three of our colleagues are working on a documentary illustrating how Dr. Peter Anderson, a specialist in Pediatric Oncology at M.D. Anderson Cancer Center in Houston, uses narrative to help guide his interaction with patients. While interviews with Dr. Anderson serve as a foundation for much of the documentary, stories about several children who had cancer are interwoven into the program. Those stories provide human faces and

ORAL VS. WRITTEN CULTURES AND THE USE OF EVIDENCE

Walter J. Ong, formerly a professor of rhetoric at St. Louis University, suggests that important differences exist between literary and oral cultures.[4] Literary, or writing-based, cultures tend to develop ideas in a much more linear fashion than do oral cultures. According to Ong, some cultures are primary oral cultures because they have not yet developed a written language. Aboriginal cultures throughout the world represent the last known primary oral cultures. In America, we clearly have the capacity to be a written culture; however, technology like cell phones and television causes our culture to behave as if it were an oral culture. Ong calls these types of cultures secondary oral cultures. These differences between types of cultures are important. Evidence in a written culture would look very different from evidence in an oral culture. While written cultures might prefer carefully worded and thoughtfully analyzed quotations, oral cultures might prefer examples, narratives, and stories as forms of evidence.

authentic emotion for the story of how cancer disrupts lives as well as the important ways that Dr. Anderson tries to help his patients. Narratives provide the basis for emotional connection, empathy, and relevance for many topics.

Although narratives are important parts of speeches, you should keep in mind a few things about how to use them effectively. First, good narratives are sometimes hard to find. Although you may find narratives through library research, better narratives might be collected through interviews, discussion groups, and other forms of personal contact. Second, you should be careful in how you present narratives in your speech. You should not generalize from narratives—narratives are personal stories that may not be applicable to all or even most circumstances. Narratives should also not be presented as definitive because they are often only segments of a much broader story. Finally, you should use narratives in ethical ways. You should never reveal private information without permission and you should not overrely on the emotional nature of narratives.

Surveys

Another type of supporting material commonly used during presentations is a **survey**, *a study in which a limited number of questions are answered by a sample of the population to discover opinions on issues.* You will most often find surveys quoted in magazines or journals. Audiences usually see these surveys as more credible than an example or one person's experience because they synthesize the experience of hundreds or thousands of people. Public opinion polls fall into this category. One person's experience with alcohol can have an impact on an audience, but a survey indicating that one-third of all Americans abstain, or one-third drink occasionally, or a certain percentage of college students binge drink supports your argument better. As with personal experience, you should ask some important questions about the evidence found in surveys:

1. *How reliable is the source?* A report of a survey in a professional journal of sociology, psychology, or communication is likely to be more thorough and more valid than one found in a local newspaper.

2. *How broad was the sample used in the survey?* Was it a survey of the entire nation, the region, the state, the city, the campus, or the class?

3. *Who was included in the survey?* Did everyone in the sample have an equally good chance of being selected, or were volunteers asked to respond to the questions, making the survey pool self-selected?

4. *How representative was the survey sample?* For example, readers of *The New Yorker* magazine may not be typical of the population in your state.

5. *Who performed the survey?* Was the survey conducted by a nationally recognized survey firm, such as Lou Harris or Gallup, or was it by the local newspaper editor? Was it performed by professionals such as professors, researchers, or management consultants?

6. *Why was the survey done?* Was it performed for any self-serving purpose—for example, to attract more readers—or did the government conduct the survey to help establish policy or legislation? Finding out who sponsored the survey is important.

Testimony

Testimonial evidence, a third kind of supporting material, consists of *written or oral statements of others' experiences used by a speaker to substantiate or clarify a point.* Testimonial evidence shows the audience that you are not alone in your beliefs, ideas, and arguments. Other people also support you, and their statements should help the audience accept your point of view. The three kinds of testimonial evidence you can use in your speeches are lay, expert, and celebrity.

Lay testimony is a *statement made by an ordinary person that substantiates or supports what you say.* In advertising, this kind of testimony shows ordinary people using or buying products and stating the fine qualities of those products. In a speech, lay testimony might be the words of your relatives, neighbors, or friends concerning an issue. Such testimony shows the audience that you and other ordinary people feel the same way about an issue. Other examples of lay testimony are parents speaking about curriculum changes at a school board meeting or alumni attesting to the positive qualities of their college at a recruiting session.

Expert testimony is a *statement made by someone who has special knowledge or expertise about an issue or idea.* In your speech, you might quote John McCain about the war in Iraq, the surgeon general about health care, or the president of the Sierra Club about the environment. The idea is to demonstrate that people with specialized experience or education support the positions you advocate in your speech.

Celebrity testimony is a *statement made by a public figure who is known to the audience.* Celebrity testimony occurs in advertising when someone famous endorses a particular product. In your presentation, you might point out that a famous politician, a syndicated columnist, or a well-known entertainer endorses the position you advocate.

Although testimonial evidence may encourage your audience to adopt your ideas, you need to use such evidence with caution. An idea may have little credence even though many laypeople believe in it; an expert may be quoted on topics well outside his or her area of expertise; and a celebrity is often paid for endorsing a product. To protect yourself and your audience, you should ask yourself the following questions before using testimonial evidence in your speeches:

- Is the person you quote an expert whose opinions or conclusions are worthier than most other people's opinions?

- Is the quotation about a subject in the person's area of expertise?

- Is the person's statement based on extensive personal experience, professional study or research, or another form of firsthand proof?

- Will your audience find the statement more believable because you got the quotation from this outside source?

Go to the **www.quotationspage.com** Web site and search for quotations on a topic of interest. Were any of the quotations you found effective quotations for a speech? Do you think that this method of finding quotations and testimony is an effective technique for researching in preparation for your presentation?

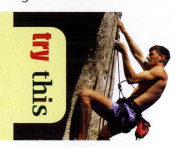

Numbers and Statistics

To use numbers and statistics effectively, you must develop basic skills in **numeric literacy**, or *the ability to understand, interpret, and explain quantitative information.* This does not mean that you have to be an expert in math; rather, you need to have a general understanding of what numbers can tell audience members and how they can be used as evidence to support a claim, prove a point, or highlight a fact. The first step in being literate with numbers is to understand what they can tell you. Generally speaking, numbers help speakers accomplish the following outcomes:

- *Precisely describe objects, concepts, and ideas.* Using descriptive statistics you can give very precise details about points you are making in your speech. How large is the national debt? How many people are without medical insurance? How many tornadoes developed in the United States last year? What percentage of Americans has college degrees? All of these are questions that can be answered with precise descriptive statistics. Because numbers are easier to interpret and understand in written form, speakers often need to simplify values for listeners. For example, instead of saying "There were 323,426 high school graduates," say, "There were over three hundred thousand graduates." You can couple descriptive statistics with meaningful comparisons to make them clearer. For instance, you could say, "There were over three hundred thousand graduates, which is about the same population as the city of Lancaster."

- *Show relationships.* Researchers are often interested in using statistics to determine relationships between things. The precise term for this is "statistical correlation." For instance, you could probably guess that there is a statistical correlation between age and reading ability, family income and education level, and city population and crime. Although most of these correlations will be found through research, you may have enough experience to determine statistical relationships on your own. For instance, if you are a small business owner or employee you might be able to determine whether there is a correlation between advertising expenses and sales, or even various factors associated with employee productivity. In fact, common spreadsheets like Microsoft Excel or Apple's Numbers allow easy calculations of correlations.

  When using correlations you should take care to carefully explain them to audience members. A line graph or scatterplot (discussed more in Chapter 9) is an effective visual aid to illustrate correlations and relationships. Also, be careful to avoid the assumption that correlation means causation. For instance, there is a correlation between outside temperature and crime—the higher the temperature the higher the crime rate. Hotter weather does not cause people to commit crimes, but more people are outside in the summer, increasing their susceptibility to being victims.

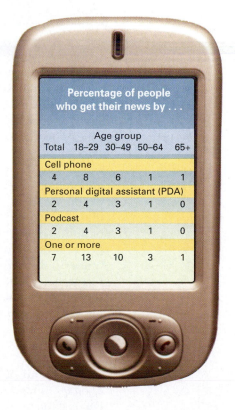

Percentage of people who get their news by . . .				
		Age group		
Total	18–29	30–49	50–64	65+
Cell phone				
4	8	6	1	1
Personal digital assistant (PDA)				
2	4	3	1	0
Podcast				
2	4	3	1	0
One or more				
7	13	10	3	1

- *Show differences.* In addition to showing relationships, numbers and statistics can also be used to show differences. What percentage of men and women graduate from high school? Do most people get their news from television, newspapers, radio, or the Internet? Are Democrats or Republicans more likely to affiliate with the Tea Party Movement? These are all questions that require numbers to show differences between groups of people. Another question of difference can relate to objects. Which auto manufacturer has the best gas mileage for family sedans? What type of computer operating system is most attacked by computer viruses? These types of questions often use descriptive statistics, but disaggregate those statistics by groupings. Bar charts are commonly used to visually illustrate this type of information.

Assume that you are preparing a speech on the rise in popularity of mobile Internet devices. As part of your speech you decided to survey eight people in your workplace to generate statistics relevant to your topic. Table 5.7 shows a summary of the results.

TABLE 5.7	SURVEY RESULTS FOR MOBILE INTERNET SURVEY		
SEX	TYPE	AGE	HOURS ONLINE PER DAY
Male	Droid	43	2
Male	iPhone	23	5
Female	iPad	18	7
Male	Droid	21	5
Female	netbook	32	1
Female	iPad	26	3
Male	iPad	21	5
Male	Droid	30	2

Using results from the survey, what can you learn? From a descriptive standpoint you could count the number of males and females, count how many people use each type of mobile Internet device, and calculate averages for both age and hours spent online each day. Do you think there is a relationship between age and hours spent online? If you create a line plot with age on one axis and hours online on the other, you will see that older members of the sample tend to spend less time online than those who are younger. What about differences? If you calculate the average age for Droid and iPad users, and compare those averages to the age for the iPhone and netbook users, you will conclude that iPad users tend to be younger, followed by iPhone users, and then Droid and netbook users. You could use a bar graph to illustrate those differences. Using a similar approach, what is the average number of hours spent online by males and females?

Knowledge of simple statistics can help you draw important conclusions from numeric data. You will likely find many statistics already calculated for you in research you uncover on your topic. Such information adds important detail and shows that you have carefully researched your topic. As with other types of supporting material, you should cite sources for statistics you use during your presentation.

Analogies

Another kind of supporting material is the analogy. An **analogy** is *a comparison of things in some respects, especially in position or function, that are otherwise dissimilar.* For instance,

Sometimes, when I'm wearing jeans on campus, I feel like a chameleon. Not because I blend in with the scenery, trees, limbs, rocks, or foliage, but because I blend in with other people—everybody wears jeans.

While providing clarification, an analogy is not a proof, because the comparison inevitably breaks down. Therefore, a speaker who argues that American society will fail just as Roman society did can carry the comparison only so far because the form of government, the time in history, and the institutions in the two societies are quite different. Likewise, you can question the chameleon–human analogy by pointing out the vast differences between the two species. Nonetheless, analogies can be quite successful as a way of illustrating or clarifying.

Definitions

Some of the most contentious arguments in our society center on **definitions**, or *determinations of meaning through description, simplification, examples, analysis, comparison, explanation, or illustration*. Experts and ordinary citizens have argued for years about definitions. For instance, when does art become pornography? Is withdrawal of life support systems euthanasia or humanitarian concern? How you define a concept can make a considerable difference in helping audience members understand your points.

Definitions in a presentation are supposed to enlighten the audience by revealing what a term means. Sometimes you can use definitions that appear in standard reference works, such as dictionaries and encyclopedias, but explaining the word in language the audience will understand is most effective. For example, say you use the term *subcutaneous hematoma* in your speech. *Subcutaneous hematoma* is jargon used by physicians to explain a blotch on the skin, but you could explain it in this way: "*Subcutaneous* means 'under the skin,' and *hematoma* means 'swelled with blood,' so the words mean 'blood swelling under the skin,' or what most of us call a 'bruise.'"

The Ethical Use of Supporting Material

Did you know national statistics show that nearly 40 percent of students report copying sentences and other material from written and electronic sources without giving appropriate credit?[5] Because of statistics like these, coupled with high-profile cases of plagiarism by students, faculty, and even prominent national figures, many institutions are now taking the issue of academic integrity more seriously than ever before. Although you should take care to understand how to act with integrity with any assignment, this obligation takes on special importance in a public speaking class.

Throughout this book we emphasize various ethical requirements for communication that stem from the National Communication Association (NCA) Credo on Ethics. Let's end this chapter by summarizing the ethical obligations faced by speakers when they use supporting materials:

> " **Not that you lied to me but that I no longer believe you—that is what has distressed me.** "
>
> [Friedrich Nietzsche, German philosopher (1844–1900)]

1. *Speakers have an ethical obligation to find the best possible sources of information.* The Internet and full-text databases certainly provide us with easy research options; however, these tools do not necessarily improve the quality of our research. Yet, your audience depends on you to present the best and most accurate information possible. The best sources of information are sometimes not available online or in full-text form. Selecting a variety of sources including print sources, Internet sources, and possibly even interviews can thus help improve the overall quality of the materials on which you base your presentation.

2. *Speakers have an ethical obligation to cite their sources of information.* In Chapter 1 a stern warning appeared against an offense called **plagiarism** or *the intentional use of information from a source without crediting that source.* A more positive reason for citing sources of information is so anyone in your audience can verify what you say. A verbal citation that reveals your source of information allows others to see for themselves that what you said was accurate.

3. *Speakers have an ethical obligation to fairly and accurately represent sources.* How often have you heard politicians and other public figures complain that the

media take their comments "out of context"? To avoid making unfair and inaccurate representations of sources, whether they are newspaper articles, Web pages, books, or even interviews, you must ensure that you fully understand the points being made by the source. Remember, for example, that two-sided arguments are often used to present a point. In a **two-sided argument** *a source advocating one position will present an argument from the opposite viewpoint and then go on to refute that argument.* To take an excerpt from a source where the opposing argument is being presented for refutation and imply that the source was advocating the opposing argument is unethical. As a speaker, you have the liberty to disagree with points made by the sources you consult; you do not have the liberty to misrepresent those same sources.

The act of plagiarizing is often discussed as an issue of ethics—indeed, the Credo on Communication Ethics explicitly states that we have an ethical obligation to credit others' ideas and words. On the other hand, when we have encountered instances of plagiarism, students rarely commit such acts with the intent of being unethical. Research conducted by Melissa Broeckelman-Post[6] found that the most common reasons for plagiarizing were: (a) I have too much work to do and not enough time to finish all of it; (b) I don't have enough time because I procrastinated; (c) I will get a better grade if I cheat; (d) If I don't get a good grade I will lose my scholarship; and (e) I don't understand the course material/assignment. Nearly all of these reasons revolve around the issue of adequate time management. As a student growing in your skills as a speaker, writer, and researcher, you must give yourself enough time to adequately research, organize, prepare, and revise your ideas.

Although it is tempting to try to expand the NCA credo to provide a definite list of suggestions on what to do or avoid with respect to academic integrity and plagiarism, such "rules" must be co-created between you and your teacher. We encourage you to have discussions with your instructor, either individually or as a class, about the following questions:

1. When should sources be cited?
2. How much information in a speech should come from other sources?
3. How should I determine whether to paraphrase or quote?
4. So long as I cite the source, can I quote/paraphrase as much information from a source as I want to?
5. Do I have to cite sources for information other than quotes (e.g., statistics, pictures, graphics, etc.)?
6. Is working on my speech with other people considered cheating?

Such discussions will provide you with valuable information about the expectations surrounding your assignment and will also allow you to experience firsthand how communication is a tool for shaping the culture in which we live.

In conclusion, locating, understanding, and incorporating supporting material is one of the most important tasks you will undertake as a presenter of information and argument. Good research affects literally every step in the process of preparing and delivering a presentation. Taking care to effectively and ethically use your information will make you a better speaker and will earn the respect of your peers and teachers.

For >> REVIEW

AS YOU READ

1. Think about how you will use research to prepare, organize, and deliver your presentation.

2. Identify personal experiences, library and Internet resources, and potential interviews that will support and be appropriate for your speech.

3. Understand how to critically evaluate Internet resources.

SUMMARY HIGHLIGHTS

▶ The research process is a common thread tying together all aspects of the speech preparation process.
- An effective research strategy means finding multiple types of sources because different books, journals, and peoples' experiences provide you with different types of supporting materials.
- Research helps you find and narrow speech topics, identify main points, support your ideas, develop effective introductions and conclusions, and deliver your speech with confidence.

▶ Students typically use four common types of sources in their speeches.
- Personal experiences can provide useful examples but should be carefully evaluated to determine whether they are useful evidence.
- Library resources include books, journals, newspapers, magazines, and government documents. Most libraries have specialized electronic databases that will enable you to find information.
- The Internet provides easy access to large quantities of information; such sources must be carefully evaluated.
- Interviewing others can provide useful details, examples, and quotations. However, preparing for and carrying out successful interviews takes time and careful planning.

▶ To evaluate sources you should ask the following questions: Is the supporting material clear? Is the supporting material verifiable? Is the source of the supporting material competent? Is the source objective? Is the supporting material relevant?

4. Practice citing information correctly in your outline and oral presentation, and gain an understanding of the ethical obligations associated with using sources and supporting materials.

▶ Once you have found your sources, you must carefully consider how you will cite the information.
- Preparation outlines should include bibliographic references, which are complete lists of sources in a "references" or "works cited" section. Your outline should also include Internet references, which are brief notations in the text of the outline indicating which bibliographic reference contains specific information.
- In your presentation, you should provide oral citations of sources so listeners will know where information came from.

▶ Presenters are obligated to follow ethical principles when selecting and using supporting material in their presentations.
- Speakers have an ethical obligation to find the best possible sources of information.
- Speakers must cite their sources of information.
- Speakers are required to present fair and accurate representations of their sources of information.

Pop Quiz

1. Data on which proof may be based is termed:
   (A) interviews
   (B) evidence
   (C) oral citation
   (D) periodicals

2. In Jacob's speech on lifeguarding, he discussed incidents that he encountered while lifeguarding. The stories were examples of:
   (A) interviews
   (B) analogies
   (C) surveys
   (D) personal experience

3. When interviewing others, you should:
   (A) wait until the last minute to contact the interviewee to set up a meeting time
   (B) be vague with regard to your purpose and the assignment
   (C) avoid planning questions so it sounds more conversational
   (D) be careful about the tone of your questions and comments

4. Holdings databases help people locate:
   (A) books, journals, and other resources
   (B) only books
   (C) online stores
   (D) e-mail addresses

5. Magazines, newspapers, and academic journals are examples of:
   (A) internal references
   (B) holdings databases
   (C) periodicals
   (D) lay testimony

6. Annie is doing an online search for information and is looking for a specific phrase. What should she do to make sure the search engine returns only sites using the specific phrase?
   (A) put the phrase in quotation marks
   (B) place NOT between the words
   (C) add OR between the words
   (D) type a single quote at the end of the phrase

7. Criteria for evaluating sources includes making sure that the source is:
   (A) subjective
   (B) irrelevant
   (C) vague
   (D) competent

8. The complete citations that appear in the "words cited" section of your speech outline are called:
   (A) internal references
   (B) bibliographic references
   (C) periodicals
   (D) oral citations

9. Joe distributed questions to a small classroom in order to find out opinions on issues. This type of supporting material is called a(n):
   (A) survey
   (B) testimony
   (C) example
   (D) analogy

10. When a source presents an argument from one viewpoint and then refutes the argument from the opposite viewpoint, the source is presenting a(n):
    (A) oral citation
    (B) plagiarized argument
    (C) two-sided argument
    (D) expert testimony

Answers: 1 (B); 2 (D); 3 (D); 4 (A); 5 (C); 6 (A); 7 (D); 8 (B); 9 (B); 10 (C)

APPLICATION EXERCISES

1. Conduct a Web search for sites discussing "dangers of cell phones." After locating a Web site on the topic, do the same search in Academic Search Premier or some other general database. Compare the conclusions of the Web site and the articles you find. Do the articles provide independent verification of the conclusions stated in the Web site? Which sources appear most credible? Why?

2. For each of the topics listed below, identify at least three databases that you would use to locate information sources at your library. Briefly explain why you selected each database.
   Global warming
   AIDS
   The war in Iraq
   Economic recession

3. Below is information about a magazine article and a book on the topic of student motivation. For each source, correctly write the citation in both APA and MLA styles.

MAGAZINE ARTICLE

AUTHOR: SANDY JOHNSTON, PHD

MAGAZINE: *PHI DELTA KAPPAN*

ARTICLE TITLE: MAKING LEARNING FUN FOR STUDENTS

YEAR: 2005

DATE: JUNE

PAGES: 34–38

BOOK

AUTHOR: KENNETH KIEWRA

TITLE: ENHANCING STUDENT MOTIVATION

EDITION: 2ND

YEAR: 2004

PUBLISHER: UNIVERSITY PRESS

PUBLISHER LOCATION: OMAHA, NE

KEY TERMS

Analogy	Internal references	Reference librarian
Bibliographic references	Lay testimony	Search engine
Celebrity testimony	Narratives	Supporting material
Definitions	Numeric literacy	Survey
Evidence	Oral citation	Testimonial evidence
Examples	Periodicals	Two-sided argument
Expert testimony	Personal experience	Virtual library
Holdings database	Plagiarism	

get involved!

Many members of community groups face an unending challenge of soliciting funding to support ongoing projects and to launch new initiatives. Many organizations solicit grant funding from a variety of agencies for such purposes. Nearly every grant application requires some analysis of literature, much like you use in your speeches. Consequently, as an experienced college student you have valuable information that can benefit agencies that regularly seek external funding.

For your speech you have selected a topic of interest to you and others in your community. Assume that you were asked to give a briefing on this topic to a community service organization (perhaps you have even identified a particular organization and have spoken with them when preparing your speech). The organization is interested in having you help them learn to gather information on the topic that they can use to apply for state, federal, and private grants. In short, they need to learn the best way to do research so that they can present credible arguments to potential funding sources. Prepare an outline of a lesson that does the following:

1. Outlines a step-by-step strategy for locating a variety of sources ranging from Internet materials to highly specialized research outlets.
2. Identifies criteria for evaluating the quality and usefulness of sources.
3. Provides examples of a variety of sources (e.g., Wikipedia entries, newspaper articles, books, etc.), shows how those sources could be evaluated according to the criteria you identify, and explains how those sources could be used to develop arguments.

As you prepare the outline for your briefing, you may want to consult these sources as well as those discussed in this chapter:

"Evaluating Internet Sources and Sites: A Tutorial," Purdue University:
http://www.lib.purdue.edu/ugrl/staff/sharkey/interneteval/

"Evaluation Criteria," New Mexico State University:
http://lib.nmsu.edu/instruction/evalcrit.html

Once you have prepared your briefing, create a cover letter and one-page summary of your presentation. In the cover letter, offer to meet with representatives of the organization to present your briefing. Either send the letter or drop it off at the organization's office.

6

ORGANIZING & OUTLINING

Good organization heightens a speaker's credibility and helps listeners better understand a presentation. In this chapter you will learn the functions of the introduction of a speech. This chapter then shows you the principles underlying organization, the application of those principles in practical outlines, and the choices you need to make in adapting your message to an audience through organization. This chapter ends by explaining the three functions of a conclusion.

YOUR PRESENTATION

As You READ

>>

1. Practice composing outlines so that they reflect a limited number of main points of equal importance, and incorporate subordination, division, and parallelism.
2. Think about how you might use the six patterns of organization in your presentations.
3. Draft a presentation outline, a keyword outline, and a formal sentence outline.
4. Recognize the critical roles played by a presentation's introduction, conclusion, and internal devices such as transitions, signposts, previews, and reviews.

Hannah Meyerson thought about the film she'd just seen. An Oscar-nominated and award-winning documentary, it told the true story of the Liberian women who had forced their corrupt president, Charles Taylor, and the country's violent warlords to go to the peace table after fourteen years of bloody civil conflict in this West African nation.

Using prayer, silent protest, and other peaceful means against competing lawless armies, Liberia's Christian and Muslim women had banded together, dressed in white, and pressed for an end to the raping, pillaging, and fighting that had devastated their country and its people. The women held firm to their purpose, even when—after they had traveled to peace talks that finally began in nearby Ghana—fresh fighting broke out in Liberia's capital city of Monrovia, endangering the family and friends they had left behind.

Hannah knows she wants to use the events depicted in the film *Pray the Devil Back to Hell* in her next assigned speech. How, though, will she organize it? Should she take her listeners through the events in historical sequence, beginning with the women's first roadside demonstration and ending with peace? Should she research and discuss the handful of individual leaders who appeared in and narrated the film? These were the women who had inspired and organized the peace movement, and Hannah finds each of their stories fascinating. Or should she focus on the climax of the story as it occurred on two separate fronts—Ghana, where the warring parties struggled toward agreement, and Monrovia, where proposals to depose Taylor sparked a new wave of violence?

What kind of organizational pattern would work best with Hannah's topic? Organizing and outlining your material is the focus of this chapter. You will learn many possible patterns of organization, and tips about which ones are most appropriate for a particular topic or purpose.

How Would *You* Do It?

Refer to the chapter opening story, and identify the patterns of organization Hannah is considering for her speech. Which one would you choose for her topic?

Why Organize?

You have already found information about your topic; now you need to arrange your message. Research on organizing speeches indicates that speakers who give well-organized presentations enjoy several advantages over those who do not. First, audience members understand the organized presentations better.[1] Second, organized presenters appear more competent and trustworthy than speakers who deliver disorganized presentations.[2] Clearly, audiences appreciate well-organized messages.

Speakers themselves also benefit from taking the time to carefully organize their presentations. First, they do not just *appear* more confident when their messages are better organized, they actually *are* more confident.[3] Second, they believe they deliver their presentations more smoothly.[4] Third, researchers found that the more students can learn and master the ability to organize ideas, the better analytical thinkers they become.[5] And good organizational skills you learn in public speaking apply equally well whenever you speak or write in this class or in others.

"The more students can learn and master the ability to organize ideas, the better analytical thinkers they become."

How Do You Introduce Your Presentation?

Whether you introduce yourself or another speaker introduces you, an **introduction**, *the beginning portion of your presentation*, serves four functions.

1. Gains and maintains favorable attention.
2. Relates your topic to your audience.
3. Relates you to the topic.
4. Previews the message by stating the purpose and forecasting the organization of the presentation.

Gaining and Maintaining Favorable Attention

The first function of an introduction is gaining and maintaining attention. Even if they appear attentive, your audience members may not be completely focused on you or your message when you begin. You need to direct their attention.

Here are ten possible ways to gain and maintain your audience's attention:

1. *Present a person or object.* A presenter brought a very muscular person to demonstrate safe weight-lifting moves during the presentation, while

another student speaking on health food gave everyone a whole-grain granola bar to eat after the presentation. A third student handed out packets of artificial sweeteners. She said, "These sweeteners will not wake us up like sugar would do, but I hope they are a wake-up call. In your hands, you hold the three leading brands of artificial sweeteners."

2. *Invite audience participation.* If you invite **audience participation**, *you make your audience active participants in your presentation.* One student who was speaking about some of the problems of poverty asked his audience to sit crowded elbow-to-elbow during his presentation to illustrate lack of living space. Or you can ask your audience a question and expect and acknowledge a reply.

3. *Imagine a situation.* You might have the audience imagine that they are standing on a ski slope, flying through the air, or burrowing underground. Kelsey Smith began her speech by having her audience imagine that they were in a recent situation:

> Imagine it is a hot summer day. Your mom packs up the car. You and your family drive down to the local pool. Only when you get there you are forbidden to enter the pool and you must go home. This may sound outrageous but to people of color of suburban Philadelphia, this happened. Many of us think that racism is a part of history and that it is not relevant today. However, this incident occurred on July 10, 2009. And, it is only one of the many examples of racism in today's world.

4. *Use audio and video.* A deputy sheriff showed a videotape of a drunken driver being arrested in a presentation on driving while intoxicated. Be sure not to let your audio or visual resource dominate your time.

5. *Arouse audience suspense.* A student began her presentation by saying, "My friend Sally died last year. Today you will learn what happened to her and what could happen to you." This is how Kellie Podliska began her speech on Ponzi schemes: "According to a CNN article by Allen Chernoff, Bernard Madoff is serving 150 years in prison for stealing $50 billion from investors. How did he do it? His crime is considered to be the largest Ponzi scheme in history. It involved thousands of investors, including his own family."

6. *Use slides, film, video, or PowerPoint.* A student who was studying big-city slums began with a rapid series of twelve PowerPoint slides showing trash heaps, crowded rooms, run-down buildings, and rats.

7. *Read a quotation.* Gretchen Barker began her speech on music therapy with this quotation: "Music speaks what cannot be expressed, soothes the mind and gives it rest, heals the heart and makes it whole, flows from Heaven to the soul."

8. *State striking facts or figures.* Facts and figures can bore your audience to tears or rouse them out of a stupor. A student speaking about minority students in higher education used Texas as an example because that state requires its 35 public colleges and universities to admit any student in the top 10 percent of his or her class. The result in 2008: The University of Texas–Austin, the largest of the public universities in Texas, attracted more minority students than they used to admit under a race-based system. Today, over 80 percent of the students at that flagship university have been admitted under the 10 percent rule established when George W. Bush was governor more than a decade ago.[6]

9. *Tell a story.* Telling a story to gain the audience's attention is one of the oldest and most commonly used methods. Your story can be actual (factual) or created (hypothetical), as long as you tell your audience which it is. A well-honed hypothetical story must be realistic and detailed.

10. *Use humor.* Although often overused, jokes or humor to gain and maintain attention can be effective, but only if the humor is related to the topic. Too often jokes are told for their own sake, whether or not they have anything to do with the subject of the speech. Another word of caution: if

you are not good at telling jokes, then you ought to practice your humor before your speech in front of the class. If the joke is offensive, you will likely lose your audience altogether. Handled well, an appropriate touch of humor will likely be welcomed by the audience. Noah Nash began his speech on absolute truth by stating, "President James A. Garfield said, 'The truth will set you free, but first it will make you miserable.'"

Relating the Topic to the Audience

The second function of an introduction is relating the topic to the audience. This introductory move assures the audience of a reason for their attention, because *there is a connection between them and the topic.* A student presenting on the ethics of changing grades related the topic to her student audience by pointing out that their own university registrar had changed thousands of grades at the request of professors—nearly always raising them. The audience listened to the presentation with more interest because the presenter took pains to relate the topic to both the men and the women in class.

Relating the topic to the audience does not need to be more than one or two sentences in length. For example, Kristen Waldock stated, "According to an article on mercola.com, the average American drinks almost 54 gallons of soft drinks each year, which adds up to a little over a gallon per week." Gretchen Barker said simply, "As college students, we all lead very stressful lives and using music to positively affect our mood is a healthy choice." Finally, Shelby Deckert began, "H1N1 bombards us in the news and it is a major concern on this campus."

Relating the Topic to the Presenter

The third function of an introduction is relating the topic to the presenter. Here are two strategies:

- *Dress for the topic and occasion.* Wear clothing that will signal your credibility on a topic and that shows your relationship to the topic and the occasion.
- *Use self-disclosure* about why or how you have knowledge about the topic. Sometimes self-disclosure, revealing something about yourself that others cannot see, is confessional: "I successfully overcame drug addiction," "I have been a relationship counselor for ten years," or "I have benefited from affirmative action programs." You do not have to reveal highly provocative or dramatic information. For example, one student shared, "As a health-conscious person, I like to know what I'm putting into my body."

Previewing the Message

Often the last part of an introduction is a revelation. The presenter reveals the purpose as well as the organization and development of her presentation. **Forecasting** *tells the audience how you are going to cover the topic.* This thesis statement is an example that clearly indicates both the specific purpose and the organization:

> Today I am going to provide three reasons why you should request generic prescription drugs instead of well-advertised, name-brand prescription drugs.

The type of presentation is persuasive. The specific purpose is clear, and the organization ("three reasons") is apparent.

Leah Fagerland provided her thesis statement and preview of her speech: "Euthanasia is a morally charged issue with blurred moral and legal boundaries; its definitions and types can be difficult to define and implement. Let us now delve into what is morally right and wrong; the difference between postponing death and prolonging life."

Kellie Podliska provided a simple preview statement: "Today we will look at Ponzi schemes, how they work, the origins of the Ponzi scheme, and other Ponzi schemes in history."

How to Organize the Body of the Presentation

The introduction, body, and conclusion are the three main components of most formal presentations. In this chapter, we first consider the organization of the *body*, the main message. Usually, we create and organize the body of the presentation before tackling the introduction and conclusion. We do that because you need to know what your main message is before you can properly introduce or conclude that message.

Emphasize Main Points

The first task in organizing the body of the presentation is to identify your main points. Examine the ideas and arguments you have gathered, and consider the key issues you want to address. If you have written down your specific purpose, you may be able to identify your main points easily. For example, Stacey Tischer, a second-year doctoral pharmacy student, gave a presentation on breast cancer[7] with these three main points:

I.   Fifteen hundred men each year contract breast cancer.
II. Black women who are diagnosed die of the disease more often than white women who are diagnosed.
III. Clinical examination can help detect the problem.

"Most messages have two to three main points, reflecting what an audience can easily remember."

By dividing your topic into main ideas you can better explain and discuss it further. The main points, as we see here, provide the skeleton for the body of the speech. They will be backed up with supporting materials, examples, evidence, and further divisions of subpoints and sub-subpoints. Section III above could be further explained with subpoints like these:

A. Looking and feeling are two parts to breast examination.
B. Detecting the difference between cancerous and noncancerous irregularities is very important.

As you are considering your topic, your specific purpose, and the main points that you will develop, remember this practical advice:

- Choose two or three main points.
- Word your main points in the same form (e.g., sentences).
- Choose main ideas that are approximately equal in importance.

Let us consider each of these suggestions in more depth.

Limit Your Main Points to Two to Three Points

Most messages have two to three main points, reflecting what an audience can easily remember. For some topics, you may come up with only two main points. On the other hand, you may find that some topics are more easily divisible into a greater number of points. For instance, if you are talking about a complex process like preparing for an audit, you could divide your talk into the five main steps of the process. Try to present only as much as your audience can remember.

An emergency medical person knows too much about health for a five-minute presentation. He could, however, address what happens in the first minutes of responding to a crisis with three main points in a presentation entitled "First Acts of the First Responder."

I. Make sure the victim's heart is beating or immediately provide cardiopulmonary therapy.
II. Make sure external blood flow is stopped with pressure or tourniquets.
III. Make sure the victim is breathing or immediately provide oxygen.

Express Your Main Points in a Parallel Manner

In speaking and writing, "parallelism" increases clarity, sounds more engaging, and lingers longer in memory. **Parallel construction** means that *you repeat words and phrases and use the same parts of speech for each item.*

Notice how the repeated words in this speech by President Obama energize the language and make it memorable:

I. Don't tell me that words don't matter.
   A. "'I have a dream'—just words?"
   B. "'We hold these truths to be self-evident, that all men are created equal'—just words?"
   C. "'We have nothing to fear but fear itself'—just words."[8]

Parallelism incorporates some or similar words repeatedly to create a kind of rhythm in the speech. Although the parallel wording may seem subtle, the wording will affect the way you develop subsequent subpoints and sub-subpoints. In general, using parallel construction in your main points encourages more logical development of supporting ideas. When your main points are organized similarly, the audience is more likely to follow them and remember them.

Ensure That Your Main Points Are Nearly Equal in Importance

One way that you can check that your main points are of equal weight is to consider how much you subdivide each main point. If one main point has several subdivisions, but the others have none, then the point with many subdivisions must be more important than the others. Merge main points or reduce subdivisions to achieve nearly equal weight. Maybe one of the subpoints is really a main point.

Similarly, when you practice your presentation later on, you may find that you do not spend equal time on each main point. Each main point need not be granted *exactly* the same amount of time, but the time you spend discussing each point should be more or less similar. If you have three main points, you should spend about 30 percent of your time on each.

Determine the Order of the Main Points

Sometimes the order of your main points seems obvious. At other times, the organizational pattern is less clear. Your purpose and topic determine your choice of organizational pattern. In this section we provide you with some alternatives you can consider for the organization of your main points.

The general purpose of your presentation will suggest potential organizational patterns. Among the possible organizational patterns, which we will discuss below, are:

"Your purpose and topic determine your choice of organizational pattern."

1. The time-sequence and spatial relations patterns found often in informative presentations.
2. The cause-effect and topical sequence patterns found in both informative and persuasive presentations.
3. The problem-solution and Monroe's Motivated Sequence patterns found often in persuasive presentations.

Time-Sequence Pattern

The **time-sequence pattern** *states the order of events as they actually occur*. Use this pattern when your primary purpose is to tell your audience how something came about over a period of time. The steps in reducing water pollution, the evolution of sexual harassment policies, and the development of smartphone technology are examples of topics based on time. This pattern is also commonly used in "how to do it" and in "either/or" presentations because the audience will be unable to "do it" unless they follow steps in the correct order. Figure 6.1 is a presentation outline on the subject of artificial sweeteners, written by Carolyn Braus, that uses the time-sequence pattern.

Artificial Sweeteners

Introduction:

I. **Gaining and maintaining favorable attention:** [While passing out packets of Equal, Sweet 'N Low, and Splenda to audience members.] Good morning! If you're tired, these sweeteners will not wake you up like sugar would do, but I hope they are a wake-up call. In your hands, you hold the three leading brands of artificial sweeteners.

II. **Relating the topic to the audience:** You may know these best by their pretty colors that you see on your table at Perkins. And I know what goes through your minds: "Would anyone notice if I just stole all of these?" But your dining table isn't the only place you will find these artificial sweeteners. They are used in many of our store-bought foods.

III. **Relating the topic to the presenter:** As a health-conscious person, I like to know what I'm putting into my body. This powered my extensive search for the stories behind artificial sweeteners.

IV. **Previewing the message:** Artificial sweeteners have been the subject of continuing controversy ever since the first one was introduced in 1879. I am here to give you some of the facts and findings concerning today's most popular artificial sweeteners: Sweet 'N Low in the pink packet, Equal in the blue packet, and Splenda in the yellow packet.

Transition:

We will start at the beginning with Sweet 'N Low, the first artificial sweetener.

Body:

I. Sweet 'N Low marked the start of the artificial sweetener age.

   A. Sweet 'N Low is composed of a synthetic chemical called saccharin, which was discovered by accident.

      1. In 1879, two researchers at Johns Hopkins University were creating new chemical dyes when one of their vessels boiled over. Forgetting to wash his hands, one of the researchers realized that the compound left on his hands tasted sweet when he sat down for his next meal.

Figure 6.1   This presentation on artificial sweeteners employs the time-sequence pattern.

2. Saccharin was approved by the FDA and put on the market as the first artificial sweetener. Today it is used in products such as chewing gum, canned fruit, salad dressings, and vitamins to supply taste without the calories. It is considered low-calorie due to the fact that it is not metabolized by the body and passes through unchanged.

B. Saccharin has had a very controversial past.

1. In the 70s, studies showed that rats who were fed saccharin had increased occurrences of bladder cancer. Because of this, the FDA proposed a ban on saccharin. Rather than banning it right away, Congress passed legislation that would protect saccharin while more safety studies were conducted. In the meantime, foods containing saccharin were required to bear a label warning of health hazards and the cause of cancer in laboratory animals.

2. Further research determined that male rats have a predisposition to bladder cancer, unlike humans. By 2001, saccharin was removed from the list of potential cancer-causing agents and saccharin-containing items no longer required a special label. Despite all this, an article out of the May 2004 issue of the *Nutrition Action Healthletter* states that one of the National Cancer Institute's own studies showed evidence of an increased risk of bladder cancer in heavy saccharin users.

Transition:

Now that we know the history and controversy of our little pink packet, we can move on to the blue packet: Equal.

II. Equal was the next to hit the market.

A. Equal is composed of aspartame, a chemical name that is probably very familiar to you all. Like saccharin, the discovery of aspartame was also an accident.

1. This time, a chemist working for a pharmaceutical company was testing a new anti-ulcer drug when he licked his finger to pick up a piece of paper.

2. The FDA approved aspartame as a food additive in 1981, and according to Equal's official Web site, Equal alone is used in over six thousand products—not to mention other brands of artificial sweeteners that contain aspartame. Aspartame is composed of three chemicals, all of which are metabolized by the body.

B. Aspartame has experienced just as much, if not more, controversy as saccharin.

1. According to a 2006 issue of *Environmental Nutrition,* hundreds of studies have affirmed that aspartame does not increase the risk of cancer in humans. Still, many doubt the safety of aspartame.

2. In 2005, a long-term study was published in which eighteen hundred rats were fed aspartame-laced or pure water over a lifetime. This large study revealed an increased rate of cancer in the rats who were given aspartame. In response, the National Cancer Institute conducted its own study of over half a million people between the ages of fifty and sixty-nine, using diet questionnaires and health monitoring to search for a link between aspartame and cancer. No such link was discovered.

3. Suspicion doesn't stop there. The phrase "aspartame disease" has developed to describe the wide range of conditions that are supposedly mimicked by reactions to aspartame. For example, adverse reactions to aspartame may mimic multiple sclerosis, arthritis, migraines, and depression. Though the FDA dismisses this idea, it has become the subject of many Internet sites that speak out against aspartame.

Transition:

There is one more sweetener in your hands that we haven't discussed. And that is the most popular sweetener of all: Splenda, in the yellow packet.

III. Splenda is the most recently developed product.

A. Splenda's discovery wasn't as accidental as that of saccharin or aspartame.

1. It is made up of the chemical sucralose, which is made through a process that starts with cane sugar and replaces three hydrogen-oxygen groups on the sugar molecule with three chlorine atoms.

2. It can withstand high temperatures and is often used for baking.

B. Splenda offers its own health concerns.

1. In a recent study, Duke University researchers found that Splenda may cause weight gain, kill good intestinal bacteria, and block the absorption of prescription drugs. Over a twelve-week period, researchers gave doses of Splenda to some

Figure 6.1   (continued)

rats and not to others. The rats given Splenda gained weight and continued to gain weight after treatment was stopped. The Splenda also appeared to cause a decrease in microflora, which synthesize vitamins and act as protection from bad microbes. However, these results can't necessarily be applied to humans.

2. A major concern with Splenda is that it has not been around long enough to know any long-term effects of the product.

Transition:

Now all the packets—pink, blue, and yellow—are accounted for.

Conclusion:

I. **The brake-light function:** There are no simple answers to many questions. Should you use artificial sweeteners or should you use sugar? If you do use artificial sweeteners, which one should you choose?

II. **The instant-replay function:** There is certainly much dispute over the safety of artificial sweeteners. This debate continues, as many loose ends seem to remain untied. To explore this, we've taken a look at the leading brands of artificial sweeteners: Sweet 'N Low, Equal, and Splenda.

III. **Action-ending function:** I hope that the next time you go out to a restaurant and you see the little glass box full of colorful packets, you will consider the information I provided to you today. At least I hope the glass box looks more significant.

References:

Belvoir Media Group, LLC. (2006, April). Ubiquitous aspartame: is it a safe sweetener or a cancer time bomb? *Environmental Nutrition, 29(4),* 7.

Calorie Control Council. (n.d.). *History of saccharin.* Retrieved October 4, 2009, from http://www.saccharin.org/history.html

Calorie Control Council. (2006). *Saccharin.* Retrieved October 4, 2009, from http://www.saccharin.org/pdf/sach_broch_final_406.pdf

The Chronicle. (2009, March/April). Splenda, the calorie-free artificial sweetener, may leave consumers with something worse than a bitter aftertaste. *Total Health,30(4),* 17.

Consumers Union of the United States, Inc. (2007, October). Aspartame and Saccharin: debate continues. *Consumer Reports, 72(10),* 17.

Henkel, J. (1999, November). Sugar substitutes. *FDA Consumer, 33(6),* 12.

Mann, D. (2005). *Are artificial sweeteners safe?* Retrieved October 4, 2009, from the MedicineNet Web site http://www.medicinenet.com/script/main/art.asp?articlekey=56064

Merisant Company. (n.d.). *Ingredients.* Retrieved October 4, 2009, from the Equal Web site http://www.equal.com/products/ingredient.html

Metcalfe, E., Martini, B., & Gold, M. (2000, June). Sweet talking. *Ecologist, 30(4),* 6.

McNeil Nutritionals, LLC. (n.d.). *Frequently asked questions.* Retrieved October 4, 2009, from the Splenda Web site http://www.splenda.com/page.jhtml?id=splenda/faqs/nocalorie.inc#q11

Schardt, D. (2004, May). Sweet nothings. *Nutrition Action Healthletter, 31(4),* 8.

Thomas, P. (2005, September). Aspartame reactions: a hidden epidemic. *Ecologist, 35(7),* 47–49.

United States Food & Drug Administration. (2006, July/August). Artificial sweeteners: no calories . . . sweet. *FDA Consumer, 40(4),* 27–28.

Walter, P. (2006, April). Sweetener: no cancer link. *Chemistry and industry, 8,* 9.

Weihrauch, M. R., & Deihl, V. (2004). Artificial sweeteners—do they bear a carcinogenic risk? *Annals of Oncology, 15(10),* 1460–1465.

Figure 6.1 **(continued)**

Spatial Relations Pattern

The **spatial relations pattern** *demonstrates how items are related in space.* Examples of presentations that could be organized using a spatial relations pattern would include using a map to show historic conservation sites over a period of time, using a grid to explain choreography in ballroom dancing, or using an architectural model to explain effective kitchen design for people who use wheelchairs. An example of the spatial relations pattern, written by football player Paul Backowski, appears in Figure 6.2.

American Football: A Game of Inches

Introduction:

Three-hundred-pound men in synchronous motion, gracefully grinding their teeth and pushing each other back and forth just to gain a couple inches of earth. Spatial relations in the game of American football is extremely important to the success of opposing players and teams. The offensive line is the group of five players who are typically the largest humans on the field. I will use concepts from the offensive line to explain spatial relations. Why do I know the game from the inside? I was a varsity football player on a major college team.

Body:

I. I want to begin by describing specific concepts that coaches teach all American football offensive linemen.

   A. Space and distance are extremely important.

   B. Offensive linemen should line up next to each other with at least a two-foot gap between the center, guards, and tackle positions.

   C. Distance between linemen is extremely important because space keeps the linemen from stepping or tripping over each other.

   D. Space allows room for linemen to gather momentum before a collision with opposing defenders, who are less than a foot away.

II. First Steps: Correct spacing is critical to success of individual plays.

   A. After establishing a two-foot gap between each player, the linemen are now ready to execute the designated play.

   B. The first step should be forward 6 inches every time, which allows the player to explode quickly.

   C. American football is a game based on speed and quickness, regardless of size and weight.

   D. The first step is extremely important. If the step is done correctly, the play will be a success. If the step is off, the play runs the risk of being a failure.

III. Practicing the stance and first steps are important to success.

   A. Repetition of stance and steps are the basics to the game of football and are extremely essential to success.

   B. Begin each day by lining up next to a partner and by maintaining a distance of two feet.

   C. Next, practice stepping 6 inches forward. Repeat these two steps over and over until this process becomes natural.

   D. These steps may seem unimportant, but they are integral to the success of every play.

Conclusion:

Spatial relations are extremely important for the success of a football team. Distance and space relationships are constantly being analyzed to increase the efficiency of every play. Stance and length of steps are just two examples of the importance of spatial relationships in the game of American football.

Figure 6.2   See how many places in the presentation refer to how things relate in space and how often the presenter uses measures and distances to convey the message.

Cause-Effect Pattern

The **cause-effect pattern** of organization *describes or explains causes and consequences*. Actually, the pattern of organization can move from cause

to effect or from effect to cause. Examples of effect to cause are the various spinoffs from *Law and Order*, such as *Criminal Intent* or *SVU*, stories in which the narrative begins with the murder (effect) and proceeds to the cause (conviction of the murderer). In a presentation on the vital topic of health you might use such a pattern by starting with someone almost miraculously free of pain (effect) and move toward the new drug (cause) that made the person pain-free. Two examples of cause to effect might be how increased exposure to sunshine, medicine, and even lights can defeat SAD (Seasonal Affective Disorder) and how taking a daily vitamin can increase your body's immunity to disease. Figure 6.3 illustrates a cause-effect pattern.

Violence and Video Games

Introduction:

Shooter Lee Boyd Malvo played the video game *Halo* before his Washington, D.C., sniper attacks. Eric Harris and Dylan Klebold, the killers at Columbine High School, loved the game *Doom*. More recently, it has been suggested that Cho Seung-Hul, who gunned down 31 members of the Virginia Tech community, allegedly played *Counter-Strike* as a high school student in northern Virginia. You have probably grown up playing video games and have not spared a second thought as to how they affect your behavior. My older brother, Matt, was a heavy user of violent video games, and he routinely talked back to his teachers, got into physical fights, and displayed anger and hostility to me and our parents. Our parents were able to get counseling for Matt, but, through the process, we learned that the video games seemed to have an effect on his behavior. Today I will explain how video games can cause violent behavior, and I will share three kinds of research studies that support this hypothesis.

Body:

I. Video games have been shown to lead to violent behavior.

   A. A great deal of research has been done on the effects of violent video-game playing and people's behaviors.

   B. Not all of the research done has been conclusive, but a considerable percentage of these studies has allowed researchers to conclude that violent video games are related to violent behavior and may, indeed, cause it.

   C. The caveat is that some people play violent video games and never commit crimes.

II. Three kinds of studies demonstrate the relationship between violent video-game playing and violent behavior.

   A. One set of studies examined the relationship between exposure and real-world aggression and demonstrated that these experiences caused negative effects on both behavior and learning.

   B. Another set of studies examined behavior over time and showed that gaming habits and belligerence were pronounced even months later.

   C. Experimental studies—like those done here at college—illustrate that people who are asked to play violent video games, as opposed to nonviolent games, are more likely to show aggressive behavior.

Figure 6.3   **Cause-effect organizational pattern.**

III. Let me dispel three myths about the relationship between viewing violence and displaying violent behavior.

   A. "Unrealistic video games will not affect behavior." Actually, cartoon-like and fantasy video games have both been shown to increase aggression.

   B. "Violent video-game watching has not been linked to serious aggression." In truth, high levels of viewing have been linked to delinquency, fighting at school and during free play periods, and violent behavior.

   C. "The effects of video-game use are relatively small." In fact, video-game effects on aggression are larger than the effect of second-hand tobacco smoke on lung cancer, than the effect of lead exposure on IQ tests in children, and than the effect of calcium consumption on bone mass.

Conclusion:

Let us summarize this discussion. Video games appear to be linked to violence. Studies have found a relationship between viewing video games and aggressive behavior. Long-term studies demonstrate that regularly using video games leads to aggression. Finally, experimental studies that randomly assigned participants to play either violent or nonviolent games found that playing the violent video games resulted in more aggressive behaviors toward the other players. My brother, like the shooters in Washington, D.C.; Colorado; and Virginia, was influenced by violent video games. As Martin Luther King, Jr., noted, "Returning violence for violence multiplies violence . . . Hate cannot drive out hate: only love can do that."

References:

Anderson, C.A., & Bushman, B.J. (2001). Effects of violent video games on aggressive behavior, aggressive cognition, aggressive affect, physiological arousal, and prosocial behavior: A meta-analytic review of the scientific literature. *Psychological Science, 12,* 353–359.

Anderson, C.A., Gentitle, D.A., & Buckley, K.E. (2007). *Violent video game effects on children and adolescents.* New York: Oxford University Press.

Howe, S., Stigge, J., & Sixta, B. (2008, Summer). Interview with Dr. Craig Anderson: Video game violence. *Eye on PSI CHI: The National Honor Society in Psychology, 12,* 32–35.

Schaffer, Amanda. (2007, April 27). "Don't Shoot: Why video games are linked to violence." *Slate Magazine,* online.

Figure 6.3   **(continued)**

Topical Sequence Pattern

The **topical sequence pattern**, a highly versatile organizational pattern, *simply divides up a topic into related parts.* Be careful not to treat the topical sequence pattern as a dumper into which you can throw anything. The main points in a topical sequence have to be related to a central idea and the main points need to be related to each other: three reasons to volunteer at the food bank, two types of hybrid vehicles, and the advantages and disadvantages of jury trials. Figure 6.4 shows an example of the topical sequence pattern.

When the Levee Breaks

Introduction:

[Start by playing Led Zeppelin's "When the Levee Breaks."] Because of tragedies like the flooding of New Orleans and the summer floods of 2009 in the Upper Midwest, many of us learned about the importance of levees.

This speech will teach you about levee breaks so that you can better understand how such devastating flooding can occur.

Body:

I. Levees are built to hold back floodwater.

   A. A levee is a type of dam that runs along a river or other body of water.

   B. Although levees can be constructed out of a variety of material, including steel and cement, most are made out of dirt with some stronger material like concrete used for reinforcement.

   C. Levees are wider at the bottom and narrower at the top.

      1. The bottom of a levee is called the feet.

      2. The top of the levee can be extended upward using temporary material like sandbags to protect against projected water crests.

II. Levee breaches can occur in a variety of ways.

   A. A breach is any type of failure of the levee to retain and hold back water.

   B. Levees fail for a variety of reasons.

      1. Overtopping is when the levee is simply too short to hold back the water—the water literally gets so high that it flows over the top of the levee. Overtopping can be exacerbated by wave action in the water.

      2. Slight overtopping can cause the entire levee to fail because of "jetting," which is when the water washes out the back side of the levee.

      3. "Piping" occurs when small seeps of water spring through the levee. Even with an intact levee, piping can become so severe that the levee essentially fails.

      4. Related to piping, when the earth becomes saturated below the levee, the entire levee is at risk of disintegrating—a process known as "liquefaction."

      5. Surface erosion is when fast-moving water washes out the front face of the levee, thereby making it weaker. Severe surface erosion can lead to slope failure, where the levee is essentially washed out by the water.

      6. The weight of water can cause levees to "slide," which means that they move backward from the water. As they move they become weaker and are prone to having segments separate from one another.

Conclusion:

Millions of people are impacted directly or indirectly by levees. Understanding what they are and how they fail can help all of us be safer and work to improve these attempts at controlling what some say is uncontrollable.

Figure 6.4 **A topical sequence pattern of organization.**
Notice that the main heads have a logical relationship with each other.

Problem-Solution Pattern

The **problem-solution pattern**, *depicting an issue and a solution*, tends to be used more often in persuasive than in informative presentations. The statement of the problem is difficult without framing the issue in some way that indicates your own perspective, a perspective that you want the audience to adopt. For example, let us say you describe the environmental issue of establishing game preserves. Your position on the issue—that the state should pay farmers to set aside land for wildlife and natural habitat—is the perspective you urge on the audience. An example of a problem-solution pattern, Puppy Mills, written by Carolyn Braus, appears in Figure 6.5. Your solution is even more likely to be perceived as persuasive because you will advocate some policy or action that you want your audience to embrace.

The problem-solution pattern raises three serious questions for the speaker: how much should you say about the problem, how much about the solution, and how ethical is the solution? Usually you can work out a proper ratio based on what the audience knows about the issue. If the listeners are unaware that a problem exists, you may have to spend more time telling them about the problem. On the other hand, if the problem is well known to all, you can spend most of your time on the solution. This pattern lends itself nicely to outlining, with the problem being one main point and the solution the other. Finally, you need to determine if your solution harms anyone.

Puppy Mills

Introduction:

I. **Gaining and maintaining favorable attention:** [Sing "How Much Is That Doggy in the Window?"] Yes, that doggy in the window *is* for sale. But do you really know the cost you will be paying if you ever consider buying a pet store puppy? That puppy may have come from what is known as a puppy mill. According to the Web site of the Humane Society of the United States, puppy mills are "mass dog-breeding operations."

II. **Relating the topic to the audience:** If you or someone you know is ever thinking of purchasing a new, lovable pet, it is important to be aware of possible risks and how to avoid them. Plus, I know that many of us already have dogs back home whom we love. You could have purchased your own dog from a puppy mill without even knowing it.

III. **Relating the topic to the presenter:** As someone who has been personally affected by this low trade, I have spent much time researching and uncovering the truths of these mass operations.

IV. **Previewing the message:** Puppy mills are inhumane, and we must play our part in putting an end to them. We'll explore this by looking at why puppy mills are a problem, the reasons they exist, and what we can do to solve the problem of puppy mills.

Transition:
First, let's look at why puppy mills are a problem.

Body:

I. Puppy mills are a serious problem.

   A. There are an estimated 10,000 puppy mills in the United States.

      1. Our part of the Midwest is not an exception. Last year in May, seventy-three puppies and dogs, including Pomeranians, bulldogs, Chihuahuas, and pugs, were confiscated from a puppy mill in Olmstead County, Minnesota. The animals were found in "deplorable and

Missouri Puppy Mill Rescue
The dogs were voluntarily relinquished by an owner who could no longer afford to feed them.

Figure 6.5   The problem-solution organization.

unsanitary conditions." A member of the Humane Society who helped collect the animals said, "They were in a barn in wire cages with cobwebs everywhere, sitting in their own feces." The owner of the mill, who had been selling these animals over the Internet for as much as $800 each, faced charges of animal cruelty. Many cases such as this surely go unnoticed.

2. Everyone is susceptible to the effects of puppy mills, even the rich and famous. According to an article in *People* magazine from January 2008, a three-month undercover investigation revealed that Pets of Bel-Air, a ritzy pet store frequented by the likes of Britney Spears and Paris Hilton, obtains many of its dogs from puppy mills.

B. Puppy millers are not concerned with their animals' well being.

1. The ultimate goal of the puppy mill owner is profit, not quality dogs. Puppy mill dogs are simply the "inventory" of these retail operations.

2. Dogs used for breeding are often forced to live in puppy mills for their entire lives.

   a) They are continually bred for years without human companionship or the hope of ever becoming part of a family.

   b) After their fertility wanes, breeding animals are commonly killed, abandoned, or sold to another puppy mill.

3. Puppy mill dogs are frequently housed in shockingly poor conditions. In her April 2009 article, Suzanne Smalley, journalist for *Newsweek* magazine, describes the typical puppy mills of Lancaster County, Pennsylvania: "Often, the animals are left outside during the frigid winters. Their feet slip painfully through the cages' wire floors—and sometimes, so does their excrement, which rains on top of the dogs below when breeders stack cages to save space. Some of the dogs are nearly as big as their cages, leaving them little room to move."

4. Because of these horrid living conditions, puppy mill puppies may suffer from many physical problems. They may have hereditary conditions like epilepsy, heart disease, and blood disorders. Or they may develop illnesses and diseases like pneumonia, distemper, and respiratory infection. Besides physical problems, these dogs may also suffer from many behavioral problems due to lack of socialization.

Transition:
Now that we know what a puppy mill is, let's look at the reasons puppy mills exist.

II. There are a couple of main reasons why puppy mills are still around.

A. Why are people supporting puppy mills by buying their puppies? Well, puppy millers have devised ways to hide their cruel business.

1. They regularly place newspaper ads boasting one specific breed to fool consumers into thinking the mill is actually a small operation.

2. They set up fancy Web sites.

3. They sell to pet stores.

   a) Pet store businesses depend on impulse buyers. That's why many pet stores are positioned in malls where people make other impulse buys.

   b) Most of the puppies sold in pet stores have been purchased from a puppy mill. The reason for this is that, frankly, puppy millers are nearly the only ones who will sell to them.

   c) Truly reputable breeders care about their animals and never sell an animal without interviewing its hopeful buyer, whether that may be through selling a dog online or through a pet store.

   d) Even a humane society requires at least two visits with a dog before adoption. Pet stores do not take these precautionary steps to ensure responsible, lifelong homes for their pets.

B. Inadequate laws and enforcement.

1. Federal law requires that certain breeders be licensed and regularly inspected by the USDA. Under the Animal Welfare Act, these breeders are required to provide only food, water, and shelter. They are not required to provide love, socialization, or freedom from confining cages.

2. There are many loopholes. If a breeder sells directly to the public but not through a pet store (for example if the breeder sells over an Internet Web site), he or she is not required to adhere to any federal humane care standards.

Figure 6.5   (continued)

3. Many licensed breeders get away with repeated violations of the Animal Welfare Act. Violators are rarely fined nor are their licenses suspended, and if suspended, breeders can often renew their licenses again and again.

4. Luckily, some advancements are being made. In 2008, Virginia became the first state to pass a law limiting the number of adult dogs a commercial breeder may possess at any one time to fifty dogs. Also in 2008, legislation was passed in Pennsylvania that increases minimum cage sizes, requires veterinary care and exercise periods, and bans wire flooring at all breeding kennels.

Transition:

Now that we know why puppy mills are still thriving, we can look at how each of us can play a part in putting a stop to them.

III. This is how we can solve the problem of puppy mills.

A. First of all, don't support puppy mills.

1. If you are looking for a dog, start by looking at an animal shelter. Not only will you save a life, but you'll ensure that your money isn't going to support a puppy mill.

2. If adoption isn't an option for you, make sure you are buying from a responsible breeder. Never buy a puppy without personally visiting the breeder's premises. And because a good breeder cares, the breeder should be screening you as much as you are screening the breeder.

B. One of the most important things you can do is to educate others.

1. Puppy mills are not a new problem. People simply aren't aware that they exist.

2. The most common response of people when they find out that their pet came from a puppy mill is "I had no idea."

3. Five years ago I bought a cocker spaniel puppy from a local pet store.

    a) Like most pet store buys, it was an impulse buy.

    b) When I became aware of this issue, I did some research and found that in 1997 the owners of the kennel from which my dog came were charged with violations of the Animal Welfare Act. Right after taking my new dog home, we realized that she had an ear infection in both ears, had loose stools, and suffered from a good deal of separation anxiety. I was affected personally because of my lack of awareness.

C. A final way you can help is through donating your time or even your money. There are always animal shelters looking for volunteers and many organizations that work to get better legislation passed that could use better funding.

Conclusion:

I. **The brake-light function:** In conclusion, puppy mills are inhumane, and we must play our part in putting an end to them.

II. **The instant-replay function:** We've explored this by looking at why puppy mills are a problem, the reasons puppy mills exist, and how we can solve the problem of puppy mills.

III. **The action-ending function:** So the next time you think, "How much is that doggy in the window?", you'll think twice.

References:

The American Society for the Prevention of Cruelty to Animals. (n.d.). *Laws that protect dogs in puppy mills.* Retrieved November 3, 2009, from the ASPCA Web site http://www.aspca.org/fight-animal-cruelty/puppy-mills/laws-that-protect-dogs.html

Dodd, J. (2008, 21 January). Hollywood pet shop scandal. *People, 69,* 144.

Estrada, H. M. (2008, May 24). 200 animals confiscated from farm. *Star Tribune,* p. 1A.

Hamilton, A., & Scully, S. (2005, December 12). Curbing the puppy trade. *Time, 166,* 62–63.

The Humane Society of the United States. (2008). *Inside a puppy mill.* Retrieved November 3, 2009, from the Stop Puppy Mills Web site http://www.stoppuppymills.org/inside_a_puppy_mill.html

The Humane Society of the United States. (2009). *Frequently asked questions.* Retrieved November 3, 2009, from the Stop Puppy Mills Web site http://www.stoppuppymills.org/frequently_asked_questions.html

Figure 6.5   **(continued)**

The Humane Society of the United States. (2009). *What you can do.* Retrieved November 3, 2009, from the Stop Puppy Mills Web site http://www.stoppuppymills.org/what_you_can_do.html

The Humane Society of the United States. (2009). *Puppy buying tips.* Retrieved November 3, 2009, from the Stop Puppy Mills Web site http://www.stoppuppymills.org/puppy_buying_tips.html

Hurdle, J. (2009, August). 2008 law leading to crackdown on Pennsylvania puppy mills. *The New York Times,* p. 12A.

Macejco, C. (2008, November). Pennsylvania puppy mill law: state forces breeders to work with DVMs. *DVM Newsmagazine, 39,* 1.

Peters, S. L. (2008, September 18). Saturday is awareness day for opponents of puppy mills. *USA Today,* p. 7D.

Peters, S. L. (2007, November 1). Taking aim at puppy mills. *USA Today,* p. 8D.

Rosen, J. (2009, August 11). Dogs in need: rescued puppy mill dogs arrive with a host of emotional scars. *McClatchy-Tribune,* p. 1B.

Smalley, S. (2009, April 13). A (designer) dog's life. *Newsweek, 153,* 52–55.

Figure 6.5 (continued)

cultural NOTE

CULTURAL DIFFERENCES IN ORGANIZATION

Most North Americans are linear; that is, they like to arrange their thoughts in a line from most important to least important, from biggest to smallest, from tallest to shortest. Other cultures use different organizational schemes. Some East Asian cultures, for example, sound to North Americans as if they are "talking around" a subject instead of getting right to the topic because they expect a rather long "warm-up" of socializing before getting down to business. Also, they may be indirect by suggesting rather than saying something directly. Imagine that you are going to speak to an audience that includes a number of Korean, Chinese, and Japanese people. The audience is predominantly American, however. You will be explaining how to enroll in classes at your college. How will you approach this topic? What adjustments might you make given the composition of the audience?

Monroe's Motivated Sequence

Monroe's Motivated Sequence[9] was developed by Alan Monroe, who applied John Dewey's work on reflective thinking to persuasion. This organizational pattern *includes five specific components: attention, need, satisfaction, visualization, and action.*

- First, capture the *attention* of your audience. You want your audience to decide that to listen to you is important.

- Second, establish the *need* for your proposal. You want to describe a problem or show why some need exists. You want your audience to believe that something must be done.

- Third, present the solution to the problem or show how the need can be satisfied. You want your audience to understand how your proposal will achieve *satisfaction*.

- Fourth, go beyond simply presenting the solution by *visualizing* the solution for the audience. You want the audience to envision enjoying the benefits of your proposal.

- Fifth and last, state the behavior that you expect of your audience. In this step, you request *action* or approval. You want your audience to respond by saying that they will do what you have asked. Your presentation should have a strong conclusion that asks for specific, but reasonable, action.

For example, the speech in Figure 6.6 concludes with basic steps anyone can take to help control climate change.

Table 6.1 on page 146 shows that each of the organizational patterns fulfills certain purposes. The time-sequence and spatial relations patterns work well in

Climate Change

Introduction:

Attention Step:

I. Everyone uses energy on a regular basis, but not everyone realizes the damage our energy use does to the environment. Last summer, I had the opportunity to work for an organization that explores energy use across the country.

Body:

I. According to the Environmental Protection Agency (EPA), the Earth's climate has frequently changed over time, going through ice ages and periods of warmth caused by activities such as volcanic eruptions, changing the composition of the Earth's atmosphere, and influencing change in the Earth's climate.

Next Step:

II. Our use of fossil fuels generates greenhouse gases that raise the Earth's temperature in ways serious enough to invite regulation.

A. Greenhouse gases prevent heat from escaping into space and are extremely important in keeping the Earth's surface warm, but in recent years they have been increasing enough to change the climate.

1. Greenhouse gases come from burning fossil fuels, such as coal and oil, and reducing forests that would normally protect us from the gases.

2. According to the NOAA and NASA, greenhouse gases are responsible for increasing the Earth's average surface temperature 1.2 to 1.4 degrees Fahrenheit in the last 100 years and are expected to increase the Earth's surface temperature by 3.2 to 7.2 degrees Fahrenheit by the year 2100.

B. Climate change affects the entire planet in different ways.

1. Climate change affects the environment with rising sea levels, melting glaciers, and developing ice on rivers and lakes later in the winter season and breaking up ice earlier in the spring.

2. According to the EPA, climate change will most likely affect human health as well, because diseases that thrive in warm environments will begin to spread, such as malaria, dengue fever, and yellow fever. Climate change will also change air quality, creating more respiratory disorders.

C. As a way to control climate change, the U.S. federal government encourages voluntary and incentive-based programs to reduce increases in greenhouse gas emissions.

Satisfaction Step:

III. Because greenhouse gases are a result of activities such as driving a car and using electricity, my solution to climate change is to educate others about what they can do to be more environmentally friendly.

A. Energy consumption can be decreased by using ENERGY STAR light bulbs, using public transportation or your bike, or the three R's—reduce, reuse, and recycle.

B. Energy consumption can be changed by using solar and nuclear energy that do not produce greenhouse gases.

Visualization Step:

IV. The world would be healthier if people reduced their carbon footprint.

A. Climate change can be slowed down.

B. Using education and effective campaigns, more people can be reached about environmental issues.

Conclusion:

Action Step:

I. Climate change is a serious issue that will affect our planet more and more each year. You can take simple steps to improve the world around you, just by biking instead of driving, by recycling instead of trashing, or by purchasing new light bulbs. Then, tell your family and friends about the importance of environmental issues.

This outline was composed by Casey J. Peterson, president of the local chapter of the Public Relations Student Society of America.

Figure 6.6

Monroe's Motivated Sequence.
Within this sequence you will see the elements of a problem-solution presentation (problem: greenhouse gases; solutions: education, alternative energy sources, and public transportation).

TABLE 6.1	PATTERNS OF ORGANIZATION LINKED TO GENERAL PURPOSES	
USUALLY INFORMATIVE	EITHER INFORMATIVE OR PERSUASIVE	USUALLY PERSUASIVE
Time-sequence	Cause-effect	Problem-solution
Spatial relations	Topical sequence	Monroe's Motivated Sequence

informative presentations. The problem-solution pattern and Monroe's Motivated Sequence work well in persuasive presentations. And cause-effect and topical sequence patterns work well in both informative and persuasive presentations.

Incorporate Supporting Materials

The main points create only the skeleton of the body of the presentation. The presenter must flesh out this skeleton with subpoints and sub-subpoints. You need to decide what information to keep and what to discard. You also need to determine where and what kind of visual resources will help your audience understand your message. Refer to Chapter 5 to review how to flesh out the skeleton with supporting materials in the form of examples, narrative, statistics, and evidence.

Now you know organizational patterns from which you can choose to make your presentation effective. You also know that any kind of outline is just the bones of the speech that you have to "beef up" with supporting materials and visual resources.

What Holds the Presentation Together?

Your methods of moving from one point to another, of telling the audience where you are in the overall presentation, where you are going next, and where you have been is the "glue" that holds your presentation together. Audience members cannot "reread" a speech as they can reread an essay if they get lost in a disorganized maze. Transitions, signposts, internal previews, and internal reviews are the mortar between the bricks. Together they allow the audience easy access to the information you are presenting.

Transitions are *statements or words that bridge previous parts of the presentation to the next part. Transitions can be signposts, internal previews, or internal reviews.* They almost always appear between main parts of the presentation (introduction, body, and conclusion), when turning to a visual aid, or when moving from an argument to evidence. For instance, transitions might look like this:

> Having explained positive purpose as the first reason for choosing a career as a nurse's aide, let us turn to the second: service to those who are in need. (Review of past point and preview of the next.)

> Now that you have heard an overview of Washington, D.C.'s scenic Mall with its reflecting ponds, let me show you a map of the many museums that are free and open to the public. (Move from main point to visual aid.)

Signposts, *like road signs on a highway, reveal where the speaker is going.* Signposts are brief transitions that do not have to point backward and forward; they have only to tell the listener where the presenter is in the message. Some examples include the following:

> My first point is that . . .
>
> One of the best examples is . . .
>
> To illustrate this point, I will . . .
>
> A second, and even more convincing, argument is . . .

Skillful use of signposts and transitions will clarify your organization and help you become a confident presenter.

Internal previews *inform listeners of your next point or points and are more detailed than transitions.* They are similar to the statements a presenter makes in the introduction of his or her presentation, although internal previews occur within the body of the presentation. Examples of internal previews include the following:

> My next point is that education correlates highly with income.
>
> I now will explain how to build community support for improving our middle schools.

Internal reviews *remind listeners of your last point or points and are more detailed than transitions.* They occur within the body of the presentation. Examples of internal reviews include the following:

> Now that we have covered the symptoms of this disease, let's move to the tests used to diagnose it.
>
> At this point, we have established that most students are honest when taking tests and writing papers.

Let's turn now to the second major topic of this chapter: outlining the presentation.

Principles of Outlining

The organization of a presentation is generally shown in outline form. Outlining is relatively easy to learn. Three principles of outlining govern the writing of an outline: *subordination, division,* and *parallelism.*

Subordination

The **principle of subordination** allows you to *indicate which material is more important and which is less important through indentation and symbols.* The principle of subordination is based not only on the symbols (numbers and letters) and indentations, but also on the content of the statements. The subpoints are subordinate to the main points, the sub-subpoints are subordinate to the subpoints, and so on. Evaluate the content of each statement to determine whether it is broader or narrower, more important or less important, than the statements above and below. Figure 6.7 presents an example of subordination, which will make the idea easy to grasp.

More important materials usually consist of generalizations, arguments, or conclusions. Less important materials consist of the supporting evidence for your generalizations, arguments, or conclusions. By less important, we of course do not mean that your supporting evidence is not vital to your presentation—just that it is more specific and detailed, and farther down in your outline. In the outline, Roman numerals indicate the main points, capital letters indicate the subpoints under the Roman numeral statements, and Arabic numbers indicate sub-subpoints under the subpoints. Figure 6.7 shows a typical outline format. Notice, too, that the less important the material, the greater the indentation from the left-hand margin.

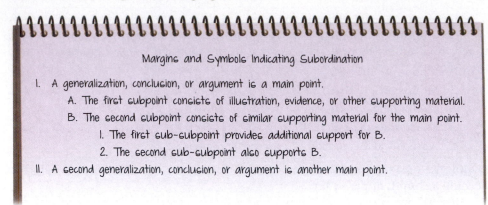

Margins and Symbols Indicating Subordination

I. A generalization, conclusion, or argument is a main point.
    A. The first subpoint consists of illustration, evidence, or other supporting material.
    B. The second subpoint consists of similar supporting material for the main point.
        1. The first sub-subpoint provides additional support for B.
        2. The second sub-subpoint also supports B.
II. A second generalization, conclusion, or argument is another main point.

Figure 6.7   **Margins and symbols indicating subordination.**

Division

The second principle of outlining is the **principle of division**, which states that, *if a point is to be divided, it must have at least two subpoints.* For example, the outline illustrated in Figure 6.7 contains two main points (I, II), two subpoints (A, B) under main point I, and two sub-subpoints (1, 2) under subpoint B. With rare exceptions, such as for a single example or clarification, items will be either undivided or divided into two or more parts.

Parallelism

The third principle of outlining is the **principle of parallelism**, which states that *main points, subpoints, and sub-subpoints must use the same grammatical and syntactical forms.* That means that in a sentence outline you would use all sentences, not a mixture of sentences, dependent clauses, and phrases. The sentences would tend to appear the same in structure, with subject followed by verb followed by object, for instance. See the explanation of parallelism on page 133.

An outline can use parallel construction without consisting entirely of sentences. For example, a keyword outline on note cards might consist of single words used to remind you of the content as you deliver your speech. To review the information on the principles of outlining, you should examine Figure 6.8, which briefly explains each of the three principles.

Subordination	Division	Parallelism
I. _____	Every "I" must have at least a "II."	Each entry must be either a complete sentence, a phrase, or a word; entries may not be a mix of sentences, phrases, and words.
A. _____	Every "A" must have at least a "B."	
B. _____		
1. _____	Every "1" must have at least a "2."	
2. _____		
a. _____	Every "a" must have at least a "b."	
b. _____		
II. _____		

Figure 6.8   **How does an outline indicate subordination, division, and parallelism?**

In the preparation outline and delivery of a speech, you generally compose three different but related kinds of outlines. In your course, your teacher will likely instruct you about which of these outlines will be required. Also your instructor might require another type of outline that is not covered in this text. First, you might create a preparation, or working, outline. Next, you will probably develop a formal outline. Finally, you might want to create a keyword outline on note cards or paper, which you can use when you deliver your presentation.

Types of Outlines

The Preparation Outline

After you have selected the topic, given it a title, developed a specific purpose, written a thesis statement, and gathered information for your presentation, you will begin to sketch out the basic ideas you wish to convey to your audience. The **preparation outline** is *your initial or tentative conception of your presentation.*

For example, imagine that you want to speak about volunteering in your community. You might start by thinking of some main point for which you can provide examples:

I. What volunteer opportunities exist in our community?
   A. Working for the local food bank
   B. Serving as a hospice volunteer
   C. Reading to immigrant children at the grade school
   D. Leading a tour of a museum

As you learn more about opportunities you can refine your list, create more main points, and delete those you deem less important. The preparation outline usually is an informal draft, a tentative plan for the points in your presentation. This type of outline is called a "working outline" because it mainly helps you sort out your initial ideas in an orderly fashion.

The Formal Sentence Outline

A **formal sentence outline** is *a final outline in complete sentence form.* An example is provided in Figure 6.9 by Brenna Smithberg. The formal outline includes the following elements:

1. The title.
2. The specific purpose.
3. The thesis statement.
4. The introduction of the presentation, which may be outlined or written out in full.
5. The body of the presentation in outline form.
6. The conclusion of the presentation, which may be outlined or written out in full.
7. A bibliography of sources and references consulted.

Since you have already covered parts one, two, and three in Chapter 3, let's briefly consider parts four through seven. At the end of this chapter, we will cover the functions and techniques of introductions and conclusions.

Introduction   The introduction of a presentation should take about 15 percent of the total time and should fulfill four functions: (1) gaining and maintaining attention, (2) relating the topic to the audience, (3) relating the speaker to the topic, and (4) previewing the message by stating the purpose and forecasting the organization of the presentation. Many presenters write out their introductions so they feel secure about beginning their talk. Others outline their introductions and deliver them extemporaneously.

Body   The body of the presentation is the main part of your message. This main portion generally consists of up to three points that account for about 75 to 80 percent of the entire talk. The body should be outlined using the principles of subordination, division, and parallelism that we discussed above.

Conclusion   The conclusion should be even shorter than the introduction. If the introduction to the presentation is about 15 percent of the entire presentation, then the conclusion should be about 5 percent of the presentation and certainly no longer than 10 percent. The functions of the conclusion include: (1) forewarning the audience of the end of the presentation, (2) reminding your audience of the main points, and (3) specifying what the audience should do as a result of the presentation.

References   The formal outline includes a **list of references**, or *the sources consulted and the sources actually used in the presentation.* Your instructor will tell you whether you should include all of your sources or only those you actually cite. In any case, you will want to provide them in correct bibliographic form. To help you, you can purchase a Modern Language Association (MLA) or an American Psychological Association (APA) style manual or *A Style Manual for Communication Majors* by Bourhis, Adams, and Titsworth.[10] You can also find examples in Figure 5.4 in Chapter 5 of this text.

Title: Poverty in America

Specific Purpose: My audience will be able to identify people who are living in poverty, will be able to explain why so many Americans are living in poverty, and will be able to identify ways that people in poverty can get help.

Thesis Statement: Poverty is a major problem in America.

Introduction:

  I. **Gaining and maintaining favorable attention:** Can you imagine worrying about the next time you will get the chance to eat or wondering if you're going to have a place to sleep at night? A total of 35.9 million people live below the official poverty line (Urban Institute). I always knew poverty was an issue in third-world countries, but right here in America? I had no idea.

  II. **Relating the topic to the audience:** One in twelve people in our community go hungry every day. You may think there is no way something like this could happen to your family, but one accident or one job layoff could have you asking yourself where you will get the money to eat.

  III. **Relating the topic to the presenter:** I have done extensive research on poverty as well as acquired hands-on experience volunteering at a local food pantry.

Figure 6.9   **A sentence outline for an informative speech with title, specific purpose, and thesis statement.**

IV. **Previewing the message:** Poverty is a growing problem in America but it could be greatly improved through awareness. Today I will inform you about who is impoverished, explore why America is in poverty, and examine ways for people in need to get help.

Transition:
I will start by looking at the face of poverty.

Body:

I. **First main point:** To understand poverty one must know who is considered "poor."

   A. The United States government measures poverty by a narrow income standard that does not include other aspects of economic status, such as debt, property, and savings (NCCP).

      1. The official poverty measure is a specific dollar amount that varies by family size but is the same across the continental United States.

      2. According to the guidelines, the poverty level in 2008 was $21,200 a year for a family of four (NCCP).

      3. The poverty guidelines are used to determine eligibility for public programs.

   B. Researchers study poverty's demographics to understand who is poor and examine poverty trends and dynamics (Urban Institute).

      1. High crime, low-performing schools, and scarce job opportunities often plague poor communities.

      2. There is a higher poverty rate among Asian Americans, African Americans, and Latinos than Caucasians in America (Poverty Trends by Race).

Transition:
Now that you know who is in poverty, I will discuss how these people became so unfortunate.

II. **Second main point**: There are numerous reasons why residents of the wealthiest nation became so impoverished.

   A. First, one must realize that by the late 1950s the great economy we inherited from World War II was drastically slipping (Understanding Poverty in America).

   B. Next, one must look at the decrease in jobs in America.

      1. Since the start of the recession in December 2007, the number of unemployed people has increased by 7.6 million to 15.1 million (Employment Situation Summary).

      2. The unemployment rate has doubled to 9.8 percent (Employment Situation Summary).

      3. A total of 35.6 percent of unemployed people were jobless for twenty-seven weeks or more (Employment Situation Summary).

   C. Finally, people find themselves in difficult situations, out of savings, and in poverty.

      1. Factors to consider when thinking of difficult situations are illness and unexpected trips to the emergency room.

      2. Health insurance is important to have so you are ready for these situations.

Transition:

Now that we know how millions of our country's people found themselves living in poverty, I will discuss ways for them to get help.

III. **Third main point:** There are two different ways people can obtain help; one is through nonprofit organizations and the other is through the government.

   A. Food pantries and homeless shelters are useful when someone needs food or a place to sleep.

      1. We have local food pantries where people can go to get free food once a month.

      2. We have shelters in our community where people with no home can sleep.

   B. Food stamps and welfare reform are important for many of the people living in poverty (An Inquiry into the Nature and Causes of Poverty in America and How to Combat It).

      1. The number of families who were eligible to receive food stamps declined dramatically between 1995 and 2000 (Valentine). This is when the poverty rate increased so much.

Figure 6.9   (continued)

2. The federal government maintains nearly a dozen different food assistance programs (Mutikani).

Conclusion:

I. **The brake-light function:** Today I raised your awareness of poverty in America.

II. **The instant-replay function:** I hope you feel well informed on the issue and better understand who is impoverished, why many Americans are in poverty, and ways for people in need to get help.

III. **The action-ending function:** Millions of people are living in poverty. Next time you read or hear something about poverty, don't overlook it. In the blink of an eye you could be in the very same situation.

Works Cited:

"Employment Situation Summary." *U.S. Bureau of Labor Statistics.* 19 Oct. 2009. http://www.bls.gov/news.release/empsit.nr0.htm.

"An Inquiry Into the Nature and Causes of Poverty in America and How to Combat It." *The Heritage Foundation—Conservative Policy Research and Analysis.* Web. 19 Oct. 2009. http://www.heritage.org/Research/Welfare/HL263.cfm.

Mutikani, Lucia. "US poverty rate hits 11-year high." *Reuters.* 10 Sept. 2009. Retrieved 11 Sept. 2009 from http://www.reuters.com/article/topNews/idUSTRE58943C20090910?pageNumber=2&virtualBrandChannel=0&sp=true.

"NCCP | Measuring Poverty in the United States." *NCCP | Home.* Web. 19 Oct. 2009. http://www.nccp.org/publications/pub_825.html.

"Poverty trends by race." *College of Behavioral and Social Sciences—University of Maryland—Behavioral & Social Sciences.* 19 Oct. 2009. http://www.bsos.umd.edu/socy/vanneman/socy441/trends/povrace.html.

"Understanding Poverty in America." *The Heritage Foundation—Conservative Policy Research and Analysis.* Web. 19 Oct. 2009. http://www.heritage.org/Research/Welfare/bg1713.cfm.

"The Urban Institute | What Works." *The Urban Institute | Research of Record.* Web. 19 Oct. 2009. http://www.urban.org/poverty/whatworks.cfm.

Valentine, Vikki. "Q & A: The Causes Behind Hunger in America: NPR." *NPR: National Public Radio: News & Analysis, World, US, Music & Arts: NPR.* 22 Nov. 2005. Retrieved 16 Sept. 2009 from http://www.npr.org/templates/story/story.php?storyId=5021812.

Figure 6.9   **(continued)**

I. New agricultural technologies
   A. Biotechnology
   B. Biosecure products

II. Precision agriculture
   A. Global positioning systems
   B. Satellites and computers

Figure 6.10   **How can a keyword outline help you remember your speech?**

The Keyword Outline

The purpose of a keyword outline is to reduce your full-sentence outline to a manageable set of cues that mainly remind you of what you are going to say and when you are going to say it. A keyword outline encourages conversational delivery instead of an oral reading of your words.

You might want to make a keyword outline on note cards or on a sheet of paper, whichever your instructor prefers. The **keyword outline** is a *brief outline with cue words that you can use during the delivery of your presentation.* The outline may include words that will prompt your memory, sources that you will cite within the presentation, or even the complete quotations of material you will repeat. The keyword outline may look sketchy to someone other than the speaker. Figure 6.10 is an example of a keyword outline.

Now we will move from "behind the scenes" outlining to actually speaking before an audience. In the next section you will learn the critical functions of concluding your presentation.

Just like the introduction, the conclusion of a presentation fulfills certain functions: (1) to forewarn the audience that you are about to stop; (2) to remind the audience of your central idea or the main points in your message; and (3) to specify what the audience should think or do in response to your presentation. Let us examine each of the functions of a conclusion in greater detail.

The **brake-light function** *warns the audience that you are about to stop.* The most blatant, though trite, method of signaling the end of a speech is to say, "In conclusion . . ." or "To summarize . . ." or "In review . . .". Another way is to physically move back from the lectern. Also, you can change your tone of voice to have the sound of finality. There are a variety of ways to say, "I'm coming to the end." For instance, you have indicated an impending conclusion as soon as you say, "Now let us take my four main arguments and bring them together into one strong statement: You should learn about the candidates before you vote."

The second function of a conclusion—*to remind the audience of the thesis of your message*—is the **instant-replay function**. You could synthesize a number of major arguments or ideas into a single memorable statement. You could simply repeat the main steps or points in the speech. For instance, a student who spoke on the Heimlich maneuver for saving a choking person concluded his speech by repeating and demonstrating the moves for saving a person's life.

The third function of a conclusion is to clearly *state the response you seek from the audience*, the **action-ending function**. If your speech was informative, what do you want the audience to remember? Tell them. If your presentation was persuasive, how can the audience show its acceptance? A student who delivered a presentation on periodontal disease concluded by letting her classmates turn in their candy for a package of sugarless gum.

What Are the Functions of a Conclusion?

Tips for Concluding

Following are some ideas for ending your presentation. Of course you can think of others that are equally effective. What works for *you* will be best.

- *End with a quotation.* Quotations provide an effective end to your talk. Confine yourself to a brief quotation or two.
- *Ask a question.* Presenters can use questions to invite listeners into their topics; they also can use questions to close their talks, encouraging the audience to learn more about the topic or to take action.
- *Tell a story.* Audience members enjoy hearing stories. Stories are especially apt in a conclusion when they serve to remind the audience of the purpose of a presentation.
- *Close with a striking statement.* In a presentation on using seat belts, the speaker ended by saying: "In an accident, it is not who is right that really counts; it's who is left."

- *Review central idea and main points.* Remind the audience what you told them.
- *Forewarn the audience that you are nearly done.* Avoid abrupt endings that leave the audience hanging.
- *Tell the audience what you expect.* What do you want them to think or do as a result of your presentation?
- *Refer back to the introduction.* Closing by reminding them how you began is a good strategy. For example, your introduction can be part of a story that ends in your conclusion.
- *End strongly in a memorable way.* You want your audience to remember what you said. Often they remember what you said last best of all.

These tips are just a few of the many ways you can draw your presentation to a close. They are provided here just to jump-start your own creativity in finding ways to end your presentation.

An Example of a Conclusion

Brake-Light Function
Instant-Replay Function

Action-Ending Function

Let me remind you of what we have discussed today. First, I addressed the problem of having "wingnuts," right-wing and left-wing ideologues, pretending to report news objectively. Second, I pointed out that right wingnuts dominate on radio while left wingnuts dominate on cable TV. Finally, I provided you with some guidelines for evaluating news so you can tell the difference between news as presented on *The Colbert Report* and CBS. I leave you with these words of wisdom from conservative author P. J. O'Rourke: "One thing talk can't accomplish is communication. This is because everyone is talking too much to pay attention to what anyone is saying."

For REVIEW >>

AS YOU READ

1. Practice composing outlines so that they reflect a limited number of main points of equal importance, and incorporate subordination, division, and parallelism.

2. Think about how you might use the six patterns of organization in your presentations.

3. Draft a presentation outline, a keyword outline, and a formal sentence outline.

4. Recognize the critical roles played by a presentation's introduction, conclusion, and internal devices such as transitions, signposts, previews, and reviews.

SUMMARY HIGHLIGHTS

► Outlining includes three important principles.
  • The principle of subordination means that the symbols and indentation of your outline should show which material is more important and which material is less important.
  • The principle of division states that when points are divided, they must have at least two subpoints.
  • The principle of parallelism states that main points, subpoints, and sub-subpoints should use the same grammatical and syntactical forms.

► Some typical ways to order or pattern your speech are the time-sequence, spatial relations, cause-effect, topical sequence, problem-solution, and Monroe's Motivated Sequence.

► You will probably create three types of outlines.
  • The preparation outline is your initial or tentative conception of your presentation.
  • A formal outline is a final outline in complete sentence form including the title, specific purpose, thesis statement, introduction of the speech, body of the speech, conclusion of the presentation, and a bibliography of sources consulted.
  • The keyword outline is a brief outline—often on note cards—created for you to use during the delivery of your presentation.

► The introduction, conclusion, and internal devices each play a critical role in a presentation.
  • The introduction usually announces the topic, relates that topic to the audience, gains the audience's attention, and forecasts the organization or development of the topic.
  • Transitions connect ideas.
  • Signposts tell the audience briefly where the speaker is within the speech.
  • Internal previews forewarn the audience of that which is to come.
  • Internal reviews remind the audience of what has already been covered.
  • The conclusion: (1) forewarns the audience of an impending ending, (2) reviews the main points, and (3) states what you expect the audience to do or remember.

Pop Quiz

1. The first task in organizing the body of the presentation is to:
   (A) write transitions
   (B) identify subpoints
   (C) determine the order of the main points
   (D) identify the main points

2. In Jenni's speech on South Dakota, she started each of her main points with the phrase, "In South Dakota . . .". This shows that Jenni used:
   (A) the brake-light function
   (B) parallel construction
   (C) transitions
   (D) time-sequence patterns

3. The time-sequence pattern:
   (A) demonstrates how items are related in space
   (B) states the order of events as they actually occur
   (C) divides up a topic into related parts
   (D) depicts an issue and a solution

4. If you are giving a speech on different bedroom configurations, the best organization to use is the:
   (A) topical sequence pattern
   (B) problem-solution pattern
   (C) spatial relations pattern
   (D) time-sequence pattern

5. When using Monroe's Motivated Sequence, *need* refers to:
   (A) presenting the solution to the problem
   (B) stating the behavior that you expect of your audience
   (C) making the audience decide to listen to you
   (D) describing a problem or showing the audience why something must be done

6. The phrase, "My second point is . . ." is an example of a:
   (A) transition
   (B) signpost
   (C) thesis
   (D) conclusion

7. Statements that remind listeners of your last point or points and are more detailed than transitions are:
   (A) internal previews
   (B) signposts
   (C) internal reviews
   (D) overviews

8. Which principle of outlining says that if a point is divided, it must have at least two subpoints?
   (A) division
   (B) parallelism
   (C) subordination
   (D) ordination

9. A final outline in complete sentence form is known as the:
   (A) preparation outline
   (B) formal sentence outline
   (C) draft outline
   (D) keyword outline

10. Which of the following is not a function of a conclusion?
    (A) action-ending
    (B) brake-light
    (C) relate topic to audience
    (D) instant-replay

Answers: 1 (D); 2 (B); 3 (B); 4 (C); 5 (D); 6 (B); 7 (C); 8 (A); 9 (B); 10 (C)

APPLICATION EXERCISES

1. Think of a topic not mentioned in this chapter that would be best organized into each of the following patterns. Write the topic next to the appropriate pattern.

ORGANIZATION PATTERN	TOPIC
TIME-SEQUENCE:	
SPATIAL RELATIONS:	
PROBLEM-SOLUTION:	
CAUSE-EFFECT:	
TOPICAL SEQUENCE:	
MONROE'S MOTIVATED SEQUENCE:	

Can you explain why each pattern is most appropriate for each topic?

2. Go to the library and find the publication *Vital Speeches of the Day*, which is a collection of current speeches. Make a copy of a presentation and highlight the transitions, signposts, internal previews, and internal reviews.

3. Take any chapter in this book and construct an outline from the various levels of headings.

KEY TERMS

Action-ending function	Internal reviews	Principle of parallelism
Audience participation	Introduction	Principle of subordination
Brake-light function	Keyword outline	Problem-solution pattern
Cause-effect pattern	List of references	Signposts
Forecasting	Monroe's Motivated Sequence	Spatial relations pattern
Formal sentence outline	Parallel construction	Time-sequence pattern
Instant-replay function	Preparation outline	Topical sequence pattern
Internal previews	Principle of division	Transitions

get involved!

Campus Compact is a nonprofit organization that has engaged over 20 million students in projects like:

- Tutoring at-risk youth in reading and math
- Building houses for low-income families
- Conducting environmental safety studies
- Caring for the sick, the hungry, the homeless, and the elderly

According to their Web site: "These students provide more than $7 billion annually in service within their communities. But they do more than volunteer. They build strong community partnerships. They lobby Congress. They start their own nonprofit agencies. They learn to apply their knowledge in ways that will bring about lasting change. And Campus Compact gives them the skills and resources to do it."

The Campus Compact story is one of students who tackle local and even global issues to prove that even one person can have a significant impact on a community.

7

DELIVERING

Have you observed how skilled presenters seem to know their topic and their audience? The best presenters make delivery look easy. They do so by practicing their presentations until they feel confident, look poised, and sound conversational.

SPEECHES

As You READ

>>

1. Identify the qualities of "effective delivery."
2. Think about how you might use each of the four modes of delivery.
3. Relate how context or situation influences the type of delivery you should choose.
4. Identify the functions of both the vocal and nonverbal aspects of delivery in presentations.

What do President Obama and Sarah Palin have in common as speakers? Let's see what commentators have to say about them first. *The Economist* is a periodical first published in 1843 to take part in "a severe contest between intelligence . . . and timid ignorance. . . ." That publication says of Obama:

One thing you can generally count on when the lanky figure of Barack Obama approaches a podium is that you will hear a good speech; and the more trouble he is in, the better the speech is likely to be.[1]

What does the press say about Palin? In April of 2010 she and other possible presidential contenders addressed the Southern Republican Leadership Conference (SRLC), a group of Republican loyalists who can make or break a political career. Here is what Salon.com said of her speech at the New Orleans conference:

Palin just finished up a 30-minute speech here, full of red meat, obnoxious jokes aimed at President Obama (and the media). . . . The crowd loved it, and Palin basked in their adoration, playing for laughs and applause whenever she could.[2]

After eight years of lackluster speeches by George W. Bush, Obama burst on the scene with speeches that inspired a majority of Americans to vote for him. Similarly, Palin joined a floundering John McCain campaign in which she emerged as a political figure on the national scene. So what do Palin and the president have in common?

Both of these speakers have excellent delivery skills. Obama is fluent, reads a teleprompter like a professional broadcaster, maintains eye contact with his audience, and engages his audience in issues that normally dull the senses. Palin, trained and experienced as a broadcaster, has a captivating style that is slightly flirtatious, often outrageous, and carefully targeted at disaffected

Americans who hate taxes, despise big government, and eschew regulations.

These two speakers, so large now on the national stage, started just the way you are starting. They learned through experience how to give good speeches. Both of them learned the basics of nonverbal communication—the use of eyes, body, facial expression, gesture, and movement—as well as the basics of voice, rhyme, and reason. They both demonstrate that the delivery skills you will learn in this chapter are important in effective communication to an audience.

How Would *You* Do It?

What are your strengths in delivery? Do you have an expressive face? Active gestures and movement? Good eye contact? A good voice?

What Is Effective Delivery?

Effective delivery is a way of presenting a speech that does not call attention to itself. Ray Grigg writes, "Too loud and we are not heard. Too bright and we are not seen. Too fancy and we are hidden. Too much and we are obscured."[3] His advice is well taken for the public presenter. If your audience is watching your gestures and your body movements and listening to your pronunciation rather than the content of your speech, you should reconsider what you are doing. Delivery should enhance the message, not distract your audience from the message.

Effective delivery appears conversational, natural, and spontaneous. Your delivery should be comfortable for you and your audience. When you speak in this manner, your audience will believe that you are speaking with them, not at them.

How can you focus on your ideas rather than on your delivery? How can you draw your audience's attention to your message rather than to your delivery? How can you sound conversational and natural? The answer to all these questions is the same. Develop your message first, and then revise your words for delivery.

To keep the focus on your message, select a topic about which you have keen interest or deep convictions. If you are committed to the ideas you present, your delivery will come naturally. If a student is upset about tuition increases, she may need no notes. The delivery naturally follows from the message. On the other hand, her emotions may interfere with effective delivery.

To begin practicing your speech, concentrate only on the basics—speaking intelligibly, maintaining eye contact, and avoiding mannerisms that will distract listeners. Be sure you are pronouncing words correctly. Avoid nervous habits such as playing with a strand of your hair, rubbing your face, tapping a pencil, or pulling on an article of your clothing. If you are practicing in front of friends, use their feedback to help you discover problems and correct them in subsequent performances.

As you continue to grow in experience and knowledge as a public presenter, you should observe how highly experienced public presenters deliver their messages. How do they appear conversational and yet inviting to their audiences through voice inflection and body movements? What do they do to enhance the impact of their ideas? Which of these techniques can you adopt in your own speeches? Which aspect of other people's speaking styles do you want to avoid? Both positive and negative examples will help you become more effective.

What Are the Four Modes of Delivery?

The four modes of delivering a presentation are (1) extemporaneous, (2) memorized, (3) manuscript, and (4) impromptu. While each mode is appropriate for different topics, audiences, speakers, and situations, your instructor will identify which mode is suitable for your assignments.

Extemporaneous Mode

In the **extemporaneous mode** *a presenter often delivers a presentation from a keyword outline or from brief notes.* This mode of delivery is most commonly taught in the public speaking classroom. Its advantages far outweigh the disadvantages for the beginning public presenter. Indeed, for most presenters, this mode is the top choice.

Extemporaneous speaking sounds conversational, looks spontaneous, and appears effortless. However, extemporaneous speaking requires considerable effort. A presenter selects a topic appropriate for the audience, completes research on the topic, organizes the main points and supporting materials, practices the presentation with a working or keyword outline, and finally delivers the presentation with maximum eye contact, appropriate gestures, and motivated movement. The presenter may occasionally glance at notes, but the emphasis is on communicating a message to an audience.

You may have experienced extemporaneous speaking without realizing it. Have you ever read the assignment for a class, caught the drift of the professor's questions, jotted a few words on your notes, and then given an answer in class? Your "speech" was extemporaneous because it included your background preparation, an organization of your ideas, brief reminders, and a conversational delivery.

An extemporaneous presentation is not practiced to the point of memorization. In fact, the presenter rarely repeats the message in exactly the same words, even in practice. The idea is to keep the content flexible enough to adapt to the audience. If the audience appears puzzled by something you say, you can add a definition, a description, or an example to clarify your position. Audience members like to be talked with, not lectured at, read to, or talked down to.

What are the *advantages* of the extemporaneous mode of delivery?

1. This mode is the most versatile: The presenter, using only brief notes, can engage in excellent eye contact. This eye contact allows careful audience analysis and immediate audience adaptation. The presenter can add or delete information based on the audience's responses.
2. Extemporaneous speaking demands attention to all aspects of public speaking preparation. The presenter has an opportunity to consider the important dimensions of selecting a topic, determining a purpose, doing careful research, identifying supporting materials, organizing the presentation appropriately, and using language in a spoken style that best communicates the message. In short, the extemporaneous presentation allows high-quality communication.
3. Extemporaneous speaking invites bodily movement, gestures, and rapid nonverbal response to audience feedback.
4. The extemporaneous presentation sounds conversational because the presenter is not reciting scripted words. The presenter is talking with the audience, not at the audience.

5. An outline is easier to use as a quick reference or guide than is a manuscript of a speech.

What are the *disadvantages* of the extemporaneous speech? If the presenter must be careful with every word, if every phrase needs to be exact, the presenter might more appropriately use another mode of speaking. Under most circumstances, however, the extemporaneous mode is the presentation method of choice.

Can you think of a current presenter who uses the extemporaneous mode of delivery effectively? The speaker who uses the extemporaneous mode of delivery can move away from the podium and walk among the audience as she speaks. Frequently, this type of speaker is given high marks for confidence.

"Extemporaneous speaking demands attention to all aspects of public speaking preparation."

Memorized Mode

The **memorized mode** of delivery is *one in which a presenter has committed a presentation to memory.* This mode entails more than just knowing all the words; the presenter also rehearses gestures, eye contact, and movement, practicing a presentation over and over in much the same way that an actor masters a dramatic script.

Oratory contests, the lecture circuit, and banquet speeches are common places to find the memorized mode. Ceremonial occasions, where little audience or topic adaptation is expected or needed, invite memorization. Politicians usually have a stock presentation they have delivered so many times that they have every word memorized. Some presenters have delivered the same presentation so many times that they even know when and how long the audience is going to applaud, laugh, or respond. In other words, memorization is best when performance to the audience is more important than communication with the audience.

What are the *advantages* of the memorized method of presenting a speech? The main advantage is that this mode permits maximum use of delivery skills: every variation in the voice can be mastered, every oral paragraph stated in correct cadence, every word correctly pronounced at the right volume. With a memorized speech, you have continuous eye contact. Because no notes are used, bodily movements and gestures are freer. While the memorized method does not eliminate the search for the next word, you are simply searching your memory instead of your notes or manuscript.

However, the memorized mode has three *disadvantages*:

1. Memorization permits little or no adaptation during delivery. The presenter is likely to focus more on the internalized manuscript than on the listeners. If the audience appears to have missed a point, the presenter has difficulty explaining the point in greater detail.
2. Recovery is more difficult if you make a mistake. If you forget a line, you have to search for the exact place where you dropped your line.
3. Especially for beginning speakers, the presentation sometimes *sounds* memorized: the wording is too smooth, the pacing too contrived, and the presentation is too much of a performance instead of a communicative experience.

The beginning presenter is more likely to be at a disadvantage than at an advantage by using the memorized method. However, some formal situations, such as commencement addresses, routine political campaign speeches, and repeated rituals and ceremonies, call for little adaptation, making memorization a good choice.

Manuscript Mode

The **manuscript mode** of delivering a presentation is *when a presenter writes out the complete presentation in advance and then uses that manuscript to deliver the speech but without memorizing it.* It is most useful when a presenter has to be precise, must avoid error, and must defend every word. A president who delivers a foreign policy presentation in which the slip of a word could start a war, a minister who carefully documents a sermon with biblical quotations, and a politician who releases information to the press are examples of presenters who might adopt this mode.

Some professors lecture from a manuscript. At some point they probably have written out their lecture. As a student it is likely that you have seen many manuscript speeches.

What are the *advantages* of the manuscript speech? Generally, the complete manuscript prevents slips of the tongue, poor wording, and distortion. Manuscripts often boost the confidence of beginning presenters who need the security of their manuscript.

The *disadvantages* outweigh the advantages, however. While using a manuscript might make the beginning presenter feel more confident, the delivery often suffers. Among the problems engendered by manuscripts are:

1. Manuscripts frequently reduce eye contact because the presenter is reading the script rather than observing the audience.
2. The manuscript method also hinders audience adaptation. The presenter is not watching the audience; to observe and respond to audience feedback is difficult.
3. The presenter may also use fewer gestures. Being bonded to the podium and the script prevents the presenter from gesturing to emphasize or illustrate points.
4. Vocal variety may be lacking as well, because much of the presentation is being read.
5. The pacing of the presentation may be too rapid or too slow for the audience. The presenter will sound inappropriate because written style is markedly different from spoken style. Instead of sounding conversational, the presentation will sound like an essay being read.

To distinguish between extemporaneous and manuscript speeches, select speeches on vital topics given by national political figures. You should select one speech that uses an extemporaneous mode of delivery (house and senate floor speeches work well) and one that uses a manuscript mode (nationally televised speeches work well). Discuss the reasons for deciding to use manuscript or extemporaneous modes of delivery in these contexts.

try this

Name a current figure who presents successfully from a manuscript. Consider actors and actresses who make presentations at awards ceremonies: How effective are they as presenters? Are they more effective when they ad-lib or add unplanned comments?

Impromptu Mode

The **impromptu mode** entails *giving a presentation without advance preparation.* Unlike the extemporaneous mode, the impromptu method uses minimal planning and preparation, and usually no practice. You may be ready for an impromptu presentation because of your knowledge, experience, and background, but you do not have any other aids to help you know what to say. The key to effective impromptu speaking is to take a moment to compose your thoughts and to identify important points instead of figuring out what you are going to say as you speak.

You have already delivered impromptu speeches. When your teacher calls on you to answer a question, your answer—if you have one—is impromptu. You were ready because you had read the assignment or had prepared for class, but you probably had not written out an answer or certain keywords. When someone asks you to introduce yourself, explain something at a meeting, reveal what you know about a particular subject, or give directions, you are delivering your answer in an impromptu fashion.

What are the *advantages* of the impromptu method? This mode reveals your skill in unplanned circumstances. In a job interview, you might be asked to answer some questions for which you had not specifically prepared. Your impromptu answers may tell a potential employer more about you than if you were given the questions ahead of time and had prepared your answers. Similarly, the student who can give an accurate, complete answer to a difficult question in class shows a mastery of the subject matter that is, in some ways, more impressive than in an exam or another situation in which the student may give partially planned answers.

Another advantage of the impromptu mode is that it provides you with opportunities to think on your feet, to be spontaneous. As you engage in impromptu speaking situations, you learn how to quickly identify the important points in the information you wish to share or the major arguments in the persuasive appeals you offer. Students might give impromptu speeches when volunteering at events or places such as blood drives or senior centers, while meeting with a student club, or while working.

The impromptu presentation also has *disadvantages*. Spontaneity discourages audience analysis, planned research, and detailed preparation. Most people who are seeking to gain employment, trying to sell a product, or aspiring to academic honors should not risk delivering an impromptu speech. Such circumstances require greater preparation. An impromptu presentation can mean a poor answer as easily as a good one. The lack of planning makes the outcome of the impromptu method of speaking uncertain.

Your mode of delivery must be appropriate for you, your topic, the audience, and the situation. Memorizing five pages of print may not be your style. A manuscript presentation is out of place in a dormitory meeting, a discussion among class members, or any informal gathering. Ultimately the method of delivery is not the crucial feature of your speech. In a study to determine whether the extemporaneous or the manuscript method is more effective, two researchers concluded that the presenter's ability is more important. Some presenters are more effective with extemporaneous speeches than with manuscript speeches, but others use both methods with equal effectiveness.[4]

"Your impromptu answers may tell a potential employer more about you than if you were given the questions ahead of time and had prepared your answers."

See Figures 7.1.a and 7.1.b for a summary of the four modes of delivery. See the Application Exercises at the end of the chapter for an impromptu presentation exercise.

Mode of Delivery	Need for Notes	Amount of Preparation	Best Use of Mode
Extemporaneous	Low	High	When every word does not need to be exact.
Memorized	None	Very high	In formal situations that call for little, or no, adaptation.
Manuscript	High	High	When every word must be precise.
Impromptu	None	None	When little planning, preparation, or practice is possible.

Figure 7.1.a   **Four modes of delivery: Need for notes, amount of preparation, and best use.**

	Advantages	Disadvantages
Extemporaneous	Sounds conversational Looks spontaneous Appears effortless Is most versatile Allows high-quality communication Invites bodily movement, gestures, and rapid nonverbal response Makes it easier to use a keyword outline as a quick reference or guide	Requires lots of practice and effort Could change the meaning because of different word choices
Memorized	Allows maximum use of delivery skills	Permits little or no adaptation To recover from mistakes is difficult Can sound memorized
Manuscript	Prevents slips of the tongue and poor wording	Reduces eye contact Hinders audience adaptation Might cause less frequent use of gestures Might affect vocal variety Might cause pacing to become too rapid or too slow
Impromptu	Requires minimal planning and practice Allows spontaneity Reveals your skill in unplanned circumstances	Discourages audience adaptation Discourages planned research Discourages detailed preparation Has uncertain outcome

Figure 7.1.b   **Four modes of delivery: Advantages and disadvantages of each.**

How Can You Use Your Voice Effectively?

Effective public presenters learn to speak in front of an audience as if they are having a conversation. Their voice and movements are a natural accompaniment for their words. In fact, some teachers believe that the best way to improve delivery is not to emphasize it directly. Instead, they encourage students to let effective delivery flow from the message, the audience, and the situation.

As you study delivery, remember that delivery and the message comprise an organic whole. If what you say is important to you and to your audience, the way you say it will not be a problem for you. You will be so busy trying to communicate your message that you will gesture, move, look, and sound like a very competent presenter.

Let's look at eight vocal aspects of delivery.

Adjust Your Rate to Content, Audience, and Situation

Rate, the first vocal characteristic of delivery, is *the speed of delivery*. Normally American speakers speak at a rate between 125 and 190 words per minute, but audiences can comprehend spoken language that is much faster. Rapid speech rate improves the speaker's credibility, and rapid speech improves persuasion.[5] In another study, students shortened their pauses and increased their speaking rates from 126 to 172 words per minute. The increased rate affected neither the audience's comprehension nor evaluation of the speakers' delivery.[6] Thus, faster speaking, up to a limit, can mean better speaking.

Beginning presenters frequently vent their anxiety by speaking too quickly. A nervous presenter makes the audience nervous as well. On the other hand, fluency comes from confidence. A presenter who is accustomed to audiences and knows the subject matter well may speak at a brisk rate without appearing to be nervous.

The essential point, not revealed by the studies, is that speaking rate needs to be adapted to the speaker, audience, situation, and content of the speech. First, become comfortable with your rate of speaking. If you normally speak rather slowly, you might feel awkward talking like a competitive debater. If you normally speak at a rapid pace, you might feel uncomfortable speaking more slowly. As you learn presentational skills, you will probably find a rate that is appropriate for you and for your audience.

Second, adapt your rate to the audience and situation. A grade-school teacher does not rip through a fairy tale; the audience is just learning how to comprehend words. A public presenter addressing a large audience without a microphone might speak more distinctly and cautiously to make sure the audience comprehends her words. A story to illustrate a point can be understood at a faster rate than can a string of statistics or a complicated argument. Martin Luther King, Jr., in his famous "I have a dream" speech, began his address at a slow rate—under 100 words per minute—but as he became more passionately involved in his topic and as his audience responded, he took on a much more rapid pace. The rate should depend on the effect you seek.

Use Pause for Effect

A second vocal characteristic is the **pause**—*a brief silence for effect*. You might begin a presentation with a question or questions: "Have you bought a cup of coffee at a coffeehouse today? [Pause] Have you had two or three? Four or five? [Pause] Do you know what your habit is costing you in a year? [Brief pause] A decade? [Longer pause] A lifetime?" The pause allows each member of the audience to answer the question in his or her own mind.

Another kind of pause—the **vocalized pause**—is really not silent at all. Instead, it is *a way of delaying with sound*. The "ahhhs," "nows," and "you knows" and "whatevers" of a novice presenter are annoying and distracting to most audiences. Unfortunately, even some highly experienced presenters have the habit of filling silences with vocalized pauses. Do not be afraid of silence; most audiences would prefer a little silence to a vocalized pause.

Use Duration for Attention

Duration is *how long something lasts*; in a speech, it can mean how long the sounds last or how long various parts of the presentation last. An anchorperson who says, "Tonight, I am speaking to you from London," is likely to say this sentence by caressing every word but might deliver other parts of the newscast in rapid-fire fashion. Dwelling on the sound of your words can have dramatic impact; the duration gives the words a sense of importance.

Similarly, duration can refer to the parts of a speech: how long you spend on the introduction, the main points, the examples, and the presentational aids. As noted earlier, the duration of most introductions is usually relatively short, the body relatively longer, and the conclusion shortest of all.

Use Rhythm to Establish Tempo

Rhythm refers to *the tempo of a speech*. All the linear arts seem to have this characteristic. A novel or play starts slowly as the author introduces the characters, establishes the plot, and describes the scene. Then the emphasis shifts to the development of the plot and typically accelerates toward a climax, which brings the novel to a close. A musical piece also has some of these characteristics, though music could be said to consist entirely of rhythm.

In a speech, the rhythm usually starts off slowly as the presenter gives clues about who she is and what she is going to speak about. During the body of the speech, the tempo accelerates, with verbal punctuation indicating what is most important. The conclusion typically slows in review as the presentation draws to a close.

We also hear the rhythm of a presentation in words, sentences, and paragraphs. **Alliteration** is *the repetition of the initial sounds of words*. For instance, it is more memorable to say "color, clarity, and carats characterize a good diamond" than to say "brightness, transparency, and weight give a diamond value." Another example of rhythm occurs in sentences when initial words are repeated: "I served my country because I am a patriot; I served my country because I saw it as my duty; and I served my country because its protection is my first concern." Similarly you can achieve rhythm with rhetorical devices, such as antithesis: "Not because I loved Octavius less, but because I loved Rome more."

Use Pitch for Expression

Pitch is *the highness or lowness of a speaker's voice, its upward and downward inflection, the melody produced by the voice*. Pitch makes the difference between the "Ohhh" from earning a poor grade on an exam and the "Ohhh" you say when you see someone really attractive. Avoid the lack of pitch changes that result in a monotone and the repetitious pitch changes that result in a singsong delivery. The best public presenters use the full range of their normal pitch. They know when to purr and when to roar, and when to vary their pitch between the two.

You learn pitch control by constant practice like an actor does. A public speaker rehearses a presentation in front of a sympathetic audience to receive feedback on whether the words are being understood as she intends them. You may not be the best judge of how you sound to others. Therefore, trust other people's evaluations of how you sound. At the same time, speakers should recognize and develop the individual strengths they already have. For example, when you focus on your message, your pitch will support or match what you say. Compare the pitch in your voice when you tell a friend about something amazing to the pitch when you recite the pledge of allegiance.

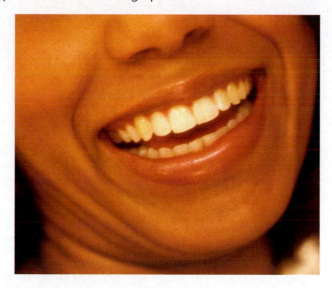

Use Volume for Emphasis

A sixth vocal characteristic of delivery is **volume**, *the relative loudness or softness of your voice.* **Projection** means *adjusting your volume appropriately for the subject, the audience, and the situation.* Variations in volume can convey emotion, importance, suspense, and subtle nuances of meaning. You whisper a secret in conversation, and you stage whisper in front of an audience to signal conspiratorial intent. You speak loudly and strongly on important points and let your voice carry your conviction.

Use Enunciation for Clarity

Enunciation, the seventh vocal aspect of delivery, is *the pronunciation and articulation of words.* **Pronunciation** is *the production of the sounds of a word.* **Articulation** is *the physiological process of creating the sounds.* Because your reading vocabulary is larger than your speaking vocabulary, you may use words in your speeches that you have never heard spoken before. To deliver unfamiliar words is risky. Rather than erring in public, first check pronunciation in a dictionary. Every dictionary, on- and offline, has a pronunciation key. For instance, the entry for the word *deification* in *Webster's New World Dictionary of the American Language* follows:

> **de·i·fi·ca·tion** (dē-ə-fə-ˈkā-shən) 1. a deifying. 2. deified person or embodiment.

The entry indicates that the word has five syllables that carry distinct sounds. The pronunciation key says that the *e* should be pronounced like the *e* in *even*, the *i*'s like the *a* in *ago*, and the *a* like the *a* in *ape*. The accent mark indicates which syllable should receive heaviest emphasis. You should learn how to use the pronunciation key in a dictionary, but you can also hear a word pronounced correctly on several online sources. For example, the Web page found at http://aruljohn .com/voice.pl gives you the option of typing in the word and then clicking on the "hear word" option. This feature is especially useful to students who speak English as a second or third language.

Another way to improve your enunciation is to prolong syllables. Such prolonging makes your pronunciation easier to understand, especially if you are addressing a large audience assembled outside or in an auditorium with no microphone. The drawing out of syllables can be overdone, however. Some radio and TV news announcers hang onto the final syllable in a sentence so long that the device is disconcertingly noticeable.

e-NOTE

Delivery Skill and Production Values in a Newscast

One of the more popular YouTube videos in 2010 was Charlie Brooker's spoof of how the news is produced (search **youtube.com** for "How to Report the News"). Notice how he demonstrates the newscaster's face, demeanor, movement, and gestures. See how he reveals the way the newscaster is supposed to modulate his voice and end his segment with a question. The entire video takes only two minutes, but it is a critical video about how newscasters do their job. Much of the video is about delivery skills run amok.

See Figure 7.2 for some common articulation problems. Articulation errors are so common that humorous stories are often based on them. Many **malapropisms**, or *mistaking one word for another*, are based on articulation errors.

A newspaper article on malapropisms mentioned these:

"Making an obstacle of themselves" for "Making a spectacle of themselves."
"Go for the juggler" for "Go for the jugular."
"He took milk of amnesia" for "He took milk of magnesia."[7]

Addition occurs *when an extra sound is added.* For example, a person says "pic-a-nic" instead of "picnic," "ath-a-lete" instead of "athlete," "real-ah-toor" instead of "realtor."

Deletion occurs *when a sound is dropped or left out of a word.* Examples of deletion are "rassberry" for "raspberry," or "liberry" for "library." Deletion also commonly occurs when people drop the final sounds of words such as "reveren'" for "reverend," "goin'" for "going," or "comin'" for "coming." Finally, deletion occurs when individuals drop the initial sounds of words such as "'possum" for "opossum."

Substitution occurs *when one sound is replaced with another.* For instance, when speakers use the word "git" for "get," "ruff" for "roof," or "tomata" for "tomato," they are making substitution errors.

Transposition occurs *when two sounds are reversed.* College students who call their teachers "perfessor" instead of "professor" or persons who say one "hunderd" instead of one "hundred" are making an error of transposition.

Figure 7.2   **Four common articulation problems.**

Use Fluency for Fluidity

The eighth vocal characteristic of delivery is **fluency**—*the smoothness of delivery, the flow of the words, and the absence of vocalized pauses.* Fluency cannot be achieved by looking up words in a dictionary or by any other simple solution. It is not necessarily very noticeable, except by its absence. Listeners are more likely to notice errors than to notice the seemingly effortless flow of words and intentional pauses in a well-delivered speech. Fluency can be improved and is related to effective communication.[8]

To achieve fluency, you must be confident in the content of your speech. If you know what you are going to say, and if you have practiced the words, then disruptive repetition and vocalized pauses are unlikely to occur.

EYE CONTACT VARIES WITH CULTURE[9]

European Americans tend to use more eye contact than do African Americans when speaking to a white audience, a difference that can lead to misunderstanding. European Americans can misinterpret averted eyes as a lack of respect. African Americans can interpret a European American's more intent eye contact as aggressive or as staring. Some Latin Americans, Southern Europeans, and Arabs tend to stand close and look directly into another person's face. Many people from India, Pakistan, and Scandinavia turn their bodies toward the person to whom they are speaking but avoid steady focus on the other person's face.

cultural NOTE

How Can You Use Your Body to Communicate Effectively?

Eye contact, facial expression, gestures, movement, and physical appearance are five bodily aspects of speech delivery—nonverbal indicators of meaning—that are important to the public speaker. When you observe two people busily engaged in conversation, you can judge their interest in the conversation without hearing their words. Similarly, in public speaking, the nonverbal aspects of delivery reinforce what the speaker is saying. Researchers have found that audiences who can see the speaker, and his or her behavior, comprehend more of the presentation than audiences who cannot (such as those listening by radio or audiotape).[10]

Use Eye Contact to Hold Audience Attention

Eye contact is *the way a presenter observes the audience while speaking.* With experience, individuals become more capable of using eye contact.[11] Audiences prefer the maintenance of good eye contact,[12] and it improves the credibility of the presenter.[13] Eye contact is one way you indicate to others how you feel about them. You may be wary of a person who will not look at you in conversation. Similarly, if you rarely or never look at audience members, they may be resentful of your seeming lack of interest. If you look over the heads of your audience or scan them so quickly that you do not really look at anyone, you may appear to be afraid. The proper relationship between you and your audience should be one of purposeful communication. You signal that sense of purpose by treating the audience members as individuals to whom you wish to communicate a message and by looking at them for responses to your message.

How can you learn to maintain eye contact with your audience? One way is to know your presentation so well and to feel so strongly about the topic that you have to make few references to your notes. A presenter who does not know the material well tends to be manuscript-bound. You can encourage yourself to keep an eye on the audience by delivering an extemporaneous presentation from an outline or keywords.

Other ways of learning eye contact include scanning or continually looking around at your entire audience, addressing various sections of the audience as you progress through your speech, and concentrating on the individuals who overtly indicate whether your message is coming across or not. These individuals usually nod "yes" or "no" with their heads. You may find that you can enhance your delivery by finding the friendly faces and positive nodders who signal when the message is getting through to them.

Use Facial Expression to Communicate

"Facial expression shows how we feel, and body orientation (leaning, withdrawing, turning) expresses the intensity of our emotion."

Another nonverbal aspect of delivery is facial expression, using the eyes, eyebrows, forehead, and mouth for expression. Facial expression shows how we feel, and body orientation (leaning, withdrawing, turning) expresses the intensity of our emotion.[14] Children between 5 and 10 years of age learn to interpret facial expressions, and those interpretations improve with age.[15] Researchers found male/female differences in expressivity and self-regulation, even at six months of age, with males having more difficulty being expressive than females.[16]

Some experts believe that the brain connects emotions and facial expressions and that culture determines what activates an emotion and the rules for displaying an emotion.[17] Presenters who vary their facial expression are viewed as more credible than those who do not.[18] Generally, women use more facial expressions and are more expressive than men; women smile more than men; women are more apt to return smiles; and women are more attracted to others who smile.[19]

Because facial expressions communicate, public presenters need to be aware of what they are communicating. Smiling can indicate both good will and submissiveness. Chimpanzees smile when they want to avoid a clash with higher-status chimpanzees. First-year students smile more than do upper-class students.[20] Constant smiling may communicate submissiveness or nervousness instead of friendliness, especially if the smiling seems unrelated to the presentation's content.

You can practice in front of a mirror, videotape your practice session, or speak in front of friends who will help you. The goal is to have facial expressions consistent with your intent and your message.

Use Gestures to Reinforce Message

Gestures are *motions of the hands or body for emphasis or expression*. Effective use of gestures distinguishes outstanding speaking from the more mundane.[21] Although you probably are unaware of your arms and hands when you converse with someone, they may become bothersome appendages when you stand in front of an audience. You have to work to make public speaking look easy, just as skillful athletes or graceful dancers make their performances look effortless.

Angry workers sometimes appear on television to protest low prices and poor working conditions. Although they are untutored in public speaking, these impassioned people deliver their presentations with gusto and determined gestures. They have a natural delivery because they are much more concerned about their message than about when they should raise their clenched fists. You can deliver the material more naturally if your attention is focused on your message. Self-conscious attention to your own gestures may be self-defeating: the gestures look studied, rehearsed, or slightly out of sync with your message. Selecting a topic that you really care about can have the side effect of improving your gestures, especially if you concentrate on your audience and message.

Gestures differ with the size of the audience and the formality of the occasion. With a small audience in an informal setting, gestures are more like those you would use in ordinary conversation. With large audiences and in formal speaking situations, gestures are larger and more dramatic. In the classroom, the situation is often fairly formal and the audience relatively small, so gestures are ordinarily larger than they would be in casual conversation but not as exaggerated as they would be in a large auditorium.

Another way to learn appropriate gestures is to practice the material in front of friends who are willing to make constructive comments. Actresses and actors spend hours rehearsing lines and gestures so that they will look spontaneous on stage. You may have to appear before many audiences before you learn to speak and move naturally, but with practice, you will learn which natural arm, head, and hand movements seem to help.

Use Bodily Movement for Purpose

The fourth nonverbal aspect of delivery is **movement**, or *what you do with your entire body during a presentation*. Do you lean forward as you speak, demonstrating how serious you are about communicating your message? Do you move out from behind the lectern to show that you want to be closer to the audience? Do you move during transitions in your presentation to signal physically to the audience that you are moving to a new location in your presentation? These are examples of purposeful movement in a public presentation. Movement must occur with purpose. You should not move just to work off your own anxiety.

Always try to face the audience even when you are moving. For instance, even when you need to write information on the board, you can avoid turning your back by putting your notes on the board before class or by putting your visual material on posters. You can learn a lot about movement by watching your classmates and professors when they speak. Notice what works for others (and for you) through observation and practice. Avoid purposeless movement such as rocking back and forth or side to side or the "caged lion" movement in which a presenter circles the front of the room like a big cat in a zoo.

The environment in which you give your presentation helps determine which movements are appropriate. The distance between the presenter and the audience is significant. A great distance suggests presenter superiority or great respect. That is why pulpits in most churches loom high and away from the congregation. A presenter often has a choice about how much to move toward or away from the audience. In the classroom, a presenter who clings to the far wall may appear to be exhibiting fear. Drawing close suggests intimacy or power. Large people can appear threatening or aggressive if they approach the audience too closely, and small people behind large podiums tend to disappear from sight. You need to decide what distances make you and your listeners most comfortable and make you as a presenter most effective.

Wear Appropriate Attire

Clothing and **physical appearance** *(the way a person looks)* make a difference in public speaking situations within and outside the classroom. Following are some suggestions for choosing appropriate attire for the classroom setting:

1. Wear clothing that is typical for your audience, unless you wish to wear clothing that makes some point about your presentation. An international student speaking about native dress could wear clothing unique to her country, for example.
2. Avoid wearing clothing or jewelry that is likely to distract your audience from your message: pants that are cut too low; shirts that are too short; or too many rings in too many places.
3. Wear clothing and accessories that contribute to your credibility, not ones that lower your standing in the eyes of the audience: avoid provocative or revealing clothing.

Public speaking outside the classroom is clearly more complicated because you have to dress for the topic, the audience, and the occasion. Violate audience expectations and they will tend to respond negatively. For example, if you were to wear provocative clothing for a presentation at an assisted-living facility, the audience would likely be distracted from the message by your outfit. When in doubt, ask the people who invited you to speak how you should dress.

Before we conclude this section, we should note that a natural style is important. No one should let public speaking immobilize them; natural instinct is important. If you use many gestures in conversation, you can effectively take it up a notch in public speaking. If you use less bodily movement when you talk, but are very expressive with voice and facial expression, then that may serve you best in public speaking. The information provided in this chapter should enhance, rather than detract from, your natural style.

Question-and-Answer Sessions

Some presentations allow for a question-and-answer session. Even if your classroom speeches do not include a question-and-answer period, you may encounter this format when you speak in other settings. In this section, we offer basic guidelines for preparing for these opportunities and for handling the questions when you are presented with them.

In advance of the question-and-answer period, you should consider possible questions that others might ask. If you have friends or classmates who will listen to your speech beforehand, ask them to pose questions that occur to them. Imagine, too, what a critic might say about your presentation. Once you have determined some of the likely questions that others might ask, prepare thoughtful and thorough responses to the questions. From these answers, practice a succinct response that captures the essence of your rejoinder.

When you actually present your talk, you may be faced with questions that you did not expect. Do not panic. Instead, listen to the question carefully. If the question is not clear, ask the audience member to repeat it or to ask it again in different words. Once you believe you have accurately heard the question, repeat it back to the entire audience: "If I understand you correctly, you are asking about. . . ." This approach will allow all of the members of the audience to hear the question and will also provide you with additional time to formulate an answer.

Even though a question may appear to be antagonistic, do not become defensive or angry. Keep in mind that an audience member has to exhibit a certain amount of courage to ask a question in front of everybody and therefore should be treated with respect. In addition, questions generally signal interest on the part of the audience, which is an indirect sign of a job well done on your part. Be gracious and positive as you respond to what may seem like a critical or hostile question.

Be as truthful and sincere in your answer as you can. Do not be flippant or sarcastic. Do not fabricate an answer if you honestly do not know the answer to the question. Be straightforward and candid in explaining that you simply do not know the precise answer to the audience member's question.

Finally, be aware that some audience members may have a particular agenda. They may have attended your speech to be heard, rather than to listen. If an audience member raises his or her hand to ask a question, do not be surprised if she or he launches into a long anecdote, reports contrary information, or begins to dominate the question-and-answer period. Be prepared to thank that person for his or her comments in a congenial but clear manner, and to move the question-and-answer period to other audience members. As the speaker, you are in charge not only of the presentation but of the question-and-answer period as well.

How Can You Improve Your Delivery?

A student confessed that he had not followed instructions. Told to write a brief outline from which to deliver a speech, the student instead had written out every word. Afraid to speak in front of the class without his manuscript, he practiced by reading it word for word. After rehearsing many times, he wrote the entire speech using a tiny font so it would appear to be delivered from a brief outline on small sheets. However, as he began his speech, he found that he could not read the tiny print so he delivered the whole speech without using any written cues. All the practice had helped him; the small font manuscript had not.

To help you improve your own delivery, you might follow these helpful steps:

1. Start with a detailed working outline that includes the introduction, the body, and the conclusion. Remember to include all main points and supporting materials.
2. Distill the working outline into a speaking outline that includes only reminders of what you intend to include in your speech.
3. Practice your speech alone first, preferably in front of a mirror, so you will notice how much or how little you use your notes. Ideally, you should deliver 80 to 90 percent or more of your speech without looking at notes.
4. Practice your speech in front of your roommate, your spouse, your kids, or colleagues. Try again to maintain eye contact as much as possible. After the speech, ask your observers to explain your message—and seek their advice for improving the speech.
5. Practice your speech with minimal notes in an empty classroom or a similar place that allows you to become accustomed to its size and the situation. Focus on some of the more sophisticated aspects of delivery, such as facial expression, vocal variety, gestures, and movement.
6. Use past critiques from your instructor or classmates to provide direction for improvement on delivery.
7. If possible, watch a videotape of your own performance for feedback. If practice does not make perfect, at least the rehearsal will make you confident. You will become so familiar with the content of your speech that you will focus more on communicating your message to your audience.

For
REVIEW >>

AS YOU READ

1. Identify the qualities of "effective delivery."

2. Think about how you might use each of the four modes of delivery.

3. Relate how context or situation influences the type of delivery you should choose.

4. Identify the functions of both the vocal and nonverbal aspects of delivery in presentations.

SUMMARY HIGHLIGHTS

▶ Effective delivery is presenting a talk by not calling attention to how you say the message.

▶ Four methods of delivery are extemporaneous, manuscript, memorized, and impromptu.
  • The method of delivery that most speech professors prefer for classroom instruction is the extemporaneous mode.
  • The extemporaneous mode allows for minimal use of notes but invites spontaneity and maximum focus on message and audience.

▶ The type of delivery you should choose depends on the situation.
  • The extemporaneous mode of delivery is most commonly taught in the public speaking classroom. The idea is to keep the content flexible enough to adapt to the audience.
  • The memorized mode of delivery is one in which a presenter has committed a presentation to memory. Oratory contests, the lecture circuit, and banquet speeches are common places to find the memorized mode.
  • The manuscript mode is most useful when a presenter has to be precise, must avoid error, and must defend every word.
  • The impromptu mode entails giving a presentation without advance preparation.

▶ The vocal aspects of delivery are rate, pause, duration, rhythm, pitch, volume, enunciation, and fluency.
  • You can orchestrate these vocal characteristics into a symphony of sound and movement attractive to the audience.
  • Use dramatic pause (a planned pause for effect).
  • Monotony and unintended verbal blunders, such as the dreaded vocalized pause, are the enemies of effective delivery.

▶ Nonverbal aspects of delivery are eye contact, facial expression, gestures, movement, and physical appearance.
  • The keys to delivery are naturalness, sincerity, and sensitive responsiveness to the audience.

Pop Quiz

1. Which of the following statements regarding the extemporaneous mode of speaking is *true*?
   (A) The extemporaneous mode allows for very little eye contact.
   (B) An extemporaneous presentation is practiced to the point of memorization.
   (C) The extemporaneous presentation sounds scripted rather than conversational.
   (D) Extemporaneous speaking invites rapid non-verbal response to audience feedback.

2. Writing out the complete presentation and using that text to deliver the speech is speaking using the mode of delivery known as:
   (A) manuscript
   (B) extemporaneous
   (C) impromptu
   (D) memorized

3. Lack of audience analysis and lack of planned research are disadvantages of which mode of speaking?
   (A) memorized
   (B) manuscript
   (C) impromptu
   (D) extemporaneous

4. An advantage of manuscript speaking is that it:
   (A) sounds conversational
   (B) allows spontaneity
   (C) utilizes a keyword outline
   (D) prevents poor wording

5. If you say that sources should be "current, credible, and comprehensive," you are using:
   (A) alliteration
   (B) pronunciation
   (C) a change in pitch
   (D) transposition

6. If you pronounce sophomore as "soph-uh-more," you are committing the articulation error of:
   (A) deletion
   (B) substitution
   (C) transposition
   (D) addition

7. When speaking to an audience, you should:
   (A) look over the heads of your audience
   (B) rarely look at the audience
   (C) scan the audience quickly
   (D) maintain eye contact

8. "You know," "uhhh," and "like" are examples of:
   (A) fast tempos
   (B) vocalized pauses
   (C) changing pitch
   (D) alliterations

9. The smoothness of delivery, the flow of the words, and the absence of vocalized pauses refer to delivery's:
   (A) fluency
   (B) rhythm
   (C) projection
   (D) pitch

10. In question-and-answer sessions, you should:
    (A) become defensive if someone offends you
    (B) criticize foolish questions
    (C) manage overbearing audience members
    (D) use sarcasm

Answers: 1 (D); 2 (A); 3 (C); 4 (D); 5 (A); 6 (D); 7 (D); 8 (B); 9 (A); 10 (C)

APPLICATION EXERCISES

1. Examine the following topics, audiences, and situations and indicate which method of delivery would be most appropriate by placing the letter in the blank. Instead of seeking "correct answers" for these items, you should discuss them with your classmates or teacher and defend your choices based on the message, the audience, and the situation.

   A = Manuscript method   **B = Extemporaneous method**

   C = Impromptu method   **D = Memorized method**

   _____ You have to answer questions from the class at the conclusion of your speech.

   _____ You have to describe the student government's new statement of policy on student rights to a group of high-level administrators in the college.

   _____ You have to deliver the same speech about student life at your college three times a week for 16 weeks to incoming first-year students.

   _____ You have to give parents a "walking tour" of the campus, including information about the buildings, the history of the college, and the background of significant places on campus.

   _____ You have to go door-to-door, demonstrating and explaining a vacuum cleaner and its attachments that you are selling to individuals, couples, and even groups of roommates.

2. The Impromptu Presentation. Practice impromptu speaking in your class to develop the skills of thinking on your feet, telling illustrative stories, and improving delivery. Prepare by placing topics like the ones listed below on single slips of paper from which the speakers each draw a topic as they would select a playing card from a spread in someone's hand. Then each speaker has two minutes maximum to address the topic in front of the class. The best of the presenters stick to the topic and either explain it or develop a narrative about it. The exercise invites you to not only think on your feet but to quickly develop a theme or story from your own experience. Fluency or smoothness of delivery, eye contact, movement, and gesture are other goals for the activity. Here are some possible topics for an impromptu presentation. You and others can think of many more.

   Tell about a person who positively influenced your life

   Reveal your favorite holiday and why

   If you could live anywhere, where would it be and why?

   Where would your dream vacation be and why?

   Do you believe in love at first sight—why or why not?

   What famous person do you most admire and why?

   If you could go back in time, what would you change?

   What do you think are three keys to happiness?

   Describe your ideal home including details

   If you could live in anyone else's shoes for one day, who would it be and why?

   How old should people be to drink or to drive and why?

3. For your next speech, have a classmate, friend, or relative observe and evaluate your speech for delivery skills. Have your critic use this scale to fill in the following blanks.

   1 = Excellent   2 = Good   3 = Average   4 = Fair   5 = Weak

   Vocal Aspects of Delivery

   _____ Pitch: highness and lowness of voice, upward and downward inflections

   _____ Rate: words per minute, appropriate variation of rate for the difficulty of content

   _____ Pause: intentional silence designed to aid understanding at appropriate places

   _____ Volume: loud enough to hear, variation with the content

   _____ Enunciation: correct pronunciation and articulation

   _____ Fluency: smoothness of delivery; lack of vocalized pauses; good pacing, rhythm, and cadence without being so smooth as to sound artificial, contrived, or glib

   Nonverbal Aspects of Delivery

   _____ Gestures: natural movement of the head, hands, arms, and torso consistent with the presenter, topic, and situation

   _____ Facial expression and smiling behavior: consistent with message, used to relate to the audience, and appropriate for audience and situation

   _____ Eye contact: natural, steady without staring, includes entire audience, and is responsive to audience feedback

   _____ Movement: purposeful, used to indicate organization, natural, without anxiety, use at podium and distance from audience

   _____ Physical appearance: appropriate for the occasion, presenter, topic, and audience

KEY TERMS

Addition	Gestures	Projection
Alliteration	Impromptu mode	Pronunciation
Articulation	Malapropism	Rate
Deletion	Manuscript mode	Rhythm
Duration	Memorized mode	Substitution
Enunciation	Movement	Transposition
Extemporaneous mode	Pause	Vocalized pause
Eye contact	Physical appearance	Volume
Fluency	Pitch	

get involved!

As you continue to learn more about public speaking and effecting change, you begin to determine the importance of **making campus connections**. As you completed the exercises for the last chapter, you may have determined that others across the globe share your issue of interest. Now is the time to learn if others across your campus share your concern.

What organizations and groups exist on your campus that might share your issue of interest? Identify all of the groups that exist. Talk with representatives of those that might focus on problems similar to the one that you have identified. If your concern is substantially different from the existing organizations, how can you create a new group? Learn about the guidelines and rules for creating a new group from your school's Web site.

8

CHOOSING
YOUR

In this chapter, you will learn how language functions in a public presentation. This chapter will help you avoid word problems, help you choose the right words, and encourage you to use words ethically.

WORDS

As You READ

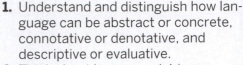

1. Understand and distinguish how language can be abstract or concrete, connotative or denotative, and descriptive or evaluative.
2. Think about how you might use language techniques to clarify meaning and enliven your presentation.
3. Compare and contrast written and spoken language.
4. Describe how you will use respectful and ethical language in your presentations.

Words matter. One reason they do is that what we call things can influence how we think about them. Companies like Walmart that want their employees to feel like valued members of the corporate team call them "associates," for instance, not lowly clerks or cashiers. Researchers who need to establish some distance from the people they study call them subjects and refrain from using their names. Social workers serve clients, not "the poor," and those who use wheelchairs are people with disabilities, not the handicapped. Even the AARP no longer goes by its old name, the American Association of Retired People, since many of its members are only in their fifties and not yet retired.

Words matter, too, when you need to motivate others to work with you and not against you. Consider, for instance, the difference between saying to a fellow team member who's in danger of missing a deadline, "*You* have a problem. What are you going to do about it?" and saying, "*We* have a problem. What are we going to do about it?"

When you speak at work, whether on the loading dock or in the classroom or the boardroom, your words matter. In this chapter you will learn how language works and how to use words responsibly.

How Would *You* Do It?

Refer to the chapter opening story and think about how written and spoken language differ. Select a recent news story from a newspaper or Web site and jot down at least three wording changes you would expect to find in the first paragraph if you heard this story broadcast as a verbal report on the evening news.

Word Power

Language is a powerful symbol system used to organize and classify what our senses detect and to shape thought. We will explore the general characteristics of language to better understand its function in our presentations.

Language Is Symbolic

The 19th-century U.S. American author Nathaniel Hawthorne once said: "Words—so innocent and powerless as they are, standing in a dictionary, how potent for good and evil they become, in the hands of one who knows how to combine them."[1] Like your name, which is a representation of you, words are **symbolic** in that *they represent the concrete and objective reality of objects and things as well as abstract ideas.* Thus the word *computer* conjures up a CPU, monitor, and keyboard, and the words *cellular phone* evoke a small handset and tiny screen.

Language Is Powerful

When words fail, wars begin. When wars finally end, we settle our disputes with words.

—Wilfred Funk[2]

Diplomats, lawyers, mediators, and negotiators use words to solve the world's political issues, business problems, and legal cases. Speakers, broadcasters, PR professionals, and journalists—the world's communicators—love and depend on words. You will learn to love words too as you learn more about how words work. But first you may need to be convinced that words are powerful.

Think, for example, of the old saying, "Sticks and stones will break my bones, but words can never hurt me." Although the statement asserts that sticks and stones can be harmful but words cannot, you may remember children using that saying to fend off the sting of words. Actually, you might agree more that "bones heal, but wounds from words can last forever." You probably remember the words of someone who insulted you, treated you with disrespect, or commented negatively about you in front of others.

Words can cause fights, but they can mend relationships as well. Words like "I'm sorry," "You were right," "I was wrong," and "I did not mean what I said" are mending words. Words like "You did a great job," "I'd hire you any time," and "You have a fine future with this company" are words that most people would like to hear. Words can make you feel wonderful—or awful. Let us see what else words can do.

Words Organize and Classify

Words allow us to organize and classify, to group and cluster individual items into larger, more manageable units. Instead of having to identify every individual thing with a specific word, we cast them into a larger group. So we refer to cars, tables, chairs, houses, cities, states, and countries. We also use words to classify. Imagine you are trying to get your friend to locate someone in a crowd. The conversation might go something like this:

"I just saw a guy from my public speaking class."

"Which one is he?"

"The tall one."

WORD DIFFERENCES

Not all languages share words with similar meanings or even a word at all for some people or things. Until South Koreans were westernized (mostly by movies), they had no word for "kiss" and considered such behavior unhygienic. Laplanders have many words to describe snow, but no generic name like the English *snow.* Brazilian Guarani live among palm trees and parrots and have many words for them, but no generic name for all of them as we do in the English language.[3]

"The blond guy with the red cap?"

"No, the one with a shaved head and sunglasses."

Words quickly allow you to limit your friend's search for your fellow student by gender, height, body type, hairstyle, and accessories.

Your presentations allow you to organize and classify your reality. Examine this excerpt from a talk by varsity basketball player Jason Crawford:

My uncle Johnny grew up in a well-educated family. He moved on to college where he earned a degree in engineering, a profession he pursued to the fullest. This man was alcohol-free the first 23 years of his life. Then one day he decided to pick up a drink. Little did he know that first drink would lead to many episodes down the line.

After a time he became more addicted and became an alcoholic. Johnny found himself driving home from a local bar one night and was pulled over by the police. Unable to function, Johnny decided that he was going to play a little game of cat and mouse. As the police officer approached the car, Johnny sped off. While trying to get away, he crashed into another car, killing two innocent victims. Johnny was also hurt, not physically but mentally. This episode would scar Johnny for the rest of his life. Uncle Johnny is now looking at life from behind bars.[4]

Jason's presentation begins with broad organizational categories—well-educated families, alcoholics, police, and victims—and moves through classifications: an engineer, a nondrinker, a drinker, an alcoholic, an arrest resister, a killer, and a criminal. Your speeches also will use words to organize and classify.

Words Shape Thought

Have you ever thought about how words shape the way you think? We have many more words about war than about peace. D. C. Smith lists some examples: "to beat a hasty retreat," "to get off on the wrong foot," and "to mark time."[5] We have many more words describing violence than describing cooperation. Are we a more warlike culture because our vocabulary reflects more concern for conflict than cooperation?

In *Prometheus Unbound*, Percy Shelley, the English Romantic poet, says of his hero, Prometheus, who gave humanity fire, culture, and science: "He gave man speech, and speech created thought, which is the measure of the Universe."[6]

"Our language determines to some extent how we think about and view the world."

A similar notion comes to us from the **Sapir-Whorf hypothesis**, a theory that suggests that *our language determines to some extent how we think about and view the world.*[7] Apparently having a large vocabulary is not only handy when you take a college entrance examination but also when you try to think of an idea and how to express it. The availability of words for a concept speeds up thought and expression, two vital processes in communication.

Language Grows and Changes

Some words die from lack of use, like "33 ⅓," which refers to the slow speed on a record player (another archaic term). Other words change in meaning, like "gay," which went from meaning "happy" to "homosexual orientation." But our constantly changing language also grows as entertainers, youth, writers, the military, and even gangs add new words to our vocabulary.

In 2008, the *Merriam-Webster Collegiate Dictionary* recognized some of the recent changes in language by introducing more than 100 new words. Here are a few examples, along with the date that the editors found for first use in print.[8]

> "Wing nut"—someone who takes extreme positions politically. The word *wing* refers to *left-wing* or *right-wing*. In use since around 1900, the expression was finally included in the dictionary over 100 years later.

> "Pescaterian" (1993)—a vegetarian whose diet includes fish.

> "Pretexting" (1992)—presenting yourself as someone else to gain private information.

Other terms that made the list included *dirty bomb*, *subprime*, and *supercross*, words used by the military, loan officers, and motorcycle racers, respectively.

What you should know and remember about this section on the organic nature of language is that words die, words are born, and words change over time. Notice also that you and your friends make changes to the language long before the dictionaries catch on. We do not have words for everything, and different cultures and ethnic groups often have words that other groups do not. Think of the language used in your workplace: would someone who does not work there know what you are talking about? The more experience we have together using the same words to refer to the same or similar things, the more likely we are to achieve high-fidelity communication with each other.

Levels of Abstraction

An **abstraction** is a *simplification standing for a person or thing*. The word *building* cannot capture the complexity of engineering, design, plumbing, electrical networks, glass, and steel that make up a "building."

Scholars called **semanticists**, *people who study words and meaning*, thought of a way to envision **levels of abstraction**, *the degree to which words become separated from concrete or sensed reality*. One prominent semanticist, S. I. Hayakawa,[9] introduced the "ladder of abstraction" to demonstrate that words have degrees of abstractness and concreteness. The ladder of abstraction should look like a stepladder. As an example, see Figure 8.1, where the bottom of the ladder, at the most abstract level, is "living being," followed up the steps by "mammal," "omnivore," "human," "female," "teenager," and "Rebekah." Does referring to Rebekah as an "omnivore" seem the same to you as calling her by her own particular name, "Rebekah"?

While **abstract words** tend to be *general, broad, and distant from what you can perceive through your senses*, **concrete words** tend to be *specific, narrow, particular, and based on what you can sense*. At a recent class reunion, a classmate described his current occupation by saying "I'm in transportation," encouraging listeners to perceive him as anything from a pilot to a train engineer to a ship's captain— all of whom are "in transportation"—but the more specific and concrete term, *city bus driver*, turned out to be a more accurate representation.

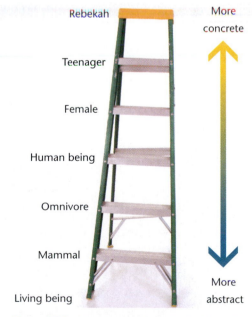

Figure 8.1 **How is Hayakawa's "ladder of abstraction" a useful metaphor for gauging concrete and abstract concepts?**

Audiences respond more predictably to concrete than to abstract language. Consider the broad possibilities of the abstract words as opposed to the concrete words.

Abstract	Concrete
I love sports.	I'm a soccer player.
I drive a late-model vehicle.	I drive a Subaru Outback.
Some foods make me ill.	I'm allergic to milk products.
I use drugs.	I take an aspirin each day.
I'm a homemaker.	I stay at home and raise two children.

The more abstract terminology leaves much more of the meaning to chance. The concrete terms are more likely to evoke the intended meanings in the listeners.

Denotative and Connotative Words

Public speakers need to be aware of the varied meanings evoked by their words. One means of understanding varied meanings is to distinguish between denotative and connotative meanings. **Denotative meaning** is *the direct, explicit meaning or reference of a word*. Keep in mind that dictionary meanings are really a historical listing of how words are used, not necessarily the current meanings. Our everyday use of words can be well ahead of the dictionary meanings.

The denotative meaning of the words *anorexia nervosa* might be "the pursuit of thinness through self-starvation," but to victims, their family, and friends, the term has emotional connotations as well. The **connotative meaning** of a term, *the idea suggested by a word other than its explicit meaning*, portrays "my sister who spent three years battling anorexia while she almost shriveled up and died." Compare in Table 8.1 the denotative meaning with one connotative meaning of several words to help you understand this concept. Notice that you may disagree or agree with the connotative meanings in the right-hand column—that is, words have various connotations for all of us. A practical piece of advice is that in your speeches, you need to consider not only the denotative but also the connotative power of words on your audience.

TABLE 8.1	DENOTATIVE AND CONNOTATIVE MEANINGS OF WORDS	
	DENOTATIVE MEANING	ONE CONNOTATIVE MEANING
Wolf	Wild canine in the dog family	Man who aggressively pursues women
Bigot	Someone who despises people who are different	Someone who despises people that I like
History	A record of human events	A false account of events as depicted by those in power

Communicators who are sensitive to others favor descriptive over evaluative language. **Descriptive language** *attempts to observe objectively and without judgment.* **Evaluative language** is *full of judgments about the goodness or badness of a person or situation.*

Descriptive and Evaluative Language

Descriptive Words	Evaluative Words
High-energy person	A person wound too tight
Expensive automobile	Overpriced, high-maintenance showmobile

You can see why evaluative words can invite trouble, and how descriptive words can help you avoid negative audience reactions. In public presentations, a speaker is wise not to use hot-button terms that cause a strong, negative reaction in the audience because an outraged listener might very well disrupt your entire presentation.

Comparison and Contrast

Speakers often use comparisons and contrasts to clarify their messages. One beginning speaker, when asked to distinguish himself from others in an "I Am Unique" speech early in the course, first compared and then contrasted his appearance to that of others in the class:

Comparison: I then looked at my physical make-up. I am 5'7'' tall, weigh roughly 155 lbs., and have short brown hair. I think I just described 90 percent of the male population at the university.

Contrast: I thought distinguishable marks might help separate me a little. I have over 70 stitches that have left scars, along with two scars from stab wounds. The most distinguishable mark on me is a tribal tattoo on my back, which I had done in England.[10]

A **comparison** *shows how much one thing is like another*; a **contrast** *shows how unlike one thing is from another.* You can use both for clarification for your audience.

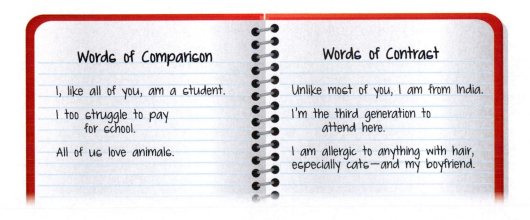

Words of Comparison	Words of Contrast
I, like all of you, am a student.	Unlike most of you, I am from India.
I too struggle to pay for school.	I'm the third generation to attend here.
All of us love animals.	I am allergic to anything with hair, especially cats—and my boyfriend.

"My use of language is part and parcel of my message."

[Theo Van Gogh (1822–1885),
brother of Dutch painter Vincent Van Gogh]

Using the power of language is knowing how to use comparison and contrast for clarifying your intended meaning.

Literal and Figurative Language

Language can be both literal and figurative. **Literal language** *uses words to reveal facts*, whereas **figurative language** *compares one concept to another analogous but different concept*. To say that a fighter hit his opponent 25 times in a round is literal; to say that he fought like a tiger is figurative. Literal language is what you usually find in news reports in newspapers and magazines or text-based news sources on the Internet. Figurative language is found in the lyrics of songs, in poetry, and in feature articles in magazines. The best speakers know how to use figurative language to add succulent spices to an otherwise bland broth of literal language.

Written and Spoken Language

Written and spoken language differ enormously. Table 8.2 highlights these differences. Figure 8.2 gives tips on how language can be used to increase clarity.

Using Language Respectfully

An important aspect of becoming an effective public communicator is to use language respectfully. That is, you need to use words that include people, that do not establish in-group and out-group identities, and that regard people without negative judgment based on ethnicity, gender, sexual orientation, or worldview.

TABLE 8.2 COMMUNICATION DIFFERENCES AMONG SPEAKERS, LISTENERS, WRITERS, AND READERS

	SPEAKER	LISTENER	WRITER	READER
Sentence length	Uses short sentences instead of long ones	Understands short sentences better than long ones	Typically can use longer sentences than a speaker can	Can read long sentences multiple times to achieve understanding
Pace	Sets the pace	Must adjust to pace	Sets no "real-time" pace	Reads at own pace
Repetition	Reiterates ideas to optimize understanding	Needs repetition to catch meanings	Might reiterate ideas to optimize understanding	Rereads if needed for better understanding
Message transmission	Conveys verbal and nonverbal messages	Receives verbal and nonverbal messages	Conveys verbal messages	Receives verbal messages
Feedback and adaptation	Can adapt immediately to feedback	Sends and responds to feedback	Receives no feedback when writing	Sends no feedback while reading

1. Define terms in your speech so your audience will understand the denotative and connotative meanings of your words.
2. Use descriptive language instead of evaluative language to avoid misunderstanding and conflict.
3. Clarify your ideas by comparison and contrast.
4. Use literal language to convey facts and figurative language for creative expression.
5. Spoken language, as opposed to written language, invites shorter sentences, more repetition, and some simplification.

Figure 8.2   **Using words for clarity.**

Use Inclusive Language

Another way to articulate this rule of artful and ethical speaking is to say that you should use **inclusive language**, *language that does not leave out groups of people.* One good principle to follow in public discourse is to call people what they themselves want others to call them. Many of our words for others come from those who dominate in a culture. Since men have dominated North American culture historically, you will find many more derogatory words for women than for men. Additionally, Native Americans did not name themselves "Indians." European explorers gave them that name when they mistakenly thought they had reached India.

"Call people what they themselves want others to call them."

You also can avoid sexist language by using inclusive language. When you consider the list below, can you add several more examples?

Finally, you can increase your chances of being inclusive by avoiding slang, because this type of language often is understood only by certain groups of people. When you use slang, you risk alienating those audience members who are not part of the group that typically is acquainted with those words and expressions.

Sexist	Inclusive
Mankind	Humankind
Manmade	Handmade
Fireman	Firefighter
Mailman	Mail carrier
Chairman	Chair

Use Approved Names

Notice also that the principle says that you should "call people what they themselves want others to call them." Sometimes people within a co-culture call each other by names that are forbidden to people outside that co-culture. Women can call each other "girls," but they probably do not want their employer to call them by that name. African Americans often call each other by names that would be deeply insulting if used by someone else. You are most likely to succeed as a public presenter if you use language that includes, honors, and respects others.

Stereotypes and Differences

The word *stereotype* was first used in 1922 by Walter Lippmann in his book *Public Opinion*. Lippmann borrowed the term from the new machine at the time that printed the same sheet of print over and over, a machine called a "stereotype." Today, **stereotype** has come to mean *the misjudging of an individual by assuming that he or she has the characteristics of some group—that every single individual is just exactly like the others* as in the case of the stereotype machine.

Every campus has more than its fair share of stereotypes about students who study too much, students who study too little, students who are athletes, and students who are more mature than others. We have stereotypes of professors, accountants, and engineers. But public speakers need to avoid stereotypes to avoid offense.

Similarly, you should avoid calling attention to irrelevant differences. When you describe someone as a *female* judge, a *Hispanic* professor, a *woman* doctor, or the city council member *in a wheelchair*, you are emphasizing irrelevant qualifiers about them. The implication might be that people who are female are rarely judges or doctors, that people of Hispanic origin are generally not professors, and that individuals in wheelchairs are typically not elected to city council. Or, even worse, a listener might assume that you do not believe that people from such groups ought to be in such positions.

What Words Should You Use?

You may be wondering what words you can use in your presentations. Try to use words that explain, clarify, and enlighten the audience by following the advice below.

Use Words That Simplify

You will often know more about your topic than do the people in your audience. However, you must be careful not to use language that reduces understanding. This writer, for example, is describing Senator John McCain, Republican from Arizona:

> He would see the heavens fall rather than court Iowa by supporting ethanol subsidies; who, ever an oak, never a willow, insouciantly goes his own way. . . . The media call McCain a "maverick," even though he seems to be, oxymoronically, a predictable maverick.[11]

George F. Will, a Ph.D. from Princeton, is a politically conservative commentator who, nonetheless, attacks many a Republican. His phrase "ever an oak, never a willow" is a clever way to describe the unshakeable McCain, but many readers may have foundered on "insouciantly" and "oxymoronically," which are designed more to highlight Will's high I.Q. than to enlighten his audience. The effective public speaker tries to simplify, to render the words understandable to the audience.

Notice how Andrew Robinson, a physiology major and veteran runner, uses simple, everyday words with lots of concrete, specific detail in this health-related presentation.

> You and your friends decide to play a late night game of basketball. You throw on an old pair of tennis shoes and eight of you head to the recreation center. After you have been playing for forty-five minutes or so, sweat is dripping down your face and back, and you are huffing and puffing from running up and down the court. You get stuck guarding this quick kid who moves instantly from one spot to the next before you can react. He drives toward the baseline with you right on him. As he nears the bottom of the key, he crosses over to his left to get around you. You try to stop, but as you plant your left foot, you feel your ankle roll as pain shoots up your leg, and you fall to the ground.[12]

Andrew was warming up to a speech not about basketball but about selecting the correct shoes for the sport. By the time Andrew finished his speech, with more agonizing stories about painful hips, sprained ankles, and sore toes, he had convinced his audience to discard their "old pair of tennis shoes" and buy shoes dedicated to their sport. He accomplished his purpose with simple, direct words.

Use Substitutions and Definitions

George Will could have substituted simpler words for "insouciantly" and "oxymoronically." He could have said "indifferently" or "uncaringly" instead of "insouciantly," and he simply could have left out the word "oxymoronically," which means contradictory, or two words with opposing meanings, as in "predictable maverick." The skillful presenter chooses words that listeners will understand or defines the terms so they will understand.

Another move toward clarity is to define any language that may seem unfamiliar or potentially confusing to an audience. For example, the term "social justice" could be made clear by describing it as an effort that seeks to establish a society in which basic needs are met and all people flourish.

"The skillful presenter chooses words that listeners will understand."

Use Synonyms and Antonyms

Another method of clarifying a word or concept for an audience is to use **synonyms**, *words that mean more or less the same thing,* or **antonyms**, *words that are opposite in meaning. House* and *home, office* and *workplace,* and *film* and *movie* are examples of synonyms. *Beautiful* and *ugly, dry* and *humid,* and *hired* and *fired* are examples of antonyms. A quick way for you to locate both synonyms and antonyms on the Internet is to access Synonym.com or Thesaurus.com. Both sites are free.

e-NOTE

Synonyms

A **thesaurus** is a source for synonyms; *Roget's International Thesaurus,* for example, has around a quarter of a million synonyms, including thirty-six for the word *thief.* The source is accessible on the Internet at **http://thesaurus.reference.com.**

Reveal the Origin of the Word

The *origin of a word* is called its **etymology**. Often a word's etymology will help an audience remember the term. For example, the word *psychology* means "study of the mind." Psychology comes from the Greek words *psykhe,* which means "soul," and *logia,* which means "the study of."

Telling a more complete story about a word is more likely to make it more memorable. Every dictionary has a brief etymology of the words, but some sources tell a more complete and compelling story. Books by William Safire[13] and by A. H. Soukhanov[14] reveal the stories behind the words, stories that help an audience remember the meaning and the significance of the words in your presentation. Use etymologies sparingly so you do not sound pedantic.

Look up the word *assassin* to see how much of the history of the word the dictionary includes. Do the same for the word *Crusades* to see when they occurred.

try this

Use Words That Evoke Images

An effective speaker uses creativity to paint word pictures in the audience's minds. Many speakers have used the following illustration to help their audience understand the world population:

> If we could shrink the earth's population to a village of 100 people and maintain the existing human ratios, the village would look like this:
> 57 Asians
> 21 Europeans
> 14 from the Western Hemisphere
> 8 Africans
> 51 females
> 70 non-white
> 70 non-Christian
> 80 living in substandard housing
> 70 illiterate
> 50 suffering from malnutrition, and
> 1 with a college education

These words create a picture in people's minds that makes the concept of "world population" more concrete, specific, and easy to understand.

Doug Burch, an army veteran, had these words to say about his eight years in the armed forces. Notice how his words create images in your mind about his experience:

> I have traveled to and from different countries and have seen the most glorious sunsets. I have watched the sun rise one too many times after being up all night. I have sailed around the Spanish Isles and snorkeled among its reefs. I have shared stories and drink with dockhands along the way. I have sat in pubs and bars with strangers who do not speak English and have tried to carry on a conversation. I have learned about many cultures, and that just because ours is one of the most advanced does not mean it is the best. I am starting to feel unique because I have learned about life, and I can still smile.[15]

Colorful words create vivid images in our minds.

Use Correct Grammar

The way you talk affects your credibility with an audience. Paula LaRocque, writing for *The Quill*, says:

> Language misuse ranks high in terms of the negative reaction and irritation it can elicit from people. Most people give considerable value to their native language and their perceptions of its proper use. Thus, people who mis-utilize language are often accused of maiming, massacring, brutalizing or butchering it. Society's inherent understanding of being civilized apparently means, in part, the ability to communicate well with grace, accuracy and without offense.[16]

Bad grammar is much like having a bit of spinach in your front teeth: Everyone sees that spinach, but nobody bothers to tell you it is there. Outside your speech class you are unlikely to encounter anyone, including your boss, who will actually say, "We are holding you back from responsible management positions because you constantly misuse the language." Nonetheless, consistent correct use of language gives a speaker credibility because other people assume the person is educated. See Figure 8.3 for some common grammatical errors.

Use Repetition

Repetition, *repeated sounds*, has striking effects in speaking because the audience gets caught up in the cadences, or rhythms, of linguistic structure. Usually, repetition is accompanied by increased volume, increased energy, and increased forcefulness as the repeated forms build toward some climactic ending.

Incorrect	Correct
He (or she) don't	He (or she) doesn't
You was	You were
I done it	I did it
Between you and I	Between you and me
I been thinking	I've been thinking
I've already took algebra	I've already taken algebra
We seen it	We saw it
Him and me went	He and I went

Figure 8.3 **Common grammatical errors.**

Adapted from *Public Speaking for College and Career*, 5th ed. by Hamilton Gregory, 1999. Used by permission of McGraw-Hill.

Observe how repetition works in this speech by Chris Meek, an engineering student and co-owner of Combat Creek Paintball:

> Do you want to get involved in America's fastest growing sport?
>
> Do you want to get involved in a sport in which size, age, and even sex make no difference?
>
> Do you want an ultimate stress reliever in which communication and quick wits make the difference between winning and losing?
>
> Then I have the sport for you, an adult version of capture-the-flag—paintball.[17]

Using repetition makes your speech easier to remember, makes your speech more energetic, and makes your speech more memorable.

Alluring Alliteration

Alliteration *means the repetition of an initial consonant.* Professional speakers use alliteration because repeated sounds make words memorable. "The Fabulous Facts about Foster Care" was Lacey Schneider's title. She began her speech by saying "Before I begin my fact-filled speech about fabulous foster care. . . ."[18] All those repeated "F" sounds are alliteration. Also used in advertising, repeated sounds attract attention and help listeners to remember.

Figure 8.4 on the next page summarizes ways that words can be used to add to the audience's experience of a presentation.

Using Words Ethically

Author Aldous Huxley said, "Thanks to words, we have been able to rise above the brutes; and thanks to words, we have often sunk to the level of demons." You already know that one of the central ethical issues in the use of language in speeches is to acknowledge through oral footnotes the use of another person's words. Violating that rule can result in a failing grade for the class or even expulsion from most colleges and universities. You might be less aware that words themselves can be used unethically. Three examples here will illustrate the point: (1) exaggeration, (2) oversimplification, and (3) perspective taking.

Exaggeration and Oversimplification

Another word for exaggeration in language is **hyperbole** (hi-PURR-bull-ee), which is *a kind of overstatement or use of a word or words that exaggerates the actual situation.* To call a relatively normal fire "the biggest conflagration this city has ever seen" is an example. The ethical speaker exercises care in describing events, people, and situations. You should use vivid, concrete language as long as the words do not overstate or exaggerate. In the heat of a persuasive speech you might be tempted to state your side of the issue with exaggerated or overstated importance.

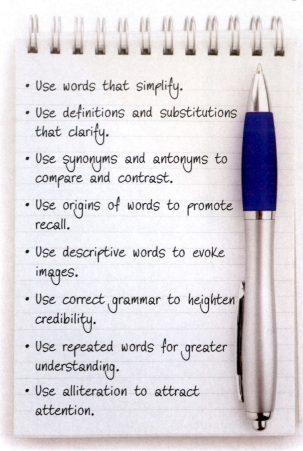

Figure 8.4 **Words to use in your presentation.**

- Use words that simplify.
- Use definitions and substitutions that clarify.
- Use synonyms and antonyms to compare and contrast.
- Use origins of words to promote recall.
- Use descriptive words to evoke images.
- Use correct grammar to heighten credibility.
- Use repeated words for greater understanding.
- Use alliteration to attract attention.

- Avoid exaggeration.
- Avoid oversimplification.
- Recognize that your language reveals your perspective.

Figure 8.5 **How to use words ethically.**

A second ethical error in language is **oversimplification**, *describing a complex issue as a simple one*. Political campaign speeches are full of examples. The candidate for the senate says, "We'll solve this crime problem with more prisons." The candidate for the state house of representatives says, "No new taxes." And the candidate for governor says, "Welfare reform!" Bumper sticker slogans rarely solve problems, and neither do sound bites. The ethical speaker tries to examine issues thoroughly, states them as descriptively as possible, and provides sound reasons for why the audience should adopt a certain position on the issue without exaggeration or oversimplification.

All of us use and misuse words with alarming frequency. Can you learn to use words so they have the effect you seek instead of drawing an unexpected negative response that forces an apology? The purpose of this chapter is to make you thoughtful about the words you use.

Language and Perspective Taking

Your words reflect your **perspective**, *your point of view or perception*. The words you choose in public speaking indicate to others how you see the world, whether you intend them to or not.

Imagine you are giving a speech about taxation. If you choose to talk about "rich people," "poor people," and "middle-class people," you are using language that divides America into economic classes. That is a particular perspective. If you talk about the "struggling young people" and "the Social Security set," you are dividing Americans by age—another perspective. Talk of the "marriage penalty" and high taxes on single wage earners divides the adult population into those who are married and those who are not. No matter how you discuss the issue, you use language that indicates your perspective.

How is this concept related to ethical speaking? Consider the connotations of the words that you can use to describe individuals who earn over $100,000 annually: "top 10 percent in income," "rich people," "wealthy individuals," "fat cats," or "privileged class." Each description indicates a perspective, but some of them—like the last two—indicate a medium to strong negative connotation that may or may not be fair to high-earning individuals. In other words, the words you choose can indicate prejudice, bias, or unfairness toward individuals or groups. Figure 8.5 lists three ways to make sure you use words ethically.

try this

Given your own worldview or perspective because of who you are, you should try to think of individuals or groups that your own words tend to treat less than fairly. For example, how do you refer to a person in a wheelchair, a refugee or immigrant, or individuals from a culture other than your own? To learn more about the importance of understanding others' points of view, type the term "perspective taking" into a search engine and review several of the results.

ASIAN AND HISPANIC: "BAGGY LABELS"

People in the United States use some terms for others that are *baggy labels* because the words try to include too much: *the words are so abstract, so unspecific, that they are not highly useful.* The word *Asian*, for example, refers to people from Japan, India, Malaysia, China, Thailand, Pakistan, Bangladesh, Cambodia, and Vietnam; people who are Muslim, Christian, Buddhist, Hindu, and many other religions; and people who have every possible skin color. All of these varied people, the biggest population groups in the world, we lump under the label "*Asian.*" Similarly, the word *Hispanic* is a baggy label that refers variously to European Americans (e.g., Spanish), "Indians" (another misnomer) who originally inhabited South and Central America, Cubans, Puerto Ricans, Mexicans, and practically anyone else who speaks Spanish and lives in North or South America. What should we call people? **The best advice is to call people what they like others to call them.**

Tips for Using Language in Presentations

Here are four practical suggestions for managing the words in your presentation.

1. *Choose language at a level that is appropriate for the specific audience.* Speak with a level of formality that is right for the audience and the situation. Nearly always, the language of public speaking is elevated above that which you would use on the street or in conversation with close friends. You might call it enlightened conversation.

2. *Choose language that the audience will understand.* Words the audience cannot comprehend might impress the audience with your vocabulary, but they neither inform nor persuade. If you must use words that the audience is unlikely to understand, then define, explain, or provide examples.

3. *Choose language consistent with yourself, the topic, and the situation.* If you do not normally use legal or medical terms, you will feel and look uncomfortable using them in a presentation. Your language needs to fit the topic and be consistent with your level of knowledge and experience. Using overly dramatic words unwarranted by the topic constitutes exaggeration; understating complex problems indicates a lack of analysis. The situation or occasion may dictate a certain kind of language—you don't speak the same way in a mosque, synagogue, or church as you do at a football game.

4. *Choose language that meets high ethical standards.* Choose words that neither exaggerate nor oversimplify. Recognize that words reflect a perspective. Avoid language that offends others because of their race, sex, sexual orientation, or physical or mental disability. Your task is to inform, persuade, or entertain, not to offend.

For >>
REVIEW

AS YOU READ

1. Understand and distinguish how language can be abstract or concrete, connotative or denotative, and descriptive or evaluative.

2. Think about how you might use language techniques to clarify meaning and enliven your presentation.

3. Compare and contrast written and spoken language.

4. Describe how you will use respectful and ethical language in your presentations.

SUMMARY HIGHLIGHTS

▶ Language operates at different levels of abstraction with specific, concrete words evoking more targeted meanings.

▶ Words have denotative and connotative meaning; they describe or evaluate and make judgments.

▶ Words can be literal (based on facts) or figurative (based on fancy).

▶ Use words that simplify, use substitutions and definitions, use synonyms and antonyms, know the origins of words, use words that evoke images, use correct grammar, and use parallelism and repetition.

▶ Tips for using language in a presentation:
  • Choose language at a level appropriate for the specific audience.
  • Choose language consistent with yourself, the topic, and the situation.
  • Choose language that meets high ethical standards.

▶ Spoken language and written language differ from each other.
  • Spoken language tends to use shorter sentences and simpler words.
  • The spoken word is personal because the speaker is part of the message in a way that an unseen and unheard author is not.
  • The spoken word offers multiple ways of communicating a message through words, movement, gestures, facial expressions, and voice inflection, whereas the written word looks pretty much the same on the screen and on paper.

▶ Avoid problems with your words by using language respectfully, which includes calling people what they wish to be called and choosing inclusive language.

▶ You can use words ethically by:
  • Avoiding exaggeration and oversimplification.
  • Understanding that language always emerges from a perspective.

Pop Quiz

1. What does "language is symbolic" mean?
   - (A) Words allow us to cluster individual items into larger units.
   - (B) Words are powerful.
   - (C) Words determine how we think about the world.
   - (D) Words represent the concrete and objective reality of objects as well as abstract ideas.

2. A theory that suggests that our language determines to some extent how we think about and view the world is called the:
   - (A) semantic theory
   - (B) Sapir-Whorf hypothesis
   - (C) ladder of abstraction
   - (D) Hyperbole theory

3. Which of the following terms is the *most concrete*?
   - (A) mammal
   - (B) carnivore
   - (C) Shih Tzu
   - (D) male

4. The denotative meaning of a term is:
   - (A) the idea suggested by a word other than its explicit meaning
   - (B) full of judgments about the goodness or badness of a person or situation
   - (C) the direct, explicit meaning or reference of a word
   - (D) general, broad, and distant from what you can perceive through your senses

5. How is spoken language different from written language?
   - (A) Spoken language uses longer sentences than the written language.
   - (B) Written language needs to repeat phrases so the reader can catch meanings.
   - (C) Written language is affected by feedback.
   - (D) Spoken language conveys verbal and nonverbal messages.

6. Labels such as "policeman" or "chairman" are not:
   - (A) inclusive
   - (B) concrete
   - (C) literal
   - (D) descriptive

7. "Exciting" and "exhilarating" are examples of:
   - (A) substitutions
   - (B) antonyms
   - (C) synonyms
   - (D) stereotypes

8. An overstatement or use of a word that exaggerates the actual situation is termed:
   - (A) oversimplification
   - (B) hyperbole
   - (C) etymology
   - (D) alliteration

9. In presentations, you should choose language that:
   - (A) is above the formality level that is appropriate for the audience and situation
   - (B) is made up of large vocabulary words
   - (C) exaggerates concepts
   - (D) is consistent with you and the topic

10. By revealing a word's origin, you are revealing its:
    - (A) alliteration
    - (B) hyperbole
    - (C) etymology
    - (D) synonym

Answers: 1 (D); 2 (B); 3 (C); 4 (C); 5 (D); 6 (A); 7 (C); 8 (B); 9 (D); 10 (C)

APPLICATION EXERCISES

1. Translate the abstract terms in the column on the left into more concrete terms in the blanks on the right.

   Now examine each of the words you have placed in the blanks and place a check after each one that may be a poor choice because it skews the audience's response in a negative or unduly positive direction. In other words, the word lacks honesty and accuracy.

   a. A recent article   _____

   b. An ethnic neighborhood   _____

   c. A good professor   _____

   d. A big profit   _____

   e. A distant land   _____

   f. A tough course   _____

   g. A tall building   _____

   h. He departed rapidly   _____

   i. She dresses poorly   _____

   j. They are religious   _____

2. Examine the words in the column on the left. Write in the blank after each word its denotative meaning and its connotative meaning. Remember that the denotative meaning is a descriptive definition; the connotative meaning is the feeling or emotion evoked by the term. In the columns to the right of letters f., g., and h., add three words and establish denotative and connotative meanings for each.

	Denotative Meaning	Connotative Meaning
a. Girl	_____	_____
b. Terrorist	_____	_____
c. Environmentalist	_____	_____
d. Developer	_____	_____
e. Senator	_____	_____
f.	_____	_____
g.	_____	_____
h.	_____	_____

3. Using any sources available, see if you can find the story behind the word or phrase.

   a. O.K.

   _____

   _____

   b. Trojan horse

   _____

   _____

   c. Baby boomers

   _____

   _____

   d. Eye candy

   _____

   _____

   e. Curse of the Bambino

   _____

   _____

KEY TERMS

Abstraction	Descriptive language	Perspective
Abstract words	Etymology	Repetition
Alliteration	Evaluative language	Sapir-Whorf hypothesis
Antonym	Figurative language	Semanticist
Comparison	Hyperbole	Stereotype
Concrete words	Inclusive language	Symbolic
Connotative meaning	Levels of abstraction	Synonym
Contrast	Literal language	Thesaurus
Denotative meaning	Oversimplification	

get involved!

Your audience can remember you and your words better if you follow your speech with a handout or brochure that repeats and possibly illustrates your main points. Here is an example adapted from the University of Scranton's Best Practices in Service Learning[1]:

> Best Practices for Reflection
> Reflection means thinking about and seeing the relevance of civic engagement through service learning. The "best practices" for reflection include but are not limited to:
> 1. Students should participate in planning the service-learning experience.
> 2. Students should see how the service-learning project relates to course objectives.
> 3. Students should be encouraged to think about the project in different ways that reflect their different learning styles (visual, auditory, etc.)
> 4. Students should thoughtfully reflect on the service-learning project before, during, and after the experience.
> 5. Teachers should provide continual feedback to encourage critical thinking.

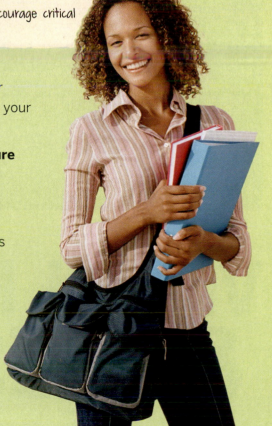

Your handout should be simple and direct with photos or images, not just lots of text. For ideas on how to develop your own brochure, visit these online sources:

http://microsoft.com/education/persuasionbrochure /mspx details how to create a brochure using Microsoft Publisher.

http://btc.montana.edu/CERES/html/MarsQuest /Quemarsbrochure/html is Montana State University's guidelines for creating a brochure for an organization or group.

http://www.servicelearning.org/resources /index.php is the Web site of the National Service-Learning Clearinghouse, a site that has plenty of information on Best Practices.

[1] http://academic.scranton.edu/department/cps/ service_learning/best_practices.shtml is the site from which the sample handout, above, was adapted.

VISUAL RESOURCES & PRESENTATION

Stimuli bombard us from the time we wake up until the serenity of sleep envelops our consciousness. Even when we are asleep, vivid—and sometimes frightening—visual imagery permeates our subconscious mind. Indeed, images captivate and inspire, all the while evoking emotions ranging from fear to exuberance. In this chapter, you will learn how to create and integrate visual imagery and other sensory aids into your presentation.

TECHNOLOGY

As You READ

>>

1. Clarify why sensory aids are important to presentations.
2. Identify how information can be made more vivid by graphs, tables, and charts.
3. Think about how you might incorporate visual aids into your presentations, such as objects, handouts, videos and audio, slides and overheads, and even other people.
4. Practice generating various types of visuals by hand and by using software such as PowerPoint.

A dora Svitak is a literary giant and not even in high school. By the age of seven Adora had already published a book sold internationally, and now, at the age of twelve, she is in high demand to speak in front of teachers to help them understand how to instill reading and writing skills in children. Adora reads and writes at a level eclipsing most adults. Her grasp of language is enviable. Adora's body of work as a writer, teacher, and speaker shows that age is less important than determination in predicting success.

A presentation by Adora is posted on TED, an online site with speech videos from influential speakers with "ideas worth spreading." You can find Adora's speech at http://www.ted.com/talks/lang/eng/ adora_svitak.html. In her presentation, Adora develops the argument that adults are constrained by their own socially created conventions of rational thought. Adora argues that children are different because they have the "audacity to imagine." She further notes that adults tend to inhibit children from learning because they "don't trust them" and restrict them to learning in the way that adults think children should learn. Her speech is insightful, and it illustrates how our "adult" ways of speaking, teaching, and communicating likely result in less creative and less interesting ideas.

Watching Adora's speech, her point was explicitly illustrated by the visual aids that she used. Although Adora used a computer and projector to display her visual aids, she did not use lists of bullets on PowerPoint slides like those you see every day in classrooms and business meetings. Rather, Adora presented creative visual imagery and cleverly designed textual messages to add interest, variety, and emphasis. If you take a few minutes to view her presentation you will see that visual aids do not need to be confined to predetermined PowerPoint templates. A little creativity and attention to aesthetic design can enhance presentations in ways that make conventional PowerPoint-type presentations look as contemporary as mullets and mood rings. This chapter teaches you about the use of visual aids, both the conventional and, following the advice of Adora Svitak, the more creative.

How Would *You* Do It?

For a speech in which you want to use a visual aid, how could you design a visual image to illustrate both holistic and detailed information about your topic?

How You Can Benefit from Using Sensory Aids

Even inexperienced speakers can guess that good presentations consist of more than just the speaker talking. One way to enhance any presentation is to use **sensory aids**, which are *resources other than the speaker that stimulate listeners and help them comprehend and remember the presenter's message.* Although sensory aids can appeal to any of the five senses, the most common ones stimulate sight. These **visual aids** are *any observable resources used to enhance, explain, or supplement the presenter's message.* They include pictures, diagrams, charts, graphs, video, and even demonstrations by actual people. In fact, some might argue that presenters are always visual aids for their messages because they use nonverbal messages to enhance their verbal statements. Nonvisual sensory aids can include music, touchable materials with different textures, and even food—with its pleasant aroma and good taste.

You have many good reasons to use sensory aids in your presentation. First, people learn better through **dual coding**, *the use of words accompanied by other sensory stimuli.*[1] Because people learn through each of their senses—seeing, hearing, touching, tasting, and smelling—presentations that use more than one sense can open a completely different channel through which learning can occur.

Create a list of the most effective visual aids that you have seen teachers use. What do you remember about these visual aids? What made them effective in your opinion? Do you feel that you learned from them?

try this

Second, people remember information better when they use sensory aids. Researchers have found that after listening to presentations in which visual aids are used, audience members remember approximately 85 percent of the content three hours later and 65 percent of the content after three days.[2] The same presentation without visual aids results in lower recall. Audience members remember only 70 percent of the information after three hours and only 10 percent of the information after three days. The lesson of this research is simple: using a visual aid can have a significant impact on whether audiences remember your message.

Third, in addition to helping audience members learn and remember information from your presentation, sensory aids hold their attention and motivate them to listen.[3] Because we think much faster than others talk, much of our mental energy is wasted anticipating or daydreaming during presentations when the speaker talks the entire time. By using sensory aids you are better able to build interest and maintain audience members' attention.

Finally, effective sensory aids result in clearer messages. Using a picture or model to illustrate a complex idea can do wonders to help audience members understand your point. Moreover, by taking time to carefully locate or create your sensory aids, you will likely gain valuable knowledge that will help you explain the concept more effectively. In short, sensory aids have the potential to dramatically improve your presentation.

Types of Visual Aids and Other Sensory Resources

Because the technology has become so accessible, presenters have grown to rely on computers as a primary resource for visual and sensory aids. Of course, other options—posters, music, videos, and even handouts—still exist. This section discusses when to use each type.

Electronic and Multimedia Resources

Computers are particularly useful for presenting **multimedia materials**, which are *digital or electronic sensory resources that combine text, graphics, video, and sound into one package.* Of course, not every multimedia presentation combines all these elements. Presenters commonly use computers to show text and images to the audience; using the computer to present video and sound is less common, although the use of YouTube and podcasts are certainly becoming a viable option for many speakers.

A variety of methods can be used to present multimedia material using a computer and projector or large-screen display. The most common approach is to use Apple's Keynote or Microsoft's PowerPoint. However, as illustrated by Adora Svitak's speech on the TED Web site, viable and perhaps more effective alternatives are emerging. In this section you will learn about two types of programs available to you. Slide-deck programs like PowerPoint and Keynote are discussed first, and holistic design programs, like Prezi, are discussed second.

Slide-Deck Programs

Slide-deck programs like Microsoft's PowerPoint and Apple's Keynote are similar because they rely on a series of slides. *Like cards in a deck, you can arrange slides in a particular order and then display those slides to the audience.* Your job as a speaker is to determine the content on each slide and then arrange the order of slides to fit your presentation. The content of slides can vary widely, although most slides tend to be one of six types: text, tables, charts, flowcharts, pictures, and multimedia. Before discussing the general advantages and disadvantages of the slide-deck approach, we will first explore examples of these types of slides.

Text Slides

How many times have you been in a class where the teacher shows one "bullet" list after another? Are those classes more exciting because of the colorful slides with text? Or not? Were you able to take notes more effectively because of them? Did the teacher seem more spontaneous or more restricted because of the slides? These questions

Collecting Survey Data

- Surveyed 8 people at work
  - 5 males
  - 3 females
- Average age was 26.75 years old
- Respondents spent average of
  3.75 hours per day online

Figure 9.1   **Text slide with bullet list.** Text slides help emphasize key ideas and provide details for audience members.

highlight the dilemma presenters face when deciding whether or not to use a substantial number of text slides in their presentation. Simply defined, a **text slide** *relies primarily on words and phrases to show audience members information.*

Figure 9.1 shows how text can be arranged on a slide, in bullet form, to highlight important concepts. If you recall the survey data reported about use of mobile Internet devices in Chapter 5, the bullet slide summarizes the process used to collect data.

Text slides do some things well and other things not so well. Research consistently demonstrates that when written messages accompany oral information, as when text slides are used, people tend to remember the information more easily; however, research also suggests that written messages do little to motivate and inspire listeners.[4] Because too many text slides can actually be distracting for the listener, you should avoid using more than a few during your presentation; you are better off limiting their use to your most important or most difficult information. When using text slides, placing information into "bullet points" is often more effective than using paragraphs and complete sentences. Second, make sure that you spend enough time explaining each point on the slide. Listeners become frustrated if you spend too much time on one bullet and ignore others. Finally, avoid placing extraneous information on your slides. Extraneous material can distract or even confuse listeners, thus counteracting any advantage of using the visual aid in the first place.

Tables

Tables *use text and/or numbers to efficiently summarize, compare, and contrast information.* When you insert a table into PowerPoint, you will need to know in advance the number of columns and rows that you need—including any rows or columns for headings and labels. For that reason, we recommend that you draw a rough sketch of your table so that you know the exact dimensions before you attempt to create it on the computer.

Practice making a table by sketching out the rows and columns necessary to compare and contrast the right for people to assemble, speak freely, and practice their religious preferences in China, Mexico, and the United States. When creating your table, you will need to create headings for your rows and columns to clearly distinguish the topics being organized.

try this

Figure 9.2 **Table comparing mobile Internet device use by males and females.** Tables efficiently summarize, contrast, and compare information.

Mobile Internet Device Use by Males and Females

	Males	Females
Droid	3	0
iPhone	1	0
iPad	1	2
netbook	0	1

Tables combine text and numbers to allow comparisons. The mobile Internet device data from Chapter 5 was used to create the table shown in Figure 9.2. Notice how the table allows easy comparisons between males and females' use of mobile Internet devices.

When using tables, practice discussing the information. As you can tell from the sample table, these types of slides contain a great deal of information, and presenters often underestimate the amount of time necessary to explain them adequately. Limiting your tables to key information and making them well organized can help you explain them more efficiently. As a rule of thumb, plan on spending about two minutes discussing tables.

Charts

Charts are *useful for visually displaying quantitative or statistical information.* Recall from Chapter 5 that numbers and statistics are most commonly used to describe things, show relationships, and show differences. The bullet list slide and table shown previously are useful for describing things; charts are more effective at showing relationships and differences. Using the mobile Internet device survey from Chapter 5, the following charts could be created.

1. *Bar and column charts.* **Bar and column charts** typically *illustrate differences between categories of information.* In the example shown in Figure 9.3 you can see the average time spent online by Droid, iPhone, iPad, and netbook users. In this case the column chart provides a quick and clear visual indication of that information.

Figure 9.3 **Column chart showing hours online by device.** Column charts help illustrate differences in categories.

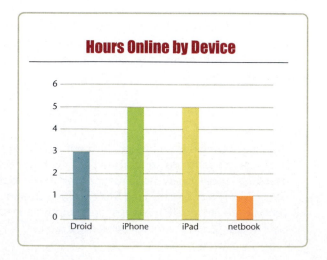

Hours Online by Device

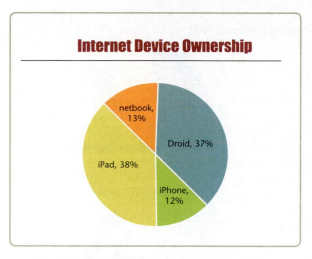

2. *Pie charts.* **Pie charts** are *used to show percentages of a whole.* In the mobile Internet device data, we know that a total of eight people responded to the survey. The pie chart shown in Figure 9.4 shows the percentage of people who owned each type of device. Information used to create this pie chart came from Figure 9.2.

3. *Line charts.* **Line charts** *show trends in quantitative data.* Line charts could be used to show trends over time. For example, you could plot the number of Internet users each year for the past twenty years to show how Internet use has consistently increased each year. A special type of line chart is called a **scatterplot**, which *plots related values on an X–Y axis and then creates a line showing how those values are related.* Figure 9.5 shows a scatterplot using the mobile Internet device data. Each person's scores for both "hours per day on the Internet" and age were plotted on the chart. If you look at the plots and connect them with a line you see that younger respondents tend to be online more than older respondents.

Flowcharts

Flowcharts are *diagrams that represent a hierarchical structure or process.* Flowcharts might be used to illustrate various positions within a company or organization. For instance, the organizational flowchart in Figure 9.6 shows the leadership positions within a student club. You might also use a flowchart to represent a

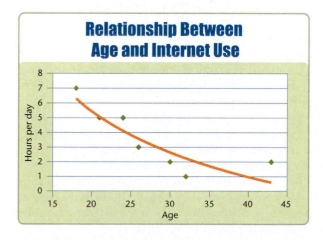

Figure 9.5   **Scatterplot showing relationship between age and Internet use.** A scatterplot is a specialized type of line plot used to show relationships between values.

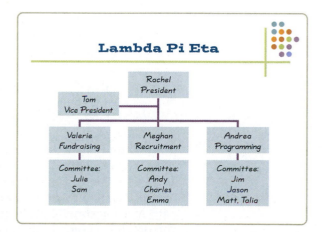

Figure 9.6   **Organizational flowchart for Lambda Pi Eta, the communication studies honor society, sponsored by the National Communication Association.**

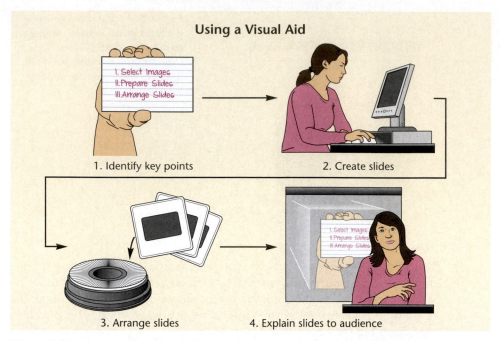

Figure 9.7 **A process-oriented flowchart showing use of a visual aid.** Flowcharts help audience members learn step-by-step actions.

process, as in the example illustrating how to use a visual aid during a presentation. This type of flowchart is illustrated in Figure 9.7.

Pictures

Presentations are often enhanced by using pictures to show audience members objects, places, and even people being discussed. However, most public speaking teachers warn students that passing pictures around during a presentation is not a good idea because the activity becomes very distracting. Moreover, most pictures are so small that not everyone can see the picture if it is held by the speaker. Fortunately, PowerPoint is an easy way to display pictures so that everyone can see them.

Presenters have three basic options for using PowerPoint to display pictures. First, many pictures are available via the Internet. For instance, you can use Google.com to search for pictures related to keywords associated with your topic. Remember that using a picture from the Internet is just like using a quotation—you must credit the source for the picture. Another option is to use a digital camera to take a picture. With the price of digital cameras plummeting to less than a hundred dollars, finding someone with access to one is relatively easy. Finally, if you have conventional photographs and access to a scanner, you can scan photos directly into PowerPoint. If you are unfamiliar with how to work with pictures in PowerPoint, we recommend that you ask your instructor for the location of a lab or resource person on campus. Remember that if you need to find or take pictures for use during your presentation, you will need to build extra time into your preparation process.

Regardless of what type of picture you want to show—photos, computer-generated graphics, or even drawings—the methods of inserting the pictures into PowerPoint remain the same. You can even use PowerPoint to create very basic pictures. Figures 9.8 and 9.9 show two slides used by José, a second-generation "mainlander" of Puerto Rican descent, in a presentation about his grandfather's unit in World War II. The first figure combines the crest of the 65th Infantry Regiment with text that briefly explains the history of the unit. The second picture shows the places his grandfather traveled to during his time in the service.

Multimedia

Presenters have traditionally used videotape to present full-motion video during their presentations. Of course, this option still exists, and most digital projectors

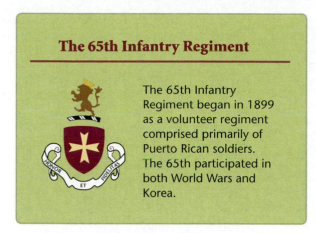

Figure 9.8   A picture combined with text in PowerPoint.

Figure 9.9   A picture used as a visual aid.

can accommodate input from a VCR or DVD player. However, incorporating video into PowerPoint is easy, and if the clips are short (which they should be), there are advantages to using PowerPoint to display the video. Gaining access to digital video is easy if you have a digital camcorder or if you have a video converter attached to your computer. Digital camcorders are still somewhat expensive but digital video converters are typically less than $100. Many campuses have multimedia computer labs equipped to convert standard videotape to digital video.

Once you have digital video, incorporating the video into PowerPoint is no different from incorporating a picture. When you play the slide and use the mouse to click on the video, the clip will play automatically. The advantage of using PowerPoint to play the video is that you do not have to worry about switching the projector from PowerPoint (the computer) to the VCR and back again. Also, by creating and editing the digital video, you have complete control over how long the clip is and what the audience is able to see.

Students and teachers are commonly using YouTube and other online video sources during presentations. Remember that using a video is no different than using any other type of Internet-based information: You must take care to ensure accuracy and give proper credit to sources.

General Tips on Using Slide-Deck Programs

Although PowerPoint and similar programs have been available to speakers for decades, relatively little research exists to document how to best use computer-generated presentation aids to promote recall and attitude change. However, a recent study conducted by researchers at the University of Central Florida provides evidence that PowerPoint is, indeed, beneficial. In that study, several groups of students watched a speech where PowerPoint was used and were compared to a control group that viewed the same speech without PowerPoint.[5] The groups viewing the speeches with PowerPoint remembered more than the group viewing the speech without PowerPoint. Of those who viewed the speech with PowerPoint, participants remembered more when the bullets on each slide were shown all at once rather than one at a time using a "build" transition effect.

"Having so many slides that you cannot possibly talk intelligently about any of them is a problem many presenters face."

Much more research must be done to fully understand the effects of PowerPoint and other computer-generated presentation aids in speeches. Until such research has been accomplished, the following suggestions might help you avoid some of the most common PowerPoint blunders (blunders that can happen with any computer presentation software).

1. *Don't overload the number of slides.* Having so many slides that you cannot possibly talk intelligently about any of them is a problem many presenters face. The ease with which we can create slides often makes including "one more" too tempting. As a general rule of thumb, you should not have more than one slide per minute. One slide every two minutes is an even better average.

2. *Don't overload any one slide.* The number of words, figures, or pictures on one slide should not exceed the amount a person can process in 30 seconds. As a practical matter, a maximum of four or five lines of text is a good rule to follow.

3. *Use a large type font.* Slides should never use less than a 28-point font. Smaller type fonts are difficult to see for people sitting more than a few rows back. Also, you should stick to fonts like Times, Courier, or Arial rather than fonts based on script or handwritten typefaces, which are harder to read at a distance.

4. *Select colors with contrast.* Although PowerPoint provides many options for preset templates, take care to use coloring schemes that allow for substantial contrast between text and the background. Also take care when creating graphs and charts so that lines, bars, and pie pieces effectively contrast with the background. Keep in mind, too, that dark slides shown in a darkened room can lull audience members to sleep!

5. *Avoid unnecessary images and effects.* Using too many clipart images or several fancy animation schemes can cause your presentation to appear shallow. Allowing PowerPoint slides to draw attention away from you, the presenter, is a common mistake made by inexperienced speakers. Your message, rather than the PowerPoint slides, should be the centerpiece of your presentation.

6. *Have a backup plan.* Computers fail, files get lost or corrupted, and projectors sometimes do not turn on. Most teachers will expect you to be prepared to make your presentation on the day assigned regardless of whether PowerPoint is cooperating. Taking time to print slides and copy them onto color transparencies is wise.

7. *Do not read slides to the audience.* Inexperienced presenters often forget that the audience can read. Reading text to the audience is time wasted in a presentation. Explaining points on a slide, providing conclusions that should be drawn from information on a slide, and talking about how the information on the slide bolsters your central idea and main points is a much more valuable use of time.

8. *Use blank slides to hide your presentation.* One rule, which we discuss later, is that visual aids should not be visible when you are not referencing them. PowerPoint seemingly makes this difficult because you do not want to turn the projector on and off during the presentation. However, you can easily insert blank slides between slides with content, so that a blank background is being displayed when you are not specifically referencing slides. Of course, these blank slides do not "count" toward the 1–2 slides-per-minute rule.

9. *Practice, practice, practice.* This suggestion is certainly not new, nor will this be the last time you read it. Yet, the importance of practicing your presentation takes on new urgency with the use of PowerPoint. Besides becoming used to the technology, you will want to determine how long you will need to explain and analyze each slide that you present.

POWERPOINT, LINEAR THINKING, AND BREAKING THE MOLD

Cultural critics have long argued that traditional Western views on rhetoric have emphasized an overly linear progression of ideas during presentations. In this instance the term "linear" is used with some negative connotation, because it implies that information is given in an overly simple and predictable manner. As noted by researchers Ian Kinchin, Deesha Chadha, and Patricia Kokotalio, PowerPoint reinforces this linear approach. As they point out, the use of bullet slides in a relatively linear sequence not only presents information in a linear way, but also segments related ideas across slides. They suggest that to break out of the cultural tendency toward linear thinking teachers and presenters should use PowerPoint in more dynamic ways. For instance, rather than emphasizing bullet lists, focus on models of interactive processes, show visual images that can allow listeners to arrive at multiple meanings, and use concept mapping to show how experts would envision interrelationships among ideas. PowerPoint does much to reflect our cultural comfort with linear thinking, but can also do much to challenge those cultural norms by helping listeners approach ideas from multiple perspectives and meanings.

SOURCE: Kinchin, I. M., Chadha, D., & Kokotalio, P. (2008). Using PowerPoint as a lens to focus on linearity in teaching. *Journal of Further and Higher Education, 32,* 333–346.

Slide-deck programs are common, easy to use, and improve speeches if used effectively. However, these types of programs have disadvantages. Slide-deck programs like PowerPoint and Keynote force the speaker and audience to adapt to a very linear progression of isolated facts, concepts, and ideas. Because each slide is separate from the others, a sense of the whole is lost and information can easily become decontextualized. Think of how often you have become lost when a teacher gets twelve or even twenty slides into a class lecture using PowerPoint! Slide-deck programs also give you very little control over the aesthetics of your presentation. You are gen-

erally limited to the templates and layouts built into the program. In essence, you are forced to adapt your presentation to the way Microsoft and Apple programmers built the software rather than using it as a tool for your own creativity.

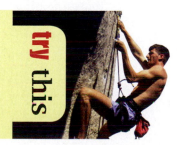

try this

Develop a sensory/visual aid plan for your presentation. Start by listing the number of content slides you intend to use. Then, identify how many blank slides you will need so that all content slides are visible only when you are talking about them. How many slides should you create in total for your presentation?

Holistic Design Programs

Whereas PowerPoint and Keynote emphasize the linear progression of discrete ideas, **holistic design programs** *allow you to work from a broader picture down to specific ideas and back again.* Think of these types of programs as giving you a zoom button for ideas. You start with a big picture, zoom in to view details, fly from one detail to the next, and zoom out to see the big picture again. You have probably done this before, but in a different context. As a child did you ever take a magnifying glass out to explore your yard? Using that simple tool you were able to explore dimensions from the broad to the micro—think of how different that experience is in comparison to a slide-by-slide PowerPoint. Like a magnifying glass, holistic programs add the dimension of depth. Rather than moving through ideas, you move into ideas.

These types of programs are very new. Although more and more are emerging, the one we have had the most experience with is Prezi, which can be found at Prezi .com. Prezi is a Web-based program that allows you to create "Prezis," which allow you to present ideas using depth and simple animation. This sounds complicated, but Prezi is, in many ways, easier to use than PowerPoint and Keynote. Students and faculty can obtain free accounts to experiment with and use Prezi. Showing you an example of a Prezi here is impossible because printed books cannot illustrate movement "into" ideas. For now, you should take time to visit Prezi's Web site and watch several of the showcase examples to get a better idea of what they look like and how they might be used to enhance presentations. Also, if you watched the speech by Adora Svitak mentioned at the beginning of the chapter, you saw Prezi in action. Although we are still experimenting with how to best use Prezi during presentations, here are some tips to start:

1. *Think about design.* The exciting potential of Prezi is that the program allows you to make greater use of visual appeal. Communication researcher Dale Cyphert recommends that you use visual images to create a larger visual narrative supplementing your spoken words.[6] Although PowerPoint and Keynote can be adapted for this purpose, Prezi seems more up to the task. For example, you can use Prezi to create a virtual landscape of your ideas. As you walk audience members through the landscape you narrate what they should learn from what they see. Although Prezis are programmed to follow a linear progression of images, they also easily depart from that script so that you can adapt to audience questions or highlight images out of order. In that sense, the Prezi design allows you to break away from the linear script if necessary.

2. *Emphasize the visual.* PowerPoint and Keynote are visual aids; ironically, they are most commonly used to present words to the audience. In our own

experience with Prezi we have been drawn more toward using images and less toward using bullet points and text. Take time to think about various types of visual images, sometimes augmented with labels and other text, to emphasize ideas and help you tell a story.

3. *Think about the big picture.* Our biggest concern with slide-deck programs is that they isolate ideas. Prezi allows the holistic picture to drive presentations. For example, much like the details you discovered about your yard with the magnifying glass, you can use Prezi to embed details and other information inside a larger image related to your topic. Use that feature to help your audience remain aware of the big picture of your speech before delving into details.

Prezi and other holistic presentation programs provide an exciting alternative to PowerPoint and Keynote. Prezi is not perfect. Some aspects of Prezi's design options are limited, and the process of creating a Prezi is different from slide-deck-based programs. However, if you take time to learn this option for multimedia presentations you will be on the cutting edge and can approach your use of visual aids in ways that are more dynamic and engaging for audience members.

Other Visual and Sensory Resources

Computers have become very popular tools for use in presentations. Now let's look at other options available to you as a presenter for incorporating visual and sensory aids. Of course, the decision on which type of visual/sensory aid to use should be determined by your specific objective for the presentation. You should avoid using the chalkboard/dry erase board or hand-drawn posters because these types of visual aids often lack professionalism and detract from your credibility as a presenter.

Yourself as a Visual Aid

When presenting on topics with which you have significant personal experience, you are often your best visual aid. Amelia, a public communication student, was a black belt in the martial arts and used herself and a friend to demonstrate simple self-defense techniques. Because her presentation described actions and "moves," such personal demonstration was necessary. Amelia even asked for volunteers from the audience to practice several of the techniques as the presentation progressed.

When you use yourself as a visual aid you are essentially performing a narrative of your experiences for your audience. Amelia, for example, performed a personal narrative of how she learned martial arts as she enacted different moves and behaviors for the audience. When performing your personal narrative, you do have some unique ethical obligations toward your audience. As explained by one scholar, there is a "reportability paradox" with any personal narrative: If the personal narrative is easy to tell it may lack credibility and authenticity with the audience—that is, they may not believe the narrative to be absolutely true.[7] To successfully blend reportability and credibility, speakers must carefully merge their own story or narrative with a more abstract explanation of others' experiences. So, for example, when telling about learning martial arts Amelia may need to focus on broad principles of how one learns and interject her own experiences as affirming or counter illustrations of those principles. This balance of particular and universal narratives should be considered whenever you use yourself as a focal point in a presentation, whether you are acting as a visual aid or simply telling a story.

Objects

Any type of physical object can be used as a visual aid. When presenting a speech on percussion in rock music, David set up a drum set to show different pieces of equipment used by modern drummers. Teachers throughout the building were particularly impressed with the solo performed for his attention-getter. Other objects could include tools, historical artifacts, equipment used to play sports, devices like a hand-held computer, or water and air filters for the home.

Presenters sometimes pass objects around during their presentation. Although this approach can provide a memorable experience for audience members, you should avoid passing around valuable or breakable objects. Also, remember that objects will not reach all audience members while you are referencing them unless you have several of them. Jamie effectively used this approach during her presentation on the geology of the Flint Hills region of Kansas. She passed around several (10 or more) rocks with fossils. After showing how to identify the fossils, Jamie pointed out that the fossils provided evidence that Kansas was once a thriving seabed. Each audience member was able to see—and feel—what Jamie was talking about because she had nearly enough objects so that each audience member could look at them during her description. Be sure to check with your instructor before planning to pass around objects— some instructors discourage their use because audience members may become distracted.

Use common sense when selecting objects for use in your speech. You should never bring potentially dangerous objects like live animals or weapons. Audience members are always uncomfortable during presentations with live snakes, fencing swords, knives, and firearms. Depending on the expectations of your university, other objects might also be inappropriate. For instance, would displaying a condom be considered acceptable or unacceptable at your university or in your particular classroom? This question reinforces the importance of audience analysis—visual aids require careful forethought on your part about the audience and the situation.

"Use common sense when selecting objects for use in your speech. You should never bring potentially dangerous objects like live animals or weapons."

Models

Sometimes bringing an actual object is not feasible. Very few classrooms can physically accommodate whales, nuclear submarines, cars, homes, cities, ancient ruins, or wind farms. In such cases, a model might be a better option. **Models** are *scaled representations of an actual object or objects.* You encounter models all the time in classes. Rarely do anatomy and physiology students get to play *CSI* on a cadaver; however, models of the human body commonly populate these classrooms. Do you remember the tried-and-true science fair project of building a working volcano out of clay, baking soda, food coloring, and vinegar? These types of models can be both informative and interesting for audiences.

Locating or preparing a model can take a great deal of time and models may be very expensive. Taking time to plan well in advance is therefore necessary for this approach. Even the decision to make your own model (say of a city or of a rainforest ecosystem) is very time consuming. Allow at least a week to plan and prepare such visual aids.

Audio and Video

Computers offer a number of options for finding and playing audio and video. If your classroom does not have a computer or if the computer cannot play your files, you must find other means. And, sometimes it is just more practical to avoid using PowerPoint. Taking time to prepare a PowerPoint presentation when all you want to do is show a 30-second clip from a TV show would be a poor use of your time. Of course, if you intend to use PowerPoint regardless, adding the clips to your PowerPoint file makes sense.

Audio and video can effectively spice up a presentation when used correctly. Joel gave an informative presentation on Led Zeppelin's influence on modern rock and effectively used short clips of songs to introduce unique aspects of Led Zeppelin's music. Joel took care to use only short clips and tried to play instrumental sections of songs so that he could still speak over the music. In her presentation on the formation of black holes, Kim used a short clip from a documentary by astrophysicist Stephen Hawking to explain how black holes are detected.

Avoid using more than a few clips throughout your presentation, and limit the clips to 20 or 30 seconds. Plan in advance how you intend to play the clips. If your classroom is equipped with a DVD player, make sure you know how the unit works—classrooms are often set up differently from your home entertainment system. If you intend to use audio, make sure that you can find a way of playing the clip so that everyone can easily hear the sound.

Slide Transparencies

Although slide transparencies are becoming increasingly outdated because of computer technology, professionals in fields like the sciences, history, and theater often use slides to display pictures and photographs. Other professors might have such resources available if you do not have slides of your own. Trey, a theater major, showed slides obtained from his lighting design professor to illustrate lighting concepts used during the previous theater season at his university. You should follow many of the same suggestions we provided for using PowerPoint if you intend to use slide transparencies.

Handouts

Handouts helped Sally convince audience members to attend a "Race for the Cure" walk held to raise awareness about breast cancer. She provided listeners with information about the event and also gave them the Web address for the American Cancer Society. In this case, handouts helped Sally make direct appeals to the audience for their support for breast cancer prevention.

However, presenters must plan carefully when using handouts. Detailed notes and lengthy, technical information can distract listeners from the actual message. Even the act of passing materials around can be distracting for both the presenter and the listener. Hand out materials either right before or right after the presentation. Regardless of when you distribute materials, make sure that you reference them during your presentation. For instance, "The pamphlet that I passed around before identifies the location where the rally will take place," and "At the end of my presentation I will provide you with a flier identifying the Web address for the American Cancer Society" are ways to effectively reference your handout while speaking. You should also consider asking one or two members of the audience to pass out the materials so you can concentrate on your presentation.

Tips on Using Visual and Sensory Aids

Now that you can identify several options for using visual and sensory aids during your presentation, you should devote particular attention to using them effectively and ethically. This section provides tips and advice for integrating visual and sensory resources into your talk.

1. *Be audience-centered when selecting sensory aids.* When presenting a persuasive presentation on the need to eliminate "junk mail," Katherine passed around several perfume and cologne samples found in popular magazines. Several of the audience members were overwhelmed by the smells—nearly to the point of having to leave the classroom. Katherine unwittingly caused some of the annoyance that she was trying to argue persuasively against. Remember to think like an audience member when selecting sensory aids for your presentation.

2. *Be ethical.* Using inappropriate, dangerous, or unpleasant sensory aids can detract from your message and destroy your credibility. Indeed, presenters have an ethical responsibility not to use or display dangerous, obscene, or offensive materials. Some teachers require that you get approval for all sensory resources used during your presentation. Even if your teacher does not require formal approval, a short discussion about your plans could help you avoid problems when you give your presentation.

3. *Keep the content of your sensory aid clear and relevant.* Although you are responsible for explaining all visual and sensory aids, most should be easily understood by audience members after a few moments of reflection. Remember that irrelevant sensory aids can do more to confuse, rather than enhance, your presentation.

4. *Explain your visual aids.* The time spent carefully crafting a chart or graph is wasted if you do not explain what the graph means. Presenters often fail to explain what conclusion should be drawn from visual aids. Even pictures should be explained well enough so that audience members understand what they represent. Seeing well-done visual aids and not getting appropriate explanation is frustrating for listeners.

5. *Understand that using sensory aids takes time.* Besides the significant time involved in locating and/or creating sensory aids, such resources take time during the presentation. A 7-minute presentation can easily become a 15-minute presentation with the addition of three or four detailed visual aids. Though different types of sensory aids take different amounts of time to explain, allowing at least two minutes for the presentation and explanation of sensory aids is wise.

6. *Avoid being too simple or too complex.* Sensory aids should be professional, but they should not overwhelm the message. Hand-drawn posters, lists of ideas on the chalkboard, or hastily created PowerPoint slides cause your presentation to appear unprofessional and insincere. Likewise, trying to use every feature in PowerPoint, including animated transitions and the ever-popular "machine gun" sound for list builds, may be entertaining in your dorm room at two in the morning but will do little to impress audience members. Special effects can even be annoying if used to the extreme.

7. *Strive for professionalism.* Take care to ensure that your visual aids are easy to read. If you use audio and/or video, make sure that the audio is loud enough to be heard easily and that the video is of the highest quality possible. Practicing your talk with the sensory aids is essential for giving a professional-looking presentation.

8. *Hide your visual aid when not in use.* Whether you are using an object, PowerPoint file, or even another person to help you demonstrate something, do your best to display the visual aid only when necessary. Asking your partner to step to the side of the classroom, placing the object behind the lectern, or using blank slides in PowerPoint are all ways you can accomplish this. Audience members might be tempted to look at the visual aid rather than at you if you do not remove the temptation.

How might your use of visual or sensory aids differ for the following types of audiences?

- A group of very young children
- A group of international visitors who speak English as a second language
- A group of college students

try this

Remember Your Purpose

Although it is an important skill, using visual and sensory aids is secondary to your main goal of communicating with audience members—such aids are simply one of many means to that end. Remember that your use of visual and sensory aids should not take the place of effective delivery, attention to organization and style, and good research. Presentation aids are just that—they supplement the message that you have already created. Your presentation is likely to be better with them than without them, but good visual aids will do little to make up for an otherwise poorly done presentation.

If you opt to use visual or sensory aids, make sure you use them to full advantage. Using PowerPoint to display several bullet points is less effective; using something like Prezi to enhance your narrative is more effective. Think about the design and aesthetics of your sensory aids to obtain the greatest impact. This is exactly the principle advocated by Adora Svitak in her speech on creativity mentioned at the beginning of the chapter.

For
REVIEW >>

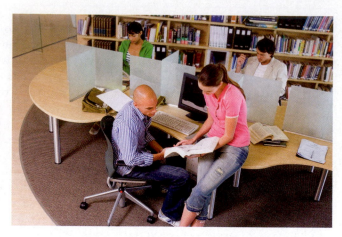

AS YOU READ

1. Clarify why sensory aids are important to presentations.

2. Identify how information can be made more vivid through graphs, tables, and charts.

3. Think about how you might incorporate visual aids into your presentations, such as objects, handouts, videos and audio, slides, and even other people.

SUMMARY HIGHLIGHTS

▶ Sensory aids improve presentations because they help listeners learn more and stay more involved with the message.
- Sensory aids are resources other than the presenter that stimulate listeners. The most common type is visual aids.
- Sensory aids improve presentations because people learn better from multiple media, they are more motivated to listen, and they perceive your message more accurately.

▶ With a computer and digital projector you can use PowerPoint to display a variety of types of visual and sensory aids.
- Text slides use words and phrases to provide audience members with information.
- Tables combine text and numbers to efficiently present information. They are particularly useful when you want to compare and contrast two or more things.
- Charts efficiently display pictures of quantitative data. Bar or column charts, line charts, and pie charts are among the most common types of charts.
- Flowcharts are diagrams that represent a hierarchical structure or process.
- By using images from the Internet, a digital camera, or a scanner, you can easily integrate pictures into your PowerPoint slides.
- Audio and video can be integrated into your PowerPoint presentation by using a digital camcorder or a digital converter attached to a computer. Audio and video clips should be short.
- Use holistic programs like Prezi as an alternative to slide-deck-based programs like PowerPoint.

▶ Based on your topic, consider using objects or scaled models to illustrate things you are talking about.

▶ If appropriate, use yourself as a visual aid by demonstrating some skill, action, or behavior for the audience.

▶ Although you should generally avoid using handouts because they can be distracting, handouts can provide audience members with key "takeaway" information.

▶ Use multimedia like video and audio to illustrate and accentuate points, but plan carefully for how you will use them.

4. Practice generating various types of visuals by hand and by using software such as PowerPoint.

▶ Slides should be clear, easy to read, and simple. Have a backup plan in case your PowerPoint file cannot be used, and concentrate on preparing and delivering an effective presentation rather than relying on "PowerPoint pizzazz" to impress your audience.

▶ Create visual aids that are professional and help clarify and highlight your message.

Pop Quiz

1. The use of words accompanied by other sensory stimuli is called:
   (A) stimuli
   (B) sensory aiding
   (C) confirmatory explanation
   (D) dual coding

2. A slide that relies primarily on words and phrases to show information is a:
   (A) table
   (B) text slide
   (C) flowchart
   (D) pie chart

3. When using text slides, you should:
   (A) use as many slides as possible
   (B) let the slide speak for itself; there is no need to explain the slide
   (C) use paragraphs and complete sentences
   (D) avoid placing extra information on the slides

4. Charts used to illustrate the differences between categories are:
   (A) pie charts
   (B) line charts
   (C) bar charts
   (D) flowcharts

5. Ryan wants to show how the sale of VHS tapes decreased over time. Which type of chart would best illustrate this trend?
   (A) bar chart
   (B) line chart
   (C) flowchart
   (D) pie chart

6. To represent the organizational hierarchy at her job, Marcy should utilize a:
   (A) pie chart
   (B) line chart
   (C) flowchart
   (D) bar chart

7. One tip to follow when using Microsoft Power-Point is to:
   (A) use blank slides to hide your presentation
   (B) use as many slides as possible
   (C) use as many words, figures, or pictures on a slide as will fit
   (D) read the slides to the audience

8. J. R. wants to give his speech on the topic of karate. Which sensory aid would best illustrate different karate positions?
   (A) charts
   (B) J. R. as a sensory aid
   (C) models
   (D) transparencies

9. What is one guideline to follow when using visual and sensory aids?
   (A) Be speaker-centered.
   (B) Avoid explaining the visual aid.
   (C) Be very simple.
   (D) Hide your visual aid when not in use.

10. Which statement about using visual and sensory aids is *false*?
    (A) Visual and sensory aids are secondary to your main goal.
    (B) Your presentation is likely to be better with visual aids.
    (C) Use of visual aids can take the place of effective delivery and organization.
    (D) Presentation aids should supplement the message.

Answers: 1 (B); 2 (B); 3 (D); 4 (C); 5 (B); 6 (C); 7 (A); 8 (B); 9 (D); 10 (C)

APPLICATION EXERCISES

1. Practice creating a PowerPoint presentation that integrates pictures from the Internet. Assume that your task is to create a short, five- to seven-minute presentation on your university for new students. Using PowerPoint and your university Web site, locate and integrate pictures and graphics that you could use in your presentation. Remember that the source of each graphic should be identified on the slide where it is used—you can use a text box to create the reference.

2. Using the following data, create an appropriate graph or table to use during a presentation. You may have enough data to create more than one graph or table:

   A poll conducted by a nonprofit group attempted to determine differences in people's perceptions about crime depending on whether they watched more or less than 20 hours of television per week. Those who watched more than 20 hours per week were labeled as high-rate viewers, and those who watched less than 20 hours per week were labeled low-rate viewers. Results of the poll found that 30 percent of the low-rate viewers perceived crime to be increasing whereas 81 percent of high-rate viewers did. When broken down by age, high-rate viewers over the age of 35 had the highest percentage, believing crime to be on the rise, with 87 percent, followed by high-rate viewers under 35 with 75 percent, low-rate viewers under 35 with 32 percent, and low-rate viewers over 35 with 28 percent. When asked to comment on their perceptions, high-rate viewers typically responded with something like, "Crime is everywhere—you see it every night when you turn on the news." Low-rate viewers typically responded, "I feel safe in my neighborhood—I know everyone and we look out for each other."

3. A necessary skill when creating text slides is identifying key information so that the number of text slides can be limited. Create one or more text slides using the information covered in the sections "General Tips on Using Slide-Deck Programs" on pages 209–211, and "Tips on Using Visual and Sensory Aids" on pages 216–217.

KEY TERMS

Bar and column charts

Charts

Dual coding

Flowcharts

Holistic design programs

Line charts

Models

Multimedia materials

Pie charts

Scatterplot

Sensory aids

Slide-deck programs

Tables

Text slide

Visual aids

get involved!

Traditional approaches to using visual aids involve finding visual materials—pictures, graphics, figures, etc.—created by others and integrating those into your presentation. Because digital cameras are so inexpensive and easy to use, you should now feel more empowered to create your own visual aids. For this activity, use a digital camera to take pictures on your campus or in your community that illustrate something about your presentation. For instance, if your speech is about consumption and waste, you might ask to take pictures at a local landfill or at the dumpsters behind a student apartment complex. If your speech is about medicine, you could ask a local hospital if you could take pictures in the hospital. You should take care to get permission before entering any private property to take pictures, and you should obtain written permission from any people prominently displayed in the picture before using their image in your presentation.

After taking the pictures, develop a plan for how you will incorporate them into your presentation. For each picture, develop a few points that you want to convey to explain what the picture is showing and what audience members should learn from the image. If you would like to see examples of how pictures can be used to advance social causes, view Ellen Shub's Web page at:

**http://photography.ellenshub.com/Common/
commonpage.php?gallery=socialActivism**

To learn more about the ethical and legal responsibilities surrounding the use of photographs, visit these sites:

http://www.photosecrets.com/tips.law.html

**http://www.uky.edu/PR/UK_News/Sept_6_2004/
photo_consent.html**

10

PRESENTING

You know a great deal of useful information and you have a number of useful skills. As you learn more in college and in life, you may find yourself communicating your knowledge to your children, colleagues, clients, or community. The purpose of this chapter is to examine the primary means of communicating information to other people: the informative presentation.

TO INFORM

As You READ

>>

1. Apply the principles and purposes of informative presentations to a topic you are considering for your informative presentation assignment.
2. Identify how you will incorporate the principles of learning into your presentation to optimize its effectiveness with your audience.
3. Reflect on the ethical dimensions of an informative presentation.

With box office receipts approaching $3 billion worldwide, James Cameron's multimillion-dollar fantasy *Avatar* (2009) is the highest-grossing film of all time. It earned nine Oscar nominations, showcased revolutionary special effects technologies, delighted critics and audiences everywhere, and spurred talk of a sequel. It also appears to have changed Cameron's life forever.

Although he has been an avid environmentalist for many years, Cameron was drawn to take more direct action following the film's success as a result of a trip he made to the Amazon jungles of Brazil, which inspired *Avatar*'s faraway environment. The 55-year-old director was determined to use his fame and *Avatar*'s global popularity to draw attention to the plight of a real Amazonian tribe facing a threat to its preindustrial way of life. The Brazilian government's plans to build the world's third-largest dam will flood hundreds of miles of the Amazon area and parch nearby land along the Xingu River, where a number of indigenous communities live.

Cameron is determined to stop the dam, calling on Brazil's president to reconsider the project and planning return trips with *Avatar* cast members to continue the meetings with tribal leaders

that he has already begun. He calls the dam a "quintessential example of the type of thing we are showing in *Avatar*— the collision of a technological civilization's vision for progress at the expense of the natural world and the cultures of the indigenous people that live there."

How would you prepare an informative speech about the dam, its potential effects on Brazil's native peoples, and Cameron's efforts to help them? Rather than taking a position on the issue and supporting it, try to learn as much as you can about the project. You will probably find that it is multifaceted and not easy to summarize. In this chapter you'll learn how to consider questions like this one and how to use the answers to prepare an effective informative presentation.

How Would *You* Do It?

Refer to the chapter opening story, and think about the possible purpose of an informative presentation about James Cameron's efforts to block the Brazilian dam. Which of the four purposes in the chapter do you think is most appropriate to this topic?

Principles of Informative Presentations

Two fundamental rhetorical principles should guide your informative presentations. These are *to relate the presenter to the topic* and *to relate the topic to the audience*. Although they are important to any presentation, these principles require special emphasis in informative presentations because they focus on the relationships between the presenter and the topic and the audience and the topic. Audiences are more likely to listen to a presentation if (1) they believe the speaker is well informed and connected to the topic, and (2) the information is relevant to them.

Relate the Presenter to the Topic

The first rhetorical principle states that you, the informative presenter, must show the audience the relationship between you and your topic. What are your qualifications for speaking on the subject? How did you happen to choose this topic? Why should the audience pay particular attention to you on this issue?

Here is an example of how one student related his topic to himself:

> You heard the teacher call my name: Gary Klineschmidt. This is a German name. My grandparents came from Germany, and the small community in which I live—New Ulm—is still predominantly German with a full allotment of Klopsteins, Kindermanns, Koenigs, and Klineschmidts. Many German customs are still practiced today in my home and in my hometown. Today I want to tell you about one German custom that has been adopted by many Americans and two German customs that are practiced primarily by people of German descent.

The presenter established a relationship between himself and his topic by stating explicitly the origins of his authority to speak on German customs.

Pat Sajak, the host of *Wheel of Fortune*, gave an address at Hillsdale College in Michigan. He related the topic to himself as he noted,

> I, of course, attended Game Show University. All the great game show hosts did. I lived in the Bob Barker Dorm. I majored in vowels and consonants. It was a tough program. In the *Jeopardy* course, I had to know the questions instead of the answers. My thesis was called: "Lovely Parting Gifts: Are they really all that lovely?" Of course, the upside was that if I got stumped during finals, I was allowed to use 50/50 or phone a friend.[1]

The point is that you must relate the topic to yourself, so that the audience will respect and apply the information you communicate. Are you giving a presentation on the steps in ethical decision making? Let the audience know about your involvement with the Boy Scouts of America. Are you giving a presentation on historic preservation? If you are a student at SUNY Plattsburgh, you might talk about your involvement with Adopt-a-Block. Are you giving a presentation on the path to U.S. citizenship? At Cal State Northridge, you might share your experience with Project S.H.I.N.E., which links college students with older immigrants and refugees who hope to learn English and become U.S. citizens.

Relate the Topic to the Audience

The second rhetorical principle of informative presentations is to relate the topic to the audience early in the presentation to ensure their interest and understanding. Again, you must be explicit: specifically tell listeners how the topic relates to them. Remember, too, that many topics may be very difficult to justify to an audience. An informative presentation on taxes is lost on an audience that pays none. An informative presentation on the farming of genetically modified food could be lost on an urban audience. Analyze your audience to find out how interested they may be in your proposed topic.

This example demonstrates the rhetorical principle of relating the topic to the audience:

> Over half of you indicated on the audience analysis form that you participate in team sports. We have two football players, two varsity tennis players, one gymnast, three hockey players, and four persons in men's and women's basketball. Because you already possess the necessary dexterity and coordination for athletics here at San Antonio College, today you are going to learn how to apply your strength and flexibility to helping people with disabilities ride horseback.

This presenter carefully detailed the many people for whom the topic is appropriate.

Bob Wright, chair and CEO of NBC and the vice chair and executive officer of General Electric, delivered a presentation at the University of Virginia School of Law in Charlottesville, Virginia. The title of his talk was "No Profession Is More Honorable Than the Law." Wright observed,

> Unfortunately, you young soon-to-be lawyers about to embark on exciting careers end up paying the price. You pay the price in having a public that thinks they don't want or need your services, and a public that doesn't trust your ethics or your honesty.[2]

try this

Topics for informative speeches are everywhere. Think about subjects most Americans might know little about: other cultures, other religions, other races, other countries, other languages, court cases, mental health, payday loans, mortgages, investments, bank fees, credit card costs, home equity loans, and so on.

Can you think of topics that your classroom audience is likely to know little about? Can you take that little-known concept and teach your audience how to deal with it?

e-NOTE

Too many beginners go to Google with their topic and then quote, paraphrase, and cite the first sources that pop up. Most of those first attempts to find sources uncover more of them than you can read in a lifetime. So, the skill you want to develop is how to choose words that will greatly limit your search.

Wright recognized the importance of relating his topic of distrust of lawyers directly to the audience of law students. When you deliver your informative presentation, remember to relate the topic to yourself and your audience.

How to Identify the Purpose of Your Informative Presentations

An **informative presentation** is *one that increases an audience's knowledge about a subject or that helps the audience learn more about an issue or idea.* Four purposes of informative presentations are (1) to create information hunger, (2) to help the audience understand the information, (3) to help the audience remember the information, and (4) to help the audience apply that information. How do you decide which purposes you can meet?

"Audiences are not always receptive to new information."

Create Information Hunger

The first purpose of informative presentations is to *generate a desire for information—* to create **information hunger**. Audiences, like students, are not always receptive to new information. You have observed teachers who were skilled at inspiring your interest in poetry, advanced algebra, chemistry, or physical education. You will have an opportunity to demonstrate whether you are as skilled at communicating information to an audience of classmates.

What are some strategies for creating information hunger? Among the many possibilities are these: arouse audience curiosity, pose a puzzling question for which your presentation is an answer, and provide an explanation for an issue that has confused people.

Arouse Audience Curiosity

A useful strategy for creating information hunger is to arouse audience curiosity about your topic. Consider this speech titled "Competitive Sports: Don't Take Me Out to the Ballgame."

It is a warm, sunny day out on the baseball field. You, playing shortstop, decide to taunt the upcoming batter with such comments as, "Easy out," "This one can't hit," "He runs like a girl," and so on. All of a sudden, there is commotion in the stands. The game is called to a halt as a fistfight in the stands ends with your father in critical condition. Seems the father of the "easy out" started calling you names, and it all spun out of control. Something like this would never happen though, would it? Unfortunately, this is becoming an all-too-common scenario in the area of Little League and high school sports.

Speakers should use some caution in arousing curiosity. If the speaker's message is too mysterious or bizarre, the audience could lose interest or become distracted. For example, you should not wear a strange costume, behave in a weird manner, or present yourself in a way that is completely out of the ordinary.

Pose a Puzzling Question

One student, Ramona Anderson, induced information hunger this way:

> Have you read your "Mountain Dew" bottle? Your "Diet Pepsi" bottle? Your "Classic Coke" can? If you take the time to read your bottle or can, you will find an interesting message, sometimes in distinctive red print. That message says: "phenylketonurics: Contains Phenylalanine." Is this a message to aliens who dwell among us? Have you ever personally met a "phenylketonuric"? Today you are going to find out what this label means and why you should read the warning. My presentation is entitled "The Phenylketonurics among Us."[3]

The presenter posed a puzzling question about this mysterious word and its cryptic message. You can start an informative presentation by thinking of other puzzling questions that emerge in everyday life: Who are Sarbanes and Oxley? What is "smart medicine"? What common food is processed with benzene and other chemical solvents? Be sure that your question is truly puzzling and not trite or mundane.

Explain a Confusing Issue

A number of conflicts around the world today receive considerable news coverage without much explanation of the issues: lots of smoke and fire but little light. For example, how many people really understand what a stem cell is? Why is stem cell research controversial? Who supports stem cell research and who opposes it?

If you can locate controversy and confusion in issues like smokers' rights, privacy concerns, and immigration policies, you have found yourself the topic for an informative presentation. Remember, however, that you are trying to explain an issue—to bring light, not heat and smoke. Your purpose is *informative*, not persuasive.

"A number of conflicts around the world today receive considerable news coverage without much explanation of the issues."

Help the Audience Understand the Information

The second general purpose of informative presentations is to increase the ways in which the audience can respond to the world.

The kind of knowledge we possess affects our perception of the world. A poet can look at a boulevard of trees and write about her vision in a way that conveys nature's beauty to others. A botanist can determine the species of the trees, whether their leaves are pinnate or palmate, and whether the plants are healthy, rare, or unusual. A chemist can note that sulfur dioxide in the air is affecting the trees and estimate how long they can withstand the ravages of pollution. A knowledgeable person may be able to respond to the trees in all these ways. Acquiring more information provides us with a wider variety of ways to respond to the world around us.

Whether the audience is interested in the topic before you present may be less important than the interest they demonstrate after the presentation. Your audience analysis here should help you find out how much the individuals already know about a subject, so you do not bore the informed or overwhelm the ignorant. Narrow the topic so you can discuss an appropriate amount of material in the allotted time. Finally, apply your own knowledge to the task to simplify and clarify the topic.

How can you encourage the audience to understand your topic? Here are some ideas:

1. Remember that *audiences probably understand main ideas and generalizations better than specific facts and details.* Make certain that you state explicitly, or even repeat, the main ideas and generalizations in your informative presentation. Limit yourself to two to three main points.

2. Remember that *audiences are more likely to understand simple words and concrete ideas than complex words and abstract ideas.*[4] Review the content of your informative presentation to discover simpler, more concrete ways of stating the same ideas.

3. Remember that *early remarks about how the presentation will meet the audience's needs can create anticipation and increase the chances that the audience will listen and understand.*[5] In your introduction, be very explicit about how the topic is related to the audience members. Unless your presentation is related to their needs, they may choose not to listen.

4. Remember that *audience members' overt participation increases their understanding.* You can learn by listening and you can learn by doing, but you learn the most—and so will your audience—by both listening and doing.[6] Determine how to encourage your listeners' involvement in your presentation by having them raise hands, stand up, answer a question, comment in a critique, or state an opinion. One community member, speaking to potential donors, began her talk by asking if the members of the audience had eaten that day and if they would have a place to sleep that night. All of the audience members raised their hands. She then told them that one out of twelve people in their community had neither eaten all day nor had a home in which to sleep. Some pitfalls can occur when you involve the audience by asking them for overt participation. First, their reaction or participation might not be what you have in mind. Second, they might take more time to respond than you had intended. Third, the audience could become unruly when they are given an opportunity to talk or move around. Be aware of these potential consequences if you decide to encourage overt participation.

These four suggestions are powerful. If you observe your best teachers, you will notice that they regularly use these techniques in their lectures.

> **"In your thirst for knowledge, be sure not to drown in all the information."**
>
> [Anthony J. D'Angelo,
> *The College Blue Book*]

Help the Audience Remember the Information

The third general purpose of informative presentations is to help the audience remember important points in your presentation. How can you get listeners to retain important information?

One method is to *reveal to the audience members specifically what you want them to learn from your presentation.* A presenter can tell you about the physiology of long-distance cycling and let you guess what is important until you flounder and eventually forget everything you heard. However, if the presenter announces at the outset, "I want you to remember the three measures of athletic performance: peak use of oxygen, power

"Audiences expect important parts of the presentation to receive more than temporary attention."

at peak in watts, and average power during a four- to six-hour ride," you know what to focus on as you listen. Similarly a student presenter at West Virginia University might say, "After this presentation, I will ask you to explain the two primary goals of the West Virginia Energy Express, a service program supported by AmeriCorps." Audiences tend to remember more about an informative presentation if the presenter tells them specifically at the outset what they should remember.

The announcement of the topic can occur in the introduction of the speech or soon thereafter. Some topics encourage you to announce them later. For example, if one of your classmates states, "I want to teach you how to knit," he or she might immediately lose the bulk of the audience. By luring them into the topic before telling them what they are expected to learn, the speaker might stir more audience interest. Rather than announcing the topic right away, the student could hold up some attractive products that are the finished result of knitting and ask something like, "Would you like to own this? Would you like to give it as a present to your spouse or a family member?"

A student decided to give her informative presentation on the welfare system as viewed from a single mother's perspective. Although she regularly shared information about being a mother and had shown her classmates photos of her children, she knew that most of them did not realize that she had taken advantage of some features of public assistance in the past. She also felt that the other students probably had little experience with welfare. To be sure that the audience would focus on her specific purpose, she stated in her introduction, "At the end of my presentation, I want you to be able to identify three qualifications to apply for assistance."

A second method of encouraging an audience to remember (and one also closely tied to arousing audience interest) is to indicate clearly in the informative presentation which ideas are **main ideas**, *generalizations to be remembered*, and which are **subordinate ideas**, *details to support the generalizations*. In preparing for examinations many students highlight important points in their textbooks and notebooks with a highlighter pen. You can use the same method in preparing your informative presentation. Highlight the important parts and convey their importance by telling the audience, "You will want to remember this point . . . ," "My second main point is . . . ," or "The critical thing to remember in doing this is . . . ."

A third method that encourages an audience to retain important information includes repeating an idea two or three times during the presentation. Audiences expect important parts of the presentation to receive more than temporary attention. They expect important points to be repeated. An early study demonstrated that if you repeat important matters either infrequently (only one time) or too often (four repetitions or more), your audience will be less likely to recall your information.[7] While excessive repetition can be distracting, a second or third restatement can help the audience understand. You can and should follow the popular saying: "Tell 'em what you are going to tell 'em; tell 'em; and then tell 'em what you told 'em." Research supports the idea that this is a good recipe for the introduction, body, and conclusion of a presentation. A woman who works for the USDA is one of its labs talked to a neighborhood group about vertical farming. Since the concept was new to many in the group, she explained exactly what it was in her introduction, in her body, and in her conclusion. The audience usually expects a summary ending that recaps the main points.[8]

A fourth method of encouraging retention is the nonverbal practice of *pausing or using a physical gesture to indicate the importance of the information.* Just as repetition signals an audience that the thought was important, a dramatic pause or silence just before an important statement is also effective. Similarly, your own energy level signals importance, so using bodily movement, gesture, or facial expression can grab audience attention and underline a statement's importance.

Most of the research on retention has been conducted with middle-class, white audiences. If you are speaking to a more diverse audience, you may want to accept these conclusions cautiously. Some audiences appear to appreciate and learn more from several repetitions. Others may expect a great deal of enthusiasm.[9] How can you ensure that your audience will retain the information that you provide them? In the classroom, listen to your instructors' and classmates' informative presentations and try to determine what these presenters do to inspire you to remember the information. In other settings where you are likely to speak, similarly observe the successful informative presenters you encounter. Then see whether you can apply the same techniques in your own informative presentations.

Help the Audience Apply the Information

The fourth general purpose of informative presentations is to encourage the audience to use or apply the information. An effective presenter determines methods of encouraging the audience to use information quickly. Sometimes the presenter can even determine ways that the audience can use the information during the presentation.

Komiko Tanaka, who was delivering an informative presentation on community engagement, for example, had everyone in class write down where they had engaged in service learning. Another student presenter had classmates taste several kinds of local cheeses. Amanda Agogino invited everyone to go online to determine how many articles they could find about accountability in corporate governance. These presenters were encouraging the audience to apply the information from their presentations to ensure that they retained the information.

Why should the informative presenter encourage the audience to use the information as quickly as possible? One reason is that *information applied immediately is remembered longer*. A second reason is that *an action tried once under supervision is more likely to be tried again later*. To think of informative presentations as simply putting an idea into people's heads, of increasing the amount they know about a topic, is easy. However, the presenter has no concrete indication that increased information has been imparted except by observing the audience's behavior.

Therefore, the informative presenter may seek a **behavioral response** from the audience, *an overt indication of understanding*. What behavioral response should the informative presenter seek? Many kinds are possible. You can provoke behavioral response by inviting the audience to talk to others about the topic, to actually apply the information, or to answer questions orally or in writing. If the audience cannot answer a question on the topic before your presentation but can do so afterward, you have effected a behavioral response in your audience. One woman spoke to a lunch group at her place of work on behavioral changes they could make in "going green." She gave all of them coupons worth 15 percent off at a large department store that features products made of recycled materials and urged them to shop there after work.

The four general purposes of informative presentations, then, are to create a desire for information in the audience, to increase audience understanding of the topic, to encourage the audience to remember the information, and to invite the audience to apply the information as quickly as possible. Next we will examine five learning principles that relate to informative presentations.

PRESENTING TO THE ELDERLY

Imagine that you are going to deliver a presentation to residents of an assisted care home. The people in the facility range from age 75 to 101. They are mostly women and most have graduated from college. You have been asked to deliver an informative presentation that will be of interest to them. While 140 people live in the building, you are told that about 90 to 100 will probably attend your talk. You are given 45 minutes to give your talk and to answer questions from the audience. What topics will you consider? How can you relate these topics to yourself and to your audience? How will you create information hunger? How will you help the audience understand, remember, and apply the information you provide? Can you use humor and wit? Will presentational aids be helpful? After you have made some of these decisions, talk with a family friend who is actually in assisted care or seek permission to visit an assisted care facility and chat with some of the residents. What do they think of your ideas? How well do they believe you would do with your presentation?

Principles of Learning

Informative speaking is a type of teaching. Listening to informative presentations is a type of learning. If you expect an audience to understand your informative presentation and apply the knowledge gained, you must treat the presentation as an occasion when teaching and learning both occur. Because you, as an informative presenter, are inviting the audience to learn, you can apply these five **principles of learning** to your presentation: *building on the known, using humor and wit, using sensory aids, organizing your information, and rewarding your listeners.*

Build on the Known

One principle of learning is that people tend to build on what they already know and to accept ideas that are consonant with what they already know. An informative presentation, by definition, is an attempt to add to what the audience already knows. If the audience is to accept the new information, it must be related to information and ideas they already hold.

Let us say that you are going to give an informative presentation on the topic of depression. What do most people in your audience know about the subject? Do they know the possible causes of depression? Do they know the difference between "feeling down" or "feeling blue" and clinical depression?[10] Do they know the symptoms of depression? Do they know the profiles of the most likely victims? Your mission is to start with audience analysis to determine what the audience knows, and then build on that knowledge with new information, presented so the material will be attractive to a variety of learning styles.

Use Humor and Wit

A second principle of learning to observe in informative speaking is to use humor and wit. **Humor** is *the ability to perceive and express that which is amusing or comical,* while

wit is *the ability to perceive and express humorously the relationship or similarity between seemingly incongruous or disparate things.* Informative presentations make the information palatable to the audience. Notice that it does not have to be funny. The principle is "Use humor and wit." Wit and humor are the clever ways you make the information attractive to the audience. Wit and humor are the packaging of the content.

One student used wit in his presentation about parenting. He was unmarried, which was well known to his classmates. The audience could hardly hide its shock when he stated in the introduction to his presentation, "I did not think anything of parenting until I had my son." His "son" turned out to be an uncooked hen's egg. He was taking a course on the family in which he was required to care for his "son," the egg, for one week. When he went out clubbing, he had to find a "babysitter" to care for the egg. He had to protect the egg from breaking as he went from class to class, take the egg to meals, and tuck the egg in at night. The introduction of his "son," the egg, added wit to the wisdom of his informative presentation on parenting.

Another student began her speech, "Have you ever helped someone paint a picture of the White House using only red, orange, and blue paints?" Her presentation focused on Passion Works, a community organization that promotes artistic expression and collaboration among artists with and without developmental disabilities.

Often language choices help add wit and vigor to your presentation. Darris Snelling, who was delivering a potentially boring presentation on "TV and Your Child," enlivened his presentation with witty language by beginning this way:

> Within ten years almost everybody in this room will be married with a young one in the crib and another on the way. Do you want your youngster to start babbling with the words *sex, violence,* and *crime* or do you want him to say *Mommy, Daddy,* and *pepperoni,* like most normal kids?[11]

The presenter hit the audience with the unexpected. The words were witty, and they made his presentation more interesting.

Humor and wit must be used judiciously. Some topics are not appropriate for humor. In addition, simply adding a joke at the beginning of a talk is often misguided. As you can determine from the examples provided above, humor and wit must be appropriate for the topic and must be integrated into the entire message.

Use Sensory Aids

A third principle of learning is to *communicate your message in more than one way because members of the audience have different learning styles.* Verbal/linguistic individuals learn best by listening or reading, while visual/spatial individuals learn best by seeing. Effective informative presenters recognize that different people have varied learning styles. Therefore, such presenters try to communicate their messages in a variety of ways to meet diverse learning styles. In Chapter 9, we discussed sensory aids thoroughly, and you may wish to review that material.

A student giving an informative presentation about diversity in higher education used a chart to explain to his audience four main indicators of diversity: college enrollment, college persistence, degrees conferred, and degrees conferred by fields. Because much of his explanation depended on the use of statistics to indicate trends in diversity, he and the audience found the chart necessary for the informative presentation.

You, too, can find a variety of methods of communicating your message to an audience that learns in diverse ways. Some material in an informative presentation

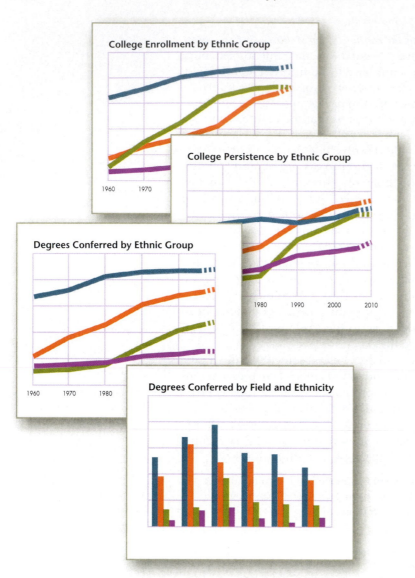

is simply too detailed and complex to present orally. You might be able to get more of the message across by presenting these complex materials in a handout to the audience at the conclusion of your presentation. Other complex data may be easier to understand through a graph, a picture, an object, a model, or a person. Consider using every ethical means necessary to get your informative message to the audience.

Organize to Optimize Learning

A fourth principle of learning is to *organize your information for easier understanding*. Organization of a presentation is more than outlining. Outlining is simply creating the skeleton of a presentation. In an informative presentation, consider other organizational possibilities. How can you try to create a proper setting for learning to take place? Where in the presentation should you reveal what you expect the audience to remember? Do you place your most important information early or late in the presentation?

No hard-and-fast answers to these questions exist, but research does hint at some good suggestions:[12]

1. *When do you create a setting for learning?* The earlier you create an atmosphere for learning, the better. Make clear to audience members early in the presentation exactly what you want them to learn from your presentation.

2. *Where should important information be placed?* Audiences remember information placed early and late in the presentation, so avoid placing your most important material in the middle of your presentation. **Primacy**, or *placing the information or main point early in the presentation*, seems to work better in presentations on controversial issues, on topics that the audience cares little about, and on topics highly familiar to the audience. **Recency**, or *placing the information or main point late in your presentation*, seems to work best when audience members care about the issue, when the issue is moderately unfamiliar, and when the topic is not terribly interesting.[13]

3. *How do you indicate which parts of your presentation are main points and which are supporting?* In writing, subordination is easy to indicate by levels of headings, but people listening to a presentation cannot necessarily visualize the structure of your presentation, which is why the effective informative presenter indicates early in the presentation what is going to be covered. This forecast sets up the audience's expectations; they will know what you are going to talk about and for approximately how long. Similarly, as you proceed through your presentation, you may wish to signal your progress by indicating

where you are in your organization through transitions. Among organizational indicators are signposts and transitions like the following:

> "My second point is . . ."
>
> "Now that I have carefully explained a brief history of democracy in the United States, I will describe how democracy is viewed today."
>
> "This story about what happened to me in Iraq will illustrate my point about obeying orders."

In each case, the presenter is signaling whether the next item is a main point in the presentation or supporting evidence for it. Chapter 6 has a thorough explanation of transitions and signposts.

"Organization of a presentation is more than outlining."

Reward Your Listeners

A fifth principle of learning is that *audiences are more likely to respond to information that is rewarding for them.* **Reward** in this context means *a psychological or physical reinforcement to increase an audience's response to information given in a presentation.* One of the audience's concerns about an informative presentation is "What's in it for me?" The effective informative presenter answers this question not only in the introduction, where the need for the information is formally explained, but also throughout the presentation. By the time a presenter is in the middle of the presentation, the audience may have forgotten much of the earlier motivating information presented, so the presenter continually needs to remind the audience how the information meets its needs.

One student began her presentation by saying the following:

> Did you realize that, at this very moment, each and every one of you could be and probably is suffering from America's most widespread ailment? It is not a sexually transmitted disease, cancer, or heart disease, but a problem that is commonly ignored by most Americans—the problem of being overweight.

As the presenter proceeded through her information on nutrition, she kept reassuring the audience members that they could overcome the problem in part by knowing which foods to eat and which to avoid. The audience benefited by learning the names of foods that could improve or weaken health.

In this example, the reinforcement was in the form of readily usable information that the audience could apply. But rewards come in many forms. A presenter can use other, more psychological, forms of reward. "Do you want to be among the few who know what a credit card interest rate is?" The presenter who confidentially tells you about credit card debt is doing you a service because you will no longer be ignorant and you will be in the special category of those few "in the know."

Figure 10.1 reviews the five principles of learning.

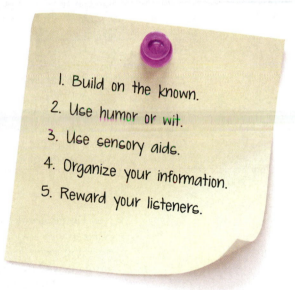

Figure 10.1   **Principles of learning.**

Skills for the Informative Presenter

Informative speaking employs a number of skills that help make a presentation effective. In informative speaking, those skills include defining, describing, explaining, and demonstrating. Let us explore for a moment how these skills work in an informative presentation.

Defining in an Informative Presentation

pat·ois
(pāt'wä, pä-twä; Fr.)

Defining is *revealing the presenter's intended meaning of a term, especially if the term is technical, scientific, controversial, or not commonly used.* Know, too, that definitions cannot substitute for other appropriate supporting materials. Presenters often forget to define the terms they use in a presentation. If a presenter has mentioned something called a "plah-see-bow" about five times without telling you what a *placebo* is, the presentation has failed to inform.

Another consideration is that the way you define a term can start a fight or establish peace. Much of the battle over end-of-life rights is centered on the medical definition of when life has ended.

Three ways to define a word are to reveal its denotation, its connotations, and its etymology. We discussed these different ways of defining a word in Chapter 8, and you may wish to review this material. For instance, the word *patois* (etymology: French, pronounced paa-TWAA) is used for the type of language spoken by many black inhabitants of the island of Jamaica in the Caribbean. A patois is a rare language that does not extend far, in this case not even to the other Caribbean islands, and that is more of a spoken than a written tongue since its grammar and spelling are not standardized. It is an informal sort of language. That would be the word's dictionary meaning, or denotation. The connotative meanings of *patois* are more complex because few white people can speak this form of language, which has been mastered by so many black people in Jamaica. Connotatively, patois suggests a private language, such as the one limited pretty much to black people who grew up in Jamaica. It may be considered less worthy because it is informal, but because it is rich in local associations and folklore, it may also be admired by outsiders.

Actually you can define words or concepts by using methods beyond denotation, connotation, and etymology. You can compare and contrast, provide an example, or provide synonyms (similar meanings) or antonyms (opposite meanings). Whatever method you use, the important point is to remember to help your audience by defining your terms.

Describing in an Informative Presentation

Describing *evokes the meaning of a person, a place, an object, or an experience by telling about its size, weight, color, texture, smell, or your feelings about it.* Describing relies on your abilities to use precise, accurate, specific, and concrete language to make your audience vividly aware.

Mark DuPont, in a public speaking class at Iowa State University, told his classmates about his hometown of Phoenix, Arizona, using the following descriptive words:

The heat cannot be escaped. As the sun beats mercilessly on the endless lines of automobiles, waves of shimmering heat drift from the blistering pavement, creating an atmosphere of an oven and making the minutes drag into eternity. The wide avenues only increase the sense of oppression and crowding as lane after lane clogs with rumbling cars and trucks. Drivers who have escaped the heat of the sun in their air-conditioned cars are overwhelmed by the heat of frustration as they do battle with stoplights and autos that have expired in the August sun. Valiant pedestrians wade through the heat, pausing only to wipe from their foreheads the sweat that stings their eyes and blurs their vision. It is the afternoon rush hour at its peak, Phoenix, Arizona, at its fiercest. The crawl of automobiles seems without end as thousands of people seek out their homes in the sweltering desert city.[14]

Explaining in an Informative Presentation

Explaining in an informative presentation *reveals how something works, why something occurred, or how something should be evaluated.* You may explain a social, political, or economic issue; you may explain a historical event; you may explain a variety of theories, principles, or laws; or you may explain by offering a critical appraisal of art, literature, music, drama, film, or presentations. A wide collection of topics may be included in "explaining." You should notice that in offering your opinion, you may come very close to attempting to persuade the audience.

Do you or your classmates understand the concept of minimal tillage in organic farming, how margarine is made, the rules of NASCAR, the qualities of Chateau Malmaison Moulis wine, a shahtoosh "ring shawl," or a lyric opera? The informative presenter takes lesser known words and concepts and renders them understandable to the audience through explanation, as illustrated in the excerpt from a speech provided below:

OEM & Non-OEM: Only Your Body Shop Knows for Sure

Until my daughter wrecked her Honda Civic, I had never thought about what happens at the body shop. In fact, a chance remark alerted me to the problem. When I stopped by the body shop after two weeks to see when the vehicle would be repaired, the person behind the desk said, "This one's going to take a while. Your insurer is recommending non-OEM parts." Probably he was not supposed to make the statement because the repair of that one relatively inexpensive car became a nightmare that revealed the cracks in our insurance/auto repair system.

OEM is an acronym for "original equipment manufacturer." A body shop that completely repairs a Honda with OEM parts is using Honda-made parts to replace the damaged portions of your vehicle. The body shop's other choices are to use salvage, that is, parts borrowed from wrecked vehicles or, more likely, to use non-OEM parts or imitations. The imitation parts could be as good as OEM parts, but they could also be misshapen, inferior in quality, and likely to peel and rust quickly. According to the February 1999 *Consumer Reports*, imitation door shells can be installed without the guard beams, with weak welds on guard beams, or with guard beams made with weaker steel. Similarly, knockoff hoods sometimes come without the crumple initiators that keep sheet metal from crashing straight through the windshield. Imitation bumpers can compromise your headlights, radiator, and even your airbags.

Demonstrating in an Informative Presentation

Demonstrating is *showing the audience an object, a person, or a place; showing the audience how something works; showing the audience how to do something; or showing the audience why something occurs.* For example, a student who was informing her classmates about the features of cellular phones used five cellular telephones as models. To help her classmates see the features on these relatively small objects, she used an instrument called an ELMO (electronic monitor, or document camera, or digital video projector), which magnified each phone on the screen in front of the classroom. Describing can accompany demonstrating.

Consider demonstrating those ideas, concepts, or processes that are too complex to be understood through words alone. Similarly, consider the wide variety of items and materials that can be used to demonstrate your topic that were discussed earlier in Chapter 9.

Some examples of presentations that invite a demonstration are

- A presentation by a health worker on how to inject insulin.
- A presentation by a civil engineering student on alternate transportation systems.
- A presentation by a library science major about how to find more and better information on the Internet.

- A presentation by a mechanic showing us how to save money on oil changes.

Consider whether your topic would lend itself to demonstration.

Ethics and Informative Presentations

Tainted or unethical information is a common problem with people who are less than honest.

What are some guidelines for positive ethical choices in an informative presentation?

1. *Be sure of the quality of your information.*

- Is the information accurate, verifiable, consistent, and placed in context?
- Have you avoided implying that you have information that you lack?
- Have you avoided making up facts or distorting information?

2. *Exercise caution when using the words of others.*

- Have you accurately quoted the sources you have cited?
- If you have summarized the words of others, have you paraphrased accurately?
- Did you cite the sources of your material?
- Have you avoided plagiarism?
- Have you kept all quotations in proper context?

3. *Be careful not to mislead your audience.*

- Have you told the audience of your association with groups whose work or purpose may be relevant to the topic?
- Have you been honest?
- Did you present all the relevant information?
- Did you tell your audience whether your examples were hypothetical or real?

- Have you used appropriate language to clarify words or concepts that the audience does not understand?

4. *Be sure the audience needs the information.*
- Are you providing the audience with new information?
- Are you allowing the audience free choice to accept or reject the information you provide?
- Can your audience make reasoned choices about the importance and accuracy of the information you are providing?

5. *Be sure that the information you are providing is in the best interests of the audience members.*
- Are you providing information that helps rather than hurts the audience?
- Are you providing information that advances rather than harms our culture and society?

Ethical choices affect your credibility as a source. If you are not ethical—if you bend the truth, twist the evidence, and shape information for selfish purposes—then your audience will find you less credible in the presentations that you give in the future. So be careful, accurate, and honest. The checklist in Figure 10.2 will help you accomplish this.

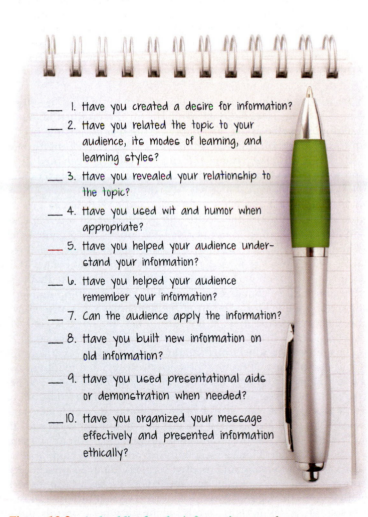

___ 1. Have you created a desire for information?

___ 2. Have you related the topic to your audience, its modes of learning, and learning styles?

___ 3. Have you revealed your relationship to the topic?

___ 4. Have you used wit and humor when appropriate?

___ 5. Have you helped your audience under-stand your information?

___ 6. Have you helped your audience remember your information?

___ 7. Can the audience apply the information?

___ 8. Have you built new information on old information?

___ 9. Have you used presentational aids or demonstration when needed?

___ 10. Have you organized your message effectively and presented information ethically?

Figure 10.2   **A checklist for the informative speech.**

An Example of an Informative Presentation

Organic Food

Using contrasts of familiar objects can arouse curiosity.

Previous experience is used to establish credibility.

Every time I walk into the grocery store I face a dilemma. Most people worry about simple things like Coke versus Pepsi, or vanilla versus chocolate ice cream. Me, I worry about one thing: conventional versus organic. You see, I grew up on a small farm in Southeast Ohio, and on that farm we practiced organic farming. My dad probably wouldn't say that he started farming organically because of a philosophical reason. We have just over 150 acres, which does not make it cost effective to invest in expensive equipment or chemicals. So, growing organic foods allows us to compete against big conventional farming operations in the central United States. This morning you will learn what organic food is as well as some tips for buying organic food. This is important information for you because it will help you make smarter choices at the grocery store—choices that could improve your health and the environment.

The central idea and primary points should be clearly previewed for the audience.

Transition and signpost for first main point.

First, you should understand what the label "organic" means when you run across it in the grocery store. The organic food market is growing rapidly as a segment of the grocery market. Kathleen Welton, writing in the February 2010 issue of the *Library Journal,* noted that global sales of organic foods exceeded $23 billion in 2008. The United States is a big part of that global organic trend. Dr. Maureen Callahan, a CNN medical correspondent, explained that in America alone, consumers spent $28 million on organic foods in 2008. Why do you think so many consumers are jumping on the organic food cart? An agronomist writing in the *Allelopathy Journal* explained that many consumers recognize the benefits of organic food in comparison to conventional food that may have been treated with pesticides and other chemicals. Also, many assume that using fewer chemicals is a benefit to the environment.

Sources of information should be identified for the audience. Depending on the source, a variety of information could be stated to establish credibility for the information, including the date, type of publication, or qualifications of the person.

So what exactly does *organic* mean?

Transitions within main points can help audience members follow points as they are developed.

The term, as used regarding food, is actually governed through the Organic Foods Production Act. The act oversees national standards for the production, handling, and processing of all foods labeled as organic. Being certified as an organic producer or processor requires certification from the United States Department of Agriculture. Mary Gold, of the Alternative Farming Systems Information Center, explained that the act authorizes food to be labeled as organic when it "promotes and enhances biodiversity, biological cycles, and soil biological diversity." Further, organic foods are based on minimal use of off-farm inputs like fertilizers, pesticides, and growth hormones. The primary objective of the act is to "optimize the health and productivity of interdependent communities of soil life, plants, animals, and people." Of course, the organic label from the FDA is not without some controversy. A 2009 *Washington Post* article explained that lobbyists have successfully gotten the FDA to relax standards on what counts as organic. For example, baby formulas now contain a synthetic additive that reportedly boosts brain power, grated organic cheese contains wood starch to prevent clumping, and organic beer can contain nonorganic hops. The article explains that aggressive lobbying, driven by significant consumer demand, has led the FDA to become more lax in its labeling standards.

Direct quotations are difficult to remember or read from notes and should be reserved for instances where precise wording is important.

Informative messages should emphasize a balanced analysis of an issue. This section shows that labeling efforts are surrounded by some controversy.

There are several reasons why farmers might choose to grow organic crops. First, the organic label tells consumers that farming practices were enacted to minimize the risk of chemical contamination. Although no food can be guaranteed to be 100 percent free of chemicals, organic foods are far more likely to be pure than are conventional foods. This certification provides a certain degree of protection to the consumer, and farmers who are organically certified are proud of the fact that their food is safer for the consumer. Second, farmers have a strong connection to the land. Although organic farming is more labor intensive, harsh chemicals are not used on the land, and more natural crop rotation methods are used to maintain enriched soil. Also, animals produced for consumption by organic farmers are treated humanely. On my family farm we focus a lot of energy on rotating crops through various tracts of land so that the soil can replenish its nutrients. By doing this we do not have to rely on chemical pest controls and fertilizers to maintain production.

When using explanation to analyze complex issues, using signposts (spoken numbers) can help maintain clarity. Visual aids can be integrated to provide even greater clarity of the points.

In this picture you can see how we use terrace farming. Terrace farming allows us to plant small crops on the side of hills, but the terraces prevent topsoil from washing down the hill. The different terraces also make it easy for us to rotate crops. Terrace farming does not necessarily mean that the resulting crops are organic, but this practice is better for the environment and makes organic farming easier to accomplish.

So now you know that organic food is more natural and probably has benefits for your health. How can you be smart when buying organic food? That's what I'll talk about next.

Because organic food can cost more than conventionally produced food, you need to be smart when shopping. First, look for the organic label. Remember that federal standards must be met before that label can be used. Also, there are no such standards for seafood of any type, so don't bother looking for organic fish, shrimp, or crabs. The vegetable and fruit aisle is where you can make your biggest impact. For fruits and veggies where you eat the outside, like celery and lettuce, buying organic is important. For other foods like bananas and melons, you will discard the outside, so the benefits of buying organic may be less significant. Also, make sure you plan before you even get to the store. If you plan menus that maximize use of organic foods, especially menus that emphasize fruits and vegetables, you can do a better job of transitioning your food consumption away from conventional food where chemicals are more common.

The Sustainable Table Web site provides some other smart suggestions for consumers. That Web site encourages us to think local and seasonal. Although not all local food will be certified as organic, because it is local it requires less transportation and does not have to be stored for long periods of time. Both of these factors mean that fewer chemicals are necessary. A trip to your local farmers' market can allow you to buy organic without having to pay higher prices. Also, buying seasonal food means that you are less likely to be eating chemically preserved food. A strawberry in January obviously requires transportation and preservation, whereas most areas of the country have plentiful local strawberries in May and June. As you can guess, the January strawberry is far more likely to be grown and preserved through use of chemicals.

If you make the decision to start buying organic food, there are several possible outcomes. According to an article in *Men's Health* by Maria Rodale, there are many potential health benefits from eating organic foods, including a reduced risk of diabetes, cancer, heart disease, and even autism among children. Margot Pollans, a recognized advocate for sustainable agriculture, also noted that the production of organic food reduces significantly the amount of pollution generated by agriculture. But, there are also drawbacks. Because it is so labor intensive and takes longer in terms of

When integrating visual aids or other supplements, take care to provide adequate explanation so that audience members understand what they are seeing or experiencing.

Transitions between main points should attempt to summarize the previous point and preview the next. This transition could be even clearer if an explicit signpost were added. How could you word that signpost to make it effective?

As your presentation unfolds, help audience members understand how they can use your information in their own lives.

For important information, find stylistic wordings like "local and seasonal" that can be easily remembered by your audience.

Concrete examples can be used to illustrate principles you are trying to teach your audience.

Rhetorical style includes the use of ornamental language. Style can be as simple as using alliteration, as with "conventionally grown cousins."

production time, organic food does cost more. A consumer could see prices for organic food that are a few cents or even a few dollars higher than those for their conventionally grown cousins.

As college students we don't often think about what we buy. For some of us a quick trip through the grocery aisles with ramen, pop, and chips defines a typical trip to the store. But many of us do try to buy healthier foods. Today you have learned what the "organic" label means on foods as well as some tips for buying organic foods. Organic food could cost a little more, but the benefits, both in terms of your own health and for the environment, could be significant. Regardless of whether you buy all organic or, like many of us, mix things up, you should understand what the label means so that you can make smarter decisions the next time you are at the grocery store.

Close the speech with a clear summary and reminder of how audience members can use the information you provided.

For REVIEW >>

AS YOU READ

1. Apply the principles and purposes of informative presentations to a topic you are considering for your informative presentation assignment.

2. Identify how you will incorporate the principles of learning into your presentation to optimize its effectiveness with your audience.

3. Reflect on the ethical dimensions of an informative presentation.

SUMMARY HIGHLIGHTS

▶ Two principles are important in informative presentations:
  • The presenter should explicitly state the relationship between himself or herself and the topic.
  • The presenter needs to link the audience to the topic.

▶ The purposes of informative presentations are to generate information hunger, to help the audience understand the information, to help the audience remember the information, and to invite the audience to apply the information from the presentation.
  • Audiences comprehend generalizations and main ideas better than details.
  • Audiences comprehend simple words and concrete ideas better than big words and abstractions.
  • A sense of anticipation can encourage listening and understanding.
  • Audience participation increases comprehension.

▶ Some principles of learning that you can use in informative presentations are:
  • Build on the known.
  • Use humor and wit.
  • Use sensory aids.
  • Organize your information.
  • Reward your listeners.

▶ The five ethical guidelines for an informative presentation are:
  • Be sure of the quality of your information.
  • Exercise caution when using the words of others.
  • Be careful not to mislead your audience.
  • Be sure the audience needs the information.
  • Be sure that the information you are providing is in the best interests of the audience members.

Pop Quiz

1. Which of the following is *not* a purpose of an informative presentation?
   (A) To shape or influence the audience's thoughts.
   (B) To create information hunger.
   (C) To help the audience understand information.
   (D) To help the audience apply the information.

2. To help your audience understand your topic, you should remember that:
   (A) the audience will understand specific facts better than main ideas
   (B) audience members do not learn by participating
   (C) audiences can understand abstract ideas better than concrete ideas
   (D) early remarks about meeting the audience's needs increase the chances that they will listen

3. Subordinate ideas should be used:
   (A) as generalizations to be remembered
   (B) to link main points
   (C) to introduce ideas
   (D) as details to support generalizations

4. You can help the audience remember information from your speech by:
   (A) letting the audience guess what you want them to learn
   (B) repeating an important idea two or three times
   (C) avoiding pauses during your speech
   (D) allowing the audience to differentiate between main and subordinate ideas

5. The principles of learning discussed in the *text* do *not* include:
   (A) using humor and wit
   (B) discouraging audience participation
   (C) organizing to optimize learning
   (D) building on the known

6. The ability to perceive and express that which is amusing or comical is termed:
   (A) humor
   (B) wit
   (C) intelligence
   (D) absurdity

7. It is not advisable to place important information:
   (A) at the beginning of the speech
   (B) late in the speech
   (C) in the middle of the speech
   (D) at the end of the speech

8. Evoking the meaning of an object by telling about its size, weight, color, or texture is called:
   (A) defining
   (B) explaining
   (C) demonstrating
   (D) describing

9. A skill that would best benefit a presentation about ballroom dance would be:
   (A) describing
   (B) demonstrating
   (C) explaining
   (D) defining

10. One guideline to follow to make ethical choices in your presentation is:
    (A) to make up facts if it will make your presentation more interesting
    (B) to cite only important sources
    (C) to present only information that supports your argument
    (D) to keep quotations in the proper context

Answers: 1 (A); 2 (D); 3 (D); 4 (B); 5 (B); 6 (A); 7 (C); 8 (D); 9 (B); 10 (D)

APPLICATION EXERCISES

1. Think of three topics about which you could give a three-minute presentation to inform. List the topics in the blanks at the left. In the blanks at the right, explain how you relate to the topic in ways that might increase your credibility with the audience.

TOPICS	YOUR RELATIONSHIP TO TOPIC
A. _____	_____
B. _____	_____
C. _____	_____

2. Consider one topic that you did not use in the previous exercise and explain how you would relate that topic to an audience of your own class in an informative presentation.

3. Write down a topic for an informative presentation that you have not used in previous application exercises. Explain in the spaces provided how you could apply each of the principles of learning to that topic.

TOPIC: _____

ONE WAY THAT I COULD RELATE THIS TOPIC TO WHAT THE AUDIENCE ALREADY KNOWS IS BY _____

_____

ONE WAY THAT I COULD RELATE WIT AND HUMOR IN AN INFORMATIVE PRESENTATION ON THIS TOPIC IS BY

_____

_____

ONE WAY THAT I COULD USE SEVERAL PRINCIPLES OF LEARNING TO GET MY MESSAGE ACROSS ON THIS TOPIC IS BY

_____

ONE WAY THAT I COULD ORGANIZE MY PRESENTATION TO HELP THE AUDIENCE LEARN MY INFORMATION IS BY

_____

ONE WAY THAT I COULD REWARD MY AUDIENCE FOR LISTENING TO MY INFORMATIVE PRESENTATION ON THIS TOPIC IS BY

_____

_____

KEY TERMS

Behavioral response	Humor	Principles of learning
Defining	Information hunger	Recency
Demonstrating	Informative presentation	Reward
Describing	Main ideas	Subordinate ideas
Explaining	Primacy	Wit

get involved!

To get involved in **creating a public information speech**, think of an informative topic of interest beyond the classroom. Using Google or Bing, see what information you can find on the topic. Then think of what audiences would be most interested in your topic.

Let us consider one example. Imagine that you are concerned about racial profiling. You learn that racial profiling is being practiced in your community. Police officers are more likely to stop some drivers than they are to stop others. Further, the questioning of potential law violators is different, based on ethnicity and gender.

You know that many people have spoken on each side of this controversial topic. However, your interest is in providing unbiased information on the topic and to look at both sides of the issue. You present a speech on this topic in your class. You receive high marks for the talk and are encouraged to speak beyond the college classroom. To whom could you deliver your speech? Consider campus organizations, community groups, and city or town councils. How can you network with people in these groups so you will be invited to provide your information to them?

11

PRESENTING PERSUASIVE

This chapter defines, analyzes, and helps you create effective persuasive messages. Much of our communication attempts to influence others. At the same time we are often the targets of persuasion. This chapter shows how to influence others through ethically responsible persuasive presentations.

MESSAGES

As You READ

1. Compare and contrast the purposes of persuasive and informative presentations.
2. Identify the principles and types of persuasive presentations.
3. Reflect on the type of change you will ask of your audience.
4. Recognize how effective persuasive presentations depend on arguments that are built upon reasoning, critical thinking, and ethics.

Most scientists and climatologists agree that the Earth's temperature has been gradually rising. What stirs controversy over global warming is disagreement over the causes, and therefore the solutions, of the change.

Many scientists and climatologists believe that human use of fossil fuels has created a dangerous buildup of greenhouse gases that trap heat near the Earth's surface. This heat appears likely to lead to global weather disruptions, water shortages, and wide fluctuations in sea level that will threaten many coastal communities. If global warming does have a human cause, an obvious solution is to start reducing polluting emissions, despite the many political and economic difficulties of such action. Other observers, however, believe that warming is not occurring, or if it is, that it is part of a natural planetary cycle that requires no action to be taken.

Advocates on both sides of the climate change issue are impassioned about their beliefs and often write and speak about their views to persuade others to share them.

Many issues engender divided views like these and provide you with opportunities to test your own persuasive skill. Do you have an opinion about climate change? Can you make an argument and support it in a way that convinces others to adopt your position? This chapter will show you how to influence others through ethically responsible persuasive presentations.

How Would *You* Do It?

Refer to the chapter opening story and the controversy over the causes of global warming. What type of persuasive speech and what strategy or strategies of persuasion would you use to convince others of your beliefs?

Persuasion permeates our culture so much that we may not be fully aware of its presence. In our democratic society today, we send and receive persuasive messages on crucial issues such as war and peace, taxation and representation, freedoms and restrictions, and readiness for disasters both natural and terrorist-related. These topics alone indicate how critical it is for us to understand persuasive speaking in our everyday lives, including:

The Role of Persuasion in Public Discourse

- How persuasion relates to you and the main types of persuasive messages
- What social science research reveals about the audience and the message in persuasive presentations
- The strategies for acceptance of persuasive messages and how to organize your persuasive presentation
- The use of inductive and deductive reasoning, argument, and evidence—the substance of many persuasive attempts
- Some of the common fallacies that unethical persuaders try to use
- The consideration of ethics in persuasion

We begin by looking at how persuasion relates to you.

You as Target of and Sender of Persuasion

We use persuasion in everything from sales to civic engagement and public deliberation. Persuasive messages bombard you every day. You are the target of many persuasive attempts. When your BlackBerry or iPhone vibrates, or a pop-up appears, you often are confronted with someone who sees you as a customer. Commercials punctuate television and radio programs every few minutes. Magazines and newspapers are filled with flashy ads designed to sell you products. Many Web sites are crammed with pop-ups and banner ads. The mall and the supermarket are designed to draw money out of your pocket. Political parties and charities vie for your loyalty and contributions. Today, more than ever, the traditional media, the Internet, and other people compete for your attention, your money, your time, your vote, or your membership. In doing so, they all use persuasion.

You are also a producer of persuasive messages. At Oakland University in Rochester, Michigan, the students use their persuasive skills for community involvement in the Brooksie Way Half Marathon, an event designed to encourage healthy lifestyles in Oakland County. At the Florissant Valley Campus of St. Louis Community College, student advocates can get involved with the North County CARES program, which provides "educational opportunities that promote individual and community growth,"[1] including a resource guide of community services in which students can engage in their community.

Your satisfaction in both private and public spheres is dependent, in great part, on your ability to be both a competent consumer and producer of persuasive messages. You do not want to be deceived by others. You want to be able to understand why you feel compelled to respond to certain messages while you disregard others. You also want to learn to be an effective and ethical persuader. Our democratic and capitalist culture thrives on persuasion. This chapter helps you to understand and to practice persuasive presentations.

Informative Presentation		Persuasive Presentation
To increase knowledge	**Presenter's Intent**	To change mind or action
To define, describe, explain, or demonstrate	**Purpose of Message**	To shape, reinforce, or change audience response
To know more than before, to advance what is known	**Listener's Response**	To feel or think differently, to behave or act differently, to critically evaluate the message
To willingly gain new knowledge	**Audience Choice**	To change behavior by choice, to be inspired or convinced by credibility, logic, or emotion

Figure 11.1   **How do informative and persuasive presentations differ?**

What Are Persuasive Presentations?

Persuasive presentations are *messages that influence an audience's choices by changing their responses toward an idea, issue, concept, or product.* Let's compare informative and persuasive presentations. Perhaps no message is completely informative or completely persuasive. In fact, persuading and informing may work to reinforce each other, but generally we are trying to do one or the other. Figure 11.1 highlights the characteristics of the two kinds of presentations.

Types of Persuasive Presentations

The three types of persuasive speeches are the speech to inspire, the speech to convince, and the speech of action.

The **speech to inspire** is a persuasive speech, although we do not often think about inspirational messages as persuasive. *The purpose of this speech is to influence listeners' feelings or motivations.* Speeches of inspiration often occur at ceremonial events. They occur in places of worship, at graduations and rallies, and on holidays or at special events. Lacey Schneider came to class very agitated about how little she and her classmates knew about politics. Her purpose was to get her listeners to be more mindful about their own political beliefs and to then follow up by voting for a candidate who represented them. These few sentences give you the flavor of her presentation:

> Did you know that only 31 percent of females under the age of 35 are likely to vote? I personally found this statistic to be disheartening. Now, with that figure in mind, how many women under 35 do you think know what they believe in? Unfortunately, even if they do know what they believe in, they are not expressing their beliefs by voting.[2]

You also can deliver a speech to inspire. Can you inspire your fellow students to join some cause in which you believe? Can you inspire them to be more spiritual, less materialistic, more focused on learning, or more concerned about their own community? Consider opportunities to deliver speeches of inspiration at your place of work. Can you inspire people to create a union, to donate money to a fellow worker who has lost a child, or to adopt more environmentally friendly practices? To experience examples of inspirational speaking, watch live or televised ministers, see politicians during campaigns, or observe individuals who believe strongly in issues related to natural resources, education, gun ownership, health care, and other causes.

The **speech to convince** is *a persuasive presentation delivered with the intent of influencing listeners' beliefs or attitudes.* You may wish, for example, to convince the audience that gender equality is beneficial to both women and men, that respectful language is a reasonable goal of a multicultural society, that all people deserve housing, or that we should care more about victims of terrorism and natural disasters.

The speech to convince encourages listeners to adopt a stronger position on an issue; they are not required to act. You ask your audience only to rethink their beliefs and attitudes.

The **speech of action** is *a persuasive speech given for the purpose of influencing listeners' behaviors and actions.* The foundation of the speech of action is the changing of listeners' beliefs and attitudes, plus acting on them. You may want listeners to join an organization, to volunteer their time at local social service agencies, to adhere to a low-fat diet, or to vote for a particular candidate. In the speech of action, the speaker seeks an overt behavioral effect, some evidence of response consistent with the presenter's intent.

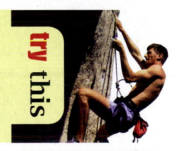

Pair with another person and help each other think of instances when you have used persuasion (a) in the home, (b) at school, (c) at work, and (d) in the community.

try this

This text has attempted throughout to emphasize "vital" topics, because public discussion of important issues—civic engagement—is at the very heart of democracy. To be effective at public discourse it would be useful to learn what works and what does not. Here are some findings about audiences and messages, which relate directly to persuasive presentations.

What Communication Research Says about Persuasion

What Should You Know about Your Audience?

- One fundamental task in persuasion is **audience analysis**, *learning enough about the listeners so that you can predict their probable response to your message.*[3]
- Every persuasive appeal has a relationship dimension. If you are too pushy about achieving your purpose, your audience might resist you more and like you less.
- The **relationship** is *how the audience feels about you as the presenter before, during, and after the persuasive appeal.* You are more likely to persuade if your audience respects you, if your integrity remains intact during your presentation, and if the audience continues to believe you are credible after they have heard your presentation.

"Public discussion of important issues— civic engagement—is at the very heart of democracy."

- Your classmates and people in your community will tend to respond in three different ways to a persuasive appeal: critically, defensively, or compliantly.[4]

  o A **critical response** *occurs when the audience focuses on the arguments, the quality of the evidence, and the truth or accuracy of the message.* In your pitch for a state-of-the-art playground for physically challenged children, your audience may want to know how many children you are talking about.

  o A **defensive response** *occurs when the audience fends off the persuader's message to protect existing beliefs, attitudes, and values.* A person proposing a tax increase for the new library may fare poorly with an audience committed to no new taxes.

  o A **compliance response** *occurs when the audience does what is socially acceptable,* including pleasing the persuader or pleasing the other listeners. An audience may go along with the idea of working with Habitat for Humanity just because they do not want to appear insensitive toward their underprivileged neighbors. They comply to be socially acceptable.

- Audiences will respond to persuasive messages depending on how motivated they are to process the message.[5]

  o Unmotivated audiences who do not take the topic seriously will respond superficially to the message. For instance, students tend to be motivated more by classes in their major than in courses they are required to complete.

  o Motivated audiences who see the topic as important to them will respond deeply by being thoughtful, analytical, and understanding. Audiences who choose to hear a presentation are more likely to respond to a message meaningfully.

  o Audiences will respond favorably to timely messages. Students about to graduate, for example, will pay more attention to a presentation on job-gaining interview skills than to a presentation on retirement possibilities. A group of people in their seventies will be more interested in ideal places to live, in healthy diets that are linked to longevity, and to Social Security benefits. Consider whether your topic is timely.

How Can You Create an Effective Message?

Once you have a purpose to direct you and an audience to listen to you, you need to create a message that uses content most likely to gain acceptance. According to current communication research, an effective persuasive presenter will:

- Employ message production *to create, organize, and deliver a persuasive appeal.*[6]

- Use the content of a persuasive appeal *to fulfill the primary goal of influencing the listeners in a predetermined direction.* The content often consists of reasons to adopt the presenter's ideas plus supporting material to bolster those claims.

- Be **explicit**, which is *the extent to which the persuader makes his or her intentions clear in the message.*[7] Often the presenter clarifies intentions at the outset—"After this presentation you will want a new water supply for our city." But, if the audience is likely to resist the presenter's purpose, then the presenter is better off preparing the audience with reasons first and making the purpose explicit later, after the audience is more prepared—"Now I think you see the need for an expensive cleanup at the site of the old fertilizer plant."

- Use **argument**, which is *the extent to which the presenter furnishes reasons for the message claims.*[8] The skillful presenter finds the reasons, the evidence, and the proof that the audience is most likely to accept.

- Use **testimonial evidence**, *the words of a cited source in support of the presenter's claims*, to produce attitude change and improve source credibility. By quoting sources whom the audience respects, the presenter will increase acceptance.

- Use **complete arguments** *including all the parts—claims and supporting material—to produce attitude change and improve source credibility.* Audiences want to know as fully as possible why they should comply.

- *Use **specific numbers**—percentages, actual numbers, averages, and ranges of numbers*—rather than saying "many," "most," or some other vague quantity. Being specific increases message effectiveness and improves source credibility.[9]

IMPLICITNESS MAY BE VALUED IN COLLECTIVIST CULTURES

James Dillard and Linda Marshall, professors of communication and family studies, respectively, say that U.S. students favor explicitness—communication that is direct and clear—and clarity over concern for others and avoidance of disapproval. In some cultures, implicitness—communication that is indirect and ambiguous—may be valued, especially in collectivist cultures where the group is given priority over the individual. Koreans, for example, prefer indirectness,[10] and Japanese advertising tends to make more indirect claims than does U.S. advertising.[11] Even some U.S. audiences who are high in social sensitivity may prefer an implicit approach. The goal of the persuader is to match presentation to listener preference on implicitness and explicitness.

Now that you know more about what communication research reveals about audiences and messages, you are ready to consider particular strategies a presenter can use to influence an audience.

Fact, Value, and Policy in Persuasive Presentations

The content of persuasive presentations often revolves around three distinct kinds of questions: questions of fact, questions of value, and questions of policy.

The **question of fact** *means that the persuasive presentation seeks to uncover the truth based on fact.* That truth or fact could be anything from who did something, why something was done, to how something was done. For instance, a federal prosecutor worked for two years on a question of fact: who leaked the name of a CIA operative, a violation of federal law? Typically you do not have two years to seek the truth, so for your persuasive presentation, you will likely choose questions of fact that take less time to uncover. Examples of such questions are "Who is responsible for a piece of legislation concerning government-backed financial aid for college students?" or "What is the reasoning behind the current law concerning the disposal of electronics?"

The **question of value** *raises issues about goodness and badness, right and wrong, enlightenment and ignorance.* Should all premature babies be kept alive even though some may face a lifetime of health issues? Should our society allow people to take their own lives when they suffer from chronic pain or incurable disease? Should we cut taxes at the same time that we reduce spending on social services? All of these are questions of value that get to the heart of our beliefs.

The **question of policy** *enters the realm of rules, regulations, and laws.* Should college students be prohibited from drinking alcohol on campus even though they are of legal age? Should restaurants be required to report the fat content of their products prominently on their walls or menus? Should our college require service learning as a graduation requirement? All of these questions are attempts to establish some policy that will regulate behaviors.

Organizing Your Persuasive Presentation

Now that you know how common persuasion is, what persuasive presentations are, how communication research has informed our knowledge of audiences and messages, and what types of questions persuasive speaking typically explores, you are ready to learn how to organize, structure, and design your persuasive presentation. Let us look first at how the introduction and the conclusion of a persuasive presentation can differ from those in other kinds of speeches.

Introducing the Persuasive Presentation

Your introduction may still consist of the four functions explained in Chapter 6: gaining and maintaining favorable attention, introducing the topic by relating the topic to the audience, relating the topic to the presenter, and previewing the organization and development of the speech. However, the persuasive presentation has one possible expansion and one possible exception.

The expansion relates to the part of the speech where the presenter or the person introducing the presenter reveals more about the credentials or credibility of the source than may be required in other kinds of presentations. Source credibility or *ethos* refers to the presenter's credentials, integrity, and positive relationship with the audience. In a persuasive presentation, a presenter's authority to speak is more significant, because who the speaker is may be one of the important reasons for a listener to respond to his or her persuasive message. Persuasive speakers should exercise considerable care in relating themselves to the topic.

The exception to the four functions with the persuasive presentation is that in informative speeches, presenters are most effective when they clearly reveal up front what they want the listeners to learn. However, in a persuasive presentation, if you are going to ask an audience to buy into some idea that would be repulsive to them without adequate preparation, then it probably would be better to gently ease listeners toward your purpose before revealing it explicitly. For instance, before your community accepts the idea of a new dump site in the immediate area—however badly needed—the people who will be affected would need considerable preparation in the form of reasons, needs, evidence, and even narratives or stories about how awful the current situation is without the dump.

Concluding the Persuasive Presentation

The conclusion of a persuasive presentation may need to be adapted so that the stated purpose—the last step in relating the topic to the audience—falls toward the end of the speech after much preparation has occurred.

Gabriella, a sales representative for a cleaning supply company, presented a persuasive message to Modern Motels of America using such an approach. She began talking to the Modern Motels executives about their long and satisfactory relationship with her company, Tidewater Supplies. She then told them about the quality of the sundries and cleaning supplies that her company had provided for their company over the years. She reminded them of how pleased their employees and customers had been with Tidewater products. Next she recollected how faithfully her company had serviced Modern Motels, never having failed to keep the motels supplied with high-quality products. Only after all of these preliminaries did Gabriella present the executives with a bid for her company's services, the persuasive purpose of her message.

Choosing Patterns of Organization for Persuasive Presentations

Chapter 6 covered organizational patterns in detail, but four patterns need attention here because presenters choose them most often for persuasive presentations.

Topical Sequence and Cause-Effect Patterns

These two patterns of organization work equally well for informative and persuasive presentations. When used for persuasion, the topical sequence pattern addresses advantages and disadvantages, lists reasons for accepting a proposition, and offers supporting material or a series of emotional stories to encourage acceptance of a proposition. The cause-effect pattern of organization, when used to persuade, first reveals the cause (too many housing developments displacing waterfront areas and barrier islands) and then the effect (no protection from flooding) in a speech aimed at encouraging new zoning regulations to stop wiping out protective areas.

Problem-Solution and Monroe Motivated Sequence Patterns

Presenters often use these two patterns of organization to persuade. The persuader who uses the problem-solution pattern first reveals the problem that creates the need for a solution: A lack of building code enforcement makes student rental properties unsafe. The presenter then moves to a possible solution: The city council is considering the addition of more inspectors and tougher consequences for violators—if citizens show support for the idea. The persuasive purpose is to encourage listeners to lobby the city council to solve the problem.

The Monroe Motivated Sequence is another pattern from Chapter 6 that presenters use mainly for persuasive presentations. This organizational pattern (1) begins by gaining attention so the listeners will focus on the topic, (2) establishes the need by demonstrating topic relevance, (3) reveals how the proposal will satisfy audience needs, (4) portrays the solution in a way that allows the audience to visualize themselves taking part, and, finally, (5) reveals what the listeners can do to make the visualization come true.

Once you understand the most commonly used patterns of organization in persuasive presentations, you need to consider how to shape the content of your presentation by considering some strategies for gaining compliance.

Persuasive Strategies

Consistency Persuades

The first principle of persuasion is that **consistency persuades**, meaning that *audiences are more likely to change their behavior if the suggested change is consistent with their present beliefs, attitudes, and values.* Risk takers like daring ideas. Competitive people are most likely to enter still other competitions. People who understand that "we are a nation of immigrants" are unlikely to discourage immigrants from moving into their neighborhood.

People tend to be relatively consistent. Past behavior is a good predictor of future behavior. The public speaker uses this notion of consistency by linking persuasive proposals to past consistencies. The presenter promotes change by showing how the promoted activity is consistent with the audience's past behavior. If

"Risk takers like daring ideas."

try this

By yourself, write down (a) a few things that you could be persuaded to change and (b) a few things that you probably would not change for anyone or anything. Why do persuaders have to be careful what they ask for?

you are speaking to a group of Republican delegates, you may show how your ideas are consistent with the right to own guns, to discourage abortions, or to toughen immigration legislation.

Small, Gradual Changes Persuade

The second principle of persuasion is that **small, gradual changes persuade**, meaning that *audiences are more likely to alter their behavior if the suggested change will require small, gradual changes rather than major, abrupt changes*. A common error of beginning persuaders is that they ask for too much change too soon for too little reason. Hostile audiences especially are resistant to persuaders who ask for too much too fast. They might respond with a **boomerang effect** in which *the audience likes the presenter and the proposal even less after the presentation*.

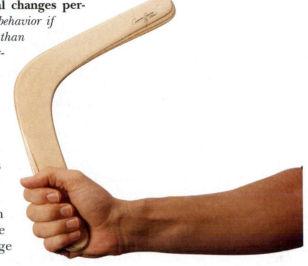

In a presentation on energy conservation, you probably would not succeed with an appeal that bluntly says "Quit using so much electricity." However, a presenter who begins with "Shut off the lights in rooms you are not using" and moves to "turn off the hot water heater when you are gone for more than a couple of days" will more likely accomplish her goal of gaining behavioral change from the audience.

Benefits Persuade

The third principle of persuasion is that *audiences are more likely to change their behavior if the suggested change will benefit them more than it will cost them*. We consider **cost-benefit analysis**, for example, every time we buy something: "Do I want this new jacket even though it means I must spend $150 plus tax? The benefits are that I will be warm and look nice. The cost is that I will not be able to replace my broken cell phone." The persuader frequently demonstrates to the audience that the benefits are worth the cost.

How can you use cost-benefit analysis in your classroom speech? Consider the costs to the audience of doing as you ask. What are the costs in money, time, commitment, energy, skill, or talent? Consider one of the most common requests in student speeches: communicate with your representative or senator about an issue. Many student speakers make that request without considering the probability that nobody in class has ever communicated with a senator or representative. Even if the speaker includes an e-mail address, the message writing will take a commitment of time and effort. Few students are willing to pay those costs. On the other hand, if the speaker comes to class with a letter already composed and simply asks for signatures from the class, then the cost is a few seconds of time, and the speaker is more likely to gain audience cooperation. Whenever you deliver a persuasive speech, consider the costs and how you can reduce them so the audience will feel the costs are worth the proposed benefits.

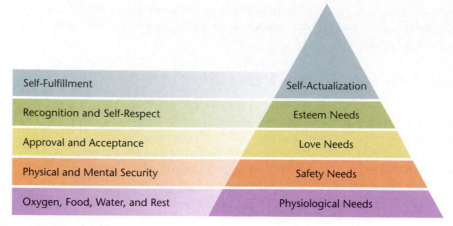

Self-Fulfillment	Self-Actualization
Recognition and Self-Respect	Esteem Needs
Approval and Acceptance	Love Needs
Physical and Mental Security	Safety Needs
Oxygen, Food, Water, and Rest	Physiological Needs

Figure 11.2   **Maslow's pyramid: A hierarchy of needs.** Can a persuader target particular human needs?

SOURCE: "Maslow's Hierarchy of Needs," from *Motivation and Personality*, 3rd ed., by Abraham H. Maslow, Robert D. Frager, and James Fadiman, © 1987. Adapted by permission of Pearson Education, Inc., Upper Saddle River, NJ.

Need Fulfillment Persuades

The fourth principle of persuasion is that audiences are more likely to change their behavior if the change meets their needs. Psychology scholar Abraham Maslow created an often-cited **hierarchy of needs,**[12] *a pyramid that builds from basic physiological needs like the need for oxygen all the way up to self-actualization needs—the realization of one's highest potential* (see Figure 11.2). Maslow's pyramid makes sense. As a human being, you do need all the items in the hierarchy, though many people never get very far above the second level shown in the figure, and few people think they have achieved complete self-actualization.

Maslow's pyramid is a useful resource for your persuasive presentations. Consider this example: Ball State University in Muncie, Indiana, initiated a project in which the students—working with a nonprofit group called TEAMwork—listened to and recorded the views and voices of poverty in their area. If you were trying to persuade students to participate in this project, you could utilize Maslow's pyramid by saying "Your family will be proud to learn that you are involved in this humanitarian concern" (Maslow's need for love, approval, and acceptance), or "You will get credit and recognition for working on this project" (Maslow's need for esteem, recognition, and self-respect), or "Working to advance the health of others will make you feel great about yourself" (Maslow's need for self-actualization and self-fulfillment). Incidentally, the "Voice and Vision: Poverty from the Inside Out" program was so good that it became a series on Indiana Public Radio. Besides the radio program, the students' community engagement taught them "the harsh realities of life on the street."

You can analyze your audience for specific needs. Do they need money? Jobs? Day care for their children or elders? Do they need help in dealing with government bureaucracies? Do they need better living conditions? Do they need to learn how to study, how to handle children, or how to live with spouses? Check out your own audience and determine what they need, because a persuasive speech that meets the audience's needs is likely to be successful.

Critical Thinking through Reasoning

A persuasive presentation can be based on ethos, pathos, or logos. Sometimes we say that others should be persuaded because an authoritative source is behind the message (ethos or source credibility): for example, the Pope, the Koran, or your boss. Sometimes we say that others should be persuaded because a touching story convinces us to take action (pathos): the homeless family, living in the city park with no blankets or food, is asking our organization for help. Still other times we argue a case for why others should be persuaded. We make a **claim**, *a conclusion of what the persuader would have the listener believe or do that invites proof or evidence.* Dillard and Marshall say that based on the research "We may assert with confidence that including evidence in a persuasive message will enhance the performance of the appeal."[13]

Using Inductive Reasoning

The kind of reasoning in which the *persuader amasses a series of particular instances to draw an inference* is known as **inductive reasoning**. The critical thinker knows that inductive reasoning is vulnerable in several ways. One weakness is that such reasoning involves an "inferential leap" in which the presenter jumps from a series of particulars to some generalization about them, e.g., the local banks have unfair rates for students. But were those particulars typical? Were they biased in that the presenter selected them while ignoring others that did not support his claim? Inductive reasoning is like circumstantial evidence: Nobody saw the killing, but the alleged killer's fingerprints were on the gun, witnesses saw him at the scene at the time of the crime, and the killer was having an affair with the victim's estranged sister. We make an "inferential leap" to the probable notion that this particular person did the killing.

Using Deductive Reasoning

Deductive reasoning *occurs when the presenter bases her claim on some premise that is generally affirmed by the audience.* Notice that the premise does not have to be true; it just has to be widely believed by the audience. So, in some communities the major premise that "God created human beings" becomes the widely believed idea that moves easily to "Human beings inhabit Kansas" (minor premise) and "therefore, God created the people of Kansas" (conclusion). This kind of reasoning is known as deductive reasoning, an argument based on a major premise, a minor premise, and a conclusion.

Like inductive reasoning, the critical thinker can attack deductive reasoning by questioning the premises on which the persuader bases the argument. Look how significantly the argument changes if the major premise is "Evolution resulted in human beings." Whether persuaders use inductive or deductive arguments, they have plenty of generalizations and premises to argue about: life begins at conception; Social Security should be privatized; wealthy people should receive tax cuts; retirement age should be raised; and rape victims should be told of the "morning-after" birth control pill.

Using Hard Evidence in Reasoning

Another feature of reasoned discourse is what you use as evidence or proof. From watching the various spinoffs of *Law and Order*, you know that some things are regarded as hard evidence: fingerprints, DNA, a weapon. On the other hand, other "proofs" are less likely to hold up: witness testimony, a grainy surveillance video, or a statement from an angry partner.

Similarly, in reasoned discourse we sometimes use arguments that are more convincing than others. A study in the *New England Journal of Medicine* is better proof than testimony from a drug company spokesperson. Statistics from an impartial source with a large, randomly selected sample are better than statistics from a company trying to show that its product is better than another's. Testimony from an authoritative source—a physician on your blood work or a chemistry professor on ionic compounds—is more convincing than the words of nonexperts. Anything that can demonstrate cause is convincing: Secondhand smoke causes increased lung cancer. Yet, scientific studies, statistics from carefully crafted research, testimony from experts, and arguments from cause are regarded as reliable forms of proof.

Using Soft Evidence in Reasoning

Less convincing, but sometimes enticing, are softer proofs like analogy, quotations, and narrative. The persuader argues that "America, like Rome, will fall because of moral decline." The persuader "proves" the case by reminding us of Roman orgies and other forms of debauchery and compares that to raves, cable TV sex shows, and our many failed marriages. The persuader uses a quotation to "prove" that she is correct in her assessment of our national security. The persuader uses narrative to persuade by telling stories of people victimized by war, people rendered homeless by natural disasters, or middle-class people bankrupted by lapsed insurance and skyrocketing healthcare costs—all examples of pathos.

An analogy is always susceptible to rebuttal because invariably an analogy is based on comparing two things that are fundamentally unlike (e.g., Roman and American society are different in countless ways). A quotation is only as good as the credibility of the person making the statement. And a narrative exhibiting pathos can be rebutted by demonstrating that the story is atypical, sensationalized, or simply beyond our ability to solve.

Using Reasoning from Cause

"Determining cause can be a challenging task."

Determining cause can be a challenging task. For example, convincing people that smoking cigarettes is a causal factor in lung cancer took decades. For many social and political issues, the causes and effects can be complex and various. Nonetheless, we use reasoning from cause often and in two directions: Sometimes we move from cause to effect and sometimes we move from effect to cause.

Reasoning from cause means that you have to demonstrate, for example, that the leading cause of lung cancer is cigarette smoking, not air pollution, not water contamination, not genetics. Causal reasoning also means that the cause must be solidly linked to the effect; otherwise, what we are witnessing would simply be correlation, two unrelated things occurring together. Scientists can prove that smoking cigarettes and getting lung cancer are solidly linked even if every smoker does not die of cigarette use. When reasoning from cause, you must be very careful to (*a*) show that the cause and effect are solidly linked and (*b*) eliminate other possible causes. Similarly, when starting with effect, you must be careful to (*a*) demonstrate that effect and cause are solidly linked and (*b*) eliminate other possible effects.

Using Reasoning from Sign

He has a backpack and he is walking across campus; therefore, he must be a student. We reason from sign every day, but we may not be correct in doing so: The guy with the backpack turns out to be an unemployed mechanic looking for a warm building for refuge. The best way to reason from sign is to reason from multiple signs. Multiple signs ordinarily lead to a better conclusion. So, if he looks like a student, acts like a student, walks across campus like a student, and appears to know others on campus, the chances are better that he is a student. In reasoning from sign, you need a sufficient number of reliable signs that do not contradict each other and are not accidental or coincidental.

Using Reasoning from Generalization

This deductive form of argument depends on the acceptance of the statement. "All spiders have eight legs," for example, is a truism since arachnids are differentiated from insects (six legs) by the number of legs. Many generalizations are less sound: "Belonging to a labor union is good." This generalization could encounter some rebuttal from those who believe that belonging to a labor union drives up the cost of products.

Normally a persuader argues from generalization by applying a generalization that is widely accepted or provable to a particular case: "All honors graduates are intelligent; Fred is an honors graduate; therefore, Fred is intelligent." However, many generalizations are not unquestionable truths. One could argue in rebuttal that many honors graduates are not highly intelligent; instead, they are people of ordinary intellect who just work harder and longer than others.

Now that you know more about how persuaders use reasoning in their presentations, let us look at fallacies, poor reasoning that you should strive to avoid.

Avoid Fallacies

A **fallacy** is *an error in reasoning that weakens an argument*. Fallacies come in many forms, but those described here are the ones we have found public speaking students to (mis)use the most.

Name Calling.   This fallacy unfairly categorizes people by slapping a label on them. Calling someone a "liberal" may be perceived as a slam, while labeling someone a "conservative" may be perceived as a compliment. As a political candidate, would you perhaps win an election by labeling your opponent as "a liberal"? How can you avoid name calling in a presentation?

- Omit the label and refer instead to the person's record.
- Decide for yourself if an idea has merit without regard for the label.

Glittering Generality.   The technique behind the "glittering generality" is to embrace a word that symbolizes some highly positive virtue. The glittering generality invites us to accept and approve an idea without examining any evidence. For example, "We need to bring democracy to country X" is a statement that exploits our very positive attitude about our form of democracy without analyzing its appropriateness to another nation or region. The critical questions to ask are:

- Does the idea in question (transplanting democracy) have a legitimate relationship to the virtuous word (democracy)?
- Is a misguided plan (transplanting democracy) being advanced simply by linking it to a positive name?

Bandwagon Technique.   With this fallacy, the speaker encourages the listener to do something because "everyone" in the same valued group is doing it. For example, you should vote for a candidate because everyone in our congregation is doing so. The critical questions to ask are:

- What is the evidence for adopting or rejecting this idea?
- Does this idea serve or hinder my interests regardless of who else allegedly is following this idea?

Circular Reasoning.   This fallacy uses two unproven propositions to prove each other. Pit bulls should be outlawed because they are vicious animals. We know they are vicious animals because they should be outlawed.

- Avoid circular reasoning by making certain that your assumptions can be proven.

Either/Or.   This fallacy assumes that everything is binary, that every issue has two opposite positions: Either you are for me or you are against me. However, someone certainly could be fairly neutral, neither for nor against. The fact is that few issues have only two opposite points of view. Most issues have multiple positions. How do you avoid this fallacy?

- Recognize that most issues are complicated enough to have multiple points of view.

Post Hoc Fallacy.   The actual name of this fallacy is *"post hoc, ergo propter hoc,"* an expression that means "after this; therefore, because of this." Fortunately, this fallacy is easier

e-NOTE

The Institute of Propaganda Analysis

Years ago, the Institute of Propaganda Analysis developed seven methods used to short-circuit critical thinking. That analysis of propaganda remains so popular today that a Google search on the Institute produces around 180,000 items about propaganda. To save time, go to **www.propagandacritic.com**, where you will find a list of propaganda techniques defined and explained.

to explain than to pronounce. For instance, I no sooner bought a new battery than my transmission failed; I met her, and my misfortunes began; and I walked under a ladder and almost immediately was splashed by a passing car. This fallacy attributes misfortunes to an event that occurred before the misfortune even though the event did not actually cause the misfortune. You can avoid this fallacy if you are always aware of the following:

- Just because two things occur closely together in time does not mean that one caused the other.
- Realize that often things occur closely in time by accident or coincidence, not because one caused the other.

Ethics and Persuasive Speaking

Persuasive presentations offer ample opportunities for positive purposes or for ethical mischief. Persuasive speaking can result in the advancement of a good cause or the purchase of a product you do not need, never wanted, and that you will never use. Distinguishing between ethical and unethical persuasive appeals is a challenging task for which the following guidelines apply:

1. *Be careful whom you trust.* The best-looking, smoothest-talking presenter can be a pathological deceiver, while an unattractive, inarticulate person can have your best interests in mind. Listeners need to watch whom they trust, and presenters need to provide credentials to show they are trustworthy. They need to demonstrate their source credibility.

2. *Analyze and evaluate messages for reasonableness, truth, and benefit to you and the community.* Many vendors try to convince you to buy in a hurry because rushing limits your reasoning. They do not want you to carefully consider whether the decision really makes sense. As a critical thinker, you will want messages to meet standards of reasonableness.

3. *You and your messages will be more persuasive if you have a long, positive history.* "The thing you get to lose once is your reputation." If your past invites others to trust you and your word; and if others tend to benefit from your messages as much or more than you do (that is, you do not seek compliance for selfish purposes), you will build credibility. Are you building a history that will help you or harm you when you attempt to persuade others?

4. *Always be respectful of your audience.* If you treat them as you would want to be treated, you will avoid many ethical problems.

5. *Avoid fallacies.* If you always strive to use sound reason tempered by critical thinking, then you will skillfully avoid those short circuits to reasonable thought that we know as fallacies.

See Figure 11.3 for a checklist that reviews the important features of the persuasive presentation, including the ethical dimension.

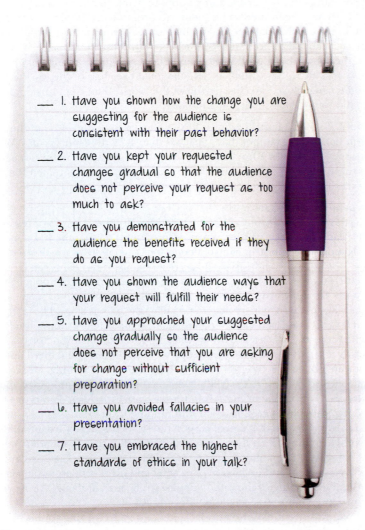

___ 1. Have you shown how the change you are suggesting for the audience is consistent with their past behavior?

___ 2. Have you kept your requested changes gradual so that the audience does not perceive your request as too much to ask?

___ 3. Have you demonstrated for the audience the benefits received if they do as you request?

___ 4. Have you shown the audience ways that your request will fulfill their needs?

___ 5. Have you approached your suggested change gradually so the audience does not perceive that you are asking for change without sufficient preparation?

___ 6. Have you avoided fallacies in your presentation?

___ 7. Have you embraced the highest standards of ethics in your talk?

Figure 11.3   **Checklist for the persuasive presentation.** What have you done on this list to help persuade your audience?

An Example of a Persuasive Presentation

Keep the Mekong Free

This is a picture of the Mekong River, on the border between Northeast Thailand and Laos. If you look to the side of the bank you will see a small pipe sticking out of the ground. This pipe is a marker for a proposed dam that will forever change the Mekong River once it is built.

Starting with a visual aid using rich verbal description is an effective way to raise audience curiosity and interest in your topic.

The speaker used personal experience to establish good will and credibility with the audience and then presented a very clear call to action.

Four main points are a lot for a shorter speech. However, some persuasive speeches may rely on more main points to clearly develop the argument(s) being presented.

This is an example of a well-worded transition statement with a signpost. Clear transitions better help audience members follow the speech as it develops, particularly when this many main points are used.

These statistics are good for providing perspective on the scope of dams; however, without using a visual aid the intricacy of the explanation could become confusing. Visual aids help make statistics clearer.

Here the speaker uses a source from an academic journal. What more could the speaker say about the source to develop stronger credibility?

Notice how the reasoning develops in this paragraph. To establish the claim that dams require international scrutiny, the speaker presents several reasons why dams have impacts beyond the home country's borders.

This is the transition and signpost to the second point.

Here the speaker uses technical language. Using your own knowledge or an online dictionary, what does "metric" mean and how could the speaker have been clearer?

Notice how the speaker uses style (the third Canon of Rhetoric) in the form of several metaphors. Stylistic devices like these can naturally increase interest in the speech. Can you identify all of the metaphors in the first two sentences of this paragraph?

This past summer I had the opportunity to visit Thailand as part of a study-abroad experience. In our program we visited two villages, one on a tributary to the Mekong where a dam had been built and one near the site of the proposed dam on the Mekong itself. In both cases, villagers explained what has happened and what could happen when dams are built.

After meeting the villagers and learning what happened after the first dam was built, I pledged to do everything possible to oppose construction of new dams on the Mekong. I hope that you will join with me in these efforts. First I'll explain why dams are used so extensively to promote economic development. Second, I will explain the scope of the proposed dam projects on the Mekong River. Next I will describe what happens to the environment and river villages when dams are constructed, and finally I will explain how you can help.

So that you can better understand why I oppose dams on a river so far away, first let's explore why dams have been used so frequently to promote economic development.

As a result of the Industrial Revolution, humans have increasingly looked to rivers as sources of raw material to promote economic growth. According to the World Dam Commission, there have been over 4,500 dams at least as high as a four-story building built across rivers worldwide. In fact, humans have dammed over half of the world's rivers. To put this in some perspective, the chairperson of the World Dam Commission explained in the introduction to the 2000 report the following:

> Less than 2.5% of the Earth's water is fresh water; of that, only 33% of the fresh water is in liquid form, and of that water less than 1.7% flows in streams. Why is this important? Basically, a fraction of a percent of the Earth's water flows from town to town, village to village, and country to country. Dams threaten the small amount of naturally flowing water that does exist.

Why do people create dams in the first place?

In a special issue of the *Journal of Environmental Management*, a group of researchers explained that dams have four primary purposes in terms of development: Dams can provide sources of irrigation; they can help control floods; they can create reservoirs to supply large bodies of water for domestic, industrial, and recreational uses; and dams can be used to create hydroelectric power. On the screen you can see a representation of how a hydroelectric dam works. Water from the artificial reservoir travels through the dam to rotate a turbine, which generates electricity. The river above and below the dam is altered because of the change in water flow. This last use, power generation, is the primary motivation behind most large-scale dam projects such as those on the Mekong River and its tributaries.

The growth of large dams has accelerated at such a large pace that international bodies are now starting to bring greater scrutiny on the practice of damming. Most dams are international concerns because rivers typically flow across national boundaries, so the actions of one country could affect one or more countries downstream. Also, dam projects are so large that they typically always require significant funding from international sources like the World Bank or private, multinational corporations. Because dams are international in scope, the World Commission on Dams was created in 2000 to act as an independent body of academics, policy makers, and other experts who can develop international guidelines for comprehensive assessment and evaluation of existing and proposed large-scale dam projects.

With this understanding of the international significance of dams, the second point explains the proposed dam projects on the Mekong River.

The Mekong River is one of the world's largest rivers. According to the United Nations Environmental Programme, the Mekong is between the tenth and twelfth largest river in the world, depending on which metric is used. The 4,200-kilometer Mekong stretches from Southern China south through Myanmar, Laos, Thailand, Cambodia, and empties into the South China Sea in Vietnam. Over 265 million people live in the Mekong River basin, with most living in Vietnam, Thailand, and Myanmar. Although economic development has been substantial over the last fifty years in Southeast Asia, people who live in the Mekong River basin are still among the poorest in the subcontinent, if not the world. Many are indigenous people who have lived along the river for thousands of years.

As explained in a 2007 *National Geographic* story, the threat to the river flows from growing economies, primarily in China, Thailand, and Vietnam. The massive flood of population, supercharged by a thirst for electricity, has led economic and political elites across the subcontinent to target the Mekong as a natural source for hydroelectric power and abundant natural resources. Despite the fact that dams already constructed along the Mekong and its tributaries have had significant negative impacts, as many as sixteen new dams are under construction or planned along the Mekong itself to meet the growing need for development in the region. Of course, my goal, and the goal for all of us, should be to see that those dams are never constructed.

Why should we care about the dam? After all, development is generally seen as good, right? Unfortunately, dams are not the environmentally safe alternative for cheap energy. First, dams catastrophically alter the river ecosystem. Speaking at a 2010 meeting of Southeast Asian leaders of state, Thai Prime Minister Abhisit Vejjajiva warned that the "Mekong River is being threatened by serious problems arising from both the unsustainable use of water and the effects of climate change." Based on experiences from other dams in the Mekong system, scientists have learned that large dams impact the environment in three significant ways.

Here the speaker uses a direct quotation because the wording is powerful and the source is highly credible. Moreover, using a government source from one of the Mekong countries can add significant power to the argument that dams are not the best source for economic development.

First, when reservoirs are created, silt that normally runs down the river collects behind the dam. This not only places greater strain on the dam itself, but also chokes the ecosystem behind the dam and robs land downstream from its natural replenishment of nutrients. Second, because the riverbank downstream is not replenished with naturally flowing river silt, valuable farmland along the banks of the river will erode away and be unusable for local production of plants and vegetables. Finally, and most dramatically, the natural fisheries along the Mekong will be destroyed. According to a 2008 report issued by a Thai nongovernmental organization called ESCR, the Pak Mun Dam, constructed in the late 1970s on a Mekong tributary, caused significant loss of natural fish species in the Mun River. Of the 265 indigenous species of fish natural to the river, only 45 were present upstream from the dam once it was completed. The problem is so bad that the Thai government has agreed to open the dam for at least four months out of the year to help maintain even a modest fish stock for villagers upstream. Even these steps have been ineffective. Villagers report fish declines of 60 to 80 percent since the dam opened.

Here the speaker relies on statistics to provide a rationale for the argument about fisheries being depleted. The argument could be strengthened with additional explanation for why a dam would harm fisheries upstream from the dam.

Of course, the impact of damming goes beyond fish and farmland. In these river villages people are connected to the river through generations. When the Pak Mun Dam was erected, small islands and sand bars were destroyed; those high spots in the river were key meeting spots for celebrations and supported active community life tied to the river. When EGAT (Eee-GHAT), the Thai energy authority, offered to relocate villagers displaced by the dam, they were given substandard housing in areas where it was impossible to grow crops or to fish. As a result, villagers lost their primary means of personal and economic prosperity. In this picture that I took, you can see one of the village elders looking over the Mun River below the dam where he used to fish. In the short clip you are about to see, one of the village elders, speaking through an interpreter, explained how the dam has harmed his community.

Here the speaker uses a picture and actual narrative from a villager to establish pathos, a form of persuasive proof. The video narrative and picture helps audience members identify with the problems faced by the villagers.

Just one dam on one tributary of the Mekong literally destroyed generations of knowledge built up around a small section of one river; imagine the effect if the Mekong itself was forever altered to quench the thirst for electricity in Bangkok, Saigon, and other metropolitan areas. Tilt, Braun, and He, an interdisciplinary group of scholars who study the impact of dams, concluded in a 2009 article that the social impact of dams on indigenous populations is equally as devastating as the ecological impact, both of which are often irreversible.

Here again, the speaker uses a metaphor to add interest to the speech.

So what can we do as Americans, thousands of miles away from the Mekong River? My final point tries to give you some practical steps that you can take to help. First, we need to make sure that our government views the issue of dams as a significant aspect of its human rights policy. We should contact our elected senators to let them know that we oppose dams so that they can take those views into consideration when debating and voting on international treaties. Second, we should contact the U.S. Department of State and encourage our international dignitaries to promote free rivers. The Department of State has significant authority to help promote human rights among indigenous populations, and our nation's diplomatic corps could have a meaningful impact on stopping some of the projects from gaining further traction. Finally, all of us should make a commitment to sign the online petition opposing dams on the Mekong River. Small steps like these show that free rivers are an international concern and they make it more difficult for economic and political elites to write off opposition to dams as the views of a few uneducated, poor river people. You can sign the petition in just a few seconds by visiting the "Save the Mekong Coalition" Web site. I'll provide you with a small slip of paper with the URL that you can use and pass along to a friend. I'll also send you an email with the URL later today.

In the final point of the speech, the speaker identifies several specific things audience members can do. Even though some of the actions may seem less effective (e.g., writing government officials), such steps could spur audience involvement, which may allow more robust steps to be taken.

Here the speaker likely saved the solution step considered most interesting to be the last. Notice how the speaker provided exact information for accomplishing this step, whereas the other steps were more vague. This persuasive strategy is often used to lead audience members to a particular desired action.

In conclusion, you have learned about the practice of damming and the threat that dams pose to the people living along the Mekong River. Unless these dams are stopped, the ecology and communities of people along the Mekong will be lost forever. Luckily, we know that voices like ours can help. In the face of informed protest, the Thai energy authority was forced to open the Pak Mun Dam to help save the threatened fisheries. With more voices from around the world, I hope that we can keep other villages from facing the same problems. You are armed with a simple action—to sign a petition. Use Facebook and email to tell your friends about this problem and get them to sign it, too. If we all voice our concern, hopefully the Mekong can remain free and the people along the river can continue to lead the life that they choose.

The speaker adds impact to the solution step by showing that "protest" has successfully helped in another circumstance. Such explanation may persuade audience members that their actions after the speech could have positive outcomes.

For REVIEW >>

AS YOU READ

1. Compare and contrast the purposes of persuasive and informative presentations.

2. Identify the principles and types of persuasive presentations.

3. Reflect on the type of change you will ask of your audience.

SUMMARY HIGHLIGHTS

▶ The purposes of informative presentations are to generate information hunger, to help the audience understand the information, to help the audience remember the information, and to invite the audience to apply the information from the presentation.

▶ The purpose of persuasive presentations is to change listeners' beliefs or attitudes and influence their feelings.

▶ Persuasive presentations change the audience.

▶ Fact, value, and policy are three types of questions around which most persuasive presentations revolve.

▶ We identified three types of persuasive speeches:
  • The speech to inspire influences listeners' feelings.
  • The speech to convince influences listeners' beliefs or attitudes.
  • The speech of action influences listeners' behaviors.

▶ We considered four strategies of persuasion:
  • Consistency persuades.
  • Small, gradual changes persuade.
  • Benefits persuade.
  • Fulfilling needs persuades.

▶ This is determined based on the subject of your presentation.

4. Recognize how effective persuasive presentations depend on arguments that are built upon reasoning, critical thinking, and ethics.

▶ Apply critical thinking through various kinds of reasoning.
- Inductive reasoning uses specific instances and an inferential leap.
- Deductive reasoning uses widely accepted premises to draw convincing conclusions.
- Hard evidence has the most credibility.
- Soft evidence can convince with more difficulty.
- Reasoning from cause can be challenging because you have to show a solid link between cause and effect.
- Reasoning from signs draws upon reliable signs that do not contradict and that are not accidental or coincidental.
- Reasoning from generalization is used when you can count on wide acceptance or when the generalization is easily provable to a particular case.

Pop Quiz

1. The persuasive speech that seeks to influence listeners' beliefs or attitudes is a:
   (A) speech of action
   (B) speech to discuss
   (C) speech to convince
   (D) speech to inspire

2. Beth wants her listeners to volunteer to donate blood. She will be giving a:
   (A) speech to inspire
   (B) speech of action
   (C) speech to convince
   (D) speech of desire

3. If an audience member responds to a persuasive message by doing what is socially acceptable, he or she is employing a:
   (A) critical response
   (B) compliance response
   (C) defensive response
   (D) motivated response

4. An audience's defensive response occurs when the audience:
   (A) fends off the persuader's message to protect existing beliefs, attitudes, and values
   (B) focuses on the arguments, the quality of the evidence, and the truth or accuracy of the message
   (C) does what is socially acceptable
   (D) takes explicit notes during the presentation

5. To create an effective message, you should:
   (A) use "many" or "most" rather than specific numbers
   (B) employ incomplete arguments
   (C) use testimonial evidence
   (D) avoid being explicit

6. "Should the university require public speaking as a graduation requirement?" is a question of:
   (A) fact
   (B) value
   (C) opinion
   (D) policy

7. An organizational pattern *not* generally used for persuasive presentations is:
   (A) topical sequence
   (B) cause-effect pattern
   (C) Monroe Motivated Sequence
   (D) spatial pattern

8. After Kenny's speech, the audience liked him and his topic less than before the presentation. This is known as:
   (A) consistency persuades
   (B) boomerang effect
   (C) speech to convince
   (D) fallacy

9. If you attempt to persuade your audience by showing them that your plan for change will benefit the audience more than it will cost them, you are using a persuasive strategy based on the fact that:

   (A) consistency persuades
   (B) small, gradual changes persuade
   (C) benefits persuade
   (D) need fulfillment persuades

10. Name calling, the bandwagon technique, and glittering generalities are examples of:

    (A) fallacies
    (B) questions of fact
    (C) speeches to inspire
    (D) testimonial evidence

Answers: 1 (C); 2 (B); 3 (B); 4 (A); 5 (C); 6 (D); 7 (D); 8 (B); 9 (C); 10 (A)

APPLICATION EXERCISES

1. Persuasive speeches often appeal to an audience's unmet needs. Since needs vary according to the community, college, class, and individual, you can make yourself more sensitive to audience needs by ranking the five unmet needs that you believe are important to your audience.

   a. _____

   b. _____

   c. _____

   d. _____

   e. _____

2. After reading the section on principles of persuasion, you should be able to identify cases in which they are correctly used. Examine the following cases and indicate which of the following principles is being observed:

   C = *Consistency persuades.*
   S = *Small changes persuade.*
   B = *Benefits persuade.*
   N = *Fulfilling needs persuades.*
   G = *Gradual approaches persuade.*

_____ a. To save my audience members considerable time and effort, I am going to provide them with a form letter that they can sign and send to the administration.

_____ b. Because I know most of my classmates are short of cash, I am going to tell them how to make some quick money with on-campus jobs.

_____ c. I plan to wait until the end of the speech to tell the audience members that the organization I want them to join will require two hours of driving per week.

_____ d. My audience of international students already believes in the value of learning public speaking, so I think the listeners will respond favorably to my recommendation for a course in voice and articulation.

_____ e. I would like my audience to cut up all their credit cards, but since they are unlikely to do so, I am instead going to ask that they try for a zero balance each month to avoid interest and fees.

Answers: a. B, b. N, c. G, d. C, e. S

KEY TERMS

Argument	Deductive reasoning	Question of value
Audience analysis	Defensive response	Relationship
Boomerang effect	Explicit	Small, gradual changes persuade
Claim	Fallacy	Specific numbers
Complete arguments	Hierarchy of needs	Speech of action
Compliance response	Inductive reasoning	Speech to convince
Consistency persuades	Persuasive presentations	Speech to inspire
Cost-benefit analysis	Question of fact	Testimonial evidence
Critical response	Question of policy	

get involved!

In a nearby city the faculty advisor for the student newspaper has been fired by the school board. The students are in an uproar because they believe he was canned for doing his job: he taught them to investigate and to report. But, like most government groups, the administration grew weary of the articles about it and sought to solve the problem by removing the teacher as faculty advisor to the student paper. Instead, the board threw fuel on the fire, which is now out of control.

The teachers' union packed a recent board meeting, the students wore T-shirts in support of their former advisor, the school board selected someone else to advise the paper, and the local newspaper charged the school board with violating freedom of the press.

A tempest in a teapot? No, this currently local issue could boil over into a state or national one. Google "freedom of the press cases" and you will find about 34 million items. Anyone interested in defending the hapless student newspaper advisor would find an abundance of information and ideas on the Internet.

Important issues come to the surface in your community, too. You can and should get involved in community issues. You can become an effective persuader on these issues by applying what you have learned about persuasion.

12

SPEAKING

Most of this book is devoted to planning, preparing, and delivering presentations for practical purposes—to teach audience members about a topic or persuade them to change in some way. Although many of our public presentations involve such objectives, another common type of speaking situation involves presentations that highlight a special event. These speeches are quite common and are generally referred to as special occasion presentations. This chapter teaches you about special occasion presentations by showing how they differ from other types of presentations, identifying the various types of special occasion presentations, and guiding you in developing your own special occasion speeches.

ON SPECIAL OCCASIONS

As You READ

1. Compare ceremonial presentations to other types of presentations.
2. Learn about nine types of ceremonial presentations.
3. Develop ideas for a ceremonial presentation that is appropriate to a specific audience, setting, and occasion.

On July 7, 2009, millions of fans from around the world watched public funeral services for Michael Jackson. The ceremony will be remembered as a defining moment in popular culture because of the significant press coverage and notoriety surrounding Jackson's life for over four decades. As the ceremony progressed, Michael Jackson was eulogized through both music and spoken word. In one speech, actress Brooke Shields walked to the microphone in tears and stated,

Michael was one of a kind . . . to us it was one of the most natural and easiest of friendships . . . we would have fun no matter where we were. We had a bond. And maybe it was because we both understood what it was like to be in the spotlight at a very young age . . . Both of us needed to be adults very early. But when we were together we were two little kids having fun.

In her eulogy, Shields was able to humanize Michael Jackson for fans who knew him only from a distance, probably through music, video, and news accounts. Shields's speech was full of genuine emotion and heartfelt admiration of her friend. More importantly, her speech was adapted to the situation in which she was speaking. Had the ceremony been a small, private function without cameras, her eulogy would have likely been different. However, within the charged atmosphere of the Staples Center in Los Angeles, Shields appropriately memorialized a beloved figure by re-envisioning his persona from the eyes of a close friend.

Most ceremonial speeches are not as emotionally trying as a eulogy, although they are also not nearly so "functional" as other types of speeches. In this chapter you will learn about the range of ceremonial speeches as well as appropriate ways to adapt your speechmaking skills to special situations.

How Would *You* Do It?

You just read about Brooke Shields's eulogy of Michael Jackson. As with other types of ceremonial speeches, eulogies are part of larger events emphasizing certain rituals and norms. If you were asked to give a eulogy, what rituals and norms would you want to emphasize in the speech?

Purpose

Recall from previous chapters that the primary purpose of an informative speech is to teach and the primary purpose of a persuasive speech is to change behaviors or beliefs. Although special occasion presentations might try to inform or persuade, these objectives are typically secondary. Rather, the primary purpose of a special occasion presentation is to perform a **ritual**, *a ceremonial act that is characterized by qualities or procedures that are appropriate to the occasion.*

All cultures have ceremonial rituals. Weddings, funerals, grand openings, awards ceremonies, and graduations are all examples of ritualized events. During such events, public presentations often punctuate important moments. At a wedding reception, for instance, the toasts to the new couple made by the "best man" and "maid of honor" are punctuating moments. The ritualistic nature of special occasion speeches is important. Such rituals help bring certainty and comfort to otherwise stressful events, they help attendees know what to expect, and they help attendees and audience members share in a common collective experience, such as wishing good tidings to a newly wedded couple or dedicating a new building to a devoted teacher. Some scholars go so far as to say that ritualized presentations at special occasions help link together the past, present, and future. That is exactly what Brooke Shields attempted to do in her eulogy for Michael Jackson.

Unique Characteristics of Special Occasion Presentations

Style

Special occasion speeches typically differ in style from more traditional informative and persuasive speeches. Recall from Chapter 2 that style refers to the clarity and ornamentation used during a presentation. Whereas a typical informative or persuasive speech might selectively use stylistic devices like narratives, metaphors, similes, or analogies, special occasion speeches might emphasize such techniques. Because special occasions are highly ritualistic, they invite the use of *highly stylized*, or **ornamental language**.

"Whereas a typical informative or persuasive speech might selectively use stylistic devices like narratives, metaphors, similes, or analogies, special occasion speeches might emphasize such techniques."

Organization

When speaking to inform or persuade, you must pay particular attention to how you organize large quantities of information. Because special occasion presentations are less concerned with information dissemination and argumentation and more concerned with setting a particular tone for the occasion, you need to handle the organization of such presentations differently than you would an informative or persuasive presentation. For instance, although special occasion presentations still should have an introduction, body, and conclusion, they typically have less obvious transitions between main points. Instead, their ornamental styling may suggest more subtle and creative ways to signal transitions between ideas. Moreover, special occasion presentations often are relatively short, and developing several main points may not be practical. In a presentation to introduce someone, for example, you should have a short introduction, provide a brief biography of the person, conclude by welcoming them, and invite applause or recognition. Taking time to "fully develop" several main points may be unnecessary and inappropriate.

SHHH. LET ME BE SILENT!

In Western culture, particularly in the field of rhetoric and public speaking, having the ability to talk and be heard is a form of power. Despite some natural tendencies to have some level of anxiousness when speaking, those who speak are viewed as more powerful than those who listen. In fact, the behavior of listening is often viewed as passive, unmotivated, and unengaged—look no further than participation grades in some classes for proof! Being silent is not viewed negatively in all cultures, though. Professor Donald Carbaugh and colleagues told a story of a Finnish foreign exchange student who was puzzled that her host family expected her to talk in the car when traveling on family outings. In Finnish culture the term "mietiskelä," which is interpreted as being contemplative and thoughtful, is part of the cultural way of being, according to Carbaugh and colleagues. They describe situations where entire groups of people can be engaged in mietiskelä at the same time. Think about times in American speaking situations when silence is explicitly called upon. At weddings the hope is that silence prevails when the officiant asks if there are any objections—in fact, silence is usually appreciated. At memorial services there are often moments of silence to honor those who have passed away. So, even in a talk-centered American culture, silence (or the Finnish concept of "mietiskelä") often becomes an important marker of special occasion speeches.

> **"Ceremony and ritual spring from our heart of hearts: those who govern us know it well, for they would sooner deny us bread than dare alter the observance of tradition."**
>
> [F. Gonzalez-Crussi, 1936–, pathologist and physician, Children's Memorial Hospital, Chicago]

Formality

Based on the previous sections, you might have guessed that special occasion speeches tend to be a bit more formal than traditional informative and persuasive presentations. Because you are taking part in a ritualized event and because you will likely try to make your style more ornamental, your special occasion speeches may appear more formal in tone.

Being formal does not mean being "stuffy." Rather, formality in this context refers more to the degree of professionalism you might use to share your ideas with your listeners. You might practice your presentation so often that you can memorize particular wordings and phrases; you might make extra efforts to use a full array of nonverbal gestures to accentuate your message; you may even, in some situations, go so far as to prepare a manuscript and practice that delivery technique. In sum, special occasion presentations are just that—special. Taking extra efforts to polish your presentation will allow you to have a more meaningful impact in setting the appropriate tone for the situation.

Types of Special Occasion Presentations

Although the potential number of different types of special occasion presentations is quite large, you will learn here about nine of the most common purposes for special occasion speaking:

- to welcome
- to pay tribute
- to introduce
- to nominate
- to dedicate

- to commemorate
- to say farewell
- to give recognition
- to entertain

These categories should provide some guidance for almost any special occasion at which you find yourself speaking.

Presentations to Welcome

Presentations to welcome are intended to *set a tone for a larger event by inviting all participants—including other presenters and audience members—to appropriately engage the event.* By "engage the event" we mean that events have a certain tone or feel, and the welcome speech should set that tone for the attendees. If the event is joyful, like an awards ceremony, the welcome speech should set a happy tone. If, on the other hand, the occasion is more serious, like an academic conference on your campus, the welcome speech should establish the professional tone necessary for that conference.

Welcome presentations typically are brief. Such presentations might try to accomplish two specific purposes. First, the presenter should typically welcome any honorees, important guests, or other noteworthy participants in the event. Second, the presenter should provide a brief message establishing the purpose of the event. During this latter stage, the presenter should use language, stories, or other stylistic devices to set the appropriate tone for the occasion.

Presentations to Pay Tribute

Presentations to pay tribute are designed to *offer celebration and praise of a noteworthy person, organization, or cause.* Speeches of tribute can be further subdivided into the following: eulogies, celebratory roasts, wedding toasts, retirement addresses, anniversary tributes, and other special events designed to celebrate the life or work of an individual or entity. For example, one of our campuses has a Campus-Community Day, established to celebrate the long heritage of the campus and community working together. Speeches at that event are tribute speeches because they honor the combined efforts of the two entities—the campus and the community.

Because tribute speeches include several different types, you should take care to fully analyze the situation to determine what focus would be most appropriate. However, nearly all tribute presentations attempt to provide some biographical sketch of the person/entity being honored. Generally speaking, tributes make extensive use of narratives to tell stories about the honoree. Such stories are effective at evoking emotion while at the same time celebrating the past. In some cases, tribute speeches might end by looking toward the future. For a retirement presentation, you might wish someone well as they take on new adventures in life; for a celebratory roast, you might encourage the honoree to "keep up the great work."

Presentations to Introduce

Speeches of introduction *are designed to tell us about the person being introduced and to help establish their ethos—in this case ethos might include credentials and/or goodwill.* Speeches of introduction usually precede a longer address, which will be presented by the person being introduced, and are typically brief.

Because the primary objective in a speech of introduction is to present information about the speaker, the majority of the speech should be devoted to the person's biography or other information relevant to the speaker's credibility. Depending on the occasion, you might also talk about the reason(s) this person was asked to speak. For this type of speech you may want to adapt the following approach:

Introduction: Use an anecdote or some story to establish audience members' emotional connection with the speaker being introduced.

Body: Discuss the speaker's biography and other qualifications. The focus of this part of your presentation should be on qualifications most relevant to the occasion but should also raise other interesting facts about the person.

Conclusion: Summarize the person's qualifications and use that summary to explain why she/he was asked to speak. End by welcoming the speaker and inviting the audience to join in the welcome by applauding.

e-NOTE

Facebook and the Death of Funeral Orations?

One type of ritual traditionally associated with public speaking is funerals. Public speaking students have practiced the "Funeral Oration" for thousands of years, primarily because speeches provided important markers and tributes of someone's passing. The funeral oration itself represents a sort of "end of life" marker of time in relation to a person's life. The traditional oration centralizes the symbolic act of grieving and paying tribute in the control of one person speaking. Modern culture, however, is starting to change that ritual. Now, social networking sites like Facebook and MySpace are changing the rules and norms for how we both mourn and celebrate life. Now, thousands of social networking pages exist for people who have died. The symbolic act of paying tribute and remembrance, traditionally reserved for a single special occasion speaker, is gradually giving way to a more ecumenical, online tribute to a deceased loved one or friend. Funeral orations may still happen, but more and more the symbolic act of paying tribute is taking place online.

Presentations to Nominate

Speeches of nomination *introduce and honor someone you wish to place in contention for an award, elected office, or some other competitively selected position.* In clubs that you belong to, officers and other leaders in the organization may be nominated for their positions through a short speech or presentation. Nomination presentations vary in length depending on the nature of the nomination. In the United States, the Republican and Democratic Party conventions, for example, feature several lengthy speeches to nominate candidates for the national presidential election. For your clubs, a very short speech might suffice to nominate officers.

Speeches of nomination should focus on two things: the qualifications of the nominee and the reason these qualifications match the characteristics of the office, position, or award to be granted.

In early 2009, former eBay CEO Meg Whitman announced her candidacy to become the Republican gubernatorial candidate in California.[1] In her speech she announced her candidacy—a form of self-nomination—and described how her experiences have prepared her for the governor's position:

> I've spent the past thirty years in business. I've worked for such great companies as Procter & Gamble, Disney, Hasbro, Stride Rite, and FTD. I've had to be confident, efficient, focused, and accountable. During the past ten years, I was the president and CEO of eBay. I built eBay from a thirty-person, $4 million company, to a company of fifteen thousand employees and nearly $8 billion in revenues.

Whitman went on to discuss, at length, her experiences in helping small businesses thrive and employment to grow—both key issues in California. Whitman's self-nomination effectively discussed her qualifications and established her as a legitimate candidate in the race. Whitman effectively talked about aspects of her background that would be perceived by voters as most important when selecting the new governor. Qualifications are strong only if they are perceived as such by listeners. Your candidate may be a great singer, but voters may not care much about that type of talent when in the voting booth.

Presentations to Dedicate

A **dedication presentation** *honors someone by naming an event, place, or other object after the honoree.* A dedication presentation could be as simple as a professional athlete saying that he or she dedicated the game to his or her parents, or as elaborate as the dedication of a Navy ship. These types of speeches will vary in length and focus depending on the setting, the honoree, and the event, place, or object being dedicated. Typically, the speaker in such presentations will talk about the dedication and the reasons why the honoree is a worthy namesake.

Presentations to Commemorate

Commemorative addresses typically are speeches that are part of some ritualized event like a graduation, a holiday, or even a unique local occasion like First Amendment Day. **Commemorative addresses** mostly are *designed to set a tone for the event—much like a welcome speech—and also usually are considered the primary, or keynote, presentation for the event.* For example, most graduation ceremonies have a graduation speaker who is supposed to give new graduates advice for their future—such speeches set a tone for the entire graduation ceremony. Of course, the highly ritualized nature of such events means that commemorative addresses are more formal and make greater use of stylistic devices.

When planning a commemorative address, analyzing the audience and situation is very important. You must carefully determine (1) what length and tone the audience expects, and (2) how to creatively highlight specific values that capture the essence of the occasion. Commemorative addresses should use subtle transitions and supporting material. Commemorative presentations should also highlight the unique ideas and thoughts of the presenter more than other types of speeches. Of course, some speakers can take this a little too far. At a recent commencement address at one of our universities, a faculty member was honored for teaching effectiveness and was asked to speak during the graduation ceremonies. As both an outstanding teacher and accomplished scholar, the person opted to talk about how passion informs inquiry and inquisitiveness—a message perfectly appropriate for a commencement address. Unfortunately, the person's research interest explored mass genocides and ethnic cleansing. Not a very uplifting message on a special day for thousands of students! Remember one of the lessons mentioned earlier in this book: topics should be appropriate for the audience and occasion!

Farewell Presentations

Farewell presentations occur in many different types of situations in which a person (either you or someone you know) is leaving. One very specific type of "farewell" might be the eulogy that is presented at a funeral. Other farewell presentations might occur when a longtime employee leaves an organization, a leader in a community organization decides to step down, or even when a notable community member or church patron moves away. The common feature among all of these **farewell presentations** is that *a person is paid tribute for his or her service before leaving.*

A farewell presentation can be delivered from two perspectives: one from the people who remain behind and another from the person leaving. If you are preparing a speech to say good-bye to someone who is leaving you should (1) create a brief introduction that establishes an emotional tone, (2) orient the body of the presentation around accomplishments and other notable qualities of

the person, and (3) wish the person well and say something to maintain an ongoing connection (for example, "we will keep you in our thoughts because . . .").

You may find yourself in a situation that calls for you to give a farewell address because you are leaving. Chances are that you will be the last to speak—those who thank and pay tribute to you will speak before you. In such situations you might begin by discussing what your time with the organization has meant; use anecdotes, stories, and other evidence to explain your feelings toward the organization; mention specific individuals who were meaningful to your experience; and conclude with gratitude (both for your experience and for the tribute) as well as warm wishes for the future.

The speech of farewell can be emotional both for those staying behind and for the person leaving. Such feelings are healthy because they provide ritualized moments to be gracious to those around us. The sincerity of a well-crafted farewell address can provide lifetime memories for all involved.

Recognition Addresses

Speeches of recognition typically are presented when one or more people are given awards. For instance, many high schools have yearly awards nights during which students receive awards for academic and extracurricular achievements. Another example is the Oscars or other entertainment awards shows. Both of these types of events are similar in that *presenters are asked to give short presentations to introduce an award recipient.*

"The sincerity of a well-crafted farewell address can provide lifetime memories for all involved."

Speeches of recognition are often very short because they are typically part of a larger program of events—for instance, there may be several other awards being presented. As such, speeches of recognition may not have explicitly developed introductions, bodies, and conclusions. The three key pieces of information necessary in these types of presentations are (1) what the award is, (2) the criteria for being honored with the award, and (3) who the recipient is and why he or she is deserving of the award. The latter point might be the most developed and may use anecdotes, stories, and other forms of support to elaborate on why the person is receiving the award. If only one award is being presented, the presentation can be developed in more detail and might resemble a traditional speech with an introduction, body, and conclusion. In such cases the organization of the speech might be adapted from that described for the speech of introduction.

Sometimes award recipients are asked to speak in acceptance of the award. Such speeches should be brief—typically about the same length as the recognition speech. When accepting the award you should discuss what the award means to you and provide appropriate thanks. People often assume that it is better to list everyone possible; in contrast, more effective speeches might explain that there are many people who deserve thanks but then focus on one or two people who were especially critical in supporting your efforts.

Presentations to Entertain

The final type of special occasion speech is a presentation to entertain. As the name suggests, **presentations to entertain** *are designed to make a point in a creative and oftentimes humorous way.* Entertainment speeches are sometimes called "after dinner speeches" because events often schedule these types of speeches as part of a social time or banquet.

Although the name suggests that the entertainment speech should be all about fun and laughs, presenters should also make some substantive point. In other words, stand-up comedy and speeches to entertain are different from each other. Generally speaking, speakers should plan their presentations by thinking about a more formal, perhaps even serious, message and then finding ways to make that message more humorous. If effectively prepared, the difference between the entertainment speech and more traditional informative and persuasive speeches will be less pronounced than between the other types of special occasion speeches. You should have a clear thesis statement as well as obvious main points, although these structural elements may be presented more subtly than one would expect in persuasive or informative presentations. After determining the point you want to make, you should find ways to interject humor that are appropriate to the audience and natural to the situation. Finally, pay particularly close attention to practicing delivery. Whether or not audience members perceive your presentation to be humorous depends on how you "sell" a line. Being able to "sell" a line involves a combination of delivery and timing. Working with others to develop humorous material and to refine your delivery is essential for a successful entertainment presentation.

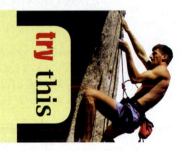

try this

Using the central idea from your informative or persuasive presentations, plan a short, one-minute entertainment speech on the same topic. Use friends and other students to help brainstorm humorous ways to approach your topic, and practice your delivery to achieve maximum impact.

How to Prepare Special Occasion Presentations

Special occasion presentations vary widely in type, purpose, and setting. As such, no textbook or class could ever prepare you for every possible special occasion speech. At the same time, the success of special occasion presentations, as is the case with other types of presentations, typically centers on one concept: how well you analyze your message in relation to the audience and situation. Figure 12.1 is a brief worksheet you can use to plan your special occasion presentations. In this figure, we use plans to dedicate the grand opening of a new campus sustainable agriculture garden as an example.

When preparing your special occasion speech you should remember that even though this type of speech is special, basic principles of ethics still apply. In fact, there are probably additional ethical principles at play *because* these speeches are special. For instance, if you use quotations or specific ideas, phrases, or even jokes from another person, you should give attribution to the source. You should not lie, fabricate, or misrepresent yourself or another person as part of your presentation. Those and other ethical principles of communication are pertinent to any speech, special or not!

In special occasion speeches, ethics also come into play with regard to adapting your speech to the occasion. Is it ethical for you to give a speech at a wedding if you think the bride or bridegroom is a creep? Would it be ethical for you to voice that during the speech, violating all audience expectations? If you were speaking at a dedication, would it be ethical for you to criticize the namesake of a building because you felt that person was involved in shady business practices? The fit between a speaker, message, and situation is something that sometimes crosses from smart practice to ethical practice in special occasions. If you do something

Figure 12.1
Worksheet for planning a special occasion presentation.

Special Occasion Presentation Worksheet

1. Define the Occasion
Describe elements of the speaking situation that will be important to the message you intend to convey in your presentation.

a. the audience:

Approximately 10 members of my class, 5–10 faculty, and 5 or so administrators. Students from other classes could attend, but I have no way of knowing.

b. the event or setting:

To provide opening remarks for the sustainable agriculture garden. The garden will open to the public for the first time after my presentation.

c. other speakers or activities before and after presentation:

Dr. Lehman will provide some introductory remarks and welcome audience members. I will speak next and the ribbon will be cut after my presentation.

2. Define the Message
Describe the ideas, emotions, or attitudes that you want to convey. List any stylistic devices like metaphors or narratives that you want to bring into your message.

a. primary message:

I want to accomplish two purposes: (1) to talk about the process of creating the garden, and (2) to dedicate the garden in Dr. Lehman's name. This will be a surprise to everyone, but the dept. chair said that such a dedication is a great idea.

b. stylistic device ideas:

Use the metaphor of "sustainable growth" to talk about Dr. Lehman as a mentor. Tell the story about how he helped me pass Plant Biology my freshman year by meeting with me and a few other students in the arboretum every Friday.

c. main points (if applicable):

Main points should follow the two parts of the primary message. Should do the dedication last to catch Dr. Lehman by surprise.

against the norm during a special occasion speech, you should consider whether you are crossing an ethical line.

Finally, those of you who work in government service and some other professions know that special events often involve gifts, and receipt of gifts by government employees can be problematic. For instance, NASA has a policy that employees cannot receive gifts exceeding $20 in value.[2] So, if you receive an award at a conference and it carries a cash honorarium, can you take it? Should you offer gifts as part of a special occasion speech? Could the mere act of honoring someone with a speech be perceived as creating a potential conflict of interest? These examples may seem far-fetched, yet they are exactly the type of situations that get people in trouble unexpectedly. When planning a special occasion speech, take care to think through professional codes of ethics related to the event!

The following example of a speech to pay tribute illustrates many of the principles you have learned about special occasion presentations. Notice how the speaker explicitly links the message to the occasion by talking about Rodney's love for his motorcycle while at the same time commemorating his accomplishments as a committed club citizen.

Sample Special Occasion Presentation

A Tribute to Rodney Freshley

Rodney Freshley is a complicated person. He is dedicated to his wife, Sally, and daughter, Samantha. He is an outdoorsman. He loves to hunt and fish.

Establishes connection between award recipient and audience.

And above all, he is fascinated by his motorcycle, the Harley-Davidson Sportster 1200 Roadster: hundreds of pounds of chrome and steel, and tons of torque. Rod is the guy who always chooses to "ride herd" on road trips. He stays in the back of the pack so he can help the group stay in formation, help anyone who has trouble, and warn the less watchful of hazards they may have overlooked.

Uses style (vivid language) to increase audience attention.

He was a pioneer in our club, one of the three founders. Now in its fifteenth year, our cycle club is the oldest and the biggest in the region. We have bikers of all ages in our club and people from many occupations, businesses, and professions. We are united in our love of the road, the wind in our face, and the adventure of the highways.

Uses past accomplishments to establish context for the recognition.

Although these accomplishments are noteworthy by themselves, Rodney deserves recognition today for a much more important reason. Each year our club sponsors a holiday toy drive for disadvantaged children. Each member of the club is responsible for obtaining at least five toys. Rodney not only met this goal, he shattered the previous record by pounding the pavement and getting over 130 toys donated. Today we celebrate Rodney's service and long-term commitment by awarding him the Outstanding Member Award.

The term "shatter" is a stylistic device (a metaphor) that helps the speaker introduce the recipient's recent accomplishment.

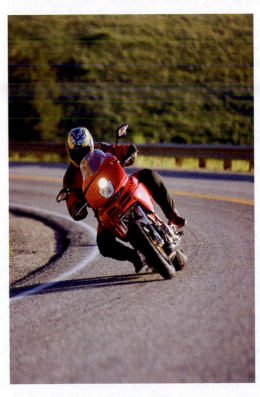

For REVIEW >>

AS YOU READ

1. Compare ceremonial presentations to other types of presentations.

2. Learn about nine types of ceremonial presentations.

SUMMARY HIGHLIGHTS

▶ Special occasion presentations differ from informative and persuasive presentations along four dimensions:
- The purpose of special occasion presentations typically is focused on setting a tone for a ritualized event like a wedding or graduation.
- The style of a special occasion presentation is typically more formal and professional. Special occasion speakers might make greater use of ornamentation like metaphors, figurative language, or narratives.
- Although special occasion presentations should have clear organization with an introduction, body, and conclusion, they may use more subtle methods for signaling transitions between main points and subpoints.
- Special occasion presentations typically try to set a more formal, professional tone. Specific types of special occasion presentations, like the speech to entertain, may emphasize light-hearted humor.

▶ There are nine common types of special occasion presentations:
- The welcome presentation sets a tone for an event and invites all participants to share in active participation.
- Speeches of tribute offer celebratory praise for a person, organization, or cause.
- Introduction presentations welcome and introduce a primary or keynote speaker. Such speeches tend to be brief and primarily focus on biographical information.
- Nomination presentations are persuasive in intent and introduce someone you wish to place in contention for an honor, award, or elected office. Such speeches emphasize qualifications of the nominee.
- Dedication presentations honor an individual or organization, usually by dedicating or naming something (a building, an event, a scholarship, etc.) in their honor.
- Commemorative presentations include graduation addresses, holiday addresses, and other speeches at festive events.
- Farewell presentations occur in situations in which someone is leaving. To say farewell you should highlight the person's accomplishments and wish him or her well. If you are the one leaving, you should discuss your feelings about the time spent with the organization and thank those with whom you worked.

- Speeches of recognition typically are presented when people receive awards. To recognize someone you should describe the award and explain why the person is being recognized with the award. If you are receiving an award, you should discuss what the award means and appropriately thank others for their support.

- Entertainment presentations use humor and levity to make a somewhat serious point. Such speeches are typically more similar to informative or persuasive presentations, but they use humor to emphasize the point of the speech.

3. Develop ideas for a ceremonial presentation that are appropriate to a specific audience, setting, and occasion.

▶ Same as objective 2.

Pop Quiz

1. The primary purpose of a special occasion presentation is:
   - (A) to inform the audience
   - (B) to change the audience's mind
   - (C) to perform a ritual
   - (D) to define terms

2. Which of the following statements about special occasion presentations is true?
   - (A) Special occasion presentations lack an introduction and have very obvious transitions between main points.
   - (B) Special occasion presentations are less formal than informative and persuasive speeches.
   - (C) The purpose of special occasion speeches is to change behaviors or beliefs.
   - (D) Special occasion speeches invite the use of ornamental language.

3. Eulogies, wedding toasts, or retirement addresses are examples of a presentation to
   - (A) welcome
   - (B) pay tribute
   - (C) introduce
   - (D) dedicate

4. A graduation speech is a presentation to:
   - (A) dedicate
   - (B) pay tribute
   - (C) commemorate
   - (D) entertain

5. Speeches of recognition are:
   - (A) designed to make a point in a creative and humorous way
   - (B) used to set a tone for an event
   - (C) presented when one or more people are given awards
   - (D) very long

6. Speeches to entertain are also called:
   - (A) after-dinner speeches
   - (B) farewell addresses
   - (C) commemorative addresses
   - (D) tribute speeches

7. The first step in preparing a special occasion presentation is:
   - (A) to define the message
   - (B) to define the occasion
   - (C) to decide on main points
   - (D) to choose stylistic devices

8. The organization of a special occasion speech:
   - (A) lacks a conclusion
   - (B) uses obvious transitions between main points
   - (C) allows the speaker to develop several main points
   - (D) differs from informative or persuasive speeches

9. One purpose of the presentation to welcome is:
    (A) to establish the purpose of the event
    (B) to praise a noteworthy person
    (C) to establish a person's ethos
    (D) to pay tribute for someone's service

10. When a celebrity presents an Oscar or Emmy to someone, they are likely giving a speech:
    (A) to commemorate
    (B) to entertain
    (C) of recognition
    (D) to introduce

Answers: 1 (C); 2 (D); 3 (B); 4 (C); 5 (C); 6 (A); 7 (B); 8 (D); 9 (A); 10 (C)

APPLICATION EXERCISES

1. Special occasion presentations tend to emphasize the use of stylistic devices. Pick a person whom you would consider a "mentor" for you. This person could be another professor or teacher, a family member, or some other individual who has helped you grow personally. After identifying that individual, create a metaphor describing how that person has helped you. For example, in Figure 12.1, Kim used the metaphor of "sustainable growth" to describe Dr. Lehman, her mentor.

2. To understand how special occasion speeches serve as ritualistic events, look only so far as your campus. Attend an event on campus that involves speeches. The event could be a public lecture, an awards ceremony, or even a commencement. List all of the speeches you heard at the event and analyze how the speeches "fit" into the ritual being enacted. Why do you think speeches are part of our rituals?

3. Practice presenting to nominate through the "class award" activity. Your class will manage an annual "Community Engagement Award." You should be prepared to nominate (and speak in favor of) a person from your community whom you would like to place in contention for the award. The recipient of the award, whom your class recommends, will be given a certificate and be invited to speak to your class.

KEY TERMS

Commemorative address

Dedication presentation

Farewell presentation

Ornamental language

Presentation to entertain

Presentation to pay tribute

Presentation to welcome

Ritual

Speech of introduction

Speech of nomination

Speech of recognition

get involved!

The CNN Heroes ceremony was created with the simple but powerful idea that ordinary people in our community can have extraordinarily positive impacts on the lives of others. Of course, the naming of the Heroes is a special occasion. Each week Heroes are introduced to CNN viewers, and those Heroes are then officially recognized at a televised awards ceremony. If you visit the CNN Heroes Web site, **http://www.cnn.com/SPECIALS/cnn.heroes/index.html**, you can view segments of the 2008 through 2010 ceremonies. As you watch these segments you will see how special occasion speeches were important parts of the ceremony as each Hero was introduced.

You can use the CNN Heroes example in two ways. First, you can use the Web site as a way to learn about the extraordinary accomplishments of the individuals recognized. In so doing, you can create your own special occasion speech introducing one of the Heroes. Besides giving you a chance to practice, the CNN event might provide you with the inspiration to do something similar in your own community. How powerful would it be for a group of college students to create a ceremony where they recognize the efforts of local heroes? If you plan an event, you will have the opportunity to decide how special occasion speeches will play a role in commemorating the work of people in your own community.

APPENDIX

WORKING & PRESENTING

Business and professional speaking situations rarely involve just one person presenting to a large audience. Especially for many entry-level and mid-management positions, most public communication involves a team or group. Although group-based presentations have many benefits, these presentations also require greater coordination and planning. This chapter teaches you how to work in groups to prepare a high-quality presentation.

AS A GROUP

The first few months of 2010 had one dominant news story: healthcare reform. The efforts of President Obama and Democratic leadership in both houses of Congress culminated in a healthcare summit held at the White House in late February. The summit, attended by key leaders from both parties, was intended as a final effort for bipartisanship; more accurately, the summit afforded both sides of the issue an opportunity to present complete cases supporting their views to the American public.

The healthcare summit began with opening comments by the president and representatives from both parties in Congress. The president described the purpose of the summit in this way:

> My hope in the several hours that we're going to be here today is that in each section that we're going to discuss—how do we lower costs for families and small businesses; how do we make sure that the insurance market works for people; how do we make sure that we are dealing with the long-term deficits; how do we make sure that people who don't have coverage can get coverage—in each of these areas, what I'm going to do is I'm going to start off by saying, "Here are some things we agree on." And then let's talk about some areas where we disagree and see if we can bridge those gaps. I don't know that those gaps can be bridged, and it may be that at the end of the day, we come out here and everybody says, "Well, you know, we have some honest disagreements. People are sincere in wanting to help, but they've got different ideas about how to do it and we can't bridge the gap between Democrats and Republicans on this."

Although the summit failed to produce bipartisan support for healthcare reform, presentations by congressional representatives and the president did much to inform the American people about the intricacies and complexities involved in reform of such magnitude. The summit illustrates how bringing groups of people together to stake out positions, debate, and test ideas can, at the very least, elevate the level of discussion beyond sound bites. As you read this appendix you will learn more about ways in which groups can be used to carry out meaningful dialogues like the healthcare summit.

How Would *You* Do It?

If you were putting together a public symposium on health care or some other significant topic, how would you structure the event? What types of speakers would you want to be present? What objectives would you have for the event?

What Are Small Groups?

Small group communication is *the interaction among three to nine people who are working together to achieve an interdependent goal.*[1]

The definition of small group communication establishes *communication* as the essential process within a small group. Communication creates a group, shapes it in unique ways, and maintains it. Like other forms of human communication, small group communication relies on verbal and nonverbal signals that are perceived, interpreted, and responded to by other people. Group members pay attention to each other and coordinate their behavior to accomplish the group's assignment. Perfect understanding between the person sending the signal and those receiving the signal is impossible; in a group, members strive to have enough understanding so that the group can achieve important objectives.

Why Are Small Groups Used for Presentations?

Small groups are increasingly used to facilitate public communication. First, important business presentations are often organized so that people with different backgrounds and skills discuss issues with which they each are familiar. So, Tate from research and development might introduce the concept for a new product, Shania from marketing might discuss how the new product compares with competitors' products, Scott from advertising might discuss initial plans for selling the product, and Emma, the project director, might discuss the timetable for rollout of the product. These types of presentations are increasingly common because many companies and organizations use **self-managed work teams**, or *groups of workers with different skills who work together to produce something or solve a problem,* to handle important issues like new product development, quality control, and human resources.

A second reason small groups are often used for public presentations is that they can make the process less stressful for everyone. Groups can help counteract many of the difficulties we face during public presentations because they satisfy our need for inclusion, affection, and control. **Inclusion** suggests that *people need to belong to, or be included in, groups with others.* As humans, we derive much of our identity, our beliefs about who we are, from the groups to which we belong. Starting with our immediate families and including such important groups as our church, mosque, or synagogue; interest groups; work teams; and social groups—all these help us define who we are. During public presentations, this need for inclusion might be particularly important

How Are Small Groups and Public Communication Connected?

"Groups can help counteract many of the difficulties we face during public presentations because they satisfy our need for inclusion, affection, and control."

because of the vulnerability that many of us feel. **Affection**, another essential need, *means that we humans need to love and be loved, to know that we are important to others who value us as unique human beings.* The emotional support from group members sharing similar experiences can build affection among group members, thus making us feel more comfortable. Finally, we have a need for **control**, or *the ability to influence our environment.* We are better able to exercise such control if we work together in groups. Preparing a good public presentation is challenging, but groups let us accomplish the task more effectively, thus satisfying our desire for control.

Although the content and format for group presentations differ, each has the following common elements:

1. *Group members share in responsibility.* Regardless of how the presentation is formatted, all group members share the task of preparing and, to some extent, presenting the presentation. Even if some group members are not responsible for the delivery of information, they might be responsible for preparing and controlling multimedia resources like PowerPoint or videos.

2. *Group members are interdependent.* As discussed at the beginning of the chapter, small groups are interdependent in the sense that all group members are essential to positive outcomes for the group. In most presentations, this interdependence is enhanced because each group member typically adds unique and necessary information about a topic. If one group member does not do his or her job, the audience will not have a complete understanding of the topic.

3. *Group presentations are more interactive.* When one presenter talks to an audience, norms and implicit rules often prevent audience members from asking questions or interrupting the speaker. Group presentations are inherently less focused on one-way transmission of information. Because multiple people speak and share ideas, a "democratic spirit" ensues and discussion in and among presenters and audience members flows more freely.

4. *Group presentations are coordinated.* Rather than having the right and responsibility of worrying about only your own message, as a member of a group you must be concerned about how your message fits within the context of other presenters' ideas. Such coordination takes careful planning.

Group presentations are enjoyable, and in many cases, more productive than individual presentations.

try this

Identify three groups that you belong to: one that meets your need for inclusion, one that meets your need for control, and one that meets your need for affection.

Key Skills for Effective Group Presentations

Although group presentations differ from traditional informative and persuasive individual presentations, there are similarities. For instance, your individual component of a group presentation should be well researched, effectively organized, and compellingly presented. For the sake of clarity, however, here are some of the unique skills that may be required for a group presentation.

1. *Creativity.* The real benefit of working on presentations as part of a group is the chance to capitalize on the collective creativity of many people. Your ability to do good research and use a clever approach for discussing your topic will be greatly enhanced through group dialogue. This implies that groups working on a presentation should devote enough time to brainstorming and discussion of the topic(s) being addressed in the presentation.

2. *Coordination.* Group presentations should be well coordinated. For instance, there should be smooth transitions from one speaker to the next; visual aids should be coordinated as a group rather than each individual having her or his own approach (for instance, using one PowerPoint file rather than several separate files); all group members should dress professionally; and group members should have a plan for where those who are not presenting should stand or sit. In short, for group presentations every small detail should be planned in advance to demonstrate a well-coordinated effort.

3. *Identification and quick resolution of conflicts.* Because group efforts of any kind—presentations included—require that members work together, identifying and resolving conflict is essential for group success. To identify and manage conflict, group members should engage in open dialogue where they can explain and check their perceptions. If conflict is actually present, all group members should take part in talking through potential causes and solutions for the conflict. Conflicts surrounding group presentations typically stem from workload distribution, scheduling, and personality clashes among individual group members.

4. *Ability to incorporate discussion.* Group presentations typically invite dialogue among presenters and between audience members and presenters. When planning group presentations, you and your team members should carefully discuss how and when to invite audience participation. You may want to prepare questions— perhaps in the form of a brief handout— that you want audience members to react to as the presentation progresses.

Planning Workflow for the Group

As you will learn, group presentations come in multiple forms. Common to each of these types of group presentations is a need for shared work and coordination. This section discusses strategies you and your group members should use to effectively plan for any type of group presentation. Specifically, you will learn about four stages that your group should go through when preparing your presentation: agreeing on a topic, dividing responsibilities, assigning presentation roles, and enacting quality control.

Agreeing on a Topic

Previous chapters have discussed the challenges that students face when selecting topics for presentations. Although some of those problems are overcome by groups, other types of problems emerge. Groups of people are effectively suited to overcoming ill-defined problems, which can include any task with undefined objectives and outcomes. For instance, groups are very good at brainstorming ideas and coming up with unique and creative ways of presenting issues to audience members. Because they allow us to feel included, groups also help us manage some of the nervousness that we naturally encounter when "flying solo" on a speech.

Although groups help us to be more creative and comfortable, those same characteristics can cause problems. Because groups tend to become highly cohesive when working on a task, groupthink can occur. **Groupthink** is when *members of the group become locked in on one way of thinking about something or carrying out a task and ignore viable (and perhaps better) alternatives.* Also, the comfort and creative energy of a group can cause members to think they are on the same page, when in fact they are not.

To maximize the benefits of working in a group while also minimizing the dangers, the first task of group members should be to carefully evaluate and agree upon a topic (or topics) for the group presentation. If you return to the discussion of the invention canon in Chapter 2 you will recall several questions that you can ask to improve topic selection; those same questions are relevant to group discussions. Another thing that should be discussed by the group is the intended outcome of the presentation. For instance, in a persuasive presentation, is the group trying to advance arguments about fact, value, or policy issues? Table A.1 shows examples of fact, value, and policy questions.

Once the group has sufficiently discussed potential topics and objectives, the group should write down an agreed-upon central idea and objective statement for the overall presentation. By taking time to discuss and record the focus of the presentations you can be sure that all group members have a clear understanding of what needs to be accomplished when working individually.

TABLE A.1　QUESTIONS OF FACT, VALUE, AND POLICY

FACT

How has the divorce rate changed in the past 15 years?

How many Hispanic students graduate from high school each year?

What percentage of college students graduate in 4 years?

How often, on average, does a person speak each day?

What occupations earn the highest annual incomes?

VALUE

Why should people seek higher education?

How should Americans treat international students?

Does our legal system provide "justice for all"?

How should young people be educated about AIDS?

What is the value of standardized tests for college admission?

POLICY

What courses should students be required to take?

Should the state's drunk driving laws be changed?

What are the arguments for and against mandatory retirement?

Should the United States intervene in foreign disputes for humanitarian reasons?

What advantages should government provide for businesses willing to develop in high-risk areas of a city?

Division of Labor

One of the benefits of working in groups is that multiple people can bring skills and assets to the task at hand. Perhaps one person in the group is great with multimedia, another a whiz at research, and another likes to coordinate and put finishing touches on outlines, visual aids, and other materials. Part of your group discussion should be devoted to finding out what skills, resources, and interests each group member has in relation to your assignment. Taking a few minutes after discussing a topic to have each group member create a personal inventory is wise.

Of course, you should not assume that division of labor means that each person has one task and works in isolation to accomplish that task. Taking such an approach does not capitalize on the benefits of group work and tends to result in poor products that lack cohesive vision. Rather, you should use the personal inventories to select task leaders who are in charge of coordinating efforts on that particular task with the help of other group members. For instance, the library expert could assign each member of the group to conduct research for different types of information, or different topics related to the overall presentation. As the research coordinator, that person could provide suggestions and help manage the overall effort of all people assigned to the research group. In essence, groups need to have many people using their expertise to take on leadership roles at various stages of the project. In so doing, the group is better able to get maximum productivity out of all group members.

Assigning Presentation Roles

Just as each person needs an assigned task during the planning of your group presentation, each group member needs to have a clearly defined task during the presentation itself. In addition to determining who will speak when, your group should also carefully plan transitions between speakers and from one section of the presentation to the next. Typically, transition periods are where a lack of coordination becomes apparent to audience members. Your teacher or the situation may dictate whether all members need equal speaking time or whether some can be involved in speaking while others take on support roles like running PowerPoint, coordinating handouts, and so on.

Quality Control

Earlier in this section you learned that one of the problems with groups is the possibility of groupthink. Although groups are generally better than individuals at making good decisions, groupthink can erode that advantage. Groupthink occurs when groups become so cohesive that they fail to consider alternative viewpoints. To combat the potential of groupthink and to generally ensure that your group achieves a strong outcome, you should plan to enact steps to maintain quality control.

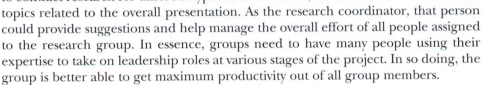

"To combat the potential of groupthink and to generally ensure that your group achieves a strong outcome, you should plan to enact steps to maintain quality control."

Perhaps the most natural method of quality control involves constant and open communication among group members. You should plan to have group members provide daily or periodic reports on their activities. The reports should be detailed in the sense that others know exactly what was done and what was accomplished. These reports might be done orally during scheduled group meetings, by e-mail, or even on Facebook. Because of the reports there will be a greater sense of responsibility to get work done, and mistakes can be caught quicker.

Using Audience Response Systems

Many types of group presentations invite feedback and responses from audience members. A method of obtaining audience feedback that has gained significant popularity is Audience Response Systems (ARS). You may have used a version of ARS in classes where teachers use "clickers" to have students answer multiple-choice questions and have aggregate responses displayed on PowerPoint slides. Because of cost, most students have little opportunity to use ARS technology for their speeches or group presentations. However, Poll Everywhere (**www.polleverywhere.com**) has a free option for use by students and faculty and allows up to thirty-two audience members to respond to questions using cell phones, Web browsers, and even Twitter—no need for clickers! These types of technologies signal that the conventionally linear mode of public speaking is giving way to more interactive presentations where audience members can participate using ubiquitous technology.

A second method of quality control is to be ethical when giving and receiving constructive criticism and feedback. When giving feedback you should be honest and avoid making unintended attributions for behaviors. People do make mistakes, and in fact, that is part of the learning process in highly hands-on classes like public speaking. Just because someone makes a mistake does not mean he or she is a poor group member. You must also commit to giving good feedback. Telling people that their work is not up to par is hollow unless you can provide authentic help to improve. When receiving critical feedback you should make an effort to learn from the feedback. Even if you disagree with the feedback, learning why another person perceives things a certain way can potentially teach you how to present your work to avoid such misperceptions.

A third approach to quality control involves assigning people specifically to that task. Some groups appoint members to be "process observers" who are charged with monitoring group communication and outcomes to make sure that the group is working effectively and accomplishing desired outcomes. Process observers might also be charged with playing devil's advocate to ideas to help ensure that multiple views are considered, thereby reducing the chances of groupthink.

Types of Group Presentations

A wide variety of group presentations exists. At the annual convention of the National Communication Association (www.natcom.org), faculty and students from around the country typically make presentations —in groups—using one of these formats: panels, discussion groups, roundtable discussions, town hall meetings, and debates. Members of a law firm trying to land a big client might use four or five representatives to carefully overview the services and expertise of the firm—following more or less a panel discussion format. At Pace University in New York, a group of students in a computer science course might prepare and present a multimedia symposium discussing and demonstrating Web site design for nonprofit organizations in their lower Manhattan community. Let's look at several common approaches to group presentations: symposia, panel discussions, and debates.

Symposia

A **symposium** is *a type of group presentation where individual members of the group divide a large topic into smaller topics for coordinated individual presentations.* Typically, one of the group members acts as a moderator for the symposium and provides an introduction and conclusion for the group in addition to brief transition statements introducing each individual presenter. The moderator might also be responsible for fielding questions from the audience.

Groups preparing for a symposium presentation must initially decide on a topic and then discuss how specific aspects of the topic can be addressed by individual presenters—taking care to ensure that each presenter has a roughly equal amount of information to cover. Consider a group choosing to do a symposium on the topic of water shortages. With five people, one person will act as a moderator. The remaining four members of the group must decide who will handle specific aspects of this relatively broad topic. After doing initial research, the group can compile a list of topics and subtopics related to water shortages. Then, after preparing a working outline of those ideas, the group can divide areas of responsibility and prepare a tentative schedule for the presentation. Figure A.1 provides a sample schedule for a 40-minute symposium.

Depending on your teacher's preference, you might be asked to do a particular type of symposium. Although each type has different content, the general format for each type is typically the same as that illustrated in Figure A.1.

Presenter	Time	Responsibility
Leslie	00:00–03:00	Opening Remarks • Attention getter • Listener relevance link • Preview the objectives of the symposium
David	03:00–09:00	Causes of Water Shortages • Increased Population • Increased Development • Drought
Karla	09:00–15:00	Current Policies Governing Water Shortages • Mandatory Rationing • Federal Policies • Treaties with Other States
Todd	15:00–21:00	Effects of Water Shortages • Diminished Water Quality • Economic Harms • Damage to Ecosystems
Alane	21:00–27:00	Potential Solutions • Recycling Storm Runoff • Desalinization • Cloud Seeding
Leslie	27:00–40:00	Concluding Remarks and Audience Questions • Summary • Call to Action • Questions (10 minutes)

Figure A.1   **Schedule for symposium on water shortages.**

GROUPS USED TO REDUCE RACIAL CONFLICT

Since 1997, Humboldt State University in California has held a Campus Dialogue on Race. As explained on its Web site (http://www.humboldt.edu/~dialogue), the purpose of the event is to invite "students, staff, faculty, administrators and community members to present and attend programs that relate to racial justice and its intersections with other forms of oppression." The 2010 dialogue included several forums on issues related to the experiences of Native Americans to Latino immigration struggles in America.

The Dialogue on Race illustrates how a series of presentations can be linked together to achieve a broader purpose. The specific mission of the Dialogue, according to the Web site, is to "promote and facilitate environmental change by engaging a diverse range of individuals, communities, and viewpoints to explore the impact of racism and its intersections with all forms of oppression." Although this same objective could guide an individual presentation, the Humboldt State Dialogue illustrates how significant social topics often require (and deserve) more sustained attention by participants.

The Campus Dialogue on Race at Humboldt State University does not happen by accident; rather, groups of people must carefully plan and execute the event.

Current Issue Symposium

The water shortage symposium in Figure A.1 is an example of a current issue group presentation. The objective of this presentation is to provide a coordinated and detailed analysis of some current event or significant issue. Much of the group's effort for this type of presentation must be devoted to brainstorming, researching, and outlining potential topics. Typically, though not always, a current issue symposium tackles topics that are somewhat broader than in an individual presentation. In addition, your teacher will probably expect you to address topics in more depth because you can draw on the research and ideas of other group members.

Multimedia Symposium

Because groups are often better at producing creative solutions to problems, some teachers assign a special type of symposium asking group members to pay particular attention to the use of multimedia resources. Angela Garcia, a sociology professor at the University of Cincinnati, asks her students to prepare multimedia symposia discussing aspects of a culture from outside the United States, including language, ethnicity, and communication.[2] Garcia requests that students incorporate music, video, art, and other multimedia resources as part of their presentations. Similar approaches could be used to examine any variety of topics.

For this type of symposium, group members should think creatively when brainstorming for multimedia resources to use and should also practice several times to coordinate all aspects of the presentation. For instance, you want to avoid playing long clips from songs or movies. Longer clips (more than 30 seconds) take attention away from the message(s) you want to relay and can actually confuse listeners. Because using multimedia resources tends to take a great deal of time, practicing the entire presentation is recommended—otherwise, one person might take substantially longer than expected and the entire time allocation plan could be destroyed. Remember that multimedia resources also take much longer to prepare than other types of presentation resources—you might need to edit video or audio, and you might need to combine your resources into a PowerPoint presentation. Finally, emphasizing creativity is important. Students often assume that showing video is the best form of multimedia. Music, art, pictures, and even people to interview (on tape) are all potential resources for a multimedia presentation.

Cultural Symposium

A third type of symposium asks each group of students to pick a unique culture or co-culture to analyze. One group of students chose to analyze the Native American co-culture for their symposium. One student in the group discussed origins of various Native American tribes; another analyzed how various bands developed unique customs, rituals, and beliefs; another traced what happened to many of the larger tribes during the 1800s when westward expansion of the white population caused many conflicts and forced evacuations; and a fourth student analyzed the current status of many of the tribes, including the issues of casino gambling on reservations and Native American mascots of sports teams. As you can see, the group analyzing Native American issues used a basic chronological arrangement to divide responsibilities among group members. Although some of the individuals used PowerPoint and other multimedia resources, others did not—but the same project could have been done as a "multimedia presentation," where all group members would have been required to use multimedia.

Teaching Symposium

Groups are particularly effective at taking complex ideas and determining how to present them to audiences. For that reason, some group assignments are designed as teaching presentations. A common approach is to ask a group to choose topics from a textbook chapter or some other resource or reading assigned by the teacher and then present information from that resource to the class. The objective of the group is to teach the class important information, skills, and strategies discussed in the chapter or reading. Although the teaching symposium is similar to the other types of symposia discussed, group meetings should pay particular attention to the best ways to teach the assigned material. Group members should discuss how to combine activities, discussion questions, multimedia, and traditional lectures so that the material will engage audience members. Although you are students, you should think like a teacher for this assignment.

Panels

Symposia are more or less similar to other types of presentations you might prepare in your class—like an informative or persuasive presentation. Symposia differ from those presentations because a group of people must coordinate their individual presentations around a common topic. **Panels** differ from symposia because they *rely less on the transmission of information between the presenter and the audience, and focus more on interaction and dialogue in and among presenters and audience members.* A typical panel presentation begins with a moderator introducing a topic for discussion, followed by brief introductory statements by panelists, and then time for interaction between and among panelists and audience members.

Presenter	Time	Responsibility
Rob	00:00–03:00	Opening remarks
Natalie	03:00–06:00	Defining student-managed farm markets
Suchita	06:00–09:00	Working with the college farm
Chris	09:00–12:00	The costs and benefits for students
Brian	12:00–15:00	How students can participate in the decision-making process
Chris	15:00–17:00	Discussion group directions Answer the following questions: • What benefits do you see for a farm market? • What drawbacks do you see in the plan? • What would you like to see in a farm market? • Other questions
	17:00–27:00	Group discussions led by members of the panel
Rob	27:00–37:00	Group reports, audience questions, and concluding remarks

Figure A.2 **A panel presentation over the plan for a new student-managed farm market.**

Figure A.2 provides a basic outline for a panel discussion on the topic of student-managed farm markets.

As you can see, this panel format builds in time for audience members to discuss issues raised by the panelists in small groups. Then, after short group discussions, the entire class returns to a general discussion of whether to propose a student-managed farm market. Using small groups to generate audience participation is wise if the panel is presenting on a topic that is controversial or that many audience members might wish to discuss. As an alternative to using small group discussions, presenters can make longer opening statements, and some of the time devoted to small group discussions could be redirected to time for audience questions.

Panel discussions are particularly effective for topics that are controversial and/or are very relevant to most audience members. These types of presentations work less well for topics about which audience members know little. They may not have enough background to effectively discuss issues or ask questions. Consequently, groups planning for a panel presentation format should carefully consider whether this format is appropriate for the audience and topic.

The moderator is very important to a panel discussion format. Besides introducing speakers, the moderator must field audience questions and know to which member of the panel to direct questions. The best moderators are those who know a great deal about the material and who are able to think on their feet quickly. Watching Sunday morning political talk shows is an excellent way to see panel discussions in action—nearly all use this format.

Debates

In a **debate**, *members of the group divide responsibilities to prepare both "pro" and "con" presentations on a controversial issue or question.* Consider this question: "Should the city create new ordinances to enact tougher penalties for individuals who have nuisance parties in their apartment or house?" Various cities have such policies.

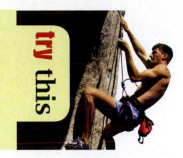

After watching one or more television shows based on a panel discussion format (consider a political talk show, a sports talk show, or even a daily talk show), identify skills that you think are important for the moderator to have. After listing the important moderator skills you observed, consider how you could use those skills to enhance your presentation.

Nuisance parties are typically defined as parties with excessive noise, underage alcohol consumption, and/or excessive public intoxication. These types of parties are most problematic in neighborhoods where "locals" and students live close together.

If your group wanted to debate the effectiveness of nuisance party ordinances, you would first need to divide group members into pro and con sides. Those individuals assigned to the "pro" side might interview local citizens, law enforcement officers, and university administrators to determine arguments in favor of such ordinances. Those on the "con" side would surely interview students, and might interview local attorneys and civil rights leaders to get opposing arguments. For many debate topics, including nuisance party laws, a great deal of information is available at the library and on the Internet.

Debate formats typically include two types of presentations: constructive presentations and rebuttal presentations. In **constructive presentations** *you initially present arguments—both for and against an idea.* In **rebuttal presentations** *presenters respond to arguments raised by the opposing side.* If you are a "con" presenter making a rebuttal, you will analyze and critique the arguments in favor of nuisance ordinances. One additional principle in debates is that the side in favor of changing the **status quo**—*the way things are currently done*—typically gets the first and last word. Figure A.3 provides a sample format for a group debate over nuisance party laws.

Notice how each side in the debate has equal time to present its ideas. In addition, notice that the amount of time devoted to James's presentation is the same as everyone else's, but that his time is divided into a first rebuttal and a concluding rebuttal. This division of time allows the "pro" side to speak first—to lay out its case for change—and last in the debate. The format described in Figure A.3 also includes a moderator and time for questions from the audience. Some teachers may require

Presenter	Time	Responsibility
Doug	00:00–03:00	Introduce topic and preview format
Steve	03:00–09:00	Constructive speech in favor of nuisance ordinance
Becky	09:00–15:00	Constructive presentation against nuisance ordinance
James	15:00–19:00	Rebuttal of Becky's "con" presentation
Andi	19:00–25:00	Concluding "con" rebuttal
James	25:00–27:00	Concluding "pro" rebuttal
Doug	27:00–40:00	Summary of key arguments and time for audience questions

Figure A.3 **Debate over nuisance party laws.**

groups to build in time for members from each side to cross-examine the other side rather than having time for audience questions. Finally, some teachers may have the audience "vote" for a winner of the debate after the last presentation has been made.

Public debate is likely one of the most challenging presentations you will make. The experience is worth the effort. Students often comment that these presentations were more enjoyable in the long run than most other types. Successful debaters know much about the topic in question so they can think on their feet. In addition, debate arguments are always based on good evidence and audience adaptation.

Evaluating Group Productivity

Using groups to accomplish any task—whether the task is organizing a dance for local seniors, planning a community health fair, or raising awareness of environmental issues on campus—involves risk. The group can fail to become interdependent and work together, or one or more members can fail to accomplish their assigned duties adequately. For that reason, observation of, reflection upon, and evaluation of group behaviors is important. Some teachers even include your reflection on group activities as a component of your grade in the course.

Observing and reflecting on your group's activities requires careful evaluation of the group as a whole as well as individual members' contributions to group tasks. Figure A.4 provides a sample progress evaluation form that your group can use to track work on your group presentation. Before adjourning each meeting, your group should discuss responses to the questions on the form. One form should be completed for each meeting.

In addition to evaluating the progress of your group as a whole, you might also be asked to evaluate the individual contributions of group members. Taking time to review previous information on leadership and group communication skills will

---

Group Progress Form

Group Members: _Sue, Jim, Andrea, Lau, and Keran_

Presentation Topic: _Still deciding_

Meeting #1   Date: _Nov 3_   **Members Present:** _All_

Objectives for Meeting: Talk about assignment
                             Brainstorm initial topics

Outcomes of Meeting:

We brainstormed an initial list of 12 topics. After thinking about them and combining some topics, we narrowed the list to 3 good topics: the environment, health and wellness, and seniors in our community.

Assignments for Next Meeting Scheduled for: _Nov 5_

Each person is supposed to find one article (or book) on each topic. At the next meeting, we will discuss the articles and select a final topic. Everyone is supposed to e-mail article citations to the rest of the group so that we do not duplicate research.

Figure A.4   **Example of a group progress form.**

help you complete this reflective evaluation. Figure A.5 provides an example of an evaluation sheet based on leadership behaviors and group communication behaviors. Notice that you rate each person, including yourself, and provide brief comments. When commenting on member performance, take care to provide descriptive feedback. Notice how Andrea provided descriptive comments about both her and Keran's behaviors during group meetings. Descriptive rather than exclusively evaluative feedback is more productive in helping people understand how others perceive their behaviors. Although the sample shows evaluations only for Andrea and Keran, your evaluation should be of each group member.

In closing, you should understand that group presentations should follow the principles and practices presented throughout this book for individual presentations. Accordingly, group presentations involve research and audience analysis. They should be organized, supported, rehearsed, and delivered effectively. The overall group presentation should also have an introduction and conclusion, which follow the guidelines provided for individual presentations. And to ensure professional delivery, groups should plan and practice how to make smooth transitions from one speaker to another and coordinate their visual aids. Group presentations do require planning and cooperation; however, the format also allows presenters to capitalize on the talents of multiple individuals. Consider this quote by U.S. anthropologist Margaret Mead: "Never doubt that a small group of committed individuals can change the world. Indeed, it's the only thing that ever has."

Group Evaluation Form

Your name: Andrea

Directions: Rate each member of your group on how well they display leadership qualities and how well they engage in group communication behaviors. Use the following scale for numeric responses and provide comments as necessary. Remember that "Self-Centered Functions and Statements" are undesirable qualities of group communicators. Consequently, a rating of "5" would indicate that the person avoids those behaviors. Write "NO" if you did not observe the person using a particular category of behaviors.

1 = Very Ineffective

2 = Ineffective

3 = Neither Effective nor Ineffective

4 = Effective

5 = Very Effective

Group Member Name	Task Functions and Statements	Maintenance Functions and Statements	Self-Centered Functions and Statements	Leadership Behaviors and Qualities
Andrea (me)	4	3	3	4
	Comments: I was the person who tried to keep the group on task. I most often used opinion giving and coordinating statements during discussions. I need to work on getting along with other group members when we have disagreements—should avoid dominating discussion. I tended to use status seeking comments because I wanted to get things done.			
Keran	4	4	4	5
	Comments: Keran was the real leader of the group. She handled conflict between Lau and me when it came up. Keran took care to schedule meetings and take notes. Keran was really good at initiating discussions and harmonizing. She was an effective leader because she made sure all of us had a say in group decisions and did not try to boss people around.			

Figure A.5 Group member evaluation example.

For
REVIEW >>

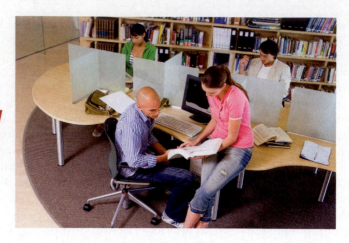

SUMMARY HIGHLIGHTS

In this appendix you have learned the following:

▶ Small groups contain between three and nine people who interact, are interdependent, and use communication to create a bond.
  • Small groups are used to facilitate public presentations because many organizations require people to specialize and, consequently, no one person can effectively know all the details necessary for a presentation.
  • Groups make the process of presenting less stressful because they help us meet our needs for affection, inclusion, and control.

▶ Group decision making involves four steps: (1) wording the discussion question, (2) discussing criteria for evaluating potential solutions, (3) brainstorming alternatives, and (4) evaluating alternatives. The group leader(s) can play an important role in helping the group maintain structure and creativity throughout this process.

▶ Various formats can be used for group presentations.
  • A symposium is a group presentation where individual members of the group divide a large topic into smaller topics for coordinated individual presentations.
  • A panel is more interactive than a symposium and relies less on the transmission of information from speaker to audience.
  • A debate involves group members presenting both pro and con messages about a controversial topic or issue.

▶ When evaluating group productivity, you should reflect on how well the group met the goals established through dialogue and planning, and you should also reflect on and evaluate how well individual members contributed to group activities.

Pop Quiz

1. How many people generally comprise a small group?
   (A) one to two
   (B) three to nine
   (C) nine to eleven
   (D) more than fifteen

2. The three needs that groups can help meet are:
   (A) intelligence, desire, liking
   (B) organization, power, direction
   (C) influence, time-management, entertainment
   (D) inclusion, affection, control

3. Which of the following is *not* a common element of a group presentation?
   (A) Group members are independent
   (B) Group members share in responsibility.
   (C) Group presentations are coordinated.
   (D) Group presentations are more interactive.

4. The question "Should State University lower tuition?" is a:
   (A) question of fact
   (B) question of value
   (C) question of policy
   (D) question of community

5. Each group member can work on different aspects of a presentation. This is referred to as the:
   (A) reciprocity principle
   (B) division of labor
   (C) specialization initiative
   (D) group work procedure

6. A presentation that focuses on interaction and dialogue in and among presenters and audience members is a:
   (A) symposium
   (B) panel
   (C) debate
   (D) seminar

7. Tanner and his group decided to work on separate parts of their topic. Each person then presented his or her part of the presentation in a coordinated manner. What type of group presentation did Tanner's group use?
   (A) panel
   (B) seminar
   (C) debate
   (D) symposium

8. The type of group presentation that builds in time for audience members to discuss issues raised by the speakers is a:
   (A) panel
   (B) conference
   (C) symposium
   (D) debate

9. Michael's group chose to assign group members into "pro" and "con" sides to present information. Michael's group is presenting a:
   (A) debate
   (B) symposium
   (C) panel
   (D) discussion

10. To evaluate group productivity, you should:
   (A) avoid focusing on individual contributions to the group
   (B) consider how well the group met the established goals
   (C) focus only on the leadership
   (D) not rate yourself

Answers: 1 (B); 2 (D); 3 (A); 4 (C); 5 (B); 6 (B); 7 (D); 8 (A); 9 (A); 10 (B)

APPLICATION EXERCISES

1. Take a moment to list the various groups you belong to and select one that illustrates the role of communication in groups. Using that group as a focal point, explain through examples and analysis how communication has both enabled and constrained the group's ability to meet its objectives. In retrospect, what advice would you give to the group to improve its communication?

2. Using one of the topics identified in the following list, write questions of fact, value, and policy relevant to that topic. Each question should be accompanied by a brief explanation of what issues would be addressed to answer that question as well as an explanation of why your question appropriately illustrates the form of question you intended (i.e., how does your question illustrate what a question of fact is supposed to address?).
   • Severe Weather
   • Flu Pandemic
   • Music File Sharing
   • Hybrid Cars
   • Plagiarism

3. Using a topic of interest, plan a symposium, panel, or debate. You should select a format for the presentation and briefly explain what each speaker should do during his or her part of the presentation. Finally, explain why you chose the format (debate, symposium, or panel) that you selected. Why was your choice of formats best in light of the other options?

KEY TERMS

Affection	Groupthink	Self-managed work teams
Constructive presentations	Inclusion	Small group communication
Control	Panel	Status quo
Debate	Rebuttal presentations	Symposium

get involved!

Small groups are powerful forces that support democracy. In fact, our very existence as a nation can be traced to a small group of revolutionaries who carried out public dialogues about injustice, tyranny, and taxation without representation. Even today, small groups of individuals serve as leaders for organizations that we join, they run businesses that employ us, and they create policies that govern our communities. Groups are everywhere and they provide a foundation for much of what we do.

A group of professors at Illinois State University recognized the power of groups when they designed a public speaking assignment requiring their students to staff tables at an "issues fair" open to campus and community people wanting to learn about topics salient to the 2008 presidential election. The assignment required students to prepare poster presentations about important issues like health care, education, and the economy, and discuss those issues with people who walked by. The issues fair was held outside on the ISU campus, which provided a wide variety of roaming "audience" members. These students helped raise awareness of how political issues were relevant to other college students. Those same teachers organized small groups of students to receive training from the county board of elections to register new voters. Those efforts not only significantly increased student voter turnout, but also persuaded the county board of elections to expand early voting locations to the ISU campus.

If you want to make a difference in your community, you will likely need to do so by forming or joining a group. An initial step might be to join a student organization or other group to learn more about issues of interest to you. As your group plans your group presentation, however, you should brainstorm ways to expand the scope of your presentation beyond your classroom. Your campus may have student research and creative activity fairs at which your group can present; you may be able to present your presentation at a community center or as part of some other event in your community. Your teacher may be able to help you make contact with community leaders who can help you find outlets for your presentation. By taking your presentation "on the road" you will gain valuable experience speaking to multiple audiences and, like the students at ISU, help promote community discussion about important topics.

A

abstract words   185
Words that are general, broad, and distant from what you can perceive through your senses.

abstraction   185
A simplification standing for a person or thing.

action-ending function   153
The third function of a conclusion, to state the response you seek from the audience.

addition   170
An articulation problem that occurs when an extra sound is added.

affection   290
Humans need to love and be loved, to know that we are important to others who value us as unique human beings.

alliteration   168, 193
The repetition of an initial consonant, a repeated sound.

analogy   118
A comparison of things in some respects, especially in position or function, that are otherwise dissimilar.

antonyms   191
Words that are opposite in meaning.

argument   253
The extent to which the presenter furnishes reasons for the message claims.

articulation   169
The physiological process of creating the sounds of a word.

audience adaptation   86
Making the message appropriate for the particular audience by using analysis and applying its results to message creation.

audience analysis   71, 251
(1) Discovering as much as possible about an audience to improve communication with them. (2) Learning enough about listeners to be able to predict their probable response to your message in a public speaking situation.

audience participation   130
The speaker makes the audience active participants in the presentation.

B

bar/column chart   206
A visual aid used to illustrate quantitative differences between categories of information.

behavioral response   231
An objective of a presentation to inform that is met when the audience shows an overt indication of understanding through action.

bibliographic references   111
Complete citations that appear in the "references" or "works cited" section of your speech outline.

boomerang effect   257
A phenomenon in which the audience likes the presenter and the proposal on the issue less after the presentation than they did before it.

brainstorming   52
Generating as many ideas for topics as you can in a limited period of time without pausing to evaluate them for quality.

brake-light function   153
Warns the audience that you are about to stop.

C

categorical brainstorming   52
Approaching the brainstorming process by beginning with categories that prompt you to think of topics.

cause-effect pattern   138
An organizational arrangement in which part of the speech describes or explains causes and consequences.

celebrity testimony   116
Statements made by a public figure who is known to the audience.

channel   10
The means of distributing your words, whether by co-axial cable, fiber optics, microwave, radio, video, or air.

chart   206
A visual aid used to visually display quantitative or statistical information.

claim   259
A conclusion of what the persuader would have the listener believe or do that invites proof or evidence.

closed or closed-ended questions   81
Questions that force a decision by inviting only a yes-or-no response or a brief answer.

co-culture   75
A group of people whose beliefs or behaviors distinguish it from the larger culture of which it is a part and with which it shares many similarities.

commemorative address   277
Designed to set a tone for an event—much like a welcome speech—and usually considered the primary, or keynote, presentation for the event.

common ground   17
Features you share with your audience.

communication   11
A transaction in which speaker and listener simultaneously send, receive, and interpret messages.

communication apprehension (CA)   19
An individual's level of fear or anxiety associated with either real or anticipated communication with another person or persons.

comparison   187
Shows how much one thing is like another by highlighting similarities.

competence   17
A thorough familiarity with your topic.

complete arguments   253
Include all parts of the argument—claims and supporting material—to produce attitude change and improve source credibility.

compliance response   252
The audience does what is socially acceptable based on the persuader's message.

concept maps   31
Pictures or diagrams that allow you to visualize main and subordinate ideas related to a more general topic.

concrete words   185
Words that are specific, narrow, particular, and based on what you can sense.

connotative meaning   186
The idea suggested by a word other than its explicit meaning.

consistency persuades   256
The concept that audiences are more likely to change their behavior if the suggested change is consistent with their present beliefs, attitudes, and values.

constructive presentations   299
Debate presentations in which arguments for both sides of the debate are initially presented.

contrast   187
Shows how unlike one thing is from another by highlighting differences.

control   290
The ability to influence our environment.

conventional wisdom   72
The popular opinions of the time about issues, styles, topics, trends, and social mores; the customary set of understandings of what is true or right.

cost-benefit analysis   257
The idea that members of an audience are more likely to change their behavior if the suggested change will benefit them more than it will cost them.

critical response   252
The audience focuses on the arguments, the quality of the message, and the truth or accuracy of the message.

current topics   53
Topics that are of interest today because they are in the news, in the media, and on the minds of people in your audience.

D

debate   298
Members of a group divide responsibilities and present both "pro" and "con" sides of a controversial topic.

dedication presentation   277
Honors someone by naming an event, place, or other object after the honoree.

deductive reasoning   259
The presenter bases his or her claim on some premise that is generally affirmed by the audience.

defensive response   252
The audience fends off the persuader's message to protect existing beliefs, attitudes, and values.

defining   236
Revealing the presenter's intended meaning of a term, especially if the term is technical, scientific, controversial, or not commonly used.

definitions   119
Determinations of meaning through description, simplification, examples, analysis, comparison, explanation, or illustration.

degree questions   81
Questions used in interviews and in audience analysis; questionnaires that ask to what extent a respondent agrees or disagrees with a question.

deletion   170
An articulation problem that occurs when a sound is dropped or left out of a word.

delivery   36
The verbal and nonverbal techniques used to present the message.

demographics   73
Audience characteristics such as gender composition, age, ethnicity, economic status, occupation, and education.

demonstrating   237
Showing the audience an object, person, or place; showing the audience how something works; showing the audience how to do something; or showing the audience why something occurs.

demonstration presentation   42
A talk intended to teach audience members how something works or how to perform some task.

denotative meaning   186
The direct, explicit meaning or reference of a word.

describing   236
When the presenter evokes the meaning of a person, place, object, or experience by telling about its size, weight, color, texture, smell, or his or her feelings about it.

descriptive language   187
Attempts to observe objectively and without judgment.

dual coding   203
Because people tend to learn words separately from other sensory stimuli, presenters can use words as one channel, and other senses as another channel through which information can be presented.

duration   168
The amount of time devoted to the parts of a speech (e.g., introduction, evidence, main points) and the dwelling on words for effect.

dynamism   18
The energy you expend in delivering your message.

E

enunciation   169
A vocal aspect of delivery that involves the pronunciation and articulation of words; pronouncing correctly and producing the sounds clearly so that the language is understandable.

ethnicity   74
People who are united through "language, historical origins, nation-state, or cultural system."

etymology   191
The origin of a word.

evaluative language   187
Language that is full of judgments about the goodness or badness of a person or situation.

evidence   100
Data on which proof may be based.

examples   113
Specific instances used to illustrate your point.

expert testimony   116
Statements made by someone who has special knowledge or expertise about an issue or idea.

explaining   237
Reveals how something works, why something occurred, or how something should be evaluated.

explicit   253
The extent to which the persuader makes his or her intentions clear in the message.

extemporaneous mode   162
A method of speech delivery in which the presenter delivers a presentation from a keyword outline or from brief notes.

eye contact   171
A nonverbal aspect of delivery that involves the speaker's looking directly at audience members to monitor their responses to the message; in public speaking, eye contact is an asset because it permits the presenter to adapt to audience responses and to assess the effects of the message.

F

fallacy   261
An error in reasoning that weakens an argument.

farewell presentation   277
A person is paid tribute for their service before leaving.

feedback   10
Verbal and nonverbal responses by the audience.

figurative language   188
Comparing one concept to another analogous but different concept.

Five Canons of Rhetoric   29
The essential skills associated with public dialogue and communication that Roman scholars synthesized from the teachings of Greek philosophers and teachers. The Five Canons are invention, organization, style, understanding, and delivery.

flowchart   207
A visual diagram representing hierarchical structures or sequential processes.

fluency   170
A vocal aspect of delivery that involves the smooth flow of words and the absence of vocalized pauses.

forecasting   131
Tells the audience how you are going to cover the topic.

formal sentence outline   149
A final outline in complete sentence form, which includes the title, specific purpose, thesis statement, introduction of the speech, body of the speech, conclusion of the speech, and a bibliography of sources.

G

gestures   172
A bodily aspect of delivery that involves motions of the hands or body to indicate emphasis, commitment, and other feelings about the topic, audience, and occasion.

groupthink   292
When members of a group become locked in on one way of thinking about something or carrying out a task and ignore viable (and perhaps better) alternatives.

H

hearing   18
Receiving sound waves.

hierarchy of needs   258
A pyramid that builds from basic physiological needs like the need for oxygen all the way up to self-actualization needs—the realization of one's highest potential.

holdings database   101
An organization system used by libraries that indexes all books, journals, periodicals, and other resources owned by the library.

holistic design programs   212
A computer-generated design program that allows the user to work from a broader picture down to specific ideas and back again.

humor   232
The ability to perceive and express that which is amusing or comical.

hyperbole   193
A kind of overstatement or use of a word or words that exaggerates the actual situation.

I

impromptu mode   164
A method of speech delivery in which the presenter has no advance preparation.

impromptu presentation   40
A type of talk that does not allow for substantial planning and practice before the presentation is given.

inclusion   289
People need to belong to, or be included in, groups with others.

inclusive language   189
Language that does not leave out groups of people.

inductive reasoning   259
The persuader amasses a series of particular instances to draw an inference.

information hunger   227
The presenter generates a desire in the audience for information.

informative presentation   227
A presentation that increases an audience's knowledge about a subject or that helps the audience learn more about an issue or idea.

inside informant   80
Someone who belongs to a group who can tell you what the group stands for.

instant-replay function   153
The second function of a conclusion, to remind the audience of the thesis of your message.

internal previews   147
Statements that inform listeners of your next point or points and are more detailed than transitions.

internal references   111
Brief notations of which bibliographic reference contains the details you are using in your speech.

internal reviews   147
Statements that remind listeners of your last point or points and are more detailed than transitions.

interviews   80
Inquiries about your audience directed at an audience member.

introduction   129
The beginning portion of your presentation.

invention   31
The art of finding information.

K

keyword outline   152
A brief outline with cue words created for you to use during the delivery of your presentation.

L

lay testimony   116
Statements made by an ordinary person that substantiate or support what you say.

levels of abstraction   185
The degree to which words become separated from concrete or sensed reality.

line chart   207
A visual aid that illustrates trends in quantitative data.

listening   18
Interpreting sounds as a message.

list of references   150
The sources consulted and the sources actually used in the presentation.

literal language   188
Words used to reveal facts.

M

main ideas   230
Generalizations to be remembered in an informative presentation.

malapropism   170
Mistaking one word for another.

manuscript mode   164
A method of speech delivery in which the presenter writes out the complete presentation in advance and then uses that manuscript to deliver the speech but without memorizing it.

memorized mode   163
A method of speech delivery in which the presenter commits the entire presentation to memory by either rote or repetition; appropriate in situations where the same speech is given over and over to different audiences.

message   10
The facial expressions seen, the words heard, the visual aids illustrated, and the ideas or meanings conveyed simultaneously between source and receiver.

models   214
Scaled representations of an actual object or objects.

Monroe's Motivated Sequence   144
An organizational arrangement based on reflective thinking that includes five specific steps: attention, need, satisfaction, visualization, and action.

movement   173
A nonverbal aspect of delivery that refers to a presenter's locomotion in front of an audience; can be used to signal the development and organization of the message.

multimedia materials   204
Digital or electronic sensory resources that combine text, graphics, video, and sound into one package.

N

narrative   114
An extended story showing how another person experienced something.

noise   11
Interference or obstacles to communication.

nonverbal messages   10
Movements, gestures, facial expressions, and vocal variations that can reinforce or contradict the accompanying words.

numeric literacy   117
The ability to understand, interpret, and explain quantitative information.

O

observation   79
A method of audience analysis based on what you can see or hear about the audience.

open-ended questions   81
Like essay questions, questions that invite an explanation and discourage yes or no responses from the person being questioned.

oral citation   112
Tells the audience who the source is, how recent the information is, and the source's qualifications.

organization   32
The arrangement and structure of a presentation.

ornamental language   273
Highly stylized and artful uses of words to convey meanings.

ornamentation   33
The creative and artful use of language.

oversimplification   194
A complex issue described as simple.

P

panel   297
Group presentations that utilize short introductory statements from panel members and then provide time for interaction and dialogue between the presenters and audience members.

parallel construction   133
Repeating words and phrases and using the same parts of speech for each item.

pause   167
An intentional silence used to draw attention to the words before or after the interlude; a break in the flow of words for effect.

periodicals   102
Sources of information that are published at regular intervals.

personal experience   100
Using your own life as a source of information.

personal inventory   52
Trying to determine a topic by considering features of your life such as experiences, attitudes, values, beliefs, interests, and skills.

perspective   194
Your point of view; the way you perceive the world, reflected in the words you choose.

persuasive presentations   250
A message delivered to an audience by a speaker who intends to influence audience members' choices by changing their responses toward an idea, issue, concept, or product.

physical appearance   173
The way we look, including our display of material things such as clothing and accessories.

pie chart   207
A visual aid illustrating percentages or components of a whole.

pitch   168
A vocal aspect of delivery that refers to the highness or lowness of the speaker's voice, its upward and downward inflection, the melody produced by the voice.

plagiarism   15, 120
(1) A speech, outline, or manuscript from any source other than you. (2) The intentional use of information from a source without crediting the source.

preparation outline   149
The initial or tentative conception of a speech in rough outline form.

presentation to entertain   278
Designed to make a point in a creative and oftentimes humorous way.

presentation to pay tribute   275
Designed to offer celebration and praise of a noteworthy person, organization, or cause.

presentation to welcome   275
Intended to set a tone for a larger event by inviting all participants—including other presenters and audience members—to appropriately engage the event.

primacy   234
Placing your best argument or main point early in the presentation.

principle of division   148
An outlining principle that states that every point divided into subordinate parts must be divided into two or more parts.

principle of parallelism   148
An outlining principle that states that all points must be stated in the same grammatical and syntactical form.

principle of subordination   147
An outlining principle that states that importance is signaled by symbols and indentation.

principles of learning   232
Principles governing audience understanding by building on the known, using humor or wit, using presentational aids, organizing information, and rewarding listeners.

problem-solution pattern   141
An organizational arrangement in which part of the speech is concerned with the problem(s) and part with the solution(s) to problem(s).

process of communication   11
The dynamic interrelationship of source, receiver, message, channel, feedback, situation, and noise.

projection   72, 169
(1) The belief that others believe as you do when they may not. (2) Adjusting your volume appropriately for the subject, the audience, and the situation.

pronunciation   169
The production of the sounds of a word.

Q

question of fact   254
The persuasive presentation seeks to uncover the truth based on fact.

question of policy   254
The persuasive presentation enters the realm of rules, regulations, and laws.

question of value   254
The persuasive presentation raises issues about goodness and badness, right and wrong, enlightenment and ignorance.

questionnaires   81
Surveys of audience opinions.

R

rate   167
A vocal aspect of delivery that refers to the speed of delivery, the number of words spoken per minute; normal rates range from 125 to 190 words per minute.

rebuttal presentations   299
Debate presentations where one side presents points in response to arguments advanced by the other side.

receiver   10
The individual or group that hears, and hopefully listens to, the message sent by the source.

recency   234
Placing your best argument or main point late in the presentation.

reference librarian   101
A librarian specifically trained to help find sources of information.

relationship   251
How the audience feels about you as a presenter before, during, and after the persuasive appeal.

repetition   192
Words repeated exactly or with slight variation.

reward   235
A psychological or physical reinforcement to increase an audience's response to information given in a presentation.

rhythm   168
The tempo of a speech, which varies by part (e.g., introductions are often slower and more deliberate) and by the pacing of the words and sentences.

ritual   273
A ceremonial act that is characterized by qualities or procedures that are appropriate to the occasion.

S

Sapir-Whorf hypothesis   184
Our language determines to some extent how we think about and view the world.

scatterplot   207
A special type of line chart that plots related values on an X–Y axis and then creates a line showing how those values are related.

search engine   103
A Web site on the Internet that is specially designed to help you search for information.

self-managed work teams   289
Groups of workers with different skills and duties who work together to produce something or to solve a problem.

semanticist   185
A person who studies words and meaning.

sensory aids   203
Resources other than the speaker that stimulate listeners and help them comprehend and remember the presenter's message.

signposts   147
Direct indicators of the speaker's progress; usually an enumeration of the main points: "A second cause is. . . ."

situation   11
The time, place, and occasion in which the message sending and receiving occurs.

slide-deck programs   204
Computer-generated programs that allow the user to arrange slides in a particular order and then display those slides to the audience.

small, gradual changes persuade   257
The principle of persuasion that says audiences are more likely to alter their behavior if the suggested change will require small, gradual changes rather than major, abrupt changes.

small group communication   289
Interaction among three to nine people working together to achieve an interdependent goal.

source   9
The originator of the message; the speaker.

source credibility   17
The audience's perception of your effectiveness as a communicator.

spatial relations pattern   136
An organizational arrangement in which events or steps are presented according to how they are related in space.

special occasion speech   59
A presentation that highlights or punctuates a special event, situation, ceremony, or occasion.

specific numbers   253
Percentages, actual numbers, averages, and ranges of numbers used instead of "many," "most," or some other vague quantity.

speech of action   251
A persuasive speech given for the purpose of influencing listeners' behaviors and actions.

speech of introduction   275
Designed to tell us about the person being introduced and to help establish their ethos.

speech of nomination   276
Introduces and honors someone you wish to place in contention for an award, elected office, or some other competitively selected position.

speech of recognition   278
Typically presented when one or more people are given awards.

speech to convince   251
A persuasive presentation given for the purpose of influencing listeners' beliefs or attitudes.

speech to inform   58
A speech that seeks to increase the audience's level of understanding or knowledge about a topic.

speech to inspire   250
A persuasive speech given for the purpose of influencing listeners' feelings or motivations.

speech to persuade   59
A speech that seeks to influence, reinforce, or modify the audience members' feelings, attitudes, beliefs, values, or behaviors.

status quo   299
The way things are currently done.

stereotype   190
A hasty generalization about an individual based on an alleged characteristic of a group.

style   33
The use and ornamentation of language.

subordinate ideas   230
Details that support the generalizations in an informative presentation.

substitution   170
An articulation problem that occurs when one sound is replaced with another.

supporting material   113
Information you can use to substantiate your arguments and to clarify your position.

survey   115
Study in which a limited number of questions are answered by a sample of the population to discover opinions on issues.

symbolic   183
Words that represent the concrete and objective reality of objects and things as well as abstract ideas.

symposium   294
A group presentation in which individual members divide a large topic into smaller topics for coordinated individual presentations.

synonyms   191
Words that mean more or less the same thing.

T

table   205
A visual aid that combines text and/or numbers to efficiently summarize, compare, and contrast information.

testimonial evidence   116, 253
Written or oral statements of others' experience used by a speaker to substantiate or clarify a point.

text slide 205
A visual aid that relies primarily on words and phrases to present and summarize information.

thesaurus 191
A source for synonyms.

thesis statement 61
A one-sentence summary of the speech.

time-sequence pattern 134
An organizational arrangement in which events or steps are presented in the order in which they occur.

topical sequence pattern 139
An organizational arrangement in which the topic is divided into related parts, such as advantages and disadvantages, or various qualities or types.

transitions 146
Statements or words that bridge previous parts of the presentation to the next part. Transitions can be signposts, internal previews, or internal reviews.

transposition 170
An articulation problem that occurs when two sounds are reversed.

trustworthiness 17
The degree to which the audience perceives the presenter as honest and honorable.

two-sided argument 120
A source advocating one position will present an argument from the opposite viewpoint and then go on to refute that argument.

U

understanding 35
The fourth Canon of Rhetoric (originally called memory) requires speakers to have a strong mental awareness of the messages they intend to present and know how to interpret facts and ideas for an audience.

V

verbal messages 10
The words chosen for the speech.

virtual library 103
Web sites that provide links to sites that have been reviewed for relevance and usability.

visual aids 203
Any observable resources used to enhance, explain, or supplement the presenter's message.

vocalized pause 167
A nonfluency in delivery characterized by such sounds as "Uhhh," "Ahhh," or "Mmmm" or the repetitious use of such expressions as "okay," "like," or "for sure" to fill silence with sound; often used by presenters who are nervous or inarticulate.

volume 169
A vocal characteristic of delivery that refers to the loudness or softness of the voice. Public presenters often project or speak louder than normal so that distant listeners can hear the message; beginning presenters frequently forget to project enough volume.

W

wit 233
The ability to perceive and express humorously the relationship or similarity between seemingly incongruous or disparate things.

CHAPTER 1

[1]Noonan, P. (1998). *Simply speaking*. New York: Regan Books.

[2]http://www.nytimes.com/2010/03/03/us/03scotus.html.

[3]http://www.chicagotribune.com/...control/11016004.topic.

[4]McCroskey, J. C. (1997). Oral communication apprehension: A summary of recent theory and research. *Human Communication Research, 4,* 78.

[5]Greene, J. O., Rucker, M. P., Zauss, E. S., & Harris, A. A. (1988). Communication anxiety and the acquisition of message production skill. *Communication Education, 47,* 337–47.

[6]Daly, J. A., Vangelisti, A. L., & Weber, D. J. (1995). Speech anxiety affects how people prepare speeches: A protocol analysis of the preparation processes of speakers. *Communication Monographs, 62,* 394.

[7]Berger, C. R. (2004). Speechlessness: Causal attributions, emotional features, and social consequences. *Journal of Language and Social Psychology, 23,* 147–69. See also Dwyer, K. K. (1998). Communication apprehension and learning style preference: Correlations and implications for teaching. *Communication Education, 49,* 137–50.

[8]MacIntyre, P. D., & MacDonald, J. R. (1998). Public speaking anxiety: Perceived competence and audience congeniality. *Communication Education, 47,* 359–65.

[9]Ayres, J. (1996). Speech preparation processes and speech apprehension. *Communication Education, 45,* 228–35. See also Menzel, K. E., & Carrell, L. J. (1994). The relationship between preparation and performance in public speaking. *Communication Education, 43,* 17–26.

CHAPTER 2

[1]Kienpointner, M. (1997). On the art of finding arguments: What ancient and modern masters of invention have to tell us about the "ars inveniendi." *Argumentation, 11.2,* 225–37.

[2]Rowan, K. E. (1995). A new pedagogy for explanatory public speaking: Why arrangement should not substitute for invention. *Communication Education, 44.3,* 236–50.

[3]Hirst, R. (2003). Scientific jargon, good and bad. *Journal of Technical Writing & Communication, 33.3,* 201–29.

[4]Keesey, R. E. (1953). John Lawson's lectures concerning oratory. *Speech Monographs, 20.1,* 49.

[5]Kopp, W. (2008). Remember the contributions you can make. *Vital Speeches of the Day, 74.7,* 311–14.

[6]Booth, P., & Davisson, A. (2008). Visualizing the rhetorical situation of Hurricane Katrina: Photography, popular culture and meaning in images [electronic journal]. *American Communication Journal, 10.* Available at http://acjournal.org.

[7]Harlman (2009, June 17). Showing political action: Images in the Iranian protests [online weblog]. *No Caption Needed: Iconic Photographs, Public Culture, and Liberal Democracy.* Accessed July 17, 2009, at http://www.nocaptionneeded.com/?p=3201.

[8]Detz, J. (2009). A thorough speech on brief speechmaking. *Vital Speeches, 75,* 447–50.

CHAPTER 4

[1]Samovar, L. A., & Porter, R. E. (2003). *Communication between cultures* (5th ed.). Belmont, CA: Wadsworth.

[2]Lustig, M. W., & Koester, J. (2003). *Interpersonal competence: Interpersonal communication across cultures.* Boston: Allyn & Bacon.

[3]Carbaugh, D. A. (1998). 'I can't do that' but 'I can actually see around corners': American Indian students and the study of public communication. In Martin, J. N., Nakayama, T. K., & Flores, L. A. (Eds.), *Readings in cultural contexts.* Mountain View, CA: Mayfield.

[4]Maurer, M. (1989). Language and the future of the blind: Independence and freedom. *Vital Speeches of the Day,* 56(1), 16–22. A speech delivered at the banquet of the annual convention, Denver, Colorado, July 8, 1989.

[5]Behnke, R. R., O'Hair, D., & Hardman, A. (1990). Audience analysis systems in advertising and marketing. In O'Hair, D., & Kreps, G. L. (1990). *Applied communication theory and research.* Hillsdale, NJ: Laurence Erlbaum Associates, pp. 203–21.

[6]Welton, M. (2002). Listening, conflict, and citizenship: Towards a pedagogy of civil society. *International Journal of Lifelong Education, 21,* 197–208.

CHAPTER 5

[1]Dominick, J. R. (1996). *The dynamics of mass communication* (5th ed.). New York: McGraw-Hill.

[2]Bourhis, J., et al. (2002). *Style manual for communication studies.* New York: McGraw-Hill.

[3]Friedman, T. L. (2005). *The world is flat: A brief history of the twenty-first century.* New York: Farrar, Straus, and Giroux.

[4]Ong, W. J. (2004). *Orality and literacy: The technologizing of the word* (1st ed.). St. Louis: Saint Louis University Press.

[5]Polnac, L., Grant, L., & Cameron, T. (1999). *Common sense.* Upper Saddle River, NJ: Prentice Hall.

[6]Broeckelman-Post, M. (2008). *Two years later: What we can learn from the third academic integrity study at OU.* Athens, OH: Ohio University School of Communication Studies.

CHAPTER 6

[1]Thompson, E. C. (1990). An experimental investigation of the relative effectiveness of organizational structure in oral communication. *Southern Speech Journal, 26,* 59–69.

[2]Sharp, H., Jr., & McClung, T. (1966). Effect of organization on the speaker's ethos. *Speech Monographs, 33,* 182–83.

[3]Greene, J. O. (1984). Speech preparation processes and verbal fluency. *Human Communication Research, 11,* 61–84.

[4]*Ibid.*

[5]Fritz, P. A., & Weaver, R. L., II. (1986). Teaching critical thinking skills in the basic speaking course: A liberal arts perspective. *Communication Education, 35,* 177–82.

[6]http://usatoday.com/oped/2008/03/post-6.html. Accessed July 18, 2008.

[7]Tischer, S. (2004, October). Presentation, North Dakota State University, Fargo, North Dakota.

[8]http://blogs.abcnews.com/politicalpunch/2008/02/obama-echoes-de.html. Accessed July 18, 2008.

[9]Gronbeck, B. E., German, K., Ehninger, D., & Monroe, A. (1997). *Principles of speech communication.* New York: Addison-Wesley.

[10]Bourhis, J., Adams, C., & Titsworth, S. (1999). *A style manual for communication majors.* New York: McGraw-Hill.

CHAPTER 7

[1]Editorial. (2010, January 28). Limits to verbiage. *The Economist,* 12. Accessed April 8, 2010, at http://www.economist.com/node/15398222.

[2]Madden, M. (2010, April 9). Sarah Palin rocks GOP in New Orleans. Accessed April 8, 2010, at http://salon.com/news/politics/SarahPalin.

[3]Grigg, R. (1988). *The tao of relationships.* New York: Bantam Books, p. 15.

[4]Hildebrandt, H. W., & Stevens, W. (1963). Manuscript and extemporaneous delivery in communicating information. *Speech Monographs, 30,* 369–72.

[5]Miller, N. (1976). Speed of speech and persuasion. *Journal of Personality and Social Psychology, 34,* 15–24.

[6]Diehl, C. F., White, R. C., & Burk, K. W. (1959). Rate and communication. *Speech Monographs, 26,* 229–31.

[7]Harden, M. (1999, April 18). Making the grade. *The Columbus Dispatch,* p. 1D.

[8]Chirumbolo, A., Mannetti, L., Pierro, A., Areni, A., & Kruglanski, A. W. (2005). Motivated closed-mindedness and creativity in small groups. *Small Group Research, 36.1,* 59–82. See also Nakatani, Y. (2005). The effects of awareness-raising training on oral communication strategy use. *Modern Language Journal, 89.1,* 76–91.

[9]Hall, E. (1959). *The silent language.* New York: Fawcett Publications.

[10]Vuilleumier, P., George, N., Lister, V., Armony, J., & Driver, J. (2005). Effects of perceived mutual gaze and gender on face processing and recognition memory. *Visual Cognition, 12.1,* 85–101.

[11]Venezia, M., Messinger, D. S., Thorp, D., & Mundy, P. (2004). The development of anticipatory smiling. *Infancy, 6.3,* 397–406.

[12]Napieralski, L. P., Brooks, C. I., & Droney, J. M. (1995). The effect of duration of eye contact on American college students' attributions of state, trait, and test anxiety. *Journal of Social Psychology, 135,* 273–80.

[13]Beebe, S. A. (1974). Eye contact: A nonverbal determinant of speaker credibility. *Speech Teacher, 23,* 21–25.

[14]Ekman, P., & Friesen, W. V. (1967). Head and body cues in the judgment of emotion: A reformulation. *Perceptual and Motor Skills, 24,* 71–74.

[15]Gosselin, P., &. Simard, J. (1999). Children's knowledge of facial expressions of emotions: Distinguishing fear and surprise. *Journal of Genetic Psychology, 160.2,* 181–93.

[16]Weinberg, M. K., Tronick, E. Z., & Cohn, J. F. (1999). Gender differences in emotional expressivity and self-regulation during early infancy. *Developmental Psychology, 35.1,* 175–88.

[17]Ekman, P. (1969). Pan-cultural elements in facial displays of emotion. *Science, 164,* 86–88.

[18]Burgoon, J. K., Birk, T., & Pfau, M. (1990). Nonverbal behaviors, persuasion, and credibility. *Human Communication Research, 17,* 140–70.

[19]Pearson, J. C., West, R. L., & Turner, L. H. (1995). *Gender and communication.* Dubuque, IA: Wm. C. Brown Publishers.

[20]*Ibid.*

[21]Movshovitz-Hadar, N., & Hazzan, O. (2004). How to present it? On the rhetoric of an outstanding lecturer. *International Journal of Mathematical Education in Science & Technology, 35.6,* 813–27. See also Singer, M. A., & Goldin-Meadow, S. (2005). Children learn when their teacher's gestures and speech differ. *Psychological Science, 16.2,* 85–89.

CHAPTER 8

[1]Lederer, R. (1991). *The miracle of language.* New York: Pocket Books.

[2]*Ibid.*

[3]Brown, R. (1968). *Words and things.* Glencoe, IL: The Free Press.

[4]Crawford, J. (1999). Killing us one by one. An unpublished presentation delivered in Interpersonal Communication 103, Public Speaking, Ohio University, Athens, Ohio.

[5]Smith, D. C. (1997, July/August). Is the use of metaphors innocuous or cause for concern? *Peace Magazine,* http://www.peacemagazine.org. See also Lakoff, G., & Johnson, M. (1981). *Metaphors we live by.* Chicago: University of Chicago Press; and Rothstein, L. (1999). The war on speech. *Bulletin of the Atomic Scientists, 55.3,* 7.

[6]Shelley, P. B. (1960). Prometheus unbound. In *John Keats and Percy Bysshe Shelley.* New York: Modern Library, p. 260.

[7]http://venus.va.com.au/suggestion/sapir.html.

[8]New words in the Merriam-Webster Dictionary. (2008, July 7). Accessed July 12, 2008, at http://www.boston.com/news/local/massachusetts/articles/2008/07/07/new_words_in_the_merriam_webster_dictionary/.

[9]Hayakawa, S. I. (1978). *Language in thought and action.* Orlando, FL: Harcourt Brace Jovanovich.

[10]Burch, D. (1999). I am unique. An unpublished presentation delivered in Interpersonal Communication 103, Public Speaking, Ohio University, Athens, Ohio.

[11]Will, G. F. (1999, August 25). Giddy over McCain. *The Washington Post,* p. A17.

[12]Robinson, A. (1999). If the shoe fits. An unpublished presentation delivered in Interpersonal Communication 103, Public Speaking, Ohio University, Athens, Ohio.

[13]Safire, W. (1972). *The new language of politics.* New York: Collier Books.

[14]Soukhanov, A. H. (1995). *Word watch: The stories behind the words of our lives.* New York: Henry Holt.

[15]Burch, D., op. cit.

[16]LaRocque, P. (1999). Between you and I, misutilizing words ranks high pet-peevewise. *The Quill, 87.3,* 31.

[17]Meek, C. (1999). Aspects of paintball. An unpublished presentation delivered in Interpersonal Communication 101, Public Speaking, Ohio University, Athens, Ohio.

[18]Schneider, L. (2004). Fabulous facts about foster care. An unpublished presentation delivered in Communication 110, Public Speaking, North Dakota State University, Fargo, North Dakota.

CHAPTER 9

[1]Gellevij, M., et al. (2002). Multimodal versus unimodal instruction in a complex learning context. *Journal of Experimental Education, 70.3,* 215–41.

[2]Zayas-Baya, E. P. (1997). Instructional media in the total language picture. *International Journal of Instructional Media, 5,* 145–50.

[3]Alley, M. (2003). *The craft of scientific presentations: Critical steps to succeed and critical errors to avoid.* New York: Springer.

[4]Kiewra, K. A. (1985). Students' notetaking behaviors and the efficacy of providing the instructor's notes for review. *Contemporary Educational Psychology, 10,* 378–86.

[5]Katt, J., Murdoch, J., Butler, J., & Pryor, B. (2008). Establishing best practices for the use of PowerPoint™ as a presentation aid. *Human Communication, 11,* 193–200.

[6]Cyphert, D. (2007). Presentation technology in the age of electronic eloquence: From visual aid to visual rhetoric. *Communication Education, 56,* 168–92.

[7]Halverson, E. (2008, January). From one woman to everyman: Reportability and credibility in publicly performed narratives. *Narrative Inquiry, 18,* 29–52.

CHAPTER 10

[1]Sajak, P. (2002, August 15). The disconnect between Hollywood and America: You possess the power. *Vital Speeches of the Day, 68(21),* 701–05.

[2]Wright, B. (2002, August 1). Enron: The inflexible obligations of the legal profession. *Vital Speeches of the Day, 68(20),* 635–38.

[3]Anderson, R. (1999). The phenylketonurics among us. An unpublished presentation delivered in Interpersonal Communication 101, Public Speaking, Ohio University, Athens, Ohio.

[4]Goh, C. C. M. (2002). Exploring listening comprehension tactics and their interactive patterns. *System, 30,* 185–206. See also Walker, I., & Hulme, C. (1999). Concrete words are easier to recall than abstract words: Evidence for a semantic contribution to short-term serial recall. *Journal of Experimental Psychology: Learning, Memory and Cognition, 25,* 1256–71.

[5]Kardash, C. M., & Noel, L. K. (2000). How organizational signals, need for cognition, and verbal ability affect text recall and recognition. *Contemporary Educational Psychology, 25,* 317–31.

[6]Springer, L., Stanne, M. E., & Donovan, S. S. (1999). Effects of small group learning on undergraduates in science, mathematics, engineering and technology: A meta-analysis. *Review of Educational Research, 69,* 21–52.

[7]Ehrensberger, R. (1945). An experimental study of the relative effectiveness of certain forms of emphasis in public speaking. *Speech Monographs, 12,* 94–111.

[8]Baird, J. E. (1974). The effects of speech summaries upon audience comprehension of expository speeches of varying quality and complexity. *Central States Speech Journal, 25,* 124–25.

[9]Perry, R. P. (1985). Instructor expressiveness: Implications for improving teaching. In Donald, J. G., & Sullivan, A. M. (Eds.), *Using research to improve teaching.* San Francisco: Jossey Bass, pp. 35–49.

[10]Beating the blues: Dealing with depression. (1999, Fall). *Inova Health Source,* 9.

[11]Snelling, D. (1999). TV and your child. An unpublished presentation delivered in Interpersonal Communication 103, Public Speaking, Ohio University, Athens, Ohio.

[12]Ehrensberger, R. (1945). An experimental study of the relative effectiveness of certain forms of emphasis in public speaking. *Speech Monographs, 12,* 94–111.

[13]Janis, I., & Feshbach, S. (1953). Effects of fear-arousing communication. *Journal of Abnormal and Social Psychology, 48,* 78–92.

[14]DuPont, M. (1980, Spring Semester). Phoenix, Arizona: My hometown. An unpublished manuscript presented in Honors Public Speaking course, Iowa State University, Ames, Iowa.

CHAPTER 11

[1]http://www.stlcc.edu/Newsroom/2008.

[2]Schneider, L. (2004, Spring Semester). Do you know where you stand? An unpublished presentation delivered in Communication 110 (Honors Section), Public Speaking, North Dakota State University, Fargo, North Dakota.

[3]Dillard, J. P., & Marshall, L. J. (2003). Persuasion as a social skill. In Greene, J. O., & Burleson, B. R. (Eds.), *Handbook of communication and social interaction skills*. Mahwah, NJ: Lawrence Erlbaum, pp. 479–513.

[4]Based on Chaiken, S., Liberman, A., & Eagly, A. H. (1989). Heuristic and systematic processing within and beyond the persuasion context. In Uleman, J. S., & Bargh, J. A. (Eds.), *Unintended thought*. New York: Guilford Press, pp. 212–52.

[5]*Ibid.*

[6]Dillard & Marshall, op. cit, p. 481.

[7]Blum-Kulka, S. (1987). Indirectness and politeness in requests: Same or different? *Journal of Pragmatics, 11*, 131–46.

[8]Dillard, J. P., Wilson, S. R., Tusing, K. J., & Kenney, T. (1997). Politeness judgments in personal relationships. *Journal of Language and Social Psychology, 16*, 297–325.

[9]O'Keefe, D. J. (1998). How to handle opposing arguments in persuasive messages: A meta-analytic review of the effects of one-sided and two-sided messages. In Roloff, M. E. (Ed.), *Communication yearbook, 22*. Thousand Oaks, CA: Sage, pp. 209–49.

[10]Holtgraves, T. (1997). Styles of language use: Individual and cultural variability in conversational indirectness. *Journal of Personality and Social Psychology, 73*, 624–37.

[11]Mueller, B. (1987). Reflections of culture: An analysis of Japanese and American advertising appeals. *Journal of Advertising Research, 27*, 51–59.

[12]Maslow, A. H. (1943). A theory of human motivation. *Psychological Review, 50*, 370–96.

[13]Dillard & Marshall, op. cit, p. 481.

CHAPTER 12

[1]Whitman, M. (2009, September 22). Californians young and old want the same thing. *Vital Speeches of the Day, 75*, 497–500.

[2]National Aeronautics and Space Administration (2010). Ethics frequently asked questions. Accessed May 5, 2010, at http://www.nasa.gov/offices/ogc/general_law/ethicsfaq.html.

APPENDIX

[1]Galanes, G., Adams, K., & Brilhart, J. (2004). *Effective group discussion: Theory and practice*. New York: McGraw-Hill.

[2]Garcia, A. (2001). Group multi-media presentations in "the sociology of language and ethnicity." *Radical Pedagogy, 3.3*, NP.

Photos

p. i: © BananaStock/JupiterImages (bottom); © Paul Burns/Getty Images (middle); **p. iii:** © PhotoDisc/PunchStock; **p. iv:** © PhotoDisc/PunchStock; **p. vi:** © Ryan McVay/Getty Images; **p. vii:** © Tetra Images/Getty Images; **p. viii:** © Stockbyte/PunchStock; **p. x:** © BananaStock/JupiterImages; **p. xi:** © Amos Morgan/Getty Images; **p. xiii:** © Rubberball/PunchStock; **p. xiv:** © PhotoAlto/PunchStock; **p. xv:** © iStockphoto.com/Cat London; **p. xvi:** © Jose Luis Pelaez Inc./Getty Images; **p. 1:** © Comstock Images/Superstock

Chapter 1, pp. 2–3: © David Young-Wolff/PhotoEdit; **p. 4:** Courtesy of Danny Wong and Blank Label; **p. 5:** © Flying Colors Ltd./Getty Images; **p. 6 (top):** © Bryan Allen/CORBIS; **p. 6 (bottom):** © JupiterImages; **p. 7:** © Jose Luis Pelaez Inc./Getty Images Inc.; **p. 8 (left):** © The McGraw-Hill Companies, Inc./Gary He, photographer; **p. 8 (right):** © Kurt Krieger/Corbis; **p. 9:** © Ambient Images Inc./PhotoEdit; **p. 10:** © Vicky Rabinowicz/Getty Images; **p. 11:** © Comstock Images/JupiterImages; **p. 12:** © William Thomas Cain/Getty Images; **p. 13 (Figure 1.1):** © Don Bayley/iStockphoto (audience) and Michael Kemter/iStockphoto (young man); **p. 13 (bottom):** Library of Congress, Prints and Photographs Division [LC-USZ62-13016]; **p. 14 (top):** © Olivier Blondeau/iStockphoto; **p. 14 (bottom):** © JupiterImages; **p. 15:** © Digital Vision/PunchStock; **p. 16:** © FPG/Getty Images; **p. 17:** © Pixtal/age Fotostock; **p. 18:** © Getty Images/Digital Vision; **p. 19:** © Barbara Penoyar/Getty Images; **p. 21:** © www.naacpldf.org; **p. 23:** © Goodshoot/PunchStock; **p. 25:** © BananaStock/JupiterImages

Chapter 2, pp. 26–27: © Colin Young-Wolff/PhotoEdit; **p. 28:** © JOSH ANDERSON/Reuters/Corbis; **p. 29:** © Bettmann/CORBIS; **p. 31 (bottom):** © Corbis; **p. 32:** © Izabela Habur/iStockphoto; **p. 33:** © JupiterImages; **p. 34 (both):** © Royalty-Free/CORBIS; **p. 36:** © PhotoDisc/PunchStock; **p. 37 (top):** © Getty Images/Digital Vision; **p. 37 (bottom):** © JupiterImages; **p. 38:** © Ian McDonnell/iStockphoto; **p. 39 (top):** © Stockbyte/Getty Images; **p. 39 (bottom):** © Sayre Berman/Corbis; **p. 40:** © Fuse/JupiterImages/Getty Images; **p. 41:** © Izabela Habur/iStockphoto; **p. 42:** © Getty Images/PhotoDisc; **p. 43:** Digital Image © The Museum of Modern Art/Licensed by SCALA/Art Resource, NY; **p. 44:** © Philadelphia Inquirer/MCT/Landov; **p. 45:** © HBSS/Corbis; **p. 47:** © BananaStock/JupiterImages

Chapter 3, pp. 48–49: © Veer; **p. 50:** © The McGraw-Hill Companies, Inc./John Flournoy, photographer; **p. 51:** © The McGraw-Hill Companies, Inc./Gary He, photographer; **p. 52:** © Image100/Corbis; **p. 53 (Table 3.1a):** © Getty Images; **p. 53 (Table 3.1b):** © Creatas/PunchStock; **p. 53 (Table 3.1c):** © David Becker/Getty Images; **p. 53 (Table 3.1d):** © PhotoDisc/Getty Images; **p. 53 (bottom):** © PhotoDisc Collection/Getty Images; **p. 55 (top):** © ColorBlind Images/Getty Images; **p. 55 (bottom):** © Bonnie Kamin/PhotoEdit; **p. 57 (top):** © Ana Sousa/iStockphoto; **p. 57 (bottom):** © JupiterImages; **p. 58:** © Royalty-Free/CORBIS; **p. 60 (top):** © Creatas/PunchStock; **p. 60 (bottom):** © S. Solum/PhotoLink/Getty Images; **p. 61:** © Brand X Pictures/PunchStock; **p. 62 (top):** © Tony Freeman/PhotoEdit; **p. 62 (bottom):** © Image Source/PunchStock; **p. 63 (Table 3.2a):** © Creatas/PunchStock; **p. 63 (Table 3.2b):** © AFP/Getty Images; **p. 63 (Table 3.2c):** © Rosanne Olson/Getty Images; **p. 64:** © Goodshoot/PunchStock; **p. 67:** © BananaStock/JupiterImages

Chapter 4, pp. 68–69: © AP Images/Charles Dharapak; **p. 70:** © Stewart Cohen/Pam Ostrow/JupiterImages; **p. 71:** © Ryan McVay/Getty Images; **p. 72 (top):** © JupiterImages; **p. 72 (bottom):** © Zhang Jun/Xinhua Press/Corbis; **p. 73:** © Jeff Greenberg/The Image Works; **p. 74 (top):** © Digital Vision/Getty Images; **p. 74 (bottom):** © G.K. & Vikki Hart/Getty Images; **p. 75:** © Digital Vision/Getty Images; **p. 76:** © Monty Rakusen/cultura/Corbis; **p. 77:** © Jose Luis Pelaez Inc./Getty Images; **p. 78:** © Digital Vision/PunchStock; **p. 79:** © Comstock Images/Alamy; **p. 80:** © Digital Vision; **p. 82:** © Angela Wyant/Getty

Images; **p. 83 (top):** © Comstock Images/Super Stock; **p. 83 (bottom):** © The McGraw-Hill Companies, Inc./Lars A. Niki, photographer; **p. 85:** © JupiterImages; **p. 86:** © Paramount/Courtesy Everett Collection; **p. 87:** © Kit Houghton/Corbis; **p. 88:** © Jan Stromme/Getty Images; **p. 89:** © Peter Mlekuz/iStockphoto; **p. 90:** © Cat London/iStockphoto.com; **p. 91:** © Getty Images; **p. 92:** © HBSS/Corbis; **p. 95:** © BananaStock/Jupiter Images

Chapter 5, pp. 96–97: © Comstock/PunchStock; **p. 98:** © Getty Images/Digital Vision; **p. 99:** © Steve Pyke/Getty Images; **p. 100 (top):** © Ingram Publishing/Alamy; **p. 100 (bottom):** © James Hardy/PhotoAlto; **p. 101:** © Andersen Ross/Blend Images (RF)/JupiterImages; **p. 102:** © iStockphoto; **p. 103:** © Veer; **p. 104:** © Dan Wilson/iStockphoto; **p. 106:** © PhotoDisc/Getty Images; **p. 108:** © JupiterImages; **p. 109:** © LWA/Getty Images; **p. 111:** © JupiterImages; **p. 113 (top):** © PhotoDisc; **p. 113 (bottom):** © BananaStock Ltd.; **p. 114:** © TANNEN MAURY/epa/Corbis; **p. 115:** © STEVE MARCUS/Reuters/Corbis; **p. 116:** © WireImage/Getty Images; **p. 117 (top):** © JupiterImages; **p. 117 (bottom):** © PhotoDisc/PunchStock; **p. 119:** © Comstock Images/JupiterImages; **p. 120 (top):** © Royalty-Free/Corbis; **p. 120 (bottom):** © iStockphoto.com/fotek; **p. 121:** © Goodshoot/PunchStock; **p. 124:** © BananaStock/JupiterImages

Chapter 6, pp. 126–127: © Andersen Ross/Getty Images; **p. 128:** © Fork Films, "Pray the Devil Back to Hell." Photo, Pewee Flomoku; **p. 129:** © iStockphoto.com/webphotographer; **p. 131:** © Vince Bucci/Getty Images Inc.; **p. 133:** © Comstock Images; **p. 134 (top):** © JupiterImages; **p. 134 (bottom):** © The McGraw-Hill Companies, Inc./Jill Braaten, photographer; **p. 136:** © Matt Sayles/Associated Press; **p. 137:** © Corbis Super RF/Alamy; **p. 138:** © UpperCut Images/Getty Images; **p. 139:** © Comstock/PunchStock Images; **p. 140:** © Jocelyn Augustino/FEMA; **p. 141:** Copyright © 2010. The American Society for the Prevention of Cruelty to Animals (ASPCA). All Rights Reserved; **p. 144:** © Stockbyte/PunchStock Images; **p. 145:** © The McGraw-Hill Companies, Inc.; **p. 146:** © Michael Scott for MMH; **p. 149:** © H. Marc Larson/Associated Press; **p. 150:** © Viviane Moos/Corbis; **p. 152:** © Ian McDonnell/iStockphoto; **p. 153:** © Alan Schein/Corbis; **p. 155:** © HBSS/Corbis; **p. 157:** © BananaStock/Jupiter Images

Chapter 7, pp. 158–159: © Jeff Greenberg/PhotoEdit; **p. 160 (top):** © The McGraw-Hill Companies, Inc./Jill Braaten, photographer; **p. 160 (bottom):** © SEAN GARDNER/Reuters/Corbis; **p. 162:** © Reuters/Corbis; **p. 163:** © AP Photo/The Oklahoman, Paul Hellstern; **p. 164:** © JupiterImages; **p. 165:** © Amanda Rohde/iStockphoto; **p. 167:** © Agence France Presse/Getty Images; **p. 168:** © Photo Spin/Getty Images; **p. 169:** © Royalty-Free/Corbis; **p. 171 (top):** © Hans Neleman/Getty Images; **p. 171 (bottom):** © Plush Studios/Getty Images; **p. 173:** © Mark Andersen/Getty Images; **p. 174:** © BananaStock/PunchStock; **p. 175:** © Don Hammond/Design Pics/Corbis; **p. 176:** © Goodshoot/PunchStock; **p. 179:** © BananaStock/JupiterImages

Chapter 8, pp. 180–181: © David Young-Wolff/PhotoEdit; **p. 182:** © Image100 Ltd.; **p. 183:** © Chip Somodevilla/Getty Images; **p. 184:** © JupiterImages; **p. 185 (top):** © Corbis; **p. 185 (bottom):** © Gerville Hall/iStockphoto; **p. 186:** © iStockphoto; **p. 187 (both):** © iStockphoto; **p. 189 (top):** © iStockphoto; **p. 189 (bottom):** © Olivier Blondeau/iStockphoto; **p. 190:** © Rob Kim/Landov; **p. 191 (top):** © The McGraw-Hill Companies, Inc./Ken Cavanaugh, photographer; **p. 191 (bottom):** © JupiterImages; **p. 192:** © Brand X Pictures/PunchStock; **p. 193 (top):** © iStockphoto; **p. 193 (bottom):** © Gary S. Chapman/Getty Images, Inc.; **p. 194 (top):** © iStockphoto; **p. 194 (middle):** © Olivier Blondeau/iStockphoto; **p. 194 (bottom):** © JupiterImages; **p. 195 (top):** © Holger Hill/Getty Images; **p. 195 (bottom):** © Kathy McLaughlin/The Image Works; **p. 196:** © HBSS/Corbis; **p. 199:** © BananaStock/Jupiter Images

Chapter 9, pp. 200–201: © Inspirestock/Corbis; **p. 202:** © TED/James Duncan Davidson; **p. 203:** © JupiterImages; **p. 204:** © Getty Images/PhotoDisc; **p. 205:** © JupiterImages; **p. 211 (middle):** © Bob Daemmrich/The Image Works; **p. 211 (bottom):** © JupiterImages; **p. 214:** © Justin Pumfrey/Getty Images, Inc.; **p. 215:** © Michael Ochs Archives/Stringer/Getty Images; **p. 216:** © Royalty-Free/Corbis; **p. 217:** © JupiterImages; **p. 218:** © Goodshoot/PunchStock; **p. 220:** © Jason Reed/Ryan McVay/Getty Images; **p. 221:** © BananaStock/JupiterImages

Text

[Index]